CONCEPTION: AN ICON OF THE BEGINNING

FRANCIS ETHEREDGE

En Route Books and Media, LLC

St. Louis, MO

En Route Books and Media, LLC
5705 Rhodes Avenue
St. Louis, MO 63109

Cover credit: TJ Burdick

Library of Congress Control Number: 2019946834

Copyright © 2019 Francis Etheredge
All rights reserved.

ISBN-13: 978-1-950108-24-4
ISBN-10: 1-950108-24-4

No part of this booklet may be reproduced, stored in a retrieval system, or transmitted in any form, or by any means, electronic, mechanical, photocopying, or otherwise, without the prior written permission of the author.

Dedication to St. John Paul II & an Opening Prayer

This book is a thanksgiving to God
for the spiritual fatherhood of the late Pope St. John Paul II; and, more generally, for the ways that papal writing and the ministry, the work and the presence of many others have enriched my life.

This book is written out of love for forgotten fathers and mothers and for my wife and eleven children, three of whom are in heaven.

Let the Fatherhood of God
be rediscovered in our world
in the daily life of the father
at work and at rest
in the family
and in society.
Amen.

Mother of the Lord and Chaste Spouse of St. Joseph,
Pray for us.
St. Joseph, Chaste Spouse and Guardian of the Redeemer[+],
Pray for us.
Jesus,
Son of the Virgin Mary and adopted son of St. Joseph,
Have mercy on us.

[+] Pope St. John Paul II, *Guardian of the Redeemer, Redemptoris Custos*, 1989. The title of this Apostolic Exhortation suggested itself as the beginning of a *Litany for fathers*.

CONTENTS

"The Creation of the Cosmos": a Poem by Grace Marie Urlakis and Biography 2

General Foreword and Biography: 5
Dr. Mary Anne Urlakis
Introduction: "Nothing Comes from nothing" 7
(Parmenides)
Icon 11
Image and Likeness 17
An Irrevocable, Covenantal Call to the Moral Life 23
Conclusion: '[A] living icon of the *imago Dei*' 27

"In the Beginning": a Poem by Grace Marie Urlakis
.... 30

"Flame of Life" and Artist's Statement by Marco Riccardo Intra Sidola 33

A Prologue in Five Parts

Part I: Exploring Expressions of the Beginning of Personhood 35
The Seed 37
We are a Present 39
A Philosophical Psalm 139 40

Part II: When does the Life of a Human Being Begin? 43

Where the Body Lives, there the Soul is, and where
both are is the Human Person.. 44
God Creates "As a Whole" 45
A Point of Departure in the Reality of our Beginning 47
The Prior-to-Thought Reality of what actually Exists... 49

Part III: A Comment on the Work as a Whole 51
Exploring the Conceptualization of the Beginning of Human
   Personhood.. 51

Part IV: The Hippocratic Oath of Kos (400 BC) 55
A Work Old and New..55
Hippocratic Oath of Kos (400 BC) 56

Part V: A General Introduction to Each Chapter 57
Chapter 1: On the Use of the Imagination............................57
Chapter 2: Scriptural Insights into the Origin of Human
Being 58
Chapter 3: What does the Church Teach "Today" about
the "Moment" of our Beginning 60
Chapter 4: Philosophical and Theological Dialogue 62
Chapter 5: The Being of the Blessed Trinity "Founds" 65
Human Being (I); the Biological Status of the Human
   Embryo (II); and The Gift and Rights of being
   Conceived-in-Relationship: We are an Icon of the
   Beginning (III).. 68

Foreword to Chapter One and Biography:
Fr. Joseph Tham, LC 71
Biography 71
Foreword to Chapter 1: On "alternative imaginations"..72
"Only a god can save us"..73
The 'beautiful icons of creation' 74
Appealing to the 'power of imagery'.................................75

"Birthright" and Artist's Statement by Eric Carson
.... 76

Chapter One: Part I of III: Sections: Ii-Iiii: On the Use of the Imagination 77
Imagine.. 79
Chapter One: Part Ii: Imagining Origins............................... 81
    The Question of Origin 81
    Each of us Begins 83
    Scripture? 85
Chapter One: Part Iii: Imagining Futures 86
Imagining the Future... 86
Starting with Personal Experience 86
Alternatively: At the "End" and the "Beginning of Life 88
What is the Difference between an Artificial and a Human Intelligence? 88
Chapter One: Part Iiii: What is the Imagination? 92
    What is the Imagination? 92

Chapter One: Part II of III: Sections IIii-IIiv: Questioning Our Existence 94
    Questioning our Existence 94
    Different ways of Questioning our Existence 94
Chapter One: Part IIii: Who Am I? 95
    Are we in a Dream? We can "Investigate" our own Existence 95
Chapter One: Part IIiii: Am I a Robot?................................. 97
    You or I could be a Robot. Are we a part of the Script or a Script Writer? 97
Chapter One: Part IIiv: Am I a Martian?............................. 99
    How do I Know that I am a Human Being and not a Being from Mars? 99

Chapter One: Part III of III: Sections IIIi-IIIvii: A New Beginning: Imagining "Body" and "Soul"...................... 101

A Reasonable Use of the Imagination 101
Chapter One: Part IIIi: "Making" Visible the Invisible 101
Chapter One: Part IIIii: Remember the "Moment" of Putting Pen to Paper 104
An Event Expressed in Material, Time, Space and Meaning 104
The Analogy or Likeness between Writing and Conception 106
Chapter One: Part IIIiii: Light: Fuelled Radiating Energy .106
The Comparison of Lighting a Candle and Conception 107
In the Shadow of a Light 108
Chapter One: Part IIIiv: Architecture and Soil 109
Architecture: from House to Home 109
From Seed-Bulb to Plant 110
Chapter One: Part IIIv: Comparing one Act of God with Another 111
The Incarnation 112
Chapter One: Part IIIvi: Word and Meaning: One "Needs" the Other? 114
Chapter One: Part IIIvii: The Need for a New Explanation of Conception: the Wholeness of Being one in "Body" and "Soul" 116
Ideas Old and New 117
A Limitation in these Ideas 117
Towards a New way of Understanding the Unity of the Person 118

Foreword to Chapter Two and Biography: Ronda Chervin, PhD 121
    Biography 122
Foreword to Chapter 2: Pondering how Philosophical Concepts concerning the Human Person can be related tn the Truth of Revelation 122
From Uncertainty to the Facts about Human Conception .124

Is Being a Woman or a Man an Essential part of the Person? 124
God's Personal Creative Love for each of us 125
The Cat and I 126

"Tatar Couple" and Artist's Statement by Bela Fishbeyn 127

Chapter Two: Scripture and the Beginning of Human Being 128
Scriptural Insights into the Origin of Human Being 128
Both Circling and Coming to the Central Texts 129

Chapter Two: Part I of XII: Drawing on General Principles of Scriptural Interpretation 132
A Note on Language: a more General Comment on Meaning and the Socio-Cultural Context of Words 135

Chapter Two: Part II of XII: The 'Word became flesh' (Jn 1:14) 136

Chapter Two: Part III of XII: Scripture Says: 'In the beginning' (Gn 1:1): Philosophy and Theology in Dialogue 140
A Brief Philosophical Look at the Question of a Beginning 141
A Brief Theological Look at the Question of our Beginning 144

Chapter Three: Part IV of XII: In the Beginning, God Created (Gn 1:1) 147
Drawing further on the Opening Chapters of Genesis for the Relationship of Creator to creature 150
Thus one is Brought to Consider the Mystery of the Holy Spirit 152
The Creation of Man, Male and Female 154
The Origin of Man in the Context of Original Sin 156

Chapter Two: Part V of XII: The Woman's Perception of Conception 158

Chapter Two: Part VI of XII: In the Light of the Woman's Perception of Conception, let us Return to *The First Book of Moses*, but also Jacob, Rachel and Job 162
Job Expresses Remarkably "Prescient" Imagery or Accounts of the Nascent Human Reality 163

Chapter Two: Part VII of XII: The Significance of Blood ... 166

Chapter Two: Part VIII of XII: Where is the Creation of the Soul in all this? 168
The Soul is, as it were, Hidden 169
The Emphasis of the Biblical Author is on the Totality of "Life" and "Death" 171

Chapter Two: Part IX of XII: The Opening Chapters of Genesis are an Expression of an Integral Gift of Life ... 173
Revisiting the Act of Creation: Time as an "Instant" and as a "Duration" of Development 174
A Second Difficulty: An Account of Making Man which is Instantaneous and an Account which "Takes" Time 177
The Help of Aristotle in Understanding the Implicit "Witness" to the Human Soul 179
Applying the Philosopher's Terminology to the Sacred Author's *Imaginative Understanding of the Beginning of Human Life* 181
A Relevant Discussion on 'Formless Matter' (Wis 11: 17) ..183
Drawing on this Meditation on Genesis 188

Chapter Two: Part X of XII: 'Your eyes beheld my unformed substance' (Ps 139: 16) 190
General observations on Psalm 139 191
This Psalm and the Personal Act of Creation 193

Particular Observations on Psalm 139 195
   Psalm 139 Echoes Genesis 1 and 2 197
The Third Stanza 199
Other Texts on the Beginning of Life Leading to the Ultimate
   Question about the Conception of Christ 200
Combining Traditions: On Conception and Fertile
   Barrenness 202

Chapter Two: Part XI of XII: A Patristic Consensus Concerning the Conception of Christ 202

Chapter Two: Part XII of XII: A Critically Rounded Account of the Conceptions of Christ, Mary and Each of Us 214
Jesus and the Fathers 215
Mary and the Fathers 217
Each of Us and the Fathers..218

Foreword to Chapter Three and Biography: Fr. Michael Baggot, LC 225
Biography 226
Foreword to Chapter 3: What does the Church Say "Today" about the Moment of our Beginning? 227
The Need for an Adequate Anthropology........................... 229
Parents Enter into a Unique Participation in the Creative power and Providential Care of the Lord of all History
   230
The Church's Inexhaustibly Rich Patrimony of Teaching on God's Plan for Marriage and the Family 232

"Matrix" and Artist's Statement by Alison Batley, USA.. 234
Chapter Three: What Does the Church Teach "Today" about the Moment of our Beginning? .235
"Today" 235
Understanding "Today" in the Modern History of the Church

A Development of Doctrine: An Ongoing Work? 237
Gaudium et Spes, 1965 238
Humanae Vitae, 1968 241
Let Me Live: the Declaration by the Sacred Congregation of the Faith on Procured Abortion, 1974 242
Familiaris Consortio, 1981 247
Making Explicit the Philosophical Implications of a Theological Reality 249
Donum Vitae, 1987 250
Address at the "University of Uppsala", 9th June, 1989 253
In the Service of Life: The Pontifical Council for the Family, 1991 254
Veritatis Splendor, 1993 257
Conversely, St. John Paul II Leaves out nothing Acceptable to Reason and Includes Everything Acceptable to Christ and His Church 262
What are the Implications of how these Issues are Treated in *Veritatis Splendor* for a Theological Understanding of the Nature of Human Conception? 265
A Letter to Families, 1994 268
Extracts from 'The Genealogy of the Person' 268
An "Incarnational" Understanding Discloses the Secret that Fulfilment is Found in "Being-in-Relationship" 274
Evangelium Vitae, 1995 275
Dignitatis Personae, 2008 280

Foreword to Chapter Four and Biography: Sr. Helena Burns, FSP 285
   Biography 285
   Foreword: Human Conception in the Context of our Culture 286
Human beginnings: A Response of Reverence, Wonder and Joy 286
Science Updates the Church's Teaching on the Sacredness of Human Life 287

Modern Science and Good Philosophy Contradict the Delayed "Personhood Theory" 288
Not a Potential Person but a Person with Potential 290

Chapter Four: How Does Philosophy help us to Understand the "Moment" of Human Beginning?
....291
Philosophical and Theological dialogue 291
Being and Beginning 293

Chapter Four: Part I of V: A Definition of Being 295
Being 295
Proceeding to a Definition of Being: Unity-in-Diversity ... 296
A Point of Departure in the Being of Christ 297
A Point of Departure in the Being of the Blessed Trinity .. 298
What are the Conceptual Requirements that an Image of Human Being, which is in the Image of the Divine Being, must Fulfil? 298
A Template of Human Being 299
An Imaginative Synthesis: 'the burning coal' (Is 6: 6) 300
The Expression of the Relationship between "Grace" and "Human Nature" and "Soul" and "Body" in Philosophical terms 301
The Soul as "Life" and the "Activity" of the Soul 304
How widely can the Principle of Unity-in-Diversity be Applied? 305
Three Conclusions on the Nature of Being 306
The First Implication: the Beginning of Creation 306
The Second Implication: Human Being 307
The Third Implication: Answering the Philosophical Problems of Uniformity or Irreconcilable Diversity ... 308

Chapter Four: Part II of V: Defining what Exists 310
Questions have Answers 310
A Working Definition of Terms 313
God 313
Person 314
Definitions and use of the term Person 318
Person and Action 322
Christ and Human Action 323
Action Manifests Being 325
The Body is Male or Female 327
The Act of Creation is a Personal Act 329
The Transmission of Life at the Origin of Bodily Expressed Personhood 330
A Personal Being: Human Being-in-Relation 333
Matter 334
Signate, Concrete or Actual "Matter" 335
'First Matter' and 'Formless Matter' 338
Genesis: 'First Matter' or 'Formless Matter' 341
Continuity and Discontinuity in the Order of Being 344
What kind of Act is an Act of Creation? 346
Discontinuity as a Principle of Design 347
How to Understand the Integration of these "Elements" in the Totality of the Whole Person 351
The Human Body: Seven Characteristics 351
Parts of a Whole 357
A Hierarchical or a Chronological Order? 358
The Essence of what Exists 362

Chapter Four: Part III of V: Form; Matter; Cause; Unity; and Personhood 366
There are Three Sections to Part III, "Exploring Ideas of 'Form'" (IIIi); "Metaphysics ... the Underlying Principles of what Exists" (IIIii); and "A PreliminaryDiscussion of the Personalization of Matter". 366

Chapter Four: Part IIIi: Exploring Ideas of 'Form' 366
Ideas as Embodied Form 367
'Form' as a Universal and 'Form' as a Particular 370
The Cause and Type of Human Form 373
The Cause of Human Personhood 375
Soul, Particularly the Human Soul 380
The Particularity of the Soul: Especially the Human Soul 384
The Principal Activities of the Soul 387
Like and unlike Life 388

Chapter Four: Part IIIii: Metaphysics ... the Underlying Principles of what Exists 391
Metaphysics 391
Revisiting 'First Matter' and 'Form' 393
Returning to "First Matter" and the Integral Nature of Human Existence 395
Accidental and Substantial Being: What Exists and the Changes it Undergoes 399
One or Three Types of 'Form' in Human Being? 401
The Progress of a "Relationship" 402
Are 'Forms' Intelligent? 403
Activity and "Intelligent" or Goal Directed Activity 403
Levels of Activity and the Coherence of the Whole 406
What if 'First Matter' is a Metaphysical Possibility because of Aristotle's Conception of Matter Being Eternal? Or a Succession of 'forms' which Require there to be a State of Matter which Makes this Possibility Possible? 408

Chapter Four: Part IIIiii: A Preliminary Discussion of the Personalization of Matter 410
The Personalization of Matter 410
Animation and the "Levels of Matter" 412
The Human Soul is the Life of the Body 412
The "Personalization" of Matter 413

The Relation of the Human Soul to Biologically Human Matter 414
A Working Definition of Human Being 416
One or Many 'Substanial Forms' to the Human Being? 418
Passive Receptivity or Reciprocal Co-Constituents of Human Being? 424
The Reciprocal Insights of "Life" and "Death" 426
Conception or Eduction? 428

Chapter Four: Part IV of V: An Analogy 433
The Whole Person 433
An Analogy: the Washing Machine 433
A Goal-Governed Process 434
The Idea as "Germ" of the Goal 435
The "Design-Form" and the "Concrete" Object: a Constant Relationship in an Ongoing Process of Change 436
The "Termini" of the Process of Change 437
Time and Change 438
The Agent-Builder and the Limitations of the Analogy 439
A number of weaknesses in this Analogy 439
Two Implications: the Relation of the Design-Form to the Material Object and the Whole Cannot but Exist in Relation to its Maker 442

Chapter Four: Part V of V: Facts, Difficulties and a Way Forward 444
Facts and Difficulties 444
Twins: a New Beginning 445
The Truth of a Principle and the Remaining Questions 446
The Possible Death of a First Child 448
The Possibility of Twins Being "Recombined" 449
Conjoined Twins imply a Real "Moment of Beginning" ... 450
How are we to Understand what Constitutes the Necessary and Sufficient Basis of the Living Body? 451
A Way Forward: the Possibility of "Common" Knowledge 453

"Baby is the Best Healing Gift" and Artist's Statement by Isao Kurihara 455

Foreword to Chapter Five and Biography: Kathleen Sweeney 457
Biography 457
Foreword: "The Trinitarian Structure of the World's Reality" 457
A Child is the Outward Expression of Spousal Love 458
We draw upon Reason and Revelation............................. 459
"Whoever welcomes one such child in my name, welcomes me" 460
Christ chose to come into the World as a Human Embryo 461

"Take My Soul" and Artist's Statement by Andrea Colella, Italy 462

Chapter Five: Finding a Place to Begin: The "Being" of the Blessed Trinity "Founds" Human Being 463
Just as the Existence of God is "Before", so the Truth about God is "Prior" to the Truth about Creation 463

Chapter Five: Part I: The "Being" of the Blessed Trinity "Founds" Human Being... 463
Naming is a Dialogue.. 464
God is the "Archetypal Form" of Being 465
The First Principle of Being is therefore 'Unity-in-Diversity" 466
A Definition of an 'Integral Vision' of Man 467
Man is made in the Image of God 469
The Beginning of an Integral Vision of Man 471

Chapter Five: Part II: General Introduction: From Relationship to Relationship by Francis Etheredge....475
The "Book" Position of this paper by Justo Aznar and Julio Tudela..................476
Where there is a Human Being there is a Human Being-in-Relationship..................476
Establishing our Common Humanity establishes the Reality of an Ethical Relationship between us 477

Biographies of Professors Justo Aznar and Julio Tudela 479

Chapter Five: Part II: The Biological Status of the early Human Embryo: When does Human Life Begin? A Paper by Professors Justo Aznar and Julio Tudela..................480
Introduction 480
Four different Positions on the early Human Embryo's Biological Nature 483
Is the early Embryo a living Being of our Species? 485
   The Genetic Identity of the Human Embryo...............485
   Is the early Human Embryo an Organized and living Human Being?..................488
A brief Review of these Biological Processes 488
The early Embryo has its own Cell Lineage, Timing, and Architecture from the Beginning 494
   The Nature of the Human Embryo obtained by Somatic Cell Nuclear Transfer (Cloning) or Parthenogenesis .. 503
   Arguments against the Position that the Zygote is a Human Individual 504
   Final Considerations 506

Chapter Five: Part III: The Gift and Rights of Being Conceived-in-Relationship: We are an Icon of the Beginning.. 508
The help of Faith and Reason.. 508
　The Gift and Rights of being Conceived 508
　Beginning an unfolding of Human Personhood (I-V). 509
What is Conception? (I)... 512
Conception in the Teaching of the Church (II) 516
Conception in the Mysteries of Mary and Jesus and each of us (III).. 518
The Fact of Human Conception (IIIi) 518
The Reciprocal Relationship between Natural and Revealed Truth (IIIii)... 519
　The Morality of Embryonic Transfer (IV) 525
Natural Arguments for Embryonic Transfer and Adoption (IVi) 525
The Supernatural Arguments for Embryonic Adoption (IVii) 527
The Adoption of the Embryonic Human Child (V) 530

The Reality of two Children: Spencer and Caroline 535

Five Conclusions 536

First Conclusion: The Virtue of Simplicity........................ 536

Second Conclusion: A Summary of the Arguments for the Existence of the Soul from Conception 539

Third Conclusion: A Summary of the Arguments against the Theory of Evolutionary Development from one kind of Being..547

Fourth Conclusion: The Social Advance of Truth Concerning Conception...556

Fifth Conclusion in Two Parts: 561
    Part I: Faith in God: Convergence from Different Philosophical and Religious Traditions........................561
    Part II: A Warning from Mother Teresa: Abortion leads to Nuclear War 566

"Death of Birthright" and Artist's Statement by Natacha Horn..573

"Blessings" 575
"Afar Women of Ethiopia" and Artist's Statement by Jerry Galea (Australia)..576

Epilogue..577

"An End Word: A New Beginning" and Biography by Elizabeth Bothamley Rex, PhD........................... 583
Biography 583
Introduction 585
A Look *"Back"*: A History of Human Fertilization and Conception from 1818 to the Present 587
A Look *"In the Book"*: Five Points from Chapter Five........ 611
A Look *"Forward"*: Starting from the 'aweinspiring and "transformative" first moment of human conception' . 615
Conclusion: A Bold New Beginning....................................621
The Light of Life 622

BIOGRAPHY
Grace Marie Urlakis

Grace Marie is a young Catholic student and writer. She is currently working towards her undergraduate degree in Theology and English in the Humanities at Holy Apostles College and Seminary. A firm lover of Eastern Christianity,

Grace Marie is also pursuing a graduate certificate through Saints Cyril and Methodius Byzantine Catholic Seminary. This love of East and West – enkindled by her passion, the Word – has led Grace Marie to compose poetry which emphasizes the vibrant theology embraced by both "lungs" of the Church.

She is the author of the following two poems: "The Creation of the Cosmos" and, following the General Foreword by her mother, "In the Beginning".

THE CREATION OF THE COSMOS

What words can speak of the beginning
Of being, er it was begun,
When yet the finite was uncreated
Glory! Eternal three in one!

"Let there be light" spoke the Word
Into the formless void,
And so it was, by your wisdom,
Light from light deployed

When yet no sun had set the sky
Nor burned within the dome
Of golds and greens the stars were born
Within your palm, their home.

You spread the heavenly tapestry,
And hung on high the stars.
Around your will they orbit
Through seasons' ceaseless hours.

Your breath swirled the galaxies,
Your hand their motion stayed,
Your arm cast the milky way
Unto horizons yet unmade.

Stroke by stroke you etched the planets
Into the dark of night,
You lit the flame of morning's star
Er walked the morning light.
Your wisdom strung the bear and bow
It fed the winged horse,
Your justice set the scales ablaze
And your mercy traced its course.

You placed in heaven prophets true
Of creation yet in mind,
Of beasts and birds, and creeping things,
Of future, past, aligned.

Then did the man in giant stride
And the virgin, young and fair,
Walk among the lamps of angels
One, in order there.

Your delight was in creation,
In the depths which none would know.
You laid aloft the pattern
And formed the ceaseless glow.

The angels saw your love, Lord,
As with the stars they played.
They marveled at your handiwork,
At the palace you had made.

Not of their merit stood these orbs
Nor shone these witless gods,
But as a beacon for the ones
Who in their light would trod.

And yet you formed a boundary
Of the depths, a floor,
Where ends the cosmic tangible
And opens heaven's door.
No being knows its entrance
- The eternal side of time -
No one can search its archway
Nor to its summit climb.

The stars sang their praise of you,
Wordless, to the Word
A symphony of being
And from the womb, creation heard.

For God set the sun on high,
And the moon to rule the night,
At His breath the day unfurled,
And lo, there was light[1].

---

[1] Grace Marie Urlakis, March 1st, 2019: A segment from "Alpha and Omega: A Canticle of Eden".

Conception: An Icon of the Beginning

Biography
Dr. Mary Anne Urlakis

Dr. Mary Anne Urlakis is the Executive Director and Co-Founder of the *Donum Vitae* Institute for Nascent Human Life. The *Donum Vitae* Institute is dedicated to defending the sanctity of human life through research, scholarship, advocacy, policy formation, and prayer. In 1994, Dr. Urlakis was the first graduate from the Medical College of

Wisconsin's Master of Arts Degree Program in Bioethics. She subsequently earned a second Master of Arts Degree in Philosophy and Applied Ethics, as well as a Doctorate in Health Care Administration and Ethics.

Dr. Urlakis holds numerous graduate certificates in bioethics and theology, including a 2015 graduate certificate in Eastern Christian Studies from Saints Cyril and Methodius Byzantine Catholic Seminary, and a 2017 graduate certificate via the joint program between the Catholic University of America and the Vatican Foundation, *Centesimus Annus Pro Pontifice* (CAPP).

In addition to her work in bioethics, Dr. Urlakis was employed for nearly a decade in Cell Culture Research for the Anatomy and Physiology Departments of the Medical College of Wisconsin. She has taught at both the graduate and undergraduate levels at Mount Mary University. Dr. Urlakis has been married for 29 years and is the mother of eight living children, three of whom are adopted. She and her husband are also parents to two little ones whose lives continue in Heaven.

GENERAL FOREWORD
Dr. Mary Anne Urlakis

"He is the image of the invisible God, the first-born of all creatures, in Him everything in heaven and on earth was created, things visible and invisible (Colossians 1:15)."

Conception: An Icon of the Beginning

Introduction: "Nothing Comes From nothing" (Parmenides)

For the reflective reader, the topics developed between the two covers of this book will evoke serious internal deliberation and discernment. Through <u>Conception: An Icon of the Beginning</u>, the thoughtful reader is invited on a multifaceted odyssey, transcending history and disciplines to consider the very essence of the nature of the human person in its inception. Like most good journeys, this one provides as many new vistas upon which to gaze as challenges with which to grapple; and when it is completed, it is likely that the contemplative pilgrim will view these topics with new found zeal.

Many months ago, when Francis Etheredge initially invited me to write a component of this remarkable text, my immediate response was: "Personhood, and the plexus among Personhood, Philosophy, Theology, Biology, Moral Anthropology and Ethics- I'm in! This is the area of research that I find the most crucial, and the most fascinating!" With my abiding love of Eastern Christianity, Etheredge's conceptualization of the human person as an icon of the beginning immediately struck a chord with me. Throughout the course of this project it has been intriguing to witness the development of *Conception: An Icon of the Beginning* – particularly to behold the way so many gifted contributors engaged the main text.

Throughout this work, Etheredge and the other contributing authors contend with complex questions regarding the very nature of the human person – questions that have perplexed thinkers throughout the ages; questions that are both particular to each individual person that has – or ever will – exist, and questions that likewise are universal, and apply to each of us bound in relationship to the human family.

The Apostolic Constitution, *Gaudium et Spes*, promulgated in 1965 by Pope St. Paul VI, addresses the relevance of this human longing:

"Meanwhile every man remains to himself an unsolved puzzle, however obscurely he may perceive it. For on certain occasions no one can entirely escape the kind of self-questioning mentioned earlier, especially when life's major events take place. To this questioning, only God fully and most certainly provides an answer as He summons man to higher knowledge and humbler probing."[2]

The most fundamental inquiries transcend time, space, ideology, and culture. Who of us has not at some point wondered: "Who am I?" "Where did I come from?" and "Why do I exist?" These queries resonate profoundly within us as they are intimately and intrinsically woven within the very essence of our being. Deeply personal – and yet also communal – they form a bedrock of moral anthropology and elucidating a myriad of implicit intricacies requires a multifaceted approach – one that considers the salient research, evidence, and argument from the philosophical, theological, biological and ethical dimensions.

It is thus, with this methodological approach that the inquiry develops. Seeking the truth, Etheredge engages the perspective of a series of collaborating authors, and utilizes the expertise of each to introduce new dimensions of the inquest.

In their introduction to part two of chapter five, entitled: "The Biological Status of the Early Human Embryo: When

---

[2] *Gaudium et Spes,* Pastoral Constitution on the Church in the Modern World, Promulgated by Pope St. Paul VI, 7 Dec 1965, Chapter 1, § 21.

does Human Life Begin?", Professors Justo Aznar and Julio Tudela state:

> "In order to determine the nature of the human embryo, we need to know its biological, anthropological, philosophical, and even its legal reality. In our opinion, however, the anthropological, philosophical and legal reality of the embryo — the basis of its human rights — must be built upon its biological reality."[3]

Like Aznar and Tudela, throughout the text, each of the collaborating authors focus the lens of the present instrument of examination through their own unique vantage and proficiency.

From the outset of *Conception: An Icon of the Beginning*, Etheredge elucidates a key principle: "Where the body lives, there is the soul, and where both are there is the person."[4] This simple maxim accurately reflects the wisdom of the ancient Church Fathers while also serving as a locus of meaning for each of the contributing authors.

In his *Physics*, Parmenides was the first to be credited with the thesis: "Nothing comes from nothing." In Greek: "τί δ' ἄν μιν καὶ χρέος ὦρσεν ὕστερον ἢ πρόσθεν, τοῦ μηδενὸς ἀρξάμενον, φῦν; οὕτως ἢ πάμπαν πελέναι χρεών ἐστιν ἢ οὐχί.[5] For millennia, the thesis "nothing comes from nothing" has found ratification among philosophers, logicians, and physicists. The Roman poet Lucretius expressed this principle in the initial book of his work *De*

---

3 Justo Aznar and Julio Tudela, in *Conception: An Icon of the Beginning*, Chapter 5, Part II.

4 Francis Etheredge, *Conception: An Icon of the Beginning*, Part II of the Prologue.

5 Parmenides, *Physics*, Fragment 8, [https://lexundria.com/parm_frag/1-19/grk, Edited by Herman Diels].

Rerum Natura, stating "nothing is created from nothing," – in Latin: "*nil posse creari de nilo,*" or *"ex nihilo nihil fit."*[6] In the disciplines of physics and chemistry, the Law of Conservation of Energy, expresses this precept. Applying this principle to the consideration of human generation, one can accurately state: "Nothing that is living comes from that which is dead." Likewise, a corpse is by definition, a body that is dead, a body that does not possess an animating spirit. Thus, if a body is indeed living, it must be united with a soul, and – as Etheredge states – where a body lives, there is a soul and so exists a person. A living person cannot come from a non-living corpse; life cannot come from death any more that what is can come from what is not, as has been observed from ancient times.

It is the analysis of the validity of this claim, replete with intrinsic ramifications, to which the enquiry of *Conception: An Icon of the Beginning* unfolds. Throughout the text, Etheredge's examination proceeds methodologically and the perspective expressed by each of the contributing authors facilitates the focusing and reorienting of the inquiry, much as a kaleidoscope is continually refocused, ever-divulging the truth, goodness, and beauty present in minuscule components. It is precisely this claim: "Where the body lives, there is the soul, and where both are is the person,"[7] that reveals the relevance of truth of nascent human personhood in time and history.

The title *Conception: An Icon of the Beginning* evokes images that are both ancient and new. Throughout the text, Etheredge engages the venerable writings of the Early Church Fathers, seeking the often-neglected relevance of

---

[6] Lucretius, *De Rerum Natura*, Book I [http://classics.mit.edu/Carus/nature_things.1.i.html, William Ellery Leonard translation].

their work to contemporary issues surrounding the beginnings of human life.

Before embarking upon this methodological investigation, it is germane to consider the meaning and historical significance of the salient terms in the title.

Icon

> "Who being the effulgence of his glory, the very image of his substance, and upholding all things by the word of his power.... (Hebrews 1:3)"

Long before I began to work in this area, I had always been fascinated by icons. Even as a youth, like most children, I intuitively knew that there was something very special about a religious icon – it was self-evident that these images were not mere religious art, but were intrinsically something far more transcendent and profound.

The term "icon" is derived from the Greek word "eikon" [εἰκών], a word meaning "image" which denotes a sign of the presence of God. An icon is a visual symbol of the reality of the invisible – an expression of spiritual realities which are inexpressible in words and inaccessible by rational discourse alone. Far from being a mere aesthetic expression of religious sentiment, the icon is an essential part of sacred tradition: the visual image of the sacred icon is equivalent to the verbal image of the Word of Sacred Scripture. As the Word of Sacred Scripture paints a mental image, so too the Sacred Image of an authentic Christian Icon is a word. Quoting St. Basil the Great, the Early Church Fathers spoke clearly in a series of Ecumenical Councils:

---

7 Francis Etheredge, *Conception: An Icon of the Beginning*, Part II of the Prologue.

"That which the word communicates by sound, a painting demonstrates silently by representation. . . . By means of these two ways which compliment one another, that is by reading and by the visible image, we gain knowledge of the same thing."[8]

From ancient times, the Church Fathers have affirmed that the icon is not merely art, illustrating Sacred Scripture, but rather it is in fact the visual equivalent of Sacred Scripture. As such, it derives its authenticity not by corresponding to the letter of the word of Sacred Scripture – or the letters of the book itself, but rather by corresponding to the *Kergyma* – the content of Sacred Scripture and most importantly to the Author of Scripture – the Word Made Flesh.

Quoting St. Basil the Great, the Early Church Fathers declared:

"The honor rendered to the image passes to its prototype, for the person who venerates an icon venerates the person who is represented on it."[9]

In a letter admonishing the Bishop of Marseille for iconoclastic activity – for destroying icons under the pretext of believing that the people were worshipping the images instead of Christ, Whom the holy icons represented, Pope St. Gregory the Great stated:

". . . we forbid you from destroying them. It is necessary to distinguish between the worship of an icon and the process of learning that which must be

---

[8] Leonid Ouspensky, *The Theology of the Icon*, Vol. I (Yonkers, NY: St. Vladimir's Seminary Press, 1992), p. 138-139.

[9] Leonid Ouspensky, *The Theology of the Icon*, Vol I, p. 140.

Conception: An Icon of the Beginning

worshipped in history. What Scripture is for the man who knows how to read, the icon is for the illiterate. Through it, even uneducated men can see what they must follow. It is the book of those who do not know the alphabet...."[10]

The icon is as old as Christianity itself – and the Church has maintained that Christ Himself manifest such images as Veronica's Veil, the Sudarium of Edessa – or, as it is known in the Orthodox Tradition – the Mandylion of Edessa[11], and the Shroud of Turin. Thus, it is the Incarnate Word Himself Who miraculously transmitted His own Holy Image to these inimitable sacred icons. It is piously believed that St. Luke the Evangelist, wrote[12] [painted] the first icons of the Blessed Virgin.[13] Yet, throughout history, there have been

---

[10] Pope St. Gregory the Great, *Epistolarum* Liber Ix, epist. Xiii, PL 77: 1128A-1130A.

[11] The Sudarium or Mandylion is a small rectangular piece of cloth on which the Divine Image of the Face of Christ appeared in a manner "not made by human hands." – the Orthodox Church celebrates the Feast of the Icon "Not Made by Human Hands" on August 16. There is controversy about the authenticity of the Mandylion, however its existence is recorded in history numerous times, first by Eusebius of Caesarea in the 4th Century, and again by Evagrius Scholastica in 593. It is piously believed that the Image was brought by St. Thaddeus of Edessa at the request of the seriously-ill King Abgar, and that the miraculous image was instrumental in the king's cure.

[12] It is important to note a distinction in terminology. Sacred Icons are *written*, not merely "painted." Sacred Icons are equal to the letter of Sacred Scripture in such a way that they express the *Kergyma* of the Gospel, the reality of the Incarnate Word. Thus, even though the Word is expressed in such physical media as paint and wood, to be precise one always refers to the *writing* of an icon – never to its "painting." This distinction is exceedingly relevant as one begins to consider the human person as an icon of the beginning.

[13] While on pilgrimage in Rome, my family and I recently had the joy of venerating sacred icons, including the *Salus Populi*

periods of violent attack against the sacred icon. Transmitted through Sacred Tradition, the icons known as Eleusa, "the Virgin of Tenderness," and Hodigitra, "She Who Shows the Way," are believed to have originated from the hand of the Evangelist, and to this day remain the pattern by which authentic sacred icons of the Virgin continue to be written. Yet, throughout history, there have been periods of violent attack against the sacred icon. Such attacks were not mere expressions of distaste regarding aesthetic nuances, but rather these were violent heretical movements which were directed against the Dogma of the Incarnation itself.

Among the most eloquent and definitive refutations of the heresy of iconoclasm is St. John Damascene's *Apology Against Those Who Decry Holy Images*. In it he states:

> "Of old, God the incorporeal and uncircumscribed was never depicted. Now, however, when God is seen clothed in flesh, and conversing with men, (Bar. 3.38) I make an image of the God whom I see. I do not worship matter, I worship the God of matter, who became matter for my sake, and deigned to inhabit matter, who worked out my salvation through matter. I will not cease from honouring that matter which works my salvation. I venerate it, though not as God."[14]

Iconoclasts cloaked their assaults against sacred icons in an erroneous charge of idolatry. However, the heretical root of their charges was the propensity to view all matter as profane, and reject the reality of the Incarnation of Christ – preferring a God Who would not condescend to truly become

---

Romani in the Basilica of Santa Maria Maggiore, attributed to originating from the hand of St. Luke the Evangelist.

[14] St. John Damascene, *Apology of St. John of Damascus Against Those Who Decry Holy Images*, Christian Classics Ethereal Library, London, Thomas Baker, 1898, p. 16.

flesh and blood, and persisting in the gnostic error that only the immaterial spiritual realm was sacred.

St. John Damascene responded:

> "How could God be born out of lifeless things? And if God's body is God by union (καθ υποστασιν), it is immutable. The nature of God remains the same as before, the flesh created in time is quickened by a logical and reasoning soul. I honour all matter besides, and venerate it. Through it, filled, as it were, with a divine power and grace, my salvation has come to me."[15]

The icon of Christ over the entrance of the Imperial Palace in Constantinople was the first of the sacred icons to be officially destroyed during the initial iconoclastic period in 730 A.D. It was destroyed by Emperor Leo III himself, after years (726-730) of futile attempts to convince Pope St. Gregory II and Patriarch St. Germanus to change Church dogma and adhere to the iconoclastic heresy.[16] Violence, bloodshed, and martyrdom continued for over a hundred years in the initial conflict.

The Church Fathers were unwavering in their defense of the sacredness of holy icons, and in the year 870 A.D., they declared at the Eight Ecumenical Council [also called the Fourth Council of Constantinople] in Canon 3:

> "We ordain that the holy icon of our Lord be venerated in the same way as the book of Gospels. Indeed, just as all receive salvation through the syllables contained in it, so do all, both learned and ignorant, draw profit from what the colors of the icon possess. For that which words announce through syllables, the colors in painting show.

---

[15] Ibid.
[16] Leonid Ouspensky, *The Theology of the Icon*, Vol. I, p. 109.

If one does not venerate the icon of Christ the Savior, let him not see His face at the Second Coming."[17]

Let those words sink in. "If one does not venerate the icon of Christ the Savior, let him not see His face at the Second Coming."[18] The image contained in a holy icon is sacred – as sacred as Scripture itself. Through the sacred image of the Icon of Christ the Savior – just as through sacred Scripture and the Magisterial teaching and tradition of the Church, one is invited to believe in the Son of God – to accept His Salvific mission, and to attest to the truth of the Creed. For each and every human person, this invitation requires a response – a response which has eternal ramifications.

The Council Fathers continued in Canon 3:

"In the same manner, we venerate and bring homage to the icon of His all-pure Mother, to those of the holy angels, painted as they are described in the words of Holy Scripture, and furthermore to those of all the saints. Let those who do not do this be an anathema."[19]

The words promulgated by the early Church Fathers in Canon 3 are as relevant and binding for us today as they were when penned in the year 870 A.D. As one reads the arguments presented by Etheredge, and each of the authors who contributed their expertise to <u>Conception: An Icon of the Beginning</u>, the sound theological underpinnings of the historical defense of the sacredness of the *Imago Dei* reflected in authentic icons becomes profoundly evident. For, just as the sacred icon derives its authenticity and

---

[17] Leonid Ouspensky, *The Theology of the Icon*, Vol II, p. 212.
[18] Ibid.
[19] Ibid.

holiness from its reflection of the *Kergyma* of the Gospel and its relationship to the Incarnate Christ, so too the human person as a union of soul and body is rendered holy by bearing the imprint of the *Imago Dei* within his very being – from the moment of conception.

Image and Likeness

> Let Us make man in our image, after Our likeness, to rule over the fish of the sea and birds of the air, over the livestock, and over all the earth itself and every creature that crawls upon it (Genesis 1:26).

Among the cornerstones in substratum of Judeo-Christian belief is the certitude that the human person was – and is – created in the Image and Likeness of Almighty God. This point of doctrine was exceptional among the pagan cultures with whom the early Jews and Christians interacted. For no other people claimed to have such an intimate and personal relationship with Divinity as to bear Its very reflection within each individual human person, and by virtue of this unmitigated privilege, to exist in a covenantal relationship with the Divine. In essence, the pagan gods existed in imitation of the of the human characteristics from which they were drawn, and human beings merely functioned to serve their material needs. This pagan view yields a sharp contrast to the Judeo-Christian contention of a human person who is created such that from the inception of his being he reveals the manifestation of the Divine Image present within his soul and body – a manifestation which in turn points to a unique and covenantal kinship. It is this axiom – that from the first instant of creation – both in the history of humanity and again reiterated in the conception of each individual, that the human person echoes the purposeful imprint of the *Imago Dei* that has remained intrinsic to Christianity. Throughout *Conception: An Icon of the Beginning*, this core doctrine is explored beautifully by Etheredge and the other contributing authors.

Unique as it is, this conviction has withstood the onslaught of error and attack throughout the centuries. In much the same way that the blessedness of the icon has been assailed by those who refuse to accept that God would reveal Himself in a personal, material, bodily and tangible manner, so too the dogma of the Incarnation has been heretically attacked by those who refuse to acknowledge that the human person is made in the Image and Likeness of God. Both the sacredness of the icon and the sacredness of the human person illuminate the reality of the Incarnation of the Second Person of the Blessed Trinity, and His Salvific mission. It is for this reason alone that both have been violently impugned throughout history.

The chronicles of St. Irenaeus (ca. A.D. 140 - ca. A.D. 202), the Second Bishop of Lyons (historically *Lugdunum, Gual*) provide the earliest, and most thorough, refutation of the gnostic heresy.[20] In his work, particularly *On the Detection and Overthrow of the So-Called Gnosis* [often referred to as simply *Adversus Haereses*], St. Irenaeus systematically refutes the gnostic doctrine – engaging and dismantling the theories of its proponents one maxim at time. Simultaneously, while pointing out the errors of the gnostic belief system St. Irenaeus methodologically presents the truths of Christian dogma. St. Irenaeus was the first theologian and philosopher to utilize the concept of the relationship of the *Imago Dei* present in each human person in a comprehensive refutation of heretical gnostic belief.

In Book V of *On the Detection and Overthrow of the So-Called Gnosis*, St. Irenaeus asserts:

---

[20] William Jurgens, *The Faith of the Early Fathers*, Volume I (Collegeville, MN: Liturgical Press, 1978), p. 84.

Conception: An Icon of the Beginning

"Now God shall be glorified in His handiwork, fitting it so as to be conformable to, and modelled after, His own Son. For by the hands of the Father, that is, by the Son and the Holy Spirit, man, and not [merely] a part of man, was made in the likeness of God. Now the soul and the spirit are certainly a *part* of the man, but certainly not *the* man; for the perfect man consists in the commingling and the union of the soul receiving the spirit of the Father, and the admixture of that fleshly nature which was moulded after the image of God."[21]

The human person is the summit of God's Creation; and it is in the human person that the glory of God shines forth as a reflection of His handiwork, sharing in the Image and Likeness of the Blessed Trinity by a unified movement of grace. It is not that the *Imago Dei* is an afterthought of the Divine handiwork – a gold-star-seal-of-approval slapped onto a fully mature human nature as a bonus. No, rather the *Imago Dei* is reflected precisely in the commingling of body and soul – the "admixture of that fleshy nature" which is constituted after the very Image of God. For St. Irenaeus and many of the ancient Church Fathers, the Image of God into which man is created is a reflection of the Divine – it is an indelible countenance and pattern according to which each human person is created – body and soul; and which is reflected by each human as a part of his or her nature. It is in the Divine Image that we are patterned and formed – body and soul – from the moment of conception, and it is because of this indelible image reflected within each of us – no matter how tiny, or aged, that we share in the sacred dignity of adopted sons and daughters of the Almighty Godhead.

---

[21] St. Irenaeus of Lyons, in *On the Detection and Overthrow of the So-Called Gnosis*, Book V; Chapter 6:1.

"The dignity of a person must be recognized in every human being from conception to natural death."[22]

Throughout the millennia, the sacred dogma of the Church has remained definitive and unwavering, articulating the same truths proclaimed by Bishop Irenaeus two millennia prior. The Catechism of the Catholic Church states:

> "Christ, . . . in the very revelation of the mystery of the Father and of his love, makes man fully manifest to himself and brings to light his exalted vocation." It is in Christ, "the image of the invisible God," that man has been created "in the image and likeness" of the Creator. It is in Christ, Redeemer and Savior, that the divine image, disfigured in man by the first sin, has been restored to its original beauty and ennobled by the grace of God."[23]

Whether a human person chooses – via an act of the will – to recognize the reality of the Divine Image in himself as well as in his neighbor, that Divine Image remains, and cannot be destroyed. Each person bears the *Imago Dei*, and the infrangible dignity that accompanies it, from the instant of conception on. In CCC 1703, the Catechism states:

> "Endowed with "a spiritual and immortal" soul, the human person is "the only creature on earth that God has willed for its own sake." From his conception, he is destined for eternal beatitude."[24]

---

[22] *Dignitas Personae*, Congregation for the Doctrine of the Faith, 22 February 1987, Section 1.

[23] CCC 1701 *Catechism of the Catholic Church*. This section of the Catechism reflects and quotes extensively from the Vatican II Document *Gaudium et Spes* – again reflecting a Magisterial teaching that has remained unbroken for millennia.

[24] CCC 1703, *Catechism of the Catholic Church*, Part 3, Section 1, Chapter 1.

Conception: An Icon of the Beginning

According to St. Irenaeus, the Divine Image is not simply a component of either body or soul, rather it is interwoven into the human person body **AND** soul. He states:

> "[T]hus also, if any one take away the image and set aside the handiwork, he cannot then understand this as being a man, but as either some part of a man, as I have already said, or as something else than a man. For that flesh which has been moulded is not a perfect man in itself, but the body of a man, and part of a man. Neither is the soul itself, considered apart by itself, the man; but it is the soul of a man, and part of a man. Neither is the spirit a man, for it is called the spirit, and not a man; but the commingling and union of all these constitutes the perfect man."[25]

For St. Ireneaus, there is a subtle distinction between the Divine Image and Likeness of the Almighty which each human person bears. The Divine *Image* refers to the Divine Countenance infused or interwoven into the intermingling of body and soul that is the human person. The Divine Image remains imperishable in each person – whether or not the individual recognizes via the intellect and will that he or she bears the *Imago Dei*. The Divine *Likeness* refers to a capacity that each human person possesses by virtue of the dignity of bearing the Divine Image. Each human person possesses the free-will to reject sin and accept Christ. In so exercising virtuous use of one's free-will, the Christian allows His Sprit to remain, thus he or she fulfills this capacity to be ultimately perfected and to grow into the Likeness of God. St. Irenaeus teaches:

---

[25] St. Irenaeus of Lyons, in *On the Detection and Overthrow of the So-Called Gnosis*, Book V; Chapter 6: 1.

"Those, then, are the perfect who have had the Spirit of God remaining in them, and have preserved their souls and bodies blameless, holding fast the faith of God, that is, that faith which is [directed] towards God, and maintaining righteous dealings with respect to their neighbours."[26]

From the inception of Christianity, dogma – grounded in firm philosophical and theological underpinnings through Sacred Tradition and Sacred Scripture - had taught that the human person possesses an inviolable and sacred dignity from the first moment of existence because each and every person is created in the Divine Image and Likeness.

Such dignity is absolute, and unique by virtue of the relationship that exists between God and man – a relationship which at its core is covenantal in nature. The consistent teachings of the Magisterium are reflected in Section 5 of *Donum Vitae*:

"From the moment of conception, the life of every human being is to be respected in an absolute way because man is the only creature on earth that God has "wished for himself" and the spiritual soul of each man is "immediately created" by God; his whole being bears the image of the Creator. Human life is sacred because its being involves "the creative action of God" and it remains forever in a special relationship with the Creator, who is its sole end."[27]

Thus, from the very beginning, each and every human person possesses an inviolable dignity – a dignity which

---

[26] Ibid.

[27] Joseph Cardinal Ratzinger, *Donum Vitae*, Congregation for the Doctrine of the Faith, 22 February 1987, Section 5.

requires recognition and compels moral obligations. Created in the *Imago Dei*, the human person is bound to discern and obey the command to love God and neighbor.

An Irrevocable, Covenantal Call to the Moral Life

> "For I am the Lord your God: be holy because I am holy (Leviticus 11: 44)."

Intrinsic to the recognition that the human person is created in the Image and Likeness of God is a moral mandate – an irrevocable call to the moral life. Flowing from the covenant relationship humanity has with God, and the natural law which is intrinsic to it, personhood confers a set of reciprocal obligations – a moral relationship which is binding from the first moment of existence. The covenantal relationship in which each and every human person is bound, is a mystical reflection of the unity of the Most Holy Trinity and the Communion of Divine Persons contained within it. The Catechism of the Catholic Church reiterates the codification of this ancient truth, stating: "The Divine Image is present in every man. It shines forth in the communion of persons, in the likeness and the unity of the Divine persons among themselves."[28]

Thus, bearing the imprint of the Divine upon his very person, the human person owes an obligation both to God who created him as well as to all other human persons who are likewise created. In alluding to the ancient covenantal relationship, Pope St. John Paul II highlights this point in the Section 39 of the Encyclical *Evangelium Vitae*:

---

[28] CCC 1702, *Catechism of the Catholic Church*, Part 3, Section 1, Chapter 1.

"Man's life comes from God; it is his gift, his image and imprint, a sharing in his breath of life. God therefore is the sole Lord of this life: man cannot do with it as he wills. God himself makes this clear to Noah after the Flood: "For your own lifeblood, too, I will demand an accounting ... and from man in regard to his fellow man I will demand an accounting for human life" (Gen 9:5). The biblical text is concerned to emphasize how the sacredness of life has its foundation in God and in his creative activity: "For God made man in his own image" (Gen 9:6)."[29]

Thus, a set of indisputable obligations flow simultaneously *from* one as a person bearing the *Imago Dei*, as well as *toward* all other persons who are likewise fashioned by the Creator bearing that unique dignity. Human persons come into being circumscribed by a covenantal kinship with God – a union and bond that is unique in all of creation, and one which necessitates an obligatory moral dimension. Such a covenantal liaison by definition reflects a relationship between persons – Divine Persons and human persons, and thus reveals a constituent set of reciprocative roles and duties. Moral rubrics presuppose a status of personhood – moral duties do not by nature occur between mere objects. Ordinary material articles, possessions, and property do not bind human persons to a moral set of obligations. While it is accurate to state that to each of these, the moral person bears responsibilities of stewardship, it is essential to note that even the actions necessitated by a good steward ultimately reflect back to a relationship between the persons. This truth can even be demonstrated when one considers the obligations one possesses toward a sacred icon. It is not to

---

[29] Pope St. John Paul, *Evangelium Vitae*, 25 March 1995, Section 39.

the wood nor paint – the mere material elements of a sacred icon – that an individual is compelled to reverence. Rather, as St. Basil the Great emphasized: "The honor rendered to the image passes to its prototype, for the person who venerates an icon venerates the person who is represented on it."[30] Likewise, as moral human persons it is not mere flesh and blood, clumps of cells and tissue, to which we owe moral consideration – it is to the living human person; a living human person created by and bearing the *Imago Dei* of the Divine Creator.

We are compelled to these correlative obligations as human persons by virtue of the Covenant relationship in which we are bound with Almighty God. The Covenant between God and man is a unique relationship – transcending both space and time, surpassing that which is physical and spiritual; of Divine origin, yet intimately human; ever ancient and ever new; encumbering all – as a people and as individual persons. It is a Covenant made between God and man, in ultimate love and mercy, ratified by the Blood of Christ Jesus. It is a Covenant that is made between God and His Creation – a Covenant between the Eternal Blessed Trinity and fallen humanity. It is a Covenant between the Three Persons of the Blessed Trinity and every person who is a member of the family of humanity. This covenantal relationship exists between God and His adopted children – as a family, as a community. The duties entailed by it are compulsory: an individual may no more "opt out" of the Covenant than he or she may abjure his or her human personhood. Timeless and transcendent, the Covenant relationship perdures, abiding in mercy and binding in accountability, regardless of the defiance of persons – individual or collective. As Pope St. John Paul illustrated in

---

[30] Leonid Ouspensky, *The Theology of the Icon*, Vol I, p. 140.

Section 39 of his Encyclical *Evangelium Vitae*, the imagery evoked in Genesis elucidates this point profoundly:

> "God blessed Noah and his sons and said to them, 'Breed, multiply, and fill the earth. . . . I give you everything with this exception: you must not eat flesh with life, that is to say blood, in it. And I shall demand an account of your life-blood, too. I shall demand it of every animal, and of man. Of man as regards his fellow-man, I shall demand an account for human life. He who sheds the blood of man, by man shall his blood be shed, for in the image of God was man created. Be fruitful and multiply, teem over the earth and subdue it." God spoke as follows to Noah and his sons, 'I am now establishing my covenant with you and with your descendants to come. . . . and I shall maintain my covenant with you (Genesis 9: 1-11).'"[31]

These obligations originate within the Covenant that exists between Almighty God and His supremely willed and loved creation – the human person. That Covenant was made between God and the entire human race – it is between God and the community, the family of humanity – sealed and irrevocably ratified with the Blood of Christ.

It is in the quintessential act of living the moral life in relationship with all other human persons, created in the *Imago Dei*, that the individual human person bears witness to the Divine reality of the sanctity of human life from the very first instant of its genesis. For Her part, the Church has unceasingly promulgated this immutable truth from Her inception. "The sacredness of life gives rise to its inviola-

---

[31] Genesis 9: 1-11, New Jerusalem Bible translation.

bility, written from the beginning in man's heart, in his conscience."[32]

Conclusion: '[A] living icon of the *imago Dei*'

"He remembers his covenant forever, the promise he made, for a thousand generations (1 Chronicles 16:15.)"

Throughout the pages of this present text the most fundamental questions of human existence are explored. From the outset of <u>Conception: An Icon of the Beginning</u>, Etheredge postulates a key principle: "Where the body lives, there is the soul, and where both are is the person."[33] Utilizing a multifaceted approach, Etheredge, with the assistance of the collaborating authors of this text investigate the legitimacy of this claim, and in so doing evince the myriad of bioethical ramifications that are contingent upon the validity of this precept. For if human conception is truly an icon of the beginning, then as human persons our obligations to the unborn – from the moment of conception – are objectively clear and irrefutable. Comprehending the human person as a living icon of the *Imago Dei* - not as a mere metaphor, but truly as an icon written in flesh and blood – reorients the discussion of the inception of human life, and its implicit doctrinal, bioethical, anthropological, biological, legal, and political implications.

Parallel to the manner in which an icon – written on wood with paint and pigment by a human agent – becomes a window to the Divine, so too the human person – woven from conception in flesh and soul reflects the icon of Christ's

---

[32] Pope St. John Paul II, *Evangelium Vitae*, 25 March 1995, Section 40.

[33] Francis, Etheredge, *Conception: An Icon of the Beginning*, Part II of the Prologue.

Incarnation. Just as the sacred icon of Christ and of His All-Holy and Immaculate Virgin Mother, and the angels and saints, are protected in Sacred Tradition and Church Law, even more so the human person who bears the iconographic Image and Likeness of God within his or her very being ought to be revered and protected. Such dignity and protection is thereby grounded in the obligations entailed by the Covenantal relationship between God and man.

Since the Church in its ancient wisdom solemnly declared at the Eighth Ecumenical Council in the year 870 A.D.,[34] that: "If one does not venerate the icon of Christ the Savior, let him not see His face at the Second Coming,"[35] how then ought one consider the indelible icon of *Imago Dei* – iconographically transcribed by the very Hand of God in flesh, blood, and soul in each human person? More specifically, if those who refuse to venerate the Image of God in Sacred Icons are anathamized,[36] how much more egregious is the refusal to recognize and venerate the imprint of the Divine Image in nascent human life – in the unborn? In the embryo?

Does not the refusal to venerate the Image and Likeness of God present within the unborn child, and the subsequent willful, violent, systematic obliteration of nascent life bearing the *Imago Dei* constitute the most egregious form of the age-old Iconoclastic Heresy? At the heart of the heresy of Iconoclasm is the refusal to acknowledge and hold sacred the

---

[34] Recall, this is also referred to as the Fourth Council of Constantinople.

[35] Leonid Ouspensky, *The Theology of the Icon*, Vol II, p. 212.

[36] Recall, Canon 3 states: "In the same manner, we venerate and bring homage to the icon of His all-pure Mother, to those of the holy angels, painted as they are described in the words of Holy Scripture, and furthermore to those of all the saints. Let those who do not do this be an anathema."

Conception: An Icon of the Beginning

Incarnation of the Second Person of the Blessed Trinity, an inward rejection of Sacred Dogma, which manifests in ostensible willed acts of destruction. Is not seeking to annihilate the very Image and Likeness of God, written in the union of the nascent body and soul of the unborn child the ultimate form of Iconoclasm?

These are the questions that we as human persons must face as we consider human conception as an icon of the beginning. It is such critical issues, paired with a sincere desire to seek the truth, which have inspired Francis Etheredge to write *Conception: An Icon of the Beginning*. May each of us who grapple with the profound nature of this query into the origin of human life and its inherent ethical implications be guided by wisdom and obtain truth.

IN THE BEGINNING[37]

Of the Word came the Beginning
From being ever, yet never begun,
Praise to you, O Trinity,
Three in Unity, Three yet One.

Out of this mystery you drew man,
Icon of your Image bound
In truth and love and good.
Called to unity profound.

When first man trod this poor earth,
Poor it was not, but good.
A sanctuary of your Presence
Of dale and river, steppe and wood.

When first you graced his breast with breath
And gave to him the land,
The birds and beasts and creeping things
Fashioned by your hand,

Then did he call each one by name,
Words from the Word within,
Then did he live through your own life,
In a world unmarred by sin.

Then was the Gardener the priest,
And the Priest the Image of God,
And man walked in His Presence
On holy ground, unshod.

---

[37] Grace Marie Urlakis, July 20th, 2018: A segment from "Alpha and Omega: A Canticle of Eden".

Yet, the one who tends was to create,
Alone this could not be so.
No animal was a fit helpmate
No beast his soul could know.

Thus, into sleep God cast man,
Where later man would, God,
Bone of bone and flesh of flesh
Across time's river, broad.

As slept man, both old and new
From that sleep was formed a bride,
Made in the Image illumined,
Drawn from an open side.

Thus, it is both will come
And to each other cleave,
And the man, his name was Adam,
And the woman he called Eve.

Still slept Adam at God's feet
When Eve saw morning bloom.
Father drew up daughter fair,
Calling softly, "Talitha Cum."[38]

Taking her hand He raised her,
Word and flesh now wed,
And as she stood before God's gaze
Was to her husband led.
Yet, first she looked upon her Maker
For His eyes impressed her soul.
Crafted in love, she loved Him,
And in loving knew her whole.

---

[38] Little Girl, Arise.

What words He spoke, none could say,
Of that brief, eternal exchange.
Marked with God's sign she turned then
At man's side arranged.

Hand in hand God placed them,
Eve, and Adam the man,
Thus, they dwelt in Eden,
In the garden, hand in hand.

Strong, in Eden worked the man,
Yet he worked now not alone.
Together, Gardener and helpmate
Stewards under the heavenly dome.

Their delight was in each other
And their sacred work now shared,
As Love's own life in Unity,
Eden's way prepared.

For when one day all was finished
And the holy labor done,
Summoned to the Mystery
Would Man and Woman come.

Still, perfect formed was newborn Eden,
Icon of what was and would,
As Man and Woman reigned together
For God pronounced them good.

Conception: An Icon of the Beginning

"Flame of Life"

by

Marco Riccardo Intra Sidola[39]

The Artist's Statement

'The moment I saw my first daughter's 3D ultrasound image, that I attach to these lines, a painting came to my mind; it is the painting you have just seen: "the Flame of Life" blazing up, winning the darkness.

The flame of a human life, portrayed in the moment of it's utmost vulnerability, that is also the moment of it's

---

[39] Oil on board, 36x60,5 cm. Unesco Chair in Bioethics and Human Rights Art Competition: Reproduced with the Permission of the Director from the Finalists of the 1st Global Art Competition: Bioethics in Art Collection. The language of the Artist's Statement is uncorrected. This picture was chosen in virtue of its very direct expression of the mystery of human life.

highest potentiality: tomorrow, this life will be able to be an help for the others and to relieve them, or to become motive of oppression for their persons, trampling their dignity. In fact, the drama of human liberty, is intrinsically deep-seated in human nature, in which also human dignity is deep-seated. The extraordinary strength that blazes up from a child who is not already born, the energy of his continuous and miraculous growing, is represented by the flame's vital heat, because every new life is able to bring with it into the world this heat, this energy and this positivity.

The darkness of Nothing has been pierced by this incredible and astonishing vital event, that wins it with its strength. To realize a "prenatal portrait" means to bring to everybody's attention the value and the dignity-as-a-person of every human being who is still not born, in every step of his growth: in fact, not things, just persons can be portrayed.'

Conception: An Icon of the Beginning

PROLOGUE: EXPLORING EXPRESSIONS OF THE BEGINNING OF HUMAN PERSONHOOD

We witness a beginning which is as old as the first person and as modern as the last: it is both a universal and a uniquely individual event.

Bearing in mind that we are a "people in dialogue", the task of an investigation is not only to trace the course of ideas as they are turned about and around, inside out and upside down; but, in the course of time, to see the need to explore ways of communicating that will turn us to talk to each other about the reality that we witness in common: that each one of us proclaims a beginning. As an expression of this dialogue, this book is wonderfully enhanced by several responses from other writers and, in addition, a variety of images which bring to life the "iconic" character of the beginning: that "we" image the mystery of our creation. In general, therefore, the author of this work has written the book to which there are a variety of responses, notably as a *General Foreword, Chapter Forewords* and as *An End Word: A New Beginning* and there are a number of images and artist's statements by way of complementary imagery; however, there is one important exception to this: Professors Justo Aznar and Julio Tudela have contributed a moving testimony to the discerning use of science in determining the beginning of human life[40].

There are various beginnings to this book; each of which, in turn, puts the basic questions in a slightly different way. Thus this Prologue divides into five parts, each a different kind of beginning to turning towards the mystery of human conception: to what can be known and to what points us to what is hidden but essential to our humanity. Just, then, as there five ways into the beginning of this book, there are five chapters which take different but complementary starting points and, indeed, are brought into dialogue with each other. In keeping, however, with the introductory nature of this book, there are two prose passages and a philosophical psalm which, in their own way, raise and address an appreciation of the whole of which conception is like the central, stunningly beautiful gem; however, unlike with the jewel, the setting of conception is not just an ornamental addition but, rather, like the rest of the body around the heart, there is the "one flesh" of marriage which brings out the fullness of the mystery involved: of person "from" person.

"The Seed" (Ii), then, communicates through the possibility of a practical exercise and its attendant reflections, followed by "We are a Present" (Ii) which introduces, briefly, that each one of us is a gift, whereas "A Philosophical Psalm 139" addresses the same subject through a mixture of theological and philosophical reflections (Iiii). "When Does the Life of a Person Begin? Where the Body Lives, there the Soul is, and where both are is the Human Person" is a more expansive introduction, beginning to explain terms and envisage, as it were, the whole subject (II). "A Comment on the Work as a Whole" raises the need to draw on the roots of the truth in a new way (III). "The Hippocratic Oath" is one of the oldest expressions of the wisdom of medicine (IV). Finally, there is an "Introduction to Each Chapter" (V).

---

40 Their contribution is the main text of Chapter V: Part II: When does the Human Being Begin?

Conception: An Icon of the Beginning

The Seed (Ii)

In the reality of everyday life it is difficult, if not impossible, to envisage how to communicate the mystery expressed in, through and by, the beginning of human life; in the first of these three introductory images, "The Seed", there is the advantage of it being possible to do a practical exercise, namely, to plant a seed. Owing to my wife needing help with the planting of vegetable seeds, I discovered a wonderful range of real-life planting activities upon which to reflect. According to the size of the original seed, so there is a corresponding "size" of initial growth. Thus the edible broad bean, which is also the vegetable to be eaten but dried and about the size of an adult thumb, grows to a very noticeable size in a short time. The more middle-sized corn of the cob grains shoot up to about the size of small matches and continue to grow and the courgette seed is about the size of an adult small finger nail, rapidly producing two, three and four largish leaves. Whereas onion, tomato and carrot seeds are tiny and start so slightly it is scarcely possible to imagine them surviving or, drawing on the etymology of the word[41], living through the experience of beginning.

This is clearly an experience that many of us need. If, in other words, anyone is in doubt about the beginning of human life, there is almost no better illustration of what is going on in the dark of the womb than planting a seed; for, just as with the conception of a child, the plant seed is different to the soil in which it is planted – upon which it draws as it lies in or on the moist soil, light and warmth making possible the growth changes that manifest the plant it is. In other words, seed and soil are significantly different

---

[41] I am indebted to Mr. Martin Higgins, MA, for this insight into 'sur' and 'vive' being a combination of 'through' and 'living': as if to speak of living through an event.

but complementary to one another; indeed, this fact is amazing enough to begin with. Just, then, as a seed needs the right conditions to "start", so is the start a radical change from being a seed; indeed, this is where there is so much excitement, as each day a watchful care oversees the temperature, water and light conditions of what is planted. Altogether, while the comparison is not without its drawbacks, watching the growth of a seed is a wonderful opportunity to consider the miracle of life: plant, animal and indeed human life!

Tomato and spring onion seeds are really tiny; dry, small and in need of a suitable place to grow. Planting them is an amazing experience if for no other reason than time, soil, a little water and a little warmth and ever so slightly, slowly, plants begin to appear above the soil. The seed is separate to the soil but needs it to grow; indeed, the seed contains all that it needs to know in terms of what to assimilate for growth. The growth is imperceptible for some time; but, gradually, there is a change in the seed and the shoots and roots appear. At any time it can be uprooted but, in general, the older it becomes the better it can cope with being transplanted, with the cold and being without water for a while; however, if the frost is too severe then the early leaves wither and endanger the whole plant. Owing to inexperience, two courgette plants which had grown on the kitchen window sill, were planted out into makeshift garden tubs and were frosted: the leaves turned white and shrivelled; and, furthermore, although they were transplanted to a more suitable bed, one of them was accidentally uprooted and rapidly pushed back down again. These two plants, as you can imagine, were not expected to survive; however, each day they were watered and, in view of a warm spell, they both began to grow new leaves.

Day in day out there are little changes that are not noticeable and then, suddenly, there is a visible change which takes us by surprise: a visible change that starts to show that what exists is definitely in development: a development that does not invent itself as it goes but discloses what it already is. Indeed, there is a kind of bursting to growth: that hidden beneath the soil or in the very stem at the root of existing leaves there is an activity that abruptly shows itself to have been going on because there is now a shoot or new leaves. I have been particularly surprised by the tomato seeds which, once they started to shoot, seemed so slow to go beyond the two leaf stage that one began to wonder if there was a lack of nutrients in the soil; but, then, one morning, I noticed a third leaf between the other two and now there are several as the number of leaves multiplies the rate of growth.

How hidden are the changes that manifest the human person and yet how marvellous is the unfolding of what begins as scarcely visible!

We are a Present (Iii)

A gift is complete, well wrapped, attractive, a thoughtful expression of the giver and ready to be given; and, at the same time, there is a "moment" to give: a birthday, an anniversary, or on getting married. The present is "within" and, at the same time, the outward expression of it is of a promise of what is good. There is, in the words which express our giving, a natural "liturgy" which celebrates an irrevocable "opening" in the giving and receiving of the gift.

Each one of us is a gift: a wholly unique expression of the human race. Just as there is a "moment" in which giving and receiving are one, so there is a "moment" of our first beginning. We have received the gift of ourselves from God; and, at the same time, we are given into the hands of others. Pondering the fact that each one of us is a gift, leads us to think of God as "Gift from Gift". Just as the Father gives himself wholly to the Son and the Son, together with the Father, give themselves wholly to the Holy Spirit, so God gives himself wholly to us; and, in God giving himself wholly to us, he brings to life the possibility of giving ourselves wholly to him and to each other in the mystery of marriage.

But just as God does not take back the gift of himself, so the giving of himself in Jesus Christ and his Church renews the original gift of man, male and female; and, in the renewal of redemption, lies the renewal of the celebration that each one of us is a gift to be given[42]: a gift to be irrevocably given.

A Philosophical Psalm 139 (Iiii)

If the first opening was a way of exploring, simply, the question of being a gift, the second opening is a summary of many years of reflection on the whole human person. Taking the fullness of Psalm 139 as a "template", this is a more philosophical account of the years of reflection; however, as the gift of human being is investigated, the more necessary it is to draw on theological thoughts of the Giver. This "Philosophical Psalm", therefore, is also a theological psalm.

---

[42] A slightly less developed version of this was first used to express, in summary form, the argument presented in an article entitled: "Being Open to Life: Abstract Norm or Embodied Word?" (http://www.hprweb.com/2018/01/being-open-to-life-abstract-norm-or-embodied-word/#comments).

A Philosophical Psalm 139[43]

Conception
Begins a biologically inscribed psychological
development
that unfolds socially.

How else do we describe the indivisibly
Existing being-in-relation,
Begotten through togetherness
Being given existence
in the *Covenant of the flesh*?

Rooted in the Un-Originate God:
Adam from the ground and Eve from his side,
both communicating the dynamic difference of the
Mystery of the Person.

Conceived in Christ from conception,
saved in the reciprocal self-giving of Christ and His
Church,
Through the Cross of Love's own choosing –
Called from Love to love.

And

Where the body lives, there is the soul,
and where both are is the person.

What is inward informs what is outward!

---

[43] This poem is now a part of a collection of Poetry and Prose called *The Prayerful Kiss* published by enroute books and media; it also includes a prose-poem account of the many difficulties and sufferings in life to which the Lord responds with help: http://enroutebooksandmedia.com/theprayerfulkiss/.

What is outward points inward!
What is invisible is made visible!

And
Where the body lives, there is the soul,
and where both are is the person.

Meaning, arising from the beginning,
Breathed again in each of us,
Takes up what is "within" and "without",
Mingling myriad impressions and possibilities,
New and old, insights ancient and modern,
Spoken, written, sung, painted, sculpted and designed,
Dialoguing from beginning to end,
In the depth and breadth
Of time and eternity.
The complete individual
is inseparably cultural!

And

Where the body lives, there is the soul,
and where both are is the person.

In the very being of the human person
is the expression of a word:

person "from" Person;
life "from" Love;
"from" Communion to Communion.

Love Unbegotten begetting
a beginning of each of us:
We are an Icon
of the Beginning.

When Does the Life of a Human Being Begin? (II)

This book, then, arose out of response to the question: When does the life of a human being begin? What kind of beginning does a human being have if, after the conception of one person, there can come into existence another person as the result of a sub-division in that first human embryo? In other words, how do we "account" for the true beginning of one person, if this is what conception really is, and the subsequent beginning of a second person at a later stage in the development of that first individual?

Thus this book[44] takes account of embryology, philosophy and theology[45], in order to explore how conception must be the actual beginning of the person, one in body and soul: 'Man, though made of body and soul, is a unity'[46]. Human embryology is the study of the human embryo: the beginning and early development of "what", without which, we would not exist; and, therefore, that which begins from the human fertilization of a human ovum[47]. Philosophy is

---

[44] Once again I am very grateful to Mr. Martin Higgins, MA, for his proof reading.

[45] Previously published work gives the background sources to the more technical aspects of human conception: Francis Etheredge, Chapter 12 of *Scripture: A Unique Word,* Newcastle upon Tyne: Cambridge Scholars Publishing, 2014, particularly pages 317-334; and cf. Francis Etheredge, "The Mysterious Instant of Conception", *National Catholic Bioethical Quarterly* (of America), Vol. 12, No. 3.

[46] Cf. *Pastoral Constitution on the Church in the Modern World, Gaudium et Spes,* 14.

[47] Cf. Christopher Gacek, "Conceiving Pregnancy: U.S. Medical Dictionaries and Their Definitions of Conception and Pregnancy", *National Catholic Bioethical Quarterly* (of America), Autumn 2009, pp. 543-557.

'the science that seeks the first causes of things'[48]; and, in contrast to others definitions, is aided by what is naturally known as well as by what is revealed. Theology, then, is "faith seeking understanding"[49].

At the same time, however, a path of research is not necessarily direct, although its meandering ways are about engaging with what grows out of turning in different directions: a kind of rumination around a theme; but, nevertheless, there is the core question: What helps to embryologically, philosophically and theologically illuminate the mystery of human beginning? Taking account of the variety of ways that a human being comes to exist, this initial research and reflection was eventually formulated in the following principle:

Where the body lives, there the soul is, and where both are is the human person.

One of the basic tasks of this research was to define the terms through which it was possible to arrive at this principle; and, as the work progressed, it became clear that orthodox Catholic doctrine can be investigated fruitfully. This fruitfulness is of two, inseparably interconnected kinds. On the one hand it is possible to identify and to develop the inheritance of the Catholic Faith; *and*, on the other hand, it is possible to call upon all that assists us to understand the moment of our beginning. In other words there is a kind of swelling to the investigation as it dwells on concepts that

---

[48] I have taken Chris John Terry's version of Aristotle's definition of philosophy and then added qualifications which he discusses but does not express in the same way: *For the Love of Wisdom: An Explanation of the Meaning and Purpose of Philosophy*, New York: Alba House, 1999, p. 2.

present both historically significant insights, like the relationship between 'form' and 'matter' and, at the same time, this terminology challenges us to think about the "imaginative" origin of these conceptual tools which, nevertheless, refer to the "whole" human being.

In terms of different accounts, then, of the beginning of the human person, the variety to be found in the Scriptures is a stimulating source of ideas; and, over time, it became clear that there is a foundational expression of the creativity of God in the opening chapters of Genesis. Considering this "initial" account of the creativity of God led to formulating the idea expressed in the title of this book, namely, that the particular "procreation" of each one of us "recapitulates", as it were, the "original" act of creation from the beginning. Each one of us, therefore, is an *icon of the beginning*. As expressive as this is, however, of the profundity of the creation of each one of us, we need to be continually reminded of the social structure of human personhood; it is, in other words, in the context of the human "we" that each one of us comes to exist. Therefore, it is possible to say: We are an Icon *of the Beginning*.

God creates "as a whole"

Just as creation was "realized" as a whole[50] so is the "procreation" of each person the creation of a whole. Or,

---

[49] Terry, *For the Love of Wisdom*, p. 8, citing St. Anselm and St. Thomas Aquinas' definition.

[50] This emphasis on the 'whole' has definite echoes in phenomenology: 'Phenomenology is an effort to "bring back into philosophy everyday things, concrete wholes, the basic experiences of life as they come to us"' (from Michael Novak, "John Paul II: Christian Philosopher," *America* 177: 12 [October 25, 1997], p. 12), quoted in George Weigel's, *Witness to Hope: The Biography of Pope John Paul II* (New York: Cliff Street Books, 1999), p. 127.

conversely, just as each one of us was created "as a whole", so is each one of us a personal expression of the Creator's love of His whole work. In other words, the integrity of the account of creation communicates an awareness of the act of God as original, originating all that exists and entailing a vision of the whole work. Thus, for example, although there are different "parts" to the universe and different kinds of creature in it, it is clear that the whole of creation is an expression of the one God; indeed, the very coherence of the whole, the fact that it "functions" and is conducive to life is an amazing witness to what is beyond coincidence. At the same time, though, there are innumerable traces of the mysterious nature of the one God in the whole of creation. Man, male and female, therefore, both communicates the mystery of the Blessed Trinity and, at the same time, the unity-in-diversity of the created orders of existence: the physical, biological, personal, psychological and the spiritual. Each person, then, comes to exist in a certain moment: Adam and Eve from the first instant of their beginning and each one of us in that unique "moment" of co-operation between the Creator and our parents.

Although, then, there is a traditional language of "soul" and "body", and even a certain tendency to think in terms of God "animating" the Adam He made from the ground (cf. Gn 2: 7), what emerges beyond the literary characteristics of biblical thought is that of God *conceiving man, male and female, as a "whole"* relationship, as it were, indicative and expressive of the mystery of the Blessed Trinity (cf. Gn 1: 26-28). In contrast to the making of the animals, then, which are created alive, complete and ordered, as it were, to their environment (cf. Gn 1: 20-23), God is more closely involved in the creation of Adam and Eve. In the case of Adam, then, it is possible to think in terms of God "making" his body and it being animated by a divine breath (cf. Gn 2: 7); but, it could be argued, what this expresses is the intimate relationship between the life of man and the life of God. Indeed, Eve is not "animated" by God but arises out of the mysterious action of God who, using the rib He removed from Adam as he slept, fashions Eve (cf. Gn 2: 21-25). Thus Eve does not live by a separate life to Adam; rather, Adam and Eve "live" out of a common life which originates with the breath of God. What arises, then, out of this foundational research is the growing perception of the work of the Creator *as the expression of an integral, embodied, relational communication of the mystery of human personhood as both individual and in-communion.*

Finally, although there are, in retrospect, many omissions and undeveloped aspects to the discussion of when each one of us "comes-to-exist" there is, nevertheless, a helpful beginning in these pages. Even if, then, numerous investigations have followed they "took flight", as it were, from this initial work; and, as such, this work acts as a kind of "point of departure" for numerous essays and constitutes, too, a stimulus to still further developments. Revisiting this earlier work also provided an opportunity to remove what has been used in subsequent works and to restate, perhaps more clearly, the ideas which began to take shape in these pages. In the sections that follow it is possible to see how the work of the Church has sowed an increasingly deeper interest in the question of human identity.

A Point of Departure in the Reality of Our Beginning

What makes the connection between the facts of life and the Church's theological reflection on them is that *this dialogue constitutes* the language of the body: a language which is addressed to us. In other words, the Church is both answering these fundamental questions and encouraging us to look with her for a deeper understanding of her answers.

Pope St. Paul VI says that 'human life is sacred' and then recalls the following words of Pope John XXIII: 'since from its first beginnings it calls for the creative action of God'[51]. What, then, is that 'creative action of God'? Is the creative action of God, from the first beginnings of human life, the creation of a soul that is at the same time the life of that body?[52] Or does the phrase: 'from its first beginnings', allow of the possibility that the body does not receive its soul immediately, but at an as yet undetermined and subsequent moment? For the *Sacred Congregation for the Doctrine of the Faith* said in footnote nineteen of its *Declaration on Procured Abortion*, six years after *Humanae Vitae* and with the approval of the same Pope: 'This declaration expressly leaves aside the question of the moment when the spiritual soul is infused. (...) For some it dates from the first instant, for others it could not at least precede nidation'[53]. The term nidation refers to the implantation[54] process by which the fertilized egg nestles[55] into the wall of the womb.

This same footnote of the *Declaration on Procured Abortion* goes on to say of this question: 'It is a philosophical problem from which our moral affirmation remains independent: (i) supposing a belated animation, there is still nothing less than a *human* life, preparing for and calling for

---

[51] Cf. footnote 13 of *Humanae Vitae*, art 13: cf. John XXIII, Encyl. *Mater et Magistra*, n. 194.

[52] Cf. *Catechism of the Catholic Church*, articles 362-366; hereafter referenced as CCC.

[53] *Let Me Live, Declaration by the Sacred Congregation for the Doctrine of the Faith on Procured Abortion*, 1974, footnote 19; hereafter, *Let Me Live*.

[54] Cf. *Concise Science Dictionary*, (Oxford: Oxford University Press, second edition, 1991), p. 341: implantation (nidation).

[55] Cf. *Collins English Dictionary*, (London: Collins, reprinted 1979), p. 993: 'nide ... from the Latin *nidus* nest.'

a soul in which the nature received from parents is completed; (ii) on the other hand, it suffices that this presence of the soul be probable (and one can never prove the contrary) in order that the taking of life involves accepting the risk of killing a man, not only waiting for, but already in possession of his soul.'

The prior-to-thought reality of what actually exists

Acknowledging, however, that the moment of the conception of the human person is a philosophical problem does not preclude the possibility of "help" from either biblical or theological sources; for, in reality, there is already a prior act of God which all research is pondering: a prior act of God which determines the existential reality to be investigated. On the one hand, the existence of the sun and the orbits of which it is a part are all an established fact and, as such, research both confirms their existence and deepens our perception of their interrelationships. On the other hand, the very position and coordination of these "planetary" relationships brings about, in part, the very conditions which make it possible for human life to exist on earth. The "intuition" of relationship, as it were, between all these facts and a cause is indeed a part of the possibility of what can be investigated. In other words, Scripture, in its own way, may well witness to the act of God which determined the structural origin of each and every person "conceived" (cf. Gn 4: 1). This does not mean that the biblical account is a "source" of a modern, embryological understanding of the origin of the human person; rather, it does mean that, in its own language, the Scripture communicates what would be a discreet implication, entailing the mystery of conception, as a part of the work of communicating the actual action of God in the history of His work of creation-salvation.

Thus it could be said that this footnote was the beginning of the thinking that led to the following possibility: that if the two orders of true knowledge[56] cannot contradict each other[57], which are in a way expressed in the complementary difference between theology and philosophy, then they can help each other. If theology, for example, is 'higher'[58] than philosophy, then can the one that is higher come to a conclusion that can then become the objective of the one that is lower? In other words, if it is theologically certain that the human person, one in body and soul, begins from the first moment of fertilization, then this conclusion could become the legitimate objective of a philosophical investigation. Paradoxically, then, *precisely because truth will not contradict truth[59], a known theological truth cannot per se prejudice the outcome of such a philosophical investigation.* Furthermore, then, it could be said that such a theological truth would be by definition an assistance to seeking a philosophical proof of the same truth. *Therefore* there emerges the following question: Does the Catholic Church teach that there is a theological certainty that the human person, one in body and soul, begins from the first moment of fertilization? To which it has to be answered that so difficult has it been to find such a statement in the docu-

---

[56] Cf. p. 45 of *The Christian Faith*, edited by J Neuner SJ and J Dupuis (New York: Alba House, revised edition 1982), art 3015 of *Dei Filius*, Vatican I, on *The twofold order of religious knowledge*; hereafter referenced as *The Christian Faith*.

[57] Cf. Vatican I, *Dei Filius*, art 3017 on *Faith and reason cannot contradict each other*, p. 46 of *The Christian Faith*.

[58] Cf. St. Thomas Aquinas *Summa Theologiae*, literally translated by the Fathers of the English Dominican Province, (New York: Benziger Brothers, Inc., 1947-8), Pt I, Qu 1, articles 1-3 and 5-8; hereafter referenced as "Benziger Brothers".

[59] Cf. Vatican I, *Dei Filius*, art 3017 on *Faith and reason cannot contradict each other*, p. 46 of *The Christian Faith*.

ments of the Magisterium, *put in precisely this way*, that an investigation of these questions has become part of the fundamental objective of this book.

In conclusion, what has emerged as a recognition of the precept, *be open to life*, has begun to swell into a *theology of the body with particular reference to the transmission and beginning of life* and which is also unfolding into a *spirituality of being open to life*. This is because, to adapt an expression of *Humanae Vitae*, the human person is a living embodiment of what it is to be 'a compound of sense and spirit' (9); and, therefore, ensuring the relationship between the generative act and its goal is about recognizing that procreation entails the expression of an attitude. Finally, reflecting on the attitude "natural" to the act of procreation, "being open to the gift of life", brings about a deepening understanding of procreation entailing a relationship to the author of life, namely, God. Thus, although it is possible to begin with the outward manifestation of human sexuality, it is impossible to reflect on it further without, at the same time, recognising *the word as a whole of which this is all a part*.

A Comment on the Work as a Whole (III)

Exploring the conceptualization of the beginning of human personhood

We need a new language to address an ancient question; indeed, the age old "usage" of body and soul, while usefully true, does not convince modern man that he is anything but biologically living. Or, conversely, we need to revitalize our understanding of their relationship so that we can see more vividly the truth that they express: that the body is the outward expression of the inwardness of human being. It seems to be all too possible to dismiss this apparently dualistic thinking, which appears to divide the biological bodily activities from the personal, communicative and relational expressions of the human person. The soul is not an inhabitant in a cellular house, a kind of electronic force field that arises out of bodily activities, nor a sort of "bridging" concept between the biological and "spiritual" expressions of the human person. On the contrary the soul is as embedded and embodied as the inside determinant of the outside of a shape; indeed, the soul is more intimate to the life of the body than the metabolic activities of the cell in that the very life of the cell is an expression of the life of the whole person. Is there, then, a modern image or way of expressing the language of the soul which is intelligible to "modern minds"? Perhaps "imagery" will help us to appreciate the need for the concept of the soul, just as our power of imagination is "evidence" of the soul's existence. For how can we envisage or "imagine" what does exist, what it is possible to invent or create or what we cannot witness coming to exist unless we possess a power that exceeds the sensory experience of existence?

To begin with, our knowledge of embryology is radically new and establishes the reality of human beginning: the beginning to which each one of us witnesses in the very fact of our existence. In the very "moment", as it were, of fertilization, what was the inert ovum or egg is now animated or "made to move" by the active influence of the sperm which has entered one of the ovum's many openings in its cellular structure. In other words, in the very moment that there is "sperm-ovum" contact there ceases to be either sperm or ovum but the human embryo: the first instant's expression of a child's existence. This is identified by the very change in what was the ovum's "open weaved" bodily structure suddenly, on contact with the sperm, closing and forming the first "outer skin" of the embryonic being. It is possible, too, that there is a faint expression of "light" arising out of the new being's beginning. Thus the "freely floating" embryo now moves to the uterus or the womb of the mother and embeds in its lining; and, as such, this is part of an amazing dialogue of messages between the embryonic child and his or her mother. On the basis of the "bodily dialogue" between the mother and the imminently present embryo, there arises the maternal consciousness of the presence of her child: the irrevocably fleshed expression of spousal love.

A "blob of cells", by contrast, generates a "reaction" but not a relationship; indeed, the very fact that a blob of cells does generate a reaction shows how intimately ordered to one another are physiological changes and psychological reactions. Therefore, if it is cancer, then distress, anxiety, the possibility of dying, the meaning of the whole event, consultation, treatment, dialogue, prayer and possibly peace follow; and, in general, because the sudden imminence of parting from the presence of all our relationships, the possible impact of death is a central effect of the coming of a "blob of cells".

But conception "generates" relationships: husband and wife are now mother and father and their parents become grandparents. In other words, just as a fatal cancer is a contributor to death and its potential impact on our relationships, so conception opens up innumerable, intergenerational connections in all directions of family life. Just as the mother and father experience joy and a whole range of other reactions, including the shrinking of their "own" time and the expanding of their "nuclear fusion", so conception comes with a whole psychological dialogue: a dialogue at first explicitly between the spouses-as-parents and, gradually, unfolding in the whole dynamism of family relationships. The very "fusion" of flesh which contributed to the outward sign of the inward act of God, bringing conception to the completion beyond its own biological power, founds the relationships which have simultaneously come into existence. Operating on cancer brings relief, however temporary, to the imminence of death; birth, by contrast, brings to the arms of the family the welcome already unfolding from the conception of personal life: life-in-relationship.

Philosophically, then, while we began with the interrelationship between body and soul what we have, in fact, is the child: the being-in-relationship; and, what is more, there is an even more ancient wisdom than body and soul, namely parent and child. In other words, each one of us is a being-in-relationship: each human person is a being-in-relationship. Whether from the very moment of conception or throughout life, human beings are essentially "beings-in-relationship": parent and child; grandparent and grandchild; siblings; aunts and uncles; nieces and nephews; and friends. In what is an incomparably simple, profound and beautiful witness to the mystery of human conception, both the writer of Genesis and Eve witness the following: 'Adam knew Eve his wife, and she conceived and bore Cain, saying, "I have gotten a man with the help of the Lord"' (RSV, Gn 4: 1). Thus the very ancient testimony turns out to possess a disarmingly simply expression of the profoundest of moments: the "continuation" of creation in procreation. The uniquely singular beginning, at once completely given by God and wholly human: the spousal love that makes explicit the implied and boldly inscribed mystery of the Blessed Trinity: creation is "relationship" from "Relationship".

Following the opening essays, designed to help us to "re-think" and to "re-imagine" the adventure of meditating on the mystery of our beginning, the work as a whole proceeds to the Scriptural witness, to the Magisterial documents, then to the philosophical tasks and, finally, to a reflection on the mystery of the Blessed Trinity, biological identity and thus to our human relationships. In other words, in a way, it is hoped that beginning with the use of our imagination and going on to the texts of Scripture, the very "concreteness" of these pages will help us to enter the more demanding work of reflecting on the Church's understanding of conception and the philosophical problems which need to be addressed.

The Hippocratic Oath (IV)

A Work Old and New: There is a work, though, at once old and new, which entails the following wisdom: 'I will not give a woman a pessary to procure abortion.' Thus we can see, even in terms of an ancient civilization, a practical wisdom which acknowledges, implicitly, the obvious: that each one of us is a witness to the beginning of being a human person: an individual being-in-relation. Thus, even if we are constantly challenged to investigate anew the beginning of human personhood, nevertheless there is a kind of obvious truth to the reality that each one of us did begin; and, just as conception means by definition a beginning, so what does not eternally exist has to have a beginning. We do not eternally exist. Therefore we have a beginning. If we have a beginning, then that beginning unfolds the reality of you and the reality of me; and, that being true, we have an equal right to exist in virtue of all of us being equally a "gift". It is right, therefore, to complement the gift of personal existence with the protection that expresses and guarantees our equality: the recognition of our common reality as expressed through the law[60].

---

[60] Cf. also, *Evangelium Vitae*, 60: 'Furthermore, what is at stake is so important that, from the standpoint of moral obligation, the mere probability that a human person is involved would suffice

Francis Etheredge

Hippocratic Oath of Kos (400 BC)

I swear by Apollo the physician, and Aesculapius, and Hygeia, and Panacea and all the gods and goddesses, making them my witnesses, that I will fulfil, according to my ability and judgment, this oath and covenant.

To hold him, who has taught me this art, as equal to my parents, and to live my life in partnership with him, and if he is in need of money to give him a share of mine, and to regard his offspring as equal to my brothers in male lineage, and to teach them this art if they desire to learn it without fee and covenant; to give a share of precepts and oral instruction and all the other learning to my sons and to the sons of him who has instructed me, and to pupils who have signed the covenant and who have taken an oath according to the medical law, but to no one else.

I will apply my knowledge for the benefit of the sick according to my ability and judgment; I will keep them from harm and injustice.

I will neither give a deadly drug to anybody if asked for it, nor will I make a suggestion to this effect. Similarly I will not give a woman a pessary to procure abortion. In purity and holiness, I will guard my life and my art.

I will not use the knife, not even on sufferers from stone, but will withdraw in favour of such men as are skilled in this work.

Whatever houses I may visit, I will come for the benefit of the sick, remaining free of all intentional injustice, of all mischief, and in particular of sexual relations with both male and female persons, be they free or slaves. What I may see or hear in the course of treatment or even outside of the treatment in regard to the life of men, which on no account

---

to justify an absolutely clear prohibition of any intervention aimed at killing a human embryo.'

ought to be spread abroad, I will keep to myself, holding such things shameful to be spoken about. If I fulfil this Oath and do not violate it, may it be granted to me to enjoy life and art, being honoured with fame among all men for all time to come; if I transgress it and swear falsely, may the opposite of all this be my lot[61].

General Introduction to Each Chapter (V)

Each *General Introduction* is repeated at the beginning of each chapter; and, in addition, according to the content and structure of the chapter, there are a number of more specific introductions.

General Introduction to Chapter 1:
On the use of the Imagination

Our culture is inundated with images and works of the imagination; and, therefore, it is almost easier for people to "invent" new possibilities than it is to think through their value, use or goodness. Is imagination so unbounded that reality has become invisible? Is our inability to engage with reality a sign of our distance from it?

The imagination, however, is both a part of the process of understanding what exists and, alternatively, a facility for extrapolating from what exists. When, for example, our subject is the beginning of life and involves, as it were, the unimaginable, we need the help of the imagination to "envision" the moment at which God acts to bring a human being to exist. In a certain sense, like striking a match, it is

---

[61] Dr. Mary Anne Urlakis provided this text for the book, *The Human Person: A Bioethical Word,* published in America by En Route Books and Media, LLC, located online at http://enroutebooksandmedia.com/bioethicalword/

easier to see that the match is lit than it is possible to say at what precise instant the match caught alight. Similarly, in that there is an act of God at the radical beginning of each one of us, it is easier to recognize that this has occurred and that a child is conceived *because there is a real event: a child now exists – than it is to say of the moment itself that it is "now"*. The "moment" of an act of God is timeless in that it "takes no time"; but, on the other hand, it lasts forever: a child is for everlasting life.

Taking up, then, that aspect of the cultural world in which we live, it is necessary to "move" through it to the questions which are really involved and which challenge us; and, therefore, we too need to take up the work of the imagination and to explore different ways of communicating the almost incommunicable. If, however, this starting point seems unfamiliar to us, consider the many ways that biblical authors and teachers use an analogy to help us make that transition from what we do not know to the "intake" of understanding; and, likewise, let us explore the vast array of inventive explanations which are, no less, an opportunity to investigate our subject!

If elsewhere it has been argued that in the "moment" of the real transmission of life, God acts to complete the spousal act of love in bringing a child to exist, here it is necessary to enable a wider and more imaginative transition to the same truth. Love seeks the fullness of truth no less than the truth seeks the fullness of love.

General Introduction to Chapter 2: Scriptural Insights into the Origin of Human Being

The Blessed Trinity is our *beginning* and our *end*; and, therefore, it is not just that the Blessed Trinity "founds" human being, it is also that communion is constituted as "being-in-relationship" with the Blessed Trinity. In view of this reality the mystery of the relationship to Jesus Christ is "pivotal" to the interrelationship between the Blessed Trinity and human being.

On the one hand, then, the marriage of Revelation and reason *in our Lord and Saviour Jesus Christ* is a fundamentally *personal* fact-in-faith. The order within this marriage is the order which is established by God: reason works with and under[62] Revelation (cf. 1 Cor. 15: 23-28). Thus the wider relationship, of the human with the divine, is *now prior for* us. The *Incarnation*, however, is not prior in view of time as it was relatively recent in human history; rather, the *Incarnation* is prior ontologically, constituting as it does the essential relationship between all of us (cf. *Gaudium et Spes,* 22). On the other hand, then, there is an implicit methodology of truth being ordered to truth, whether natural or revealed, such that truth will not contradict truth[63]. Therefore, while there is progress in reason's articulation of the problems and difficulties of a philosophical understanding of the beginning of the human person, it is possible that a consideration of Scripture will enlighten the whole discussion in a way that complements the starting points of reason: both embryological and in terms of the historical and reality refinement of ideas. In other words, enduring concepts such as "soul" and "body", imply both a radical relationship to one another and to the experience of and event of human life; and, over time, as they have born fruit in their explanatory power and usefulness, not without criticism, so they remain a helpful reference point and point of departure for further investigations.

---

[62] Cf *Gaudium et Spes,* 56.

[63] Cf. Vatican I, *Dei Filius,* 133 (or art 3017 as numbered by the editors of *The Christian Faith,* p. 46).

It is not so much, then, that reason and Revelation are absolutely different starting points, as the biblical text expresses 'a profound and indissoluble unity between the knowledge of reason and the knowledge of faith'; indeed, as St. John Paul II goes on to add in *Fides et Ratio*, 'The world and all that happens within it, including history and the fate of peoples, are realities to be observed, analysed and assessed with all the resources of reason, but without faith ever being foreign to the process' (16). Thus, while we may proceed, albeit cautiously, we can nevertheless enjoy, too, a certain confidence that the witness of God and man to the event of conception is relevant to our discussion; however, at the same time, we need to recognize that the biblical author was both perceptive according to a different, but analogous, criteria to that of contemporary embryologists and open, too, to a divine assistance in his work.

General Introduction to Chapter 3: What Does the Church Teach "Today" about the Moment of Our Beginning?

It is almost as if part of the work of the Church is clarifying the state of the question concerning the beginning of each one of us. Thus it is clear that there is not, at present, a definitive philosophical answer to the question of when ensoulment occurs: of when God creates the soul in union with the body and thus begets the beginning of human personhood.

It is, however, ingenuous to suppose that soul and body are distinct in the way that body and clothes are distinct. In other words, the bodily human person exists prior to being clothed; and, therefore, the relationship of body to clothes is not one whereby body and clothes are inescapably and inseparably one. One person can choose a variety of clothes and is still the same person. The language, then, of body and soul, can give a false impression of "parts" that are brought together. Nevertheless, this language of "body" and "soul" has a certain usefulness if it is not misunderstood. It is necessary to remember, though, that there is no human bodily life if there is no human soul; human soul and human body are so ordered to one another that one cannot exist except in relationship to the other. Thus death cannot be a complete rupture but is, nevertheless, a real "withdrawal" from the manifestation of life expressed bodily. The human body, then, having come into existence insolubly, is yet subject to the law of sin and death; and, at the same time, "lives" the God-given possibility of being reclaimed in its amazingly integral unity-in-diversity in the moment of the resurrection of the body.

The Church, then, in following the path of life, has gravitated to 'conception' as the first moment of human personhood; and, even if all the difficulties have not been overcome, there is a particular authority to this position in view of her divine-human nature and mission (cf. *Lumen Gentium*, 7-8). At the same time, however, there is a growing need to recognize the threefold nature of what comes together in the dialogue of salvation; and, therefore, while drawing upon Scripture and the Magisterium it is also necessary to turn to Tradition (cf. *Dei Verbum*, 10). While recognizing, however, that this is not an uncritical endorsement of whatever is to be found present in the Tradition, it is nevertheless an integral part of what constitutes the 'one deposit of faith' (*Dei Verbum*, 10). Thus, as will see, there is a kind of "simple"[64] apprehension of the "conception" of each human being which tends, again, to the

---

[64] I am indebted to Dr. Mary Anne Urlakis who, in her correspondence with the author, has helped to clarify this point and to show the necessity of explicitly referencing both research and appreciation of the value of the Fathers of the Church.

view that human conception is from the first instant of fertilization.

General Introduction to Chapter 4: Philosophical and Theological Dialogue

This chapter draws explicitly on *philosophy* for the inseparably complementary understanding of what a soul is and how, therefore, the human soul can be understood to be one with the body from conception. Thus it seems as if it were possible to consider an analogy of differences that yet constitute an inseparable whole: the *biblical* soul and the *philosophical* body of concepts are what *together constitute theology*. Can one any more separate this discussion on the soul from its biblical roots than one can separate it from the philosophical context *through* which it has developed? In other words, philosophy and Revelation seem to *mutually condition* each other in a way that is analogous to what is said of the relationship between the body and the soul[65]; and thus they do so in a way that does not destroy the *logical and ontological priority of Revelation to reason*[66], *which is also analogous to the logical and ontological priority of the unity of man to the plurality of his being*[67]. Therefore does the unity of a *biblically philosophical* or a *philosophically biblical* theology furnish an analogy with the unity of the person, one in soul and body?

---

[65] N. A. Luyten, *Soul-Body Relationship*, p. 472 of Vol XIII, of the *New Catholic Encyclopedia,* McGraw-Hill, 1967; hereafter this work will be abbreviated to NCE.

[66] Cf. I. C. Brady, *Soul, Human, 2. Patristic And Medieval Writers, Nemesius,* pp. 453-454 of Vol XIII, NCE.

[67] P. B. T. Bilaniuk, *Soul, Human, 5. Theology,* p. 462 of Vol XIII, NCE.

Conception: An Icon of the Beginning

While there is truth[68], which is by definition constant, it is also true that our knowledge of it develops in relation to what is contingent. In other words, as St. Thomas Aquinas suggests, it is not necessary to decide what is still insufficiently determined by the evidence[69]. By implication, then, the recognition of relevant evidence on the beginning of human being can both *refashion* one's existing understanding of it *or* extend it to the point of obtaining the *resolution* of an acknowledged difficulty - *but in neither case will what is true cease to be true nor will truth contradict truth*[70]. In other words, the accumulation of relevant evidence can be as decisive to the development of human understanding as the possession of the requisite principles. Therefore, it could be said, the development of understanding is in proportion as it were to the availability of the relevant evidence and the *remembrance*[71] of what is already known.

---

[68] Cf. *Summa Theologiae*, Benziger Brothers, Pt I, Qu 2, art 1, p. 11: to claim it is true that there is no truth is to demonstrate that it exists.

[69] Cf. Francis Copleston, *Aquinas*, Harmondsworth: Penguin Books Ltd, 1955, p. 72 and *Summa Theologiae*, a concise translation edited by Timothy McDermott, London: Methuen, 1992, Pt I, Qu 32, art 1, p. 71; hereafter, referenced as "Methuen".

[70] Vatican I, *Dei Filius*, art 3017 on *Faith and reason cannot contradict each other*, page 46 of *The Christian Faith*.

[71] It can be noted at this point, if not discussed, how 'memory' has become a significant term in the modern discussion of a variety of things, as if to say that a modern weakness lies in precisely *not remembering the past and not using the memory generally*. Cf. A. Kenny, *Aquinas*, which is part of the *Past Masters* series, Gen. ed. K. Thomas, (Oxford: Oxford University Press, 1980), pp. 28-30, where he observes a general, but not altogether complete lack of the use of the work of St. Thomas Aquinas. Cf. also Pope John Paul II, *Catechesi Tradendae*, 1979, art 55.

Finally, just as a *theological* idea like that of the person[72] drew on the Greek word for mask, *prosopon*, helping to fashion an understanding of the unitary nature of Christ and the mystery of the Blessed Trinity, so Revelation may assist us with a definition of human being which may complement the philosophical terminology necessary to the explanation of human conception. These definitions, referring as they do to the reality of human life and thought, express a fruit of that profound mystery of the activity of the Holy Spirit in the culture of man[73], which so prepares that culture that it not only contributes to the *incarnational inculturation of the Gospel*, but in some way contributes something necessary, while subordinate to it, just as the body contributes something necessary while subordinate to the soul. In other words, all truth, whether *natural* and of reason, *or supernatural*[74] and of Revelation, has its own *intrinsic relationship* to the Spirit of truth. Thus, in the end, there is a constant dialogue between the truth of Revelation and the truth as disclosed through natural reflection. In any meditation on conception, therefore, which draws on God's act of creation as revealed through reason and Revelation, there is a necessary "osmosis" of meaning as we endeavour to pass to the reality "prior" to both Revelation and reflection: the reality of conception established by the original act of the Creator.

---

[72] Cf. Henri de Lubac, "On Christian Philosophy", *Communio*, Vol. XIX, No. 3 (Fall 1992), p. 481.

[73] *Ad Gentes Divinitus*, art 9.

[74] Cf. *Dei Filius* art 3015 of Vatican Council I, p. 45 of *The Christian Faith*.

Chapter 5: Parts I-III: Towards the Renewal of Understanding Human Conception

There are three parts to this chapter, beginning with the mystery of the Blessed Trinity, going on to an examination of the biological reality of human conception and concluding with a dialogue which draws on these preliminary but essential contributions to drawing on faith and reason. Thus, in a certain way, this chapter renews the focus of the whole book and, as it were, exhorts us afresh to the necessity of a new understanding of human conception.

General Introduction to Chapter 5: Part I: The "Being" of the Blessed Trinity "Founds" Human Being

In a certain way, it could be argued, the "help" of the mystery of the Blessed Trinity to the mystery of human being is a dialogue which, once begun, is literally going to go on forever. But, preoccupied as we have been with the difficulty of "understanding" God and distracted by the manifold claims and concerns of life, perhaps we have scarcely begun to appreciate that the mystery of God Himself is a hermeneutical key to human anthropology. In other words, as we begin to recognize that God "contemplated" His own mystery in the creation of man, male and female (cf. *Letter to Families*, 6), so this invites us to co-contemplate the Blessed Trinity if we are to understand ourselves (*Gaudium et Spes*, 36). Or, to put it differently, the "question mark" that speaks through the whole search it inspires is "naturally" answered by the mystery of the Blessed Trinity. Thus Revelation is one starting point for the renewed understanding of man, male and female, and the mystery of "our" origin.

Francis Etheredge

General Introduction to Chapter 5: Part II: When does Human Life Begin? Professors Justo Aznar and Julio Tudela: Biographies and Paper

In general I have written the chapters of this book and others have wonderfully enriched it; however, there is one exception to the structure of this book. Following this General Introduction is a paper by Justo Aznar and Julio Tudela; it is a foundational text in its own right. They have written a compelling review of the collective scientific wisdom concerning the beginning of human life.

The position of this paper by Justo and Julio

Why, then, does this piece come "between" the Blessed Trinity and the more specific examination of the embryological, philosophical and theological contributions to understanding conception? In brief, this paper establishes more fully the natural foundation to understanding conception; and, indeed, traces the "process" of fertilization to the "first instant" of the changes which come about through the interrelationship between the gift of the father's sperm and the mother's egg. What is more, this paper "communicates" the equally remarkable interaction between the embryonic child and the mother. In other words, this paper introduces a "concrete" reality to the theme of conception-in-relationship: the real, reciprocal effect of the dynamic between mother and child in the earliest stages of conception and the bearing this has on the development of the child. Thus this paper provides the complementary work of reason and the discerning use of science which both expresses the "traces" of the mystery of the Creator expressed in His work and contributes to the dialogue of reason and Revelation.

Conception: An Icon of the Beginning

Where there is a human being there is a human being-in-relationship

Another way of putting this is that we are each, equally, a gift; indeed, no one gives him or herself being: each one of us has been given existence. On the basis of this reality, each one of us is conceived-in-relationship to others; and, in the unfolding of this reality, lies a profound expression of our identity as human beings: son or daughter; grandson or granddaughter; brother or sister; and the myriad relationships which spread out like light waves in all directions. We can "clothe" this human reality in all kinds of expressions; but, in the end, where there is a human being there is a human being-in-relationship: a child.

Establishing our common humanity establishes the reality of an ethical relationship between us

In the following paper Justo Aznar and Julio Tudela show in majestic detail that our humanity is in the very "grain" of what comes together at conception. Indeed, that even when there is an injustice to the human embryo, in that the child is fertilized or treated as if he or she were a "product", a "biological material" or an expendable research subject, that the reality of an embodied humanity manifests itself to the objective observer; and, were he or she to be allowed to thrive, it would be clear that what was begun, in time and through innumerable changes, is manifestly a human person present from the beginning. "Ethics", therefore, is always an expression of a relationship between us; and, in a word, establishing our common humanity establishes the reality of an ethical relationship between us.

Francis Etheredge

General Introduction to Chapter 5: Part III: The Gift and Rights of being *Conceived-in-Relationship: We are an Icon of the Beginning.*

We live between where we were and where we are going to be; and, in a sense, that defines our whole reality: a person is what I was at conception, who I am and what I am becoming. In the biblical sense, I am an unfinished work between being conceived and being resurrected from the dead; and, therefore, the whole nature of being a person encompasses both everything to do with beginning and everything expressed in the mystery of rising, God willing, with Christ. A biblical conception of person, therefore, takes account of a trans-temporal understanding of the human person and, in a word, takes us into the realm of the spiritual transformation of all that I am and all that we are: a radical transfiguration of human being.

At the same time, however, we live and work out our salvation in the present; and, in that respect, the being we are to become is also expressed in all its on-going trans-temporality. There are many ways of perceiving the human person and it is possible to view ourselves "fractionally", according to the lens of one discipline or another; however, it is necessary to strive for an adequate account of the whole human being, even amidst the kaleidoscoping fragmentation which is so often what becomes of our self-perception. This fragmentation shows itself most tragically in the reductionism which renders one person the "object" of another person's intrusive investigation, manipulation or destruction; and, therefore, there is an urgency in seeking to recover an account of the "whole" that we are which includes our relationship to God, to others and to each other.

This essay seeks to advance an integral account of the beginning of our whole human nature. At the same time it offers reasons, both religious and realistic, to recover the perception of the humanity of the frozen human embryo and to advance the possibility of housing the "homeless being" in the hospitality of a mother's nurturing womb and the relationships which stem from that beautiful fact. As a whole, while it is both urgent and timely to act for the good of another, it also necessary to widen the debate and to call for a new global ethic which defines the integral individual and social requirements of human development from the first instant of conception onwards. Thus, in this final part of Chapter Five, the resources of both reason and Revelation are brought to bear on the exciting, challenging and ever urgent question of the beginning of the human person and the way forward for the most neglected of our brothers and sisters.

CHAPTER ONE:
FOREWORD AND BIOGRAPHY

Fr. Joseph Tham, LC

Biography

Fr. Joseph Tham first majored in Mathematical Sciences and then graduated from Medical School at the University of Toronto. He joined the Legionaries of Christ and was ordained a priest in 2004. He successfully defended his doctoral dissertation with high honors under the direction of Dr. Edmund Pellegrino, former Chairman of the President's Council on Bioethics. He is former dean of the School of Bioethics in *Regina Apostolorum* where he presently teaches bioethics. He is the Editorial Coordinator of the journal *Studia Bioethica*, and a Fellow of the UNESCO Chair in Bioethics and Human Rights. He is the author and editor of numerous articles and books, including *The Missing Cornerstone* (2004), *The Secularization of Bioethics* (2007) and *Bioetica al Futuro* (2010), *Religious Perspectives on Human Vulnerability in Bioethics* (2014), *Religious Perspectives on Bioethics and Human Rights* (2017), *Sexuality, Gender and Education* (2018) and *Religious Perspectives on Social Responsibility in Health* (2018).

Foreword to Chapter 1: On "alternative imaginations"

Francis Etheredge has written a marvelous chapter on alternative imaginations on the delicate and hotly contested question of the body-soul relationship. He offers a fresh approach to the age-old question in this technological age. It calls to mind the *Question on Technology* posed by Heidegger, in his analysis of Aristotle's differentiation between the two human acts, *techne* and *poiesis*. Technology develops from *techne*, which becomes today an all-embracing and suffocating *Gestell* – a word that means an enframing or structural scaffolding which defines our mentality and lifestyles. *Gestell* imprisons our post-modern society, obsessed with efficiency, utility but shunning personal responsibility. Pope Francis names this the "throwaway culture" in his Encyclical *Laudato Si'*, where everything is ordered to manipulation and maximum enjoyment and the rest becomes disposable, including the leftover embryos!

"Only a god can save us"

Heidegger is pessimistic that we could escape the prison of technological *Gestell*, except through poetizing and contemplation. His last word on the subject was, quizzically, "Only a god can save us." While his god is probably not Christian, his insight about overcoming technocratic bondage through poetry or recovering the Aristotelian act of *poiesis* coincides with Pope Francis' call for ecological conversion that implies cultivation of virtues and a rediscovery of beauty.

Beauty and poetry, contemplation and liturgy could be our escape from the throwaway culture of utility and efficiency. The esthetic experience is akin to spiritual transcendence, as both experiences allow us to recognize the presence of others (and oneself) not as objects but subjects of relationality. Beauty transcends, as it is classically considered a transcendental together with the One, the Good and the Truth.

Hence, the unity of the trinity—truth, goodness and beauty—may be the stuff of morality. We seek the truth and goodness in every human act. For the Christian, it reminds us of another Trinity, the wholly Other consisting of a community of Persons—Creator, Redeemer and Sanctifier.

In transcendent Beauty, creation encounters creativity. Artistic creations are in fact participation of God's creative act. As an extension of God's creation, humanity also participates in it through procreation. The Three-in-One communion of Persons finds its image in the two-in-one-flesh of communion between man and woman, as John Paul II's Theology of the Body repeatedly expounds. The two become one flesh so as to make three, as Blondel is reputed to have said.

Francis Etheredge

The 'beautiful icons of creation'

In this chapter, the author uses different images to describe the origin and unity of body and soul. Some of them are philosophical, others were taken from everyday examples and others are theological. Since the title of the book uses the word icon, it draws us inevitably to consider the beautiful icons of creation.

Speaking of beauty and imaginations in the origin of human being, we naturally think of the masterpiece of Michelangelo's Sistine ceiling. His portrait of God's finger almost touching the finger of Adam is legendary, even though it is not representative of the creation account recorded in the first book of the Bible. In fact, Genesis recounts the creation of man through the creator's life-giving breath, almost evocative of a mouth to mouth resuscitation. The famed version of Michelangelo's imagination is more mechanistic, as if that fateful touch would pass on energy, electricity or life-force like that with the press of a button. Hence, multiple graphical remakes have substituted the human hand with a robotic one, arousing the *tremendum fascinans* of human unease with *techne*. The biblical image of a life-giving breath is more personal, intimate, relational and poetic, redirecting us to contemplation and *poiesis* and the mystery of transmission of new life.

We might want to ponder another icon that speaks eloquently of human origin. The Visitation represents the meeting of two saintly women, Mary and Elizabeth. Contemporaneously the fruits of their wombs also have an encounter. Her older cousin's words greeted the Mother of God carrying the Word Incarnate, "Blessed are you among women, and Blessed is the fruit of your womb." In *utero*, John leaped for joy in the presence of his cousin Jesus, the Messiah whom he will one day announce as the voice crying in the wilderness, "Prepare the way of the Lord. Make his paths straight." The visible encounter of a sterile woman with a virgin contrasts with an invisible scene where the Voice meets the Word. The jubilant salutations of the women do not surpass the silent exchanges of the fetuses. In this fruitful imagination, the body-soul union finds expressions in the mother-child relationships, kinship, virginity and maternity, feminine and masculine complementarity, and profound spirituality and theology.

Appealing to the 'power of imagery'

Francis Etheredge's appeal to the power of imagery to a more profound comprehension of the incarnate spirit, the human person, naturally derives from the Thomistic use of analogy and participation. In the dialectics between the body and the soul, he warns against a Cartesian dualism that leads to a mechanistic reductionism that Pope Francis warns about. His dialectics is not of the Hegelian brand. It is probably closer to the polar opposition of Romano Guardini, where the truths of a simple yet complex reality are found between the two poles. By examining and contrasting the two, we gain insights and knowledge.

The subject under scrutiny in this work is, therefore, the polar opposition between the body and soul. We encounter the metaphysical and physical questions of essence and existence, objectivity, and subjectivity, matter and spirit. He displays the icons of unity and diversity of man and woman in their individual and collective presence in time and space. These, in turn, raise the queries on the origins and originality, and the perennial philosophical question of the one and many. They further hint at the supernatural mysteries of Trinity and infinity and Christ's humanity and divinity. Finally, in addressing divine and human creativity and procreativity, we come back to the earlier interrogations on culture and nature, *techne* and *poiesis*.

Francis Etheredge

Above all, he has filled us with beautiful and poetic imaginations of the *Imago Dei*.

"Birthright"

by

Eric Carson

Artist's Statement

'Created specifically for this competition75, *"Birthright"* uses sacred geometry and the eight celled human embryo as

---

75 Ink on paper. Unesco Chair in Bioethics and Human Rights Art Competition: Reproduced with the Permission of the Director from the 2013 Bioethics in Art Collection. Again, like the earlier picture called "Flame of Life", this is another imaginative account

a foundation. Six major traditions of insight are represented around the common center of a fertilized egg/eye. Conflicts in these traditions often obscure the fact that they are peers on the most fundamental level: each one comes from human insight, and each develops as a culturally specific flowering. Without human life and the life sciences that create and sustain it, traditions of insight would not exist. Unity, diversity, and vulnerability come together in this piece to inspire consciousness and the responsibility that follows.'

CHAPTER ONE: IMAGINATION

General Introduction to Chapter 1: Imagination

Our culture is inundated with images and works of the imagination; and, therefore, it is almost easier for people to "invent" new possibilities than it is to think through their value, use or goodness. Is imagination so unbounded that reality has become invisible? Is our inability to engage with reality a sign of our distance from it?

The imagination, however, is both a part of the process of understanding what exists and, alternatively, a facility for extrapolating from what exists. When, for example, our subject is the beginning of life and involves, as it were, the unimaginable, we need the help of the imagination to "envision" the moment at which God acts to bring a human being to exist. In a certain sense, like striking a match, it is easier to see that the match is lit than it is possible to say at what precise instant the match caught alight. Similarly, in that there is an act of God at the radical beginning of each one of us, it is easier to recognize that this has occurred and

---

of the nascent human being; but, in addition, it makes explicit both the international nature of human life and reflection on it.

that a child is conceived *because there is a real event: a child now exists – than it is to say of the moment itself that it is "now"*. The "moment" of an act of God is timeless in that it "takes no time"; but, on the other hand, it lasts forever: a child is for everlasting life.

Taking up, then, that aspect of the cultural world in which we live, it is necessary to "move" through it to the questions which are really involved and which challenge us; and, therefore, we too need to take up the work of the imagination and to explore different ways of communicating the almost incommunicable. If, however, this starting point seems unfamiliar to us, consider the many ways that biblical authors and teachers use an analogy to help us make that transition from what we do not know to the "intake" of understanding; and, likewise, let us explore the vast array of inventive explanations which are, no less, an opportunity to investigate our subject.

If elsewhere it has been argued that in the "moment" of the real transmission of life, God acts to complete the spousal act of love in bringing a child to exist, here it is necessary to enable a wider and more imaginative transition to the same truth. Love seeks the fullness of truth no less than the truth seeks the fullness of love.

In the words of St. John Paul II: 'Today much imagination is needed if we are to learn how to speak about the faith and about life's most important questions'[76].

---

[76] St. John Paul II, *Rise, Let Us Be On Our Way*, translated by Walter Ziemba, London: Jonathan Cape, 2004, p. 107.

Conception: An Icon of the Beginning

CHAPTER ONE: PARTS Ii-Iiii: ON THE USE OF THE IMAGINATION

General Introduction to Chapter 1:
Part I: Imagine

Although the general scene of this work has been set by arguing that we need an intelligent understanding of "body" and "soul" and how that unfolds in the psychosomatic whole of human being, nevertheless we can recognize that the theme of investigating our "beginning" is as old as mankind; and, in its own way, the very opening chapters of *Genesis* are an account of that pursuit, ever old and ever new, of seeking an explanation that draws upon all that we are. Understanding human conception, then, is a part of that wondering about reality which characterizes us as human beings; and, therefore, it comes into the very fiction which purports to give a beginning to the moment that a man or a woman received a "superpower". In the context of our current culture, then, this opening essay begins with an account of that search for a beginning which is, for some, completely out of reach and for others, not only out of reach but given to us in the word of God. Imagining, then, an origin to a creature different from ourselves, whether it be Superman or his opposite, takes us into the dramatic world in which contrasts are accentuated and differences almost irreconcilable; and, therefore, we need the work of imagination to help us to step into the more difficult questions that attest to the fact that we are "called", as it were, to interrogate our existence. The very capacity to ask a question takes us beyond the horizon of matter and shows, in its own way, that through the meaning of our "word-sounds" matter itself expresses more that it can on its own.

At the same time, however, as the imagination is a kind of fictional exploration of the real questions of the human heart, a facility for envisioning how to invent a new device or explanation, it can also be a kind of "prophetic witness" to what is possible. In other words, we draw on the imagination to investigate the future before it is upon us in practice; and, in the course of that very investigation, to find the help we need to choose the developments which are, "in reality", going to develop the humanity of the human race.

The imagination, then, is itself "concrete" evidence of that transcendence of matter that the very act of imagining a range of possibilities actually entails. On the one hand, then, there is the mental grasp of an image as an integral part of apprehending the "whole" of what we are thinking. It is possible to "imagine" that conception is like communication between two people who, gradually discovering the existence of the other, start to send messages to each other: the messages making explicit the existence of a prior relationship. Thus "imagination" can help us to "visualize" what in fact is a subtle and slow process. In the "image" of two people discovering each other, it summarises a period of gradual change and development which becomes more explicitly about a relationship to an "other" as the child's identity is both discovered and disclosed to the mother and father. On the other hand, imagination can be about envisaging the "multiple" options that are entailed in deciding on a course of action; and, typically, is a very natural part of designing an object: of considering a variety of possibilities in the process of deciding on one of them. Thus the very ordered freedom of the imagination in front of the data of the design process expresses, in its own way, the freedom of the human spirit that arises from the roots of human being. In other words the imagination is a "sign", as it were, of the very presence of the transcendent human spirit in that it is possible to "envisage" what is possible in the "direction" of what already exists; and, at the same time, distinguish what works "as an imaginative account of reality" and what, otherwise, is the range of imaginative possibilities.

In this three part account of the help of imagination, there is first of all a kind of reflection on the "tendencies" of our culture to "imagine" beginnings (Ii), a second account which considers, however briefly, human imagination and the future (Iii) and then a third part which engages with the question: What is the imagination?

Imagining Origins (Ii)

Introduction to Chapter 1: Part Ii: The Question of Origin. 'Where do we come from? Where are we going? What is our origin?'[77] Why do we exist as man, male and female? (cf. Genesis 1: 27). We cannot escape questions about our identity which, in a sense, will always take us back to a "beginning". So what have superman, Scripture and experiments on the human embryo got in common?

In a story about superman, *Man of Steel*, we are taken back to his beginning on another planet and, as such, we are given a reason for the origin of his superpowers and his mission to defend the earth from evil doers. But, at the same time, we end up with another question: What is a superhero? Is it really an attempt to reintroduce the angel that left by another door? In other words, superman and those of his race who would attack and colonize the earth, are like the angelic race which, after being created, chose to be either for or against God: either for or against human beings. Thus a story becomes another vehicle to explore the mystery of good and evil and the variety of created creatures; however, the story overlooks the more basic question about why anything exists, never mind that superheroes and supervillains exist.

---

[77] CCC, 282.

Similarly we all want to know what we can about ourselves; and, indeed, some of us have had intense difficulties in coming to understand our purpose in life. It may be that a person wanted to be a writer but there were no writers in the family; and, therefore, modelling himself on many other options, led to many years of frustration and alienation, even to the point of wondering if life was worth living. What if questions just lead to more questions and not to answers? Others have suffered in other ways and, for one reason or another, have been frustrated in their desire to identify their origin, whether it was their family of origin, their parents, those who, for whatever reason, contributed to their existence[78].

Ultimately, then, we go beyond our individual needs and come to the foundational questions: Why does anything exist? On the one hand St. Thomas Aquinas said that, according to philosophy, we cannot know if there was an origin to all that exists; and, therefore, we need the help of God's word to know that there was an origin to our existence and to the universe in which we live. There remain many other questions that arise, too, that go off in many directions. How, if matter is dispersing in the universe from a "big-bang", did it ever "stop" to form a planet; and how, if it did, did it come together in just the right amount of

---

[78] A cloned human being is still a human being; and, therefore, where there is what is human God gives there to be a human being. A human being, if conceived in a different way to the plan of God, still seeks the completing wholeness of what he or she has been deprived of by being "conceived artificially". Cf, for example, a similar predicament for an advocate of real help to married couples through NaPro technology, Elizabeth Howard: "There really is an alternative": 'I was born via donor conception myself – in vivo rather than in vitro – and have struggled to come to terms with this, particularly a sense of loss of identity and being cut off from one of my parents' (p. 21, *The Catholic Herald*, June 9th, 2017).

everything to form the earth? What came first: soil or plants? If soil has plant tissue in it, how did soil come to exist without plants to help it form; but if plants need soil to grow in, then how did plants manage before soil was fully formed? Where did plants come from, anyway; and, not just plants, what about animals? Does it not take a mature kind of the species to form seeds, berries and young; and, therefore, how would a fully grown anything have emerged and survived if it had not been made so from the beginning?

Each of us begins

We come, then, to the experiments on the beginning of human life: as if each one of us did not begin as a child, a son or a daughter, a brother or a sister, with a father or a mother? How have we contradicted every witness of every human being that comes into existence and unfolds, in an amazing way, manifesting the beginning of the whole person hidden in the moment of conception or the twinning that follows? How is it possible that we cannot imagine that combining human egg and sperm with that of animals could end up "imprisoning" a human being in an inadequately human body? Where is the recognition that a human being has a right to be conceived in a human way?

As a fruit of spousal love, there is coming together of sperm and egg or ovum. In a moment there is the sealing of what was the ovum by what is not now a sperm – but together is the "walled embryo" and the beginning of a person-in-relationship: a child. In what can be called the primordial natural sacrament, God acts in the moment of "beginning", without which there is no beginning, and brings to exist a human person: whole and entire and unrepeatedly unique and yet "in-relationship" to the whole human race. The outward sign, then, of the very beginning of the bodily expression of the human person is a "witness" to a God-given moment of ensoulment within; and, just as an outward shape cannot exist without an interior, so the bodily expression of the person cannot exist without the soul.

On the one hand we are exploring the vocabulary of life and reality to communicate, as if for the first time, that everything made or created has a beginning; and, in particular, human beings have a unique beginning: a personal act of a loving God bringing each one of us to exist (cf. Gn 4: 1). Thus, although there is a purpose expressed in the very language of procreation, in that God communicates the love and mystery of being the Blessed Trinity, it is nevertheless true that every child is loved into existence by God. God knows no orphans: each of us is loved into existence – even if the evidence has dwindled and it is increasingly difficult for us to see and to believe it.

On the other hand, how helpful it is to think through the very origin of everything and, in particular, the very origin of human personhood and to discover that a human being exceeds the biological life from which it springs like creation sprang from nothingness. For just as nothing can cause itself to exist, so nothing greater can come from something lesser and nothing as uniquely personal as the human being can come from what is biological. Just, then, as the transmission of human life, in the form of an egg and a sperm, is not a human person, so the conception of a child exceeds the power of sperm and egg. Thus a child needs a cause capable of bringing about the reality of human personhood – a cause we generally identify as God.

In reality, then, there are so many more real questions which arise from the actual life of human beings; and, especially, how the very beginning of psychological identity unfolds in the natural course of embryonic development. In other words, inscribed within the very reality of embryology is the integral expression of psychological development.

Thus a child within the womb begins to recognize the parents and the parents look forward to meeting their child. How is it possible that we have so forgotten the reality of everyday life that we can no longer wonder at what actually takes place and "who" is conceived under the heart of the mother?

Scripture?

Wonderful, then, are the questions that arise. At the same time, in what way do the opening chapters of Genesis help us to understand what truth for the sake of our salvation was expressed in the Scriptures? (cf. *Dei Verbum*, 11). Contemplating everything as the writer did, did he not see the wondrous unfolding of a beginning and, at the same time, did he not see that man, male and female, uniquely expressed the mystery of "relationship" in God? Thus God, being the Blessed Trinity, created in a way that expressed the very life of God in the very relationship of complementarity: in the very relationship of man and woman and the fruit of their offspring. Each human person is an indispensible witness to the reality that God loves each one of us into existence: that each one of us is an irrevocable and irreplaceable gift of a person-in-relationship: a child of a mother and a father and a child of God.

Science fiction may explore the questions of life and even anticipate real developments; but, actually, the questions about our beginning need to be asked to the point of being answered. For, increasingly, we are walking into an uncertain future and the very identity of the human person, while remaining, is increasingly a riddle to each one of us. We need to turn again to the basic gifts of Scripture and reason, the actual insights of the life sciences, our common wisdom that everything has a beginning and a beginning is the first instant that it exists; and, at the same time, we need a new language to express the ancient wisdom of Eve who recognised, following the moment of knowing Adam: 'I have gotten a man with the help of the Lord' (Gn 4: 1).

Imagining Futures (Iii)

Introduction to Chapter 1: Part Iii: Imagining the Future. What is Artificial Intelligence? Is Intelligence Artificial? What is Intelligence?

These questions, while not answered in any chronological order, are nevertheless part of the "background" to this discussion; and, more generally, these questions involve an understanding of human anthropology: What is the Human Person?

Drawing on personal experience, education, imagination, reason and the heart's understanding of the culture in which we live, this discussion revolves around the principle that the human person is a being-in-relation. More particularly we live in a society which, increasingly, is naturally impressed by the range and versatility of machines; and, in general, it is good to recognize the tremendous value of these human achievements while, at the same time, to critically evaluate them.

Starting with personal experience

The outer swelling of a leg led to the blood test which revealed the presence of a clotting factor of 15 which, normally, is about 0.3. Thus began a whole programme of tests and investigations.

In comparison to what it was like after the Second World War, ultrasound can now produce a truly helpful, non-invasive, image of the internal structure and function of the body. A recent examination, using ultra-sound, showed very clearly a vein in the leg and the clotting that had taken place:

the clotting looked like the dust and fibre that collects in a Hoover; and, in addition, it was possible to see the slight passage of blood which managed to pulse past the side of the clot. At the same time, however, there are difficulties to visualizing the inner structure and function of the more dense parts of the leg. In other words, there are both limits to what has been done as well as an account of the wonderful progress of this technology. On the other hand, the very improvement that has been made raises the possibility of further progress and, in a certain sense, the prospect of an almost "transparent" visibility to the whole inner structure and function of the body. More generally, then, we view the possibility of the advancement of technology as an almost endless progression from what can actually be done now to what is possible in the future.

It is clear, then, that this "artifice" is a profoundly helpful aid to diagnosing the presence and, to some extent, the extent of clotting; and, in general, along with echo ultrasound scanning of the heart, x-rays of the chest, cat-scans of the lungs, there are innumerable aids to the doctor's diagnosis and treatment of the human person.

There remain, however, challenging questions: What begins the process of clotting and how early is it possible to detect it? Are there, then, always external signs to the clotting? Indeed, clotting in the lungs results in the psycho-physical symptoms of extreme weariness as well us an increasingly uncomfortable stiffness from clotting in the leg. In general, symptoms vary with the degree and mobility of the person as well as, as it were, the recognition of changes that could have been so slow as to be almost imperceptible until there is a marked interference with mobility or general well-being.

Alternatively: at the "end" and the "beginning" of life

But what if, instead of meeting the various technicians, doctors and specialists, the whole "input" was processed by a "robotic doctor" which collated everything that had gone into all these tests, including heart rate, pulse, diet and exercise, previous medical history, family history, current work and income generated over the last year and, in sum, "it" could conclude that I was ready to be scrapped. Thus, in a "moment", the room would be sealed, I would be anaesthetised and delivered into a rolling programme which, on the basis of numerous readings, salvaged and sold what was "recyclable", "trashed" the rest and, if possible, found a "market" for the remains. In other words, at a functional level, what may be an acceptable process for processing meat was "used" to assess and despatch a human being. The claim, then, would be made that the various criteria for my useful, cost-effective existence, had clearly resulted in a positive outcome for the market but a negative outcome for what was the patient.

What if, however, this mentality were to spread to the beginning of life and the whole "process" were to be a form of "supervised" production of human beings, employing all kinds of "quality control mechanisms" to determine the outcome of the products?

What about, then, the psychological and spiritual impact of this mentality on the people of the earth?

What is the difference between an artificial and a human intelligence?

On the one hand, it may be argued that artificial intelligence is, as it were, artificial because it is a calculative process abstracted from the wholeness of human being. If the "intelligence" is not only abstracted from the whole sensitivity of the humanity of the doctor but, by implication, of the person to be treated, then the outcome of a calculative process is led by market forces. In this instance, then, the machine has been programmed to deliver a "market" outcome. The whole instrumentation, however sophisticated, is completely incapable of deliberating on the meaning of the reality of being-in-relationship: of being a son; a brother; a husband; a father; a relative; a friend; a neighbour; and a living part of the whole human community. The "calculus", then, expresses a type of human intelligence: a type of human intelligence that is "built-in" to this version of the "robotic doctor". The machine, in other words, expresses what becomes of human intelligence when it is driven by "market forces" and, at the same time, does not understand the significance of being-in-relationship. Although, it could be argued, the "calculus" could be refined to take account of "active" or even existing relationships. But what scale of "usefulness" could record a person searching for the meaning of his or her suffering?

On the other hand, the *Hippocratic Oath* gives ancient expression to an understanding of the practical intelligence entailed in medicine which is, at the same time, an integrated expression of the whole humanity of the physician; indeed, it shows that the physician is "embedded" in a whole range of relationships which express both a consciousness of what is received as well as what is transmitted to others. In other words, in the midst of deadlines and costs, all of which have their place, there is a process of retaining and developing the wholeness of human being in the very practice of medicine. Indeed, it could be argued, the psychosomatic understanding of the human person is clearly an immense horizon of meaning in the dimensions of human experience: the human experience which both "entails" all kinds of suffering and responds, through the dialogue-of-relationship, to the actual "humanity-in-the-treatment", however mediated by technological aids, in the doctor-patient relationship. In the end, then, there is both the development of humanitarian aids but there is, too, the ongoing development of the humanity that aids human beings.

One feature, then, of development, is change: the possibility of discovering an unexamined premise, namely that the very communication of meaning transcends the means used to communicate it. By contrast, a machine cannot express a different mentality except in so far as it is reprogrammed to do so. In other words, a new mentality is not a program change: it is a change "beyond" program changes.

In conclusion: A bird is a "living intelligence" possessing, in its very beauty and well being, both what is necessary to the living out of a life and, at the same time, adorning our world with wondrous splendours of activity and being. The bird is both a whole unto itself and, as a part of a species, is embedded in the generations of life: past; present; and ongoing future. The bird, in other words, is orientated to life: to living and being-in-the-world; even if, in terms of its life, it is not without dangers and difficulties.

What "intelligence" a machine possesses is a reflection, ultimately, of its maker: Is it integrated into life-as-a-whole or does it express a different mentality? Culturally, we receive an immense inheritance, a kind of expression of the lived experience of the human race; and, therefore, will the generations-to-come recognize, in the "practical wisdom" we pass on, a help to the human race? There are always choices. There are choices that develop us and there are choices that undermine us. A choice that develops us entails the discipline of life: that helping and healing always demands more of us that its opposite.

Conception: An Icon of the Beginning

The intelligence, then, that enables us to understand both life-as-it-is-lived and the environment which makes it possible, inevitably suggests that there is a "building" on what we have received; and, therefore, what we receive is both what we are given and what has been done with it. Artificial Intelligence expresses both what we have understood about what exists and what it is possible to do with it; but, at the same time, developing artificial intelligence is about choosing the good that perfects human being in the very process of helping us in our relationship to one another. In other words, artificial intelligence can be redefined as an "artificial relationship" and its contribution to living relationships.

Artificial intelligence builds on our understanding of the processes that both belong to the natural world and, at the same time, express and develop the capacities that we possess. On the one hand, imagination can have a "prophetic" function in envisioning the possibilities that run on from us; however, envisioning the future is also about reflecting, ethically, on these possibilities. Ethics, however, is as inseparable to human action as it is to human being. In other words, man is a moral being whose ethical acts either develop or hinder the humanity he or she possesses. Changing towards a more humanitarian use of artificial intelligence is a possible human option. A change of mentality, however, is as remote from a machine as meaning to the word which bears it.

Artificial intelligence is also an argument for the existence of God: a wholly intelligent Being that is "expressed" in the radical intelligibility of the universe. Just as there is an immersion of an intelligent structure in the very fabric of the universe and the embodiedness of human being so, together, they indicate that the "intelligence" of God is immersed, like the beautiful intelligibility of the cosmos, in an immensely practical, intellectual Love of creation. In other words, God is "Other" than creation but, more intimately than the musician's making of music, creation "expresses" the mystery of God.

What is the Imagination (Iiii)

Introduction to Chapter 1: Part Iiii: What is the Imagination? As this work develops so it is necessary to consider the imagination itself. The very facility to "invent" an image is itself evidence of a power in the possession of the person that draws through the rootedness of our biological life and yet opens out on a terrain as vast as the universe itself. Imagination, or the development of images, has a kind of inner function within the whole of human psychology; and, at the same time, it functions as a kind of "spawning ground of possibilities". On the one hand, imagination is an integral part of perception and thought: 'We must suppose, then, that the intellect as active picks out, as it were, the potentially universal elements in the image, the synthesized reproduction in the imagination of the data of the different senses'[79]. Thus, in a certain way, there is the whole that exists in reality, of which we are both an "immersed part" and, at the same time, a "part" capable of apprehending a glimpse of being a "whole" within the "whole". The imagination contributes to the reproduction, as it were, of the existential object which we perceive. On the other hand, then, the creative imagination 'forms its object by combining elements which were separately perceived'[80]. Thus, just as there are an immeasurable number of possible combinations of what is being perceived, bearing in mind the incalculable

---

[79] Copleston, *Aquinas*, p. 176.

[80] Mark Mary de Munnynck, "Imagination." *The Catholic Encyclopedia*. Vol. 7. New York: Robert Appleton Company, 1910. 22 Nov. 2017 <http://www.newadvent.org/cathen/07672a.htm>.

number of "voices" from the past, and indeed the present, so the potential for "imaginative" connections is almost as vast as the detail of the universe itself. Imagination as creative, then, stands to reality as "seed" to thought and influences what will come to exist. Reality, therefore, in the light of imagination is as fecund as if every atom or even every particle of matter were a potential piece in a complex pattern of ideas.

What accounts for this abundance of possibilities? Seed, itself, for example, is a natural fecundity which makes the generation of plants, animals and even human beings an expression of a rich inheritance. Imagination, then, is almost a mirror of the "creativity" out of which the very universe itself emerged.

Conversely, the domination of a single idea over the whole of reality is like a tyranny which, in its resistance to the integrity of the whole, impoverishes our perception of what exists. Thus a monochromatic definition of the human being as "biological material" is both a reductive account of what exists and, at the same time, a kind of ruling out the richness of human experience. When Raskolnikov, in Dostoyevsky's *Crime and Punishment*, considers the pros and cons of murdering an old lady, it is not until he does so that he discovers the poverty of his "idea" in comparison the fullness of his own humanity or that of the woman he kills. In other words, imagination can almost work negatively in its "reduction" of the fullness of what exists. "Biological material", as applied to human being, is reductive in virtue of the fact that it excludes the obvious and richer account of reality that entails recognizing that we speak, love and search for the truth.

What concerns me in this book, however, is that work of the imagination which is both already expressed in the various accounts of the beginning of human personhood; but which, in addition, is that constant endeavour to go from what is known to what is unknown.

CHAPTER ONE: PART II: QUESTIONING OUR EXISTENCE

General Introduction to Chapter 1: Part II: Questioning Our Existence. Taking three points of departure in these brief "essays" into the question of human identity is again about taking a question from our culture and examining, briefly, the differentiation of human being: the capacity to 'interrogate our existence; the capacity to compare ourselves with a robot; and the capacity to consider what it would mean to be a Martian. These questions seem to arise frequently and, in their own way, help us to see that the radical question of human identity, of really getting to the root of what constitutes human being, is still an investigation to be pursued; and, in a certain way, an investigation that becomes ever more urgent as so much depends on a deep and abiding answer to the question posed by the very existence of a personal being.

Introduction to Chapter 1: Part II: Different ways of questioning our existence. In one sense, to question our existence is to ask if our life has a purpose, a value or a use that is entailed in "being in existence" and, as it were, illuminates it; and, at the same time, this questioning of our existence is about, almost literally, examining what we find in the "fact" of being a person. In other words, it may be too obvious to consider the "fact" of being in existence; but, on the other hand, it may be that we actually need to take time to "wonder" at being in existence. We are, as the philosophers say, contingent beings: it is not necessary that each one of us exist; but, at the same time, what if we take the opposite point of view: What if it is absolutely essential that each one of us exists? What if our very existence, in terms of the reality of human society, is an essential "point of relationship" and that without each one of us society would, as it were, have "vacant" spaces.

This is not, however, a projection of our vanity or self-importance; it is, rather, an admission that if all that exists is necessary to existence, then perhaps that includes each one of us: a gift both free and essential because we are both a gift to ourselves and to others.

But our questioning has a beginning; and, therefore, the following three pieces are, as it were, three beginnings to the question posed in the very fact of our existence.

Questioning Our Existence: Who Am I? (IIi)

Are we in a dream? Could we be in someone else's virtual reality? How do we know that we even exist?
In a certain sense we can "investigate" the very fact of our own existence

On the one hand, if I did not exist, then I could not question my own existence; and, therefore, the very fact of putting a question is evidence that I exist. Indeed, even if I put the question in a dream, both dreaming and putting a question are a part of the evidence that I exist; and, what is more, if I imagine the scenario, it is I who imagines it. Nevertheless, it is still possible to question the answer to every question and to end up, as it were, with sand in the hand; and, as such, to be subject to an almost involuntary, if not pathological questioning, evading even the fact that sand in the hand still exists. Questioning, then, does not quench itself; and, in a moment, I could discover a certain answer with which to begin again. In other words, even if I question questioning, it does not detract from the fact that it is the questioner who is questioning the asking of questions.

On the other hand, what does the very fact that I exist tell me? It tells me that I am the subject of all the changes that I undergo; and that, therefore, right from the beginning, I am the person that change manifests. In other words, all the involuntary changes of growth and development have one goal: to make me known to myself and to others; however, like any other existent in the universe, I do not bring myself to exist but I do contribute to being in existence. A rock, for example, does not bring itself into existence; but, once it exists, so the characteristics of that rock are usefully employed in building a wall, in being the basis of a sculpture or lying in splendid display of its "rockiness" in a garden. The human being, then, having come into existence, is the subject who comes to know who it is who has "given" existence to him or to her. This dialogue reflects the fact that each one of us is a "being-in-relationship"; and, as such, we share this foundational fact with all that exists in the universe.

Our path, then, if it can be called that, is to travel from coming into "being-in-relationship" to knowing those with whom I exist in relationship; and, ultimately, that includes the One who has the power to bring what does not exist into existence. The personal cannot come from the biological and, therefore, I came into existence because of one "Who" makes it possible for me to be a person; and, then, what makes it possible for me to be a person is that the psychological identity unfolds in the very nature of embryological development. But what makes it possible for the embryological development to unfold psychological development is the reality of human personhood: a reality that exceeds the biological just as the biological exceeds the material. It is, therefore, a personal act of God that brings a human person to exist; and, just as God is three persons in

Conception: An Icon of the Beginning

one God, so each human person comes to exist in relationship to others. Thus a man is a human person called to be the gift he was given to be in being given existence and a woman is a human person called to be the gift she was given to be in being given the gift of existence; and, together, men and women manifest the relational nature of human personhood, just as God reveals that He is a community of persons and 'lives a mystery of personal loving communion' (cf. *Familiaris Consortio*, 11).

But just as we fall and fail at the rail, so we discover that as empty as the crib is before Christmas, so the word of God, the sacrament of marriage, the community of the Church, come to bring the gift of Christ that makes repentance and reconciliation possible.

In one sense, then, the path of the universe is down, just as the Son of God came down to live among us, so the path up is the path down: to the humility that makes love possible between us.

Questioning Our Existence: Am I a Robot? (IIii)

You or I could be a robot; or, alternatively, we could be the non-robots in a robotic world. How do we know whether or not we are a part of the script or the script writer?

If I were a robot, however, how would I account for my own nature and, at the same time, how could I imagine what I am not: a human being? If I am not a robot, but a human being, I can imagine what it is to be a robot and I can give an account of what it is to be a human person.

On the one hand, we are incredibly well engineered, each cell a functioning whole that is integrated within the whole human system. At the same time, there is a remarkable diversification, if not specialization, whereby what is different does not "rocket off" into its own pathway and program; indeed, in virtue of the very complementarity between all the different cell types, there is a marvellous versatility and responsiveness to each other. Once begun, this organic robot develops according to its inbuilt program, absorbing what it needs and rejecting what it does not or cannot use; and, progressively, there emerges the receptivity to downloaded information and, in time, the automatic processing of this information produces language skills that "connect" with others.

On the other hand, then, the very existence of an imaginative account of what it would be like to be a robot argues against the fact that I am a robot. What is more, if I were a downloading information system, I would not be able to understand the meaning of what I am downloading; and, therefore, the very processes of thinking, writing and deliberating, are the very activities which contribute to what I am doing. Furthermore, in actual fact we do not "download" information, except on a computer; for, in the act of reading there is an on-going dialogue between "reality" and the writer. In other words, I am constantly making judgements about whether or not I understand what I read, agree with it, think that it can be improved or integrated into a more comprehensive account of reality. Thus, in the end, the inseparably personalistic response to what is happening both differentiates me from a robot and, at the same time, constitutes the "dialogical" basis for communication with my fellow human beings.

In the end, then, while the robot is a brilliant invention of a multidisciplinary team, in whatever way it may be led by a distinguished inventor, it is nevertheless an invention; and, indeed, there is the danger of investing the invention with the inventor's inventiveness. In other words, just like the "idol" makers of old, there seems to be a danger of attributing "life" to what has been made.

Conception: An Icon of the Beginning

As regards each one of us, the very expressibility of human personhood is a marvel to behold. How the artist transmits the meaning of colour, the musician the meaning of sound and the sculptor the meaning of shape. But even in the everyday actions of life, the expressibility of the human person implies such an extraordinary integration of being that could only be given at the beginning of each one of us: that the outwardness of our being human expresses the inwardness of our being a person.

Questioning Our Existence: Am I a Martian? (IIiii)

How do I know that I am a human being and not an "extra-terrestrial" being from Mars?

On the one hand, I may very well have different features to many other human beings, indeed my colour, shape, size and general appearance is, inevitably, a unique expression of me; and, therefore, hats and clothes and all the other accessories to being myself, are all relative to the unrepeatable presence that is me. The unrepeatable me is deeper than the origin of twins although, in fact, there well may be a close resemblance between the appearance of each of us. My existence, however, is not transferable: it is indistinguishably me; and, in addition, my experience is both rooted in the uniquely existent me and, at the same time, in the fact that I am immeasurably immersed in a multitude of relationships which I no more chose than the fact that I exist. In one sense, then, I am inseparable to the ends of the universe, bearing in my body the traces of what exists across the vast terrain of the multitudinous places throughout the "endless" matter amidst which we live; and, in addition, wherever I am from I am therefore of the same "universal material" of which the universe is made: I am materially "akin" to all the creatures that exist and inhabit this planetary place among the stars and other intergalactic objects.

On the other hand, what distinguishes me as a creature of this planet is the very density of identity: the very mixtures of minerals and their properties that are particularly present on earth. In other words, I am as utterly adapted to this planet as if I was made from its very substance; but, if I was, then I am also a radically new expression of it: a creature at once utterly unique and, at the same time, expressive of a common inheritance of the creatureliness to which I belong. The amazing variety of expressions of the creatureliness from which I came, in whom I am immersed as in a vast sea of "inheritable" ingredients, all of whom are capable of communication, whether instantly, through translators or other aids, all of which entail an immense wealth of cultures across the globe on which we live and in the endless variety of places which we adorn as homes and places of meeting, worship, recreation and business.

How do we express, then, that distinguishing breath that blew through the universe and transformed the very matter of its existence into the person that is both temporal and open to an eternity of being-in-relationship? Just as a child comes into existence through parents, so does that relationship endure everlastingly; and, more widely, just as we are related to each other, so each one of us is inseparably related to others, in an ever widening ripple of a really whole humanity. Just as all the characteristics and potentialities vary and yet, at the same time, come together in each human person, so like the drops of "relationship" that we are, we need the presence of One among us who, originating our mystery, knows how to help and to heal us in the gift and the task of meeting each other.

Chapter One: Part III: A New Beginning: Imagining "Body" and "Soul"

General Introduction to Chapter 1: Part III: A Reasonable Use of the Imagination. Already, then, the very possibility of enquiring about the beginning of a person has been recognized as a part of our culture and, therefore, as a part of our nature. However, not everything that is a part of our culture is also a part of our nature, except in the general sense that it all evidences what human beings do, because not all that human beings do is good; and, in view of that, it is only what is good which can be said to refer to human nature and, as regards what is not good or only imperfectly so, this refers to the many ways that we fail to recognize what fulfils us. In view, then, of the general desire to understand the existence and origin of the human person, what follows seeks to use a variety of expressions to explore how to "imagine" the problem to be investigated: that there is a mysterious moment in which each one of us begins as a whole person, one in body and soul, and that we need a gentle introduction to the difficulties of understanding this great event. Thus there follows a series of explanations, drawing on different kinds of comparison, which help us to appreciate what is involved in our task.

Introduction to Chapter 1: Part III: "Making Visible the Invisible" (IIIi). We live in a time in which it is almost impossible to discuss the conception of a human being because it is such a politically charged subject; however, the very fact of it being politically controversial and, for some, an area lacking clarity, is all the more reason to write about it in a useful variety of ways. The truth of our beginning is also surrounded by non-therapeutic experiments, none of which are for the benefit of the human embryo being experimented upon. St. John Paul II said that scientific evidence concerning human conception is 'a valuable indication for discerning by the use of reason a personal presence at the moment of the first appearance of a human life' (*Evangelium Vitae,* n. 60). At the same time, he also said that 'what is at stake is so important that, from the standpoint of moral obligation, the mere probability that a human person is involved would suffice to justify an absolutely clear prohibition of any intervention aimed at killing a human embryo' (*Evangelium Vitae,* n. 60). It is important, too, when discussing a subject as sensitive as conception, that we express that 'tenderness' which Pope Francis recommends to those who use the electronic media; and, what is more, that we do in a way that helps us to find the healing our wounds need[81]. If, understandably, a person is moved by these considerations then it would be good for them to seek help; however, in general, this is about guiding our understanding of this important subject and not entering into the many and related pastoral aspects of this question.

Even if, then, there are all kinds of problems to do with understanding the moment of our beginning, each one of us is a "witness" to that beginning; and, therefore, each one of us is evidence of who began at conception or the equivalent in the case of being one of a twin. On the basis of that evidence and employing a certain "likeness" to other events or processes, it is possible to think through the difficulties of understanding the mystery of our beginning; indeed, the very susceptibility of one kind of creature or event illuminating another, implies a marvellous integrity to all that exists: a multi-media extravaganza where one kind of

---

[81] *Message, 48th World Communication Day,* 1st June, 2014.

event enlightens us about another. Thus this series will make use of the method of comparing one kind of beginning with another. On the basis, then, of a partial likeness between two different kinds of beginning, this series will compare a number of events or "moments" with the beginning of personhood. St. Thomas Aquinas explains it in this way: "[H]uman minds, existing in bodies, know first the natures of material things, and by knowing the natures of what they see, derive some knowledge of what they cannot see"[82]. But let us not forget, though, that the reality of human conception exceeds our powers of imagination, as the beginning of each one of entails a discrete act of God. Thus it is necessary to develop an inventive "anticipation", as it were, of the actual reality of "witnessing" a truly mysterious event: the action of God at the beginning of each one of us (cf. Ps 139: 16). In this series of pieces, then, we will look at a variety of ways of understanding what we "cannot see".

Thus it is hoped that there will come together a kaleidoscopic complex of images which yet stand to the reality of human conception as glimpses of light illuminating, briefly, a reality all too hidden from our poor eyes; but, in the blazing vision of God, the beginning of each one of us is all too clearly a manifestation of His wondrous existence as "person-in-relation" (cf. Ps 139: 12-16). In what follows there are a number of arguments to help us to explore the nature of our beginning; and, if they are true, then it naturally leads to accepting the gift that each one of us is: a sparkling iconography of the unbounded generosity of the Creator among us.

In the next part of this series we take our first concrete "image": the beginning of a piece of writing and then what can be known about the "simple" case of human conception. By way of preparation, let us remember, ponder and perhaps

---

[82] *Summa Theologiae*, I. 84. 7.

even remind ourselves of the "moment" of putting pen to paper and, as we think on it, let all its aspects assume a transfiguration rather like the sun filling stained glass, briefly, and parting, ever so slightly, that veil over the invisible that we struggle to pass through.

Remember the "Moment" of Putting Pen to Paper (IIIii)

We may know the frustration of a blank page or the labour of editorial work – but this is the moment of writing. What can we learn from comparing "beginning to write" and human conception?

An Event Expressed in Material, in Time, Space and Meaning

Take a pen and write on a piece of paper. Once the pen has touched the paper there cannot but be a mark of some description unless, of course, the ink does not flow or the touch was so light that it scarcely made a visible mark; but, presupposing the contact of pen and paper, like the event of conception itself, there is then a new reality-event. Ordinarily, like the response of a key on a keyboard, there will be a letter and then a word and so the development of thought that unfolds in a piece of writing. What is more, once the actual mark is made, with or without ink, it cannot be unmade; it can be hidden, destroyed or defaced - but it cannot be unmade. The very existence of the mark entered a moment of time into the concrete act from which it is now inseparable: the mark on the page. What was, a moment before, one of many possibilities in front of the pen and the paper is now an event: an irrevocable and particular fact of a piece of writing; and, at the same time, the written mark is an event not only "in time" but also in its

Conception: An Icon of the Beginning

irreversible impact on the spatio-physical material which exists. In other words, the ink is now embedded in the paper owing to the presence of the pen and the two are now one; indeed, in a sense, I can lose the whole text or tear it up but that does not alter the fact that it came into existence and in some sense remains even if, now, as the memory of an event: but an event with existential significance - an event that struck a novel note in what exists.

Ink flows through the pen onto the paper and neither the pen nor the paper are what they are except in virtue of the maker of the pen and the paper; indeed, they are designed to be complementary precisely in order that writing can take place and that a letter, an article or a book can be written. Thus it is not a disservice to the paper that it is not a pen nor a disservice to the pen that it is not the paper. On the contrary, the paper gives the pen the opportunity to "show" itself in the writing and the pen gives the paper the opportunity to bear a message: to be the vehicle of an intricate artistry of the love between husband and wife.

As regards the writing itself, it is completely unaware of the significance of the words or, for that matter, any device which transmits it; but, nevertheless, there is a meaning which unfolds in the process of writing: a meaning integral to the words but beyond the possibility of their own comprehension of it. It is presumed, here, that the writing is communicating, as in this case, an argument: an intelligible account intended to be read and even to evoke a response of either agreement, disagreement or how the point can be developed. Thus a biological script, "if it exists", is "writing" an intelligible account of human development: not actually intelligible to itself except in the broad sense of instructions being as integral to a living process as the utilization of energy, building materials or transport systems. In other words, just as a pen had to exist before the ink could be transmitted to the paper, as indeed the paper had to exist before it could be written on, so the two together required the "agency" of the writer; and, therefore, just as everything the author brought together in a "word" presupposed all the other "ingredients", so the agency of God takes up all that comes together in that moment which begins each of us.

The Analogy or Likeness Between Writing and Conception

What, then, is the "equivalent" to the thought of the author expressed in a piece of writing? Just, then, as the author's idea is embodied in the text, so the "idea" of God is "embodied" in the existence of a human person. The meaning of the text transcends what is written to the extent that they are unintelligible to the mark on the page; and, therefore, just as the writing is a love-gift that needs to be read, so the gift of existence is implicit in the reality-event of a child's beginning. Part III of this sequence will discuss lighting a candle.

Light: Fuelled Radiating Energy (IIIiii)

The introduction to this series gives the impression that we are always working from a sense impression to an insight, from the "fact of a candlelight" to the "illumination" it brings of another kind of beginning. At the same time, however, let us realize that our looking is already "a thinking" and our perception, therefore, is already "a seeking to understand"; and, what is more, it is no different when the object of our thought is an "invisible" moment: the search for understanding is already present in the choice of imagery and the observations that we make. Nevertheless there is also a new element in that writing about a beginning entails, too, thinking about it in unexpected ways: ways that have arisen precisely because of the use of imagery. Later in this series we will address, more directly, how to understand the unity of body and soul in the human person; meanwhile, then, it will be helpful to remember that this is a background objective that, being our goal, will progressively come to the fore in the steps we take to get there. Thus it is important to recognize that no observation is without the observer who is thinking through what he or she understands about beginnings.

The Comparison of Lighting a Candle and Conception

Lighting a candle involves bringing a light to what is without one; and, therefore, there is a moment when the candle, in the flame of a match, receives a light that is now "its" own but which, in a mysterious way, is also a continuation of the light that lit it. Similarly, there is the substance of the candle, as it were, that comes together from the egg and the sperm. Unlike the candle which awaits the coming of the flame, however, the body does not exist as lifeless. In other words, while the wax and wick come together to make the candle and are inert until the moment of "lighting", the sperm is in movement and the egg is inert until they come together in the moment of fertilization. As soon as the egg and the sperm come together there is a new and independent life. The evidence for this is that the new being "closes" and the human embryo has an outward "skin". Just as the candle, however, cannot light itself, nor can there exist a human being without it being "given" a soul. Thus God, being like a "divine flame", brings the light of life to a new human being just as a flame lights a candle. In the same way, then, just as you cannot light a candle that is without wick or wax, so God creates the life of the human person in the moment that the egg and sperm come together[83]. Just as the candle becomes a candlelight in the "flame" which brings it, so the soul comes to exist in the body that begins to exist with the personal life that God gives to it.

In the Shadow of a Light

A related image is that of the shadow. Shadow and object are, at a certain moment, almost indistinguishable; but, nevertheless, a stone cannot but cast a shadow if it comes into a light. Thus, similarly, the living human body cannot but express the presence of the soul (cf. Lk 1: 35). In a certain way, then, just as a stone in a dark room "needs" another to turn the light on to be found, so turning the light on is inseparable to the stone casting a shadow; and, just as the shadow could not exist but for the light and the stone, so the human person would not exist but for the body and soul. Furthermore, just as the stone is incapable of turning the light on, so is the biological basis of human being incapable of bringing personhood to exist; and, therefore, just as there is an agent which turns the light on, so God brings the body to personal life through bringing about the integral presence of the soul.

It is difficult, then, to compare what is living with what is inert but alight or what is still but casting a shadow but, nevertheless, there are "moments" as well as key ideas which can be introduced and begun to be explained, particularly the pair popularly known as "body" and "soul". It is important to realise, at this point, though, that a human body cannot live without a soul. Just as a shadow cast by a stone is inseparable from it, and a lighted candle bears what

---

[83] The question of the absolute beginning of the human race is discussed later in the book; but, again, from the point of view of

it has received, so is the human person one in body and soul. In Part IV we will consider the thoughts that arise from the image of architecture.

Architecture and Soil (IIIiv)

We are now between the image that bears the idea indirectly and the idea that expresses it explicitly; and, therefore, we are "midway" between the opening of the discussion on the beginning of personhood and an explicit account of "body" and "soul". At the same time we are making another transition from a variety of "man-made" objects to a more natural, organic kind of image, namely the seed-bulb and the soil. The image-objects up to now have depended on the design that incorporates a range of materials and the action that brings them to "life": the act of writing and the lighting of a candle. Now we pass from an activity which requires a lot of human involvement to one which requires a little: from architect to seed-bulb planting.

Architecture: from House to Home

Next we can consider the potter and the clay; and, just as the potter does not make a random shape but a clay pot, so the processes which contribute to the formation of human identity have a goal: the revealing of the person conceived from the beginning. Similarly the architect designs the whole house and brings each part, piece by piece, to find its place in the whole; but, nevertheless, the house is incomplete without anyone living in it: the building "needs" people just as, in reality, the living body expresses personhood. At the same time, however, just as the building makes visible the

---

how it is applicable to understanding the conception of each one of us.

architect's conception of the house, so the living body makes visible the person conceived at conception. Thus the "house-home" is the bodily expression of the person: an inwardness outwardly expressed; but, in another sense, the body is not a "house" that we live in it is, rather, "making visible" what was present from the beginning. As embryological development unfolds, so the psychological relationships inherent in conception unfold, filling out the neighbourhood in which a family is known; but, just as the sky above is full of starlight, so relationships unfold unto eternity.

To take a different angle on the analogy, the partial likeness between one event and another, the architect's design is transformed into a building; and, in one sense, while the building code remains in the inheritance of each cell of the body, in another sense the body is an embodiment of a building plan. Thus, just as an architect's plan exists in "conception", in a drawing on a desk and the model, so it is given a new and unique existence in the very building which the builders have brought to exist. What is more, just as each new building, no matter how many times it is "replicated", is a different "edition" of the original, so each person bears the traces of innumerable influences: from inheritance to diet, from developmental to physiological variations and from psychological characteristics to the person-in-relationship: the unique male or the unique female.

From Seed-Bulb to Plant

On the other hand, just as a moist seed changes as it develops, so there comes a point when it needs to be planted to receive the nutrients necessary to growth; and, similarly, just as the flame of a match, once struck, needs to be fed if it is not to go out, so it needs a new source of fuel. A bulb, then, planted in the soil, not only has its own "substance" to draw upon but, as the root hairs develop, so it draws nutrition directly from the soil. Indeed, over the years, gardeners recognize the value of a plant pot, allowing the roots and the plant as a whole to develop more fully before being transplanted into the garden. Thus the human embryo, free floating down the duct from the ovary, having been fertilized, comes to rest in the "soil" of the uterus or womb. The human embryo then develops by way of a temporary aid or umbilical cord which, like the plant pot, is discarded at birth, when the child is able to be fed by his mother; indeed, whether within the womb or from the breast, the child is nurtured through the "ground" of his mother – yet the child is as different from the mother as the bulb is from the plant from which it grew.

Just as a family can walk out of the door and leave home, so there is a point of "failure" in the comparison of a house-home to the relationship between the soul and the body; for, in reality, we do not live in a body like we live in a house: death comes as life leaves the body. The body, like the language in which we express ourselves, needs the soul like words need the meaning they express. The plant, by contrast, can be transplanted and, therefore, the image "works" a little longer as "death" transplants each one of us into eternity. In Part V we compare one work of God with another.

Comparing One Act of God with Another (IIIv)

While employing imagery is a necessary aid to human understanding, there is also the possibility of comparing one act of God with another. Within Christianity as a whole, and Catholicism in particular, there are a range of mysteries whereby the timeless God has acted in time; and, while this is more about comparing one event with another: an act of God has common characteristics and is expressed in terms of created reality. Thus the *Incarnation of Christ* is a central event in the history of salvation, being discreetly anticipated in the very existence of creation expressing a word of God: '"Let there be light"; and there was light' (Gn 1: 3; and cf. St. Thomas Aquinas, *Summa Theologiae*, I, 44, 3). This is not, however, an account of biblical thought; it is, rather, a recognition that one act of God can illuminate another. Even if, then, it is possible to investigate, philosophically, the embryological beginning of each one of us, it is nevertheless helpful to have recourse to "similar" events that entail a positively creative act of God.

The Incarnation

When God became man, He took human flesh; and, therefore, from the first instant of the Son of God's human existence, He 'became flesh' (Jn 1: 14). St. Thomas Aquinas, a particularly helpful thinker in the Church, says that the incarnation was immediate if Christ was to be manifest in human flesh[84]. Although the father of Jesus Christ is God in a unique way in that the Son of God is God from God, yet we too become a human person as soon as God acts in the moment of our beginning.

The sacrament of Baptism is given and received when the word of the minister and the blessed water combine with the moment the water is poured over the head of the child. Similarly, the grace of inspiration and the author's words make one word of God; and, as such, the Church tells us that the word of God exists prior to the Church's recognition of it. In other words, the word of God comes into existence before the Church recognizes it exists; and, in the same way, the existence of the person is established by an act of God prior to any discernment the Church makes about when it has happened. Thus it is that when egg and sperm come together

---

[84] Cf. *Summa Theologiae*, III, 5, 4.

there is an act of God which brings each one of us to exist: a marvellously fitting outward sign of this act of God is the closing of the ovum wall in response to the sperm's penetration of it. In other words, an invisible act of God is "made visibly present" in the moment of the formation of the embryonic wall. At the very beginning of each one of us, then, it makes sense that the first outward sign that God acts, inwardly, to bring the person to exist, one in body and soul, is the first moment of the bodily life of the person. Just as electricity flows in nature before it is harnessed for any particular purpose, so does the matter and the energy of life exist before they are "charged" with the unfolding of the presence of the person conceived; but, once "charged", the body is integrally expressive of the person: the life of the body is the life of the human person.

Even if these analogies are more like intimations than actual arguments, they nevertheless bear out the reality to which each one of us is a witness: the reality of being so marvellously one that our origin, for all the difficulties it presents to our understanding, is indeed a wonderful occasion for an ongoing meditation on God bringing us to exist. But just as there are prejudices or errors of fact which can interfere with our judgement, so there are many reasons why we are resistant to the welcome of life, not least of which is the fear of losing what is ours; however, as we welcomed each one of our eight children, the time and energy which seemed to be taken from us has been transformed into a gift in the dialogue of everyday life. But we need, too, the simple faith that God, who created all that exists and who brings new life to the sinner, can help us all to welcome the gift of life.

The next in this series of explanations of conception takes us to a more difficult comparison between word and meaning (Part VI). Hopefully these two pieces will help us with the transition to the final piece in this series, which is on the wholeness of being one in "body" and "soul" (Part VII).

Word and Meaning: One "Needs" the Other? (IIIvi)

Imagining the mystery of conception brings us to the relationship between word and meaning. We may think of a word as an expression of thought defined in a dictionary; and, as such, a rather static and fragmentary item, not unlike a piece of a puzzle in a tray along with the rest of the "picture". Words, however, begin in thoughts (cf. Ps 139: 4); and, indeed, finding the right word can lead to the "invention" of words. However, lest we think that this is unusual, it is good for us to remember that all words, as familiar as they are, came into existence: they were the servant of a thought seeking expression. In a certain way, then, each person that comes to exist is a thought of God expressed in the totality of human being; and, somewhat in the way of words, each person is as necessary to God's conversation with us as the words we use in communion with one another. A word, then, begins in a thought.

Bringing two things together, like word and meaning, is almost automatic in that a genuine word is also intrinsically meaningful in that it has a kind of independent existence that originated with its early use. Thus, in one sense, a word preserves a certain relationship to its first use; indeed, even the development of that use brings with it a trace of its origin. The first use of the Greek word '*prosopon*', which we now translate and use as 'person', signified a mask or a role: an exterior image of a character – but a character in dialogue; and, as it was used to think through the early faith of the Church, it came to be used to express the mystery of the Blessed Trinity and the "oneness" of Christ: true man and true God[85]. In the "hand" of an author or authors, words are worked in terms of an artist's expression: a kind of "rebounding" of thinking through what exists or has been distilled through life experience - even if it is depicted as "fantasy". In other words, the author draws on what exists and fulfils a further potential to what the words already possess: a potential to "stream" in the following of an idea through all kinds of changes and developments. The author, then, recognizes the meaning inherent in words and explores the subtle nuances to navigate the path of an argument to its conclusion; but, in another sense, the author "gives" expression to a meaning in the very choice of words: a meaning not exactly repetitive of what has previously existed nor new to the point of being completely unintelligible to what has gone before. In other words, each one of us bears that trace of radical originality that distinguishes us from all others; but, on the other hand, we are all a part of a universal dialogue from which no one is excluded.

Word and meaning, then, are inseparable; and, similarly, just as there cannot be a real word without a meaning, there cannot be a living human body without a soul. Word and meaning are a natural whole; but, at the same time, they express a different kind of nature to a plant and its life. As the letters form through the hand of the writer, so they express a meaning which originates in the heart of the poet; and, just as the words make visible the thought of the writer, so embryological development manifests the identity of the person conceived. But just as word and meaning are integrally one, so a word does not come to exist as if the meaning is an addition to it; rather, word and meaning form a simultaneous whole. A jumble of words, however, does not make a sentence although an intelligent person can put

---

[85] Cf. Cardinal Ratzinger, "Concerning the Notion of Person in Theology", *Communio*, 17, (Fall, 1990).

order into it and discover various patterns, with one kind of significance or another; and, similarly, if a child is not conceived there is an intelligent explanation which needs to be elicited from the facts of what has happened or not happened. At the same time, though, where words are put together intelligently, they make a story: a beginning that works through the development of the opening ideas; and, similarly, the life of a person can be understood as a book that enters the stream of culture (cf. Ps 139: 16).

Thus the author of human life is God who, transforming the human cause of love, loves each person into existence; and, in the unfolding dynamism of a book, the development of the original idea unfolds and receives its coherence from the work as a whole. Finally, in Part VII we look at the terms "body" and "soul".

The Need for a New Explanation of Conception: the wholeness of being one in "body" and "soul" (IIIvii)

A new explanation does not mean that the whole language is new; and, therefore, there is a clear tradition of the use of "body" and "soul" in the language of Church documents. In the *Pastoral Constitution on the Church in the Modern World, Gaudium et Spes* (from the opening Latin words which mean, *Joy and Hope*), the Fathers of the *Second Vatican Council* said: 'Man, though made of body and soul, is a unity' (n. 14). YOUCAT, the *Youth Catechism of the Catholic Church*, says: 'The human soul is created directly by God' (n. 63) and 'causes the material body to be a living human body' (n. 62); and, in more obviously philosophical language, the *Catechism of the Catholic Church* says: 'spirit and matter, in man, are not two natures united, but rather their union forms a single nature' (n. 365). In these different expressions, then, we have concepts which are seeking to express the mysterious act of God in the conception of a human person. In other words, the reality of human conception exists and these are expressions of our understanding of it. In this final piece, then, the task is to bring a new understanding to the relationship of "matter" and "spirit" or "body" and "soul".

Ideas Old and New

In the history of philosophy there was an understanding of two principles, as it were, which explained human existence. On the one hand Plato argued for a soul that entered a body like a pilot steers a ship. Thus the "soul" was an intelligent pilot of a "material" ship. On the other hand, Aristotle, shortly afterwards, expressed the unity of the human being in terms of "form" and "matter". In the analogy of a piece of a wood and a template, each template unites a shape with a pre-existing material and produces an animal, plant or a human "shape". Aristotle helps us to see that there is an explanation for the different kinds of life: plant, animal and human; and, as such, the explanation lies in the combination of a different kind of soul with matter: the plant soul; the animal soul; and the human soul. Thus, according to each kind of soul, the matter has different life-characteristics. Thus plants grow, with limited movement, animals move, with a limited horizon of adaptation and, finally, the human being has growth, movement and an intelligent grasp of an immense range of activities.

A Limitation in these Ideas

As useful as these explanations are, their starting point of a "difference" between "form" and "matter" entails the introduction of a problem that cannot be solved: the problem of the division of "form" and "matter" and, if division, then the problem of understanding their unity. The philosophical "division" of "form" and "matter" is called dualism; and, without realizing it, there is tendency for philosophers to "import" dualism into their thinking. Thus "soul" and "body" seem like two "separable" parts of a whole: as if you can separate breathing and living[86]. On the one hand we need to take account of the reality of death and the possibility of the resurrection of the body. The departing light of life draws the darkness of death after it, either abruptly or slowly – but yet the breath of life can return for a while. The very uncertainty which surrounds death, it could be argued, is a "witness" to its unnaturalness. On the other hand, we need to think in terms of the psychosomatic whole that each one of us is. How to do justice, then, to the life that so irreversibly began, however briefly, which is as irrevocably one as the note that arises from a musician and his instrument?

Towards a New Way of Understanding the Unity of the Person

We have already noted, however, that the *Catechism of the Catholic Church* says: 'spirit and matter, in man, are not two natures united, but rather their union forms a single nature' (n. 365). The human person, like the note that the musician has struck, can no more be undone than a song can

---

[86] Cryopreservation raises its own problems; indeed, in forestalling death, the life of the person has not definitively ceased. It is not even clear if the arresting of normal functioning and activity will not itself induce a slower rate of deterioration rather than a complete absence of deterioration; for, indeed, the very chemicals and other agents of preservation are completely "foreign" to the natural life and state of a person. On the one hand it seems to entail a confusion about living longer, which is really only fulfilled in eternal life; and, on the other hand, it is "suspending" a life that has a natural course and the questions which need answering.

be unsung; and, like the echo, will ever rebound in the lives of others until its return to the body from which it began. Neither can meaning be separated from a spoken word, nor can an attitude be taken out of an action, nor can a drawing be other than the lines which make it. In other words, "body" and "soul" are the outward expression of what is inward, just as a man is from the ground and imitates Christ and woman is through man and imitates the Holy Spirit and both are from the unoriginate God (cf. Gn 1-2).

In reality, then, there is not a generalized matter that is then "infused" with a soul; rather, there is the specific origin of bodily, human existence, that cannot yet be called bodily if it is not the body of a human being. Thus there is a uniquely personal origin to each of us; and, in that uniquely personal origin, there is an outward sign of the wonderful originality of the whole human person who comes to exist at conception. Conception, then, is of the whole human person; and, therefore, of the whole human being-in-relationship. In other words, just as a living body manifests the human person, so the person does not exist except as a human being-in-relationship: a child of God and the human family.

CHAPTER TWO: FOREWORD AND BIOGRAPHY

**Ronda Chervin, Ph.D.,
Emerita Professor of Philosophy, Holy Apostles
College and Seminary**

Francis Etheredge

Biography

Ronda Chervin, Ph.D., has been a professor of philosophy for fifty years, having taught at Loyola Marymount University of Los Angeles, St. John's Seminary at Camarillo, California, Franciscan University of Steubenville in Ohio, Notre Dame Apostolic Institute in Virginia, Our Lady of Corpus Christi in Texas, and Holy Apostles College and Seminary in Connecticut. She is the author of numerous books in the area of philosophy and spirituality (See www.rondachervin.com).

Foreword to Chapter 2: Pondering "how philosophical concepts concerning the human person can be related to the perennial truth of Revelation"

As a retired professor, I love to read books that answer questions I never formulated succinctly but have found puzzling, almost haunting. With this in mind, what a joy to read *Conception: An Icon of the Beginning* by Francis Etheredge.

To understand the chapter you are about to read, I believe it will help to provide the specific context of myself, and many others, who have pondered questions about how philosophical concepts concerning the human person can be related to the perennial truths of Revelation.

For example:

In philosophy we think about the soul, defined from the teachings of the Greeks, sometimes as the immaterial part of the human being that is able to reason but also, just as often, as the animator of the human body. But in Scripture the soul is taught to be different from the spirit, with the spirit being closer to God.

In philosophy we talk about the human person as if masculine and feminine were less than essential to our definition. In Scripture, however, from Genesis on, we see male and female as created separately, but with differences essential to our very vocations.

In theistic philosophy, the human person, though capable of proving the existence of God, is usually viewed as separate from God in our very essence. In Scripture, however, our very being has been created "in the image and likeness of God," and our destiny is only fulfilled by a union of love with the God who not only created us, but who redeems us.

In recent times the question of the origin of human personhood has taken on a huge existential dimension in the controversy between those who consider the entity in the womb to be a person with rights only at a certain point before birth or, sometimes, after birth. In Scripture, the precious worth of the individual human being is lauded from the moment of conception.

To complicate this issue further, we have Thomas Aquinas, though always declaring abortion to be a terrible sin, yet teaching about ensoulment, the union of body and soul, following the biology of Aristotle, that it happens quite a bit after conception, and at different times for male and female. But, the philosopher Pope, John Paul II, insists that the human person begins at conception.

Now, with all this background, what could be more welcome than this brilliant, scholarly, book *Conception: An Icon of the Beginning*? In Chapter 2, Etheredge will carefully study the Scriptures and philosophy to present a consummate synthesis of faith and reason, in the tradition not only of John Paul II, but also of such saintly doctors of the Church as John Henry Cardinal Newman.

Francis Etheredge

To lapse into the colloquial, "Try it, you'll like it!"

From uncertainty to the "facts presented by the bio-ethical experts about the DNA of the newly formed conceived baby"

An introduction should not try to summarize a scholar's conclusions. The author has already done this, masterfully. Instead, I would like to offer you some ideas from my own study of related topics, so as to whet your appetite for Etheredge's more erudite and more penetrating analysis of the same themes.

Way back in the 1970's I was simultaneously teaching ethics and a newly invented course called the Philosophy of Woman. In ethics, the most timely subject was abortion. I had always assumed everyone in a Catholic University thought that human life begins at conception. Not so. Most did, but there were some who made use of the antiquated biological ideas of Aquinas, to open the door to early abortions. It was only years later that the facts presented by the bio-ethical experts about the DNA of the newly formed conceived baby would become common knowledge.

Wait until you read how Etheredge writes about this from references to Scripture!

Is "being a woman or a man an essential part of the individual person ..."?

In teaching the Philosophy of Woman, I began to wrestle with a question that concerned such Catholic writers as Dietrich and Alice Von Hildebrand (see *Man and Woman* and Alice's later book entitled *Woman, a Divine Invention*) and Edith Stein (see *Woman* – lectures given by the saint between the World Wars on women's issues). Here is the question: is being a woman or a man an essential part of the individual person, or something "accidental" – in the philosophical sense of, say, skin-color not being part of the essence of the person, but rather an external feature. Coming, myself, from an atheistic, skeptical, background, becoming a Catholic at age 21, I remember being surprised at Dietrich Von Hildebrand's way of explaining it. "What? Do you think that in heaven Jesus will be a woman and Mary will be man?" You might like to read my analysis of this and other controversial issues in my book *Feminine, Free and Faithful*, available from the publisher of this book, En Route Books and Media.

Wait until you read how Etheredge writes about this from references to Scripture!

"God's personal creative love for each of us"

The part about Chapter 2 in *Conception: An Icon of the Beginning* that I found not only intellectually helpful but also spiritually inspiring, is the way Etheredge weaves in themes about God's personal creative love for each of us.

When I first studied Catholic philosophy my idea of the human person was that we were in the image and likeness of God because, unlike the animals, we had intellect and free will. Good in itself. However, it was not until we started reading the writings of John Paul, II, that the theme of humans being in the image of the Trinity began to percolate through academe.

I think that the traditional definition of intellect and will had been subtly infiltrated by American individualism. I mean, we could think of ourselves as individually created humans, whose destiny was to fulfill ourselves through our own efforts. Pelagian, of course, but then Americans tend in that direction anyhow!

Now, reflected in Chapter 2, and developed throughout *Conception: An Icon of the Beginning* is the much richer concept that our innermost being and life is to be relational, like the Trinity. And we do so, precisely by union with Jesus, who redeems us from the selfishness that came with Original Sin. And, our vocations to be loving members of the Kingdom of God, are not simply choices we make or fail to make, but ontological parts of our creation.

The Cat and I

I want to take the risk of ending this introduction with my own humorous way of expressing these truths:

We might think sometimes, "How could God, the infinite, omnipotent being of absolute beauty, love such tiny little imperfect slobs as ourselves?"

Here is an analogy to help: There is an ontological abyss between me and my little pet-cat. But that doesn't stop me from loving her. And even if she sometimes scratches me, I readily forgive her. I try to tame her, but I never despise her.

For what it's worth.

Enjoy Chapter 2.

Conception: An Icon of the Beginning

"TATAR COUPLE",

photograph by Bela Fishbeyn[87]

Artist's Statement

'Gerontology is under-represented within the bioethics literature. There's so much focus on end of life, mostly clinically, but what about the stages before? Older adults go through many changes, physically and mentally, and receive very little support, depending on the culture and country. They are overlooked, stigmatized, an often throw-away community, as though they have already lived their lives and that should be enough. And though we must all face death, we must all face aging first. I hope we can look at older adults in a way that makes them feel valuable and worthwhile right now and not just for who they used to be.'

---

[87] Reproduced by Permission of the Director from the Unesco Chair in Bioethics and Human Rights Art Competition, 2015. This picture draws out the wonderful longevity of love's faithfulness; and, in a certain sense, makes me think of Adam and Eve.

CHAPTER TWO: SCRIPTURE AND THE BEGINNING OF HUMAN BEING

General Introduction to Chapter 2: Scriptural Insights into the Origin of Human Being. The Blessed Trinity is our *beginning* and our *end*; and, therefore, it is not just that the Blessed Trinity "founds" human being, it is also that communion is constituted as "being-in-relationship" with the Blessed Trinity. In view of this reality the mystery of the relationship to Jesus Christ is "pivotal" to the interrelationship between the Blessed Trinity and human being.

On the one hand, then, the marriage of Revelation and reason *in our Lord and Saviour Jesus Christ* is a fundamentally *personal* fact-in-faith. The order within this marriage is the order which is established by God: reason works with and under[88] Revelation (cf. 1 Cor. 15: 23-28). Thus the wider relationship, of the human with the divine, is *now prior for* us. The *Incarnation*, however, is not prior in view of time as it was relatively recent in human history; rather, the *Incarnation* is prior ontologically, constituting as it does the essential relationship between us all (cf. *Gaudium et Spes,* 22). On the other hand, then, there is an implicit methodology of truth being ordered to truth, whether natural or revealed, such that truth will not contradict truth[89]. Therefore, while there is progress in reason's articulation of the problems and difficulties of a philosophical understanding of the beginning of the human person, it is possible that a consideration of Scripture will

---

[88] Cf *Gaudium et Spes,* 56.

[89] Cf. *Vatican I, Dei Filius,* 133 (or art 3017 as numbered by the editors of *The Christian Faith,* p. 46).

enlighten the whole discussion in a way that complements the starting points of reason: both embryological and in terms of the historical and reality refinement of ideas. In other words, enduring concepts such as "soul" and "body", imply both a radical relationship to one another and to the experience of and event of human life; and, over time, as they have born fruit in their explanatory power and usefulness, not without criticism, so they remain a helpful reference point and point of departure for further investigations.

It is not so much, then, that reason and Revelation are absolutely different starting points, as the biblical text expresses 'a profound and indissoluble unity between the knowledge of reason and the knowledge of faith'; indeed, as St. John Paul II goes on to say in *Fides et Ratio*: 'The world and all that happens within it, including history and the fate of peoples, are realities to be observed, analysed and assessed with all the resources of reason, but without faith ever being foreign to the process' (16). Thus, while we may proceed, albeit cautiously, we can nevertheless enjoy, too, a certain confidence that the witness of God and man to the event of conception is relevant to our discussion. On the one hand conception entails the recognition that God acts to bring a person to exist (Gn 4: 1); and, on the other hand, it is, as it were, remote preparation for the mystery of the Incarnation of the Son of God (cf. Lk 1: 35). However, at the same time, we need to recognize that the biblical author was both perceptive according to a different, but analogous, criteria to that of contemporary embryologists and open, too, to a divine assistance in his work.

Introduction to Chapter 2: Both Circling and Coming to the Central Texts. It will be necessary, then, to begin this chapter with some specific principles concerning the study of Scripture and the possibility of taking account of its primary function of teaching 'that truth which God, for the sake of our salvation, wished to see confided to the sacred Scripture'[90]. However, even the study of Scripture has to be put in context: the context of Scripture being one of the three strands which stand together in the mystery of the Church.

Thus the Church, in her *Dogmatic Constitution on Divine Revelation, Dei Verbum,* of the *Second Vatican Council*, made a historical reality explicit when she made the following statement about Tradition, Scripture and the Magisterium. 'It is clear ... that in the supremely wise arrangement of God, sacred Tradition, sacred Scripture and the Magisterium of the Church are so connected and associated that one of them cannot stand without the others. Working together, each in its own way under the action of the one Holy Spirit, they all contribute effectively to the salvation of souls' (*Dei Verbum*, 10). Knowing, then, how indispensible it is to be clear about the beginning of life in an era of confusion, deliberate rejection or outright destruction of nascent human life, the Church is moving towards an ever clearer expression of a truth that particularly impacts on the salvation of this generation (cf. *Dei Verbum*, 11): the full reality of spousal love and the true moment and nature of human conception.

But, at the outset, it is good to remind ourselves that the Scriptural author is not an embryologist but, nevertheless, the writer is an intelligent and deeply informed, observant and "imaginative" thinker when it comes to "apprehending" a mystery that is clearly beyond the powers of human being: to actually "witness" God's creation of the whole human person, one in body and soul. Moreover, in view of a very early biblical perception of the reality of the origin of human life (cf. Gn 4: 1 but also Gn 1: 26-27; Gn 2: 7-24), it is not

---

[90] *Dei Verbum*, 11.

surprising to find that this is followed by an intra-biblical development of these initial thoughts. At the same time, however, subsequent authors have taken account of natural comparisons and observations while retaining the significance of the subject owing to the precise sense of God's involvement in it, to which Eve gave such eloquently direct testimony: 'I have gotten a man with the help of God' (Gn 4: 1). Indeed, the mystery of the conception of the human person is an utterly personal mystery; it expresses the intimate interrelationship of spousal love and the fact that, without God, no human person can come to exist. Job, even in his suffering, reflects on the mysterious nature of his origin and, at the same time, uses remarkably apt imagery given that his understanding is informed, possibly, by some kind of observation, as when he says: "Didst thou not pour me out like milk and curdle me like cheese?" (Job 10: 10).

The following twelve sections, then, take a thematic path through the wealth of Scripture, pausing here and there over those texts that are more detailed concerning the beginning of human life – both generally and specifically. However, in view of the contribution of the Church Fathers to the development of the dogma of the *Immaculate Conception*, it is possible that the Church Fathers have yet to contribute fully to the development of doctrine on the moment of conception. The last two sections of this chapter, then, draw on the Fathers of the early Church: at first specifically concerning the mystery of Christ and then ranging more widely on Christ, Mary and the conception of each one of us.

We begin, then, by recalling a number of general principles and, little by little, examining the very varied Scriptural witness to a beginning: the beginning of creation as a whole, the complementarity of human personhood and the unique identity of each human being.

Francis Etheredge

Drawing on General Principles of Scriptural Interpretation:
Part I of XII

The intention of the human author is both discernible in its own right and at the same time it exists in the context of the intention of the Divine author of Scripture[91]. The intention of the human author is expressed in every characteristic of writing which is truly human[92] and the intention of the Divine author is revealed in the act of human writing and in the work as a whole[93]: 'God ... acted in them and by them, [so that] it was as true authors that they consigned to writing whatever he wanted written and no more'[94]. The interpretation of Scripture is, as it were, embedded in the whole mystery of salvation: Scripture interprets Scripture[95] within the Tradition of the Church[96]. At the same time, however, Scripture exists in the context of the fact that Christ is 'both the mediator and the sum total of Revelation'[97]: as if Christ and His relationship to the Church is the ultimate "subject" of the word of God. Thus, as it has been said, conception is not only an occasion when God acts, *per person* (Gn 4: 1) but, as was said earlier, it has a remote bearing on preparing for the event of the Incarnation; and, in addition, on the action of God in the extraordinary

---

[91] Cf. *Dei Verbum*, 12.
[92] Cf. *Dei Verbum*, 12.
[93] Cf. *Dei Verbum*, 12.
[94] *Dei Verbum*, 11.
[95] The Pontifical Biblical Commission, *The Interpretation of the Bible in the Church*, Vatican translation, Sherbrooke: Editions Paulines, 1994, art 2, p. 115.
[96] Cf. *Dei Verbum*, 8.
[97] Cf. *Dei Verbum*, articles 2 and 25.

situation of barrenness which, in its own way, is a kind of "typological" witness to both the *Incarnation* and the nature of salvation as a gratuitous action of God in "keeping" with nature but beyond it (cf. Lk 1: 36-37[98]).

St. Augustine, in particular, warns us of either "using" Scripture to establish a point of view *which is not that of Scripture* itself[99], or of not recognizing that some things can be known for certain by reason, experience and the non-Christian[100] and that *these truths, if true, will not contradict the truth of Scripture*. On the one hand, *truth will not contradict truth*[101]. But, on the other hand, just as with the difficulty of unaided reason trying to determine whether or not the universe had a beginning, or whether or not God exists[102], so the evidence of Scripture may well help with a naturally difficult question about the "moment" that each one of us comes to exist. Moreover, it could even be a good thing to come to a question from the Scripture and to

---

[98] Cf. also Cardinal Ratzinger, subsequently Pope Emeritus Benedict XVI, *Daughter Zion*, translated by J. M. McDermott, SJ, San Francisco: Ignatius Press, 1983).

[99] St. Augustine, *The Literal Interpretation of Genesis*, p. 82, excerpt 1683, as numbered by W. Jurgens and as followed by the number of the text in brackets (1, 18, 37), *The Faith of the Early Fathers*, Collegeville, Minnesota: The Liturgical Press, 1970, Vol III; hereafter, *The Faith of the Early Fathers*.

[100] *The Faith of the Early Fathers*, Vol III, p. 82, excerpt 1684 (1, 19, 39).

[101] Cf, *The Faith of the Early Fathers*, Vol III, p. 83, excerpt 1686 (1, 21, 41) and excerpt 1687 (2, 9, 20); and *Dei Filius, Vatican I*, art 133 (art 3017 as numbered by the editors), on p. 46 of *The Christian Faith*.

[102] Cf. *Dei Verbum*, 6.

discuss it, however inconclusively[103], and then to go on to another and complementary source concerning it[104]. For Scripture has a particular purpose: it is the intention of the Spirit of God to teach what would be of use to us for our salvation[105]. On the one hand, then, we need the assistance of Scripture to begin to understand the wonderfully enthralling mystery of the beginning of life. But, on the other hand, for the sake of our salvation we need to be clear about helping people to avoid the danger of "ontological death": the utterly excruciating suffering entailed in the sin that brings about an interior death.

Therefore let us add Wisdom to wisdom and understand what we can of what exists and of what is in Scripture. Nor does this preclude recognizing that these authors knew those natural truths which were either in their capacity to know for themselves and which they did know[106], or which they could have known and did not - but for the good reason of our salvation these essentially natural truths *were* revealed to them *precisely because it pertains to our salvation to know them*[107].

---

[103] Cf. *The Faith of the Early Fathers*, Vol III, *The Literal Interpretation of Genesis*, the introduction by W. Jurgens, p. 83, and art 1683 (1, 18, 37).

[104] Cf. *The Faith of the Early Fathers*, Vol III, *The Literal Interpretation of Genesis*, p. 83, excerpt 1686 (1, 21, 41).

[105] *The Faith of the Early Fathers*, Vol III, *The Literal Interpretation of Genesis*, art 1687 (2, 9, 20), p. 84; and *Dei Verbum*, 11.

[106] *The Faith of the Early Fathers*, Vol III, *The Literal Interpretation of Genesis*, art 1687 (2, 9, 20), p. 84.

[107] Cf *Dei Verbum*, 6.

Conception: An Icon of the Beginning

A note on language: a more general comment on meaning and the socio-cultural context of words

If writing *naturally*[108] *involves a range of meaning*, rather like the production of a musical note from the oscillations of a wire, then the task of *interpretation* is at once the task of recovering that legitimate range of meaning in addition to the more *specific* task of determining the precise sense of a particular word. This is especially difficult in a period of time, and indeed a cultural place, in which so many factors that would subtly shape the meaning of words have to be reconstituted as it were from a variety of sources. However, just as a musical note is ordered to its existence in the context of the piece of music of which it is a part, so is the meaning of a word ordered to its existence in the context of the piece of writing in which it occurs. Thus the literary context could be said to be a principal *instrument* in determining the *objective thought* of which a particular word is expressive.

But this primary instrument for determining the meaning of a word is not to be severed from its living relationship to the secondary factors which contribute to its elucidation, just as the timbre of a particular note is directly related to the musician, the musical instrument, the score as a whole, the orchestra and the conductor. A musical note, furthermore, can be analysed into a *fundamental* and its corresponding *harmonics*. This *analysis*, however, of the musical note is not its reality[109]: the reality of the musical sound is the totality of all its aspects and *their "played" meaning*. Thus it is necessary to preserve a *realism* con-

---

[108] Cf. *A Catechesis on the Creed*, Vol III, *The Meaning of "Spirit" in the Old Testament*, General audience of January 3, 1990, pp. 153-154.

[109] Cf. R. E. McCall, *Substance*, p. 770 of Vol XIII, NCE.

cerning the definition of terms. On the one hand, a realism open to *the totality* of parts which go to make a particular whole and, on the other hand, a realism which includes as integral to that *whole*, the fact that language *is a fundamental of our answering response to what exists* (cf. Gn 2: 19-20).

While other factors are taken account of, then, the principal focus of this investigation are the various meanings which arise, on examination, in the course of meditating on the variety of biblical texts which take us, as it were, into the biblical authors' "imaginative" perception of conception.

The 'Word became flesh' (Jn 1: 14): Part II of XII

The particular question, concerning the moment at which the soul is *created one with the body*, is asked in the context of understanding the works of God *through* the doctrine of the *Incarnation of Christ*. This is because the creation of the soul, and the creation of the soul in union with the body, is first and foremost an act of God. Therefore, considering the beginning of human life from the perspective of it as an act of God (cf Gn 4: 1), it would seem that there is a distinct possibility that the dogma of the *Incarnation* will be relevant to understanding the act of God which is at the beginning of each one of us.

The possibility that the *Incarnation* is relevant to understanding the beginning of the life of a person is, as it were, present in an acute form in the following two quotations. The first quotation is from the *Second Vatican Council's Gaudium et Spes*: 'The Word of God, through whom all things were made, became man and dwelt among men: a perfect man, he entered world history, taking that

Conception: An Icon of the Beginning

history into himself and recapitulating it'[110]. Thus as an intrinsic part of 'taking that history into himself and recapitulating it' is that the "historical act" of beginning to exist is a fact for all creatures; and, therefore, in the case of the beginning of each human being, it is possible that the *Incarnation* can illuminate, however indirectly, the mystery of human conception. The second quotation is from *Familiaris Consortio*: 'As an incarnate spirit, that is a soul which expresses itself in a body and a body informed by an immortal spirit, man is called to love in his unified totality'[111]. In this quotation we can see the "reciprocal" nature of the body-soul totality; a totality, therefore, that it is possible to recognize as beginning in the same moment that it comes to exist. Thus, in the moment that the body comes to exist *as a human body it does so precisely because it is animated by a human soul*; and, similarly, precisely in the moment that the human soul comes to exist, it exists as expressing the animating life of the body. In this way, then, body and soul are not "two" entities; rather, body and soul are the inward and the outward expression of the one reality of the human person.

On the one hand, the *event* of the *Incarnation* of the Word of God is a wholly unique event, *precisely because* the Son of God 'has existed from all eternity'[112]; but, on the other hand, this does not seem to preclude the possibility that it is yet capable of containing within it the mystery of human conception. Not the human conception that requires the agency of a human father, although the absence of this in the *Incarnation makes present* the Fatherhood of God the Father; but, rather, the nature of human conception from

---

[110] *Gaudium et Spes*, 38.
[111] *Familiaris Consortio*, 11.
[112] *Summa Theologiae*, Methuen, Pt III, Qu 3, art 1, p. 482.

the *point of view that the creation of the soul and the soul's union with the body is necessarily an act of God: that only God can create the human person*. In other words, there seems to be no discernible reason why the soul of Christ coming to exist, and its simultaneous and immediate union with the body, is not itself *a recapitulation of the history of each one of us*. The fact that the coming into existence of the body of Christ is an event which did not require the agency of a human father, is a fact that distinguishes the creation of the body of Christ from all other human beings except that of Adam and Eve. However, the relevance of the *Incarnation* is precisely because the conception of Christ, entailed as it did, the creation of the soul of Christ and "its" union with His body. In other words, in the very creation of the soul as the life of the body, Christ is "at-one-ment" with that same mystery which is at the origin of all human beings, including that of Adam and Eve. Therefore, while there may be other reasons why a person may wish to argue that Christ's soul at conception is different with respect to that of other human beings[113], it does not follow from these exceptional characteristics of the *Incarnation*, that *the simple fact of being ensouled at conception is itself exceptional*.

In terms, then, of the nature of Christ as true God, it is true that He is God from God; however, in that Christ is also true man, His soul came to exist in the very moment His body came to exist[114]. Thus, in one sense, whatever establishes the first moment of bodily existence, establishes the first moment of the *Incarnation* of the Son of God. In addition, just as the humanity of Christ is, as it were, an expression of His divinity, so the human person is, albeit

---

[113] Cf. *Summa Theologiae*, Methuen, Pt III, Qu 34, articles 1-4, pp. 517-518.

[114] Cf. *Summa Theologiae*, Methuen, Pt III, Qu 33, article 2, p. 516.

"analogously"[115], an expression of the "image and likeness" of God (Gn 1: 26-27). Naturally, then, the very "maleness" of Christ is significant for the corresponding mystery of the Church to be enfleshed in the community of the Holy Spirit[116], as pre-eminently expressed in Mary, type of the Church[117]; and, therefore, as God is Author of both sexuality and salvation, it follows that the relationship of the manhood of Christ to the womanhood, as it were, of the Church is significant for our understanding of the complementary diversity of human personhood. One can almost imagine, then, that the complementarity is not so much that of the activity of God in us, which it is, but that of the corresponding "poles" of being: human individuality and the society of man as expressed in the life of the Church. In terms, then, of the manifestation of masculinity, it would seem that it is as necessarily embodied specifically as "womanhood" is a social expression of being a person-in-relationship; but, to avoid real people being "typologized", it is necessary to recall that in human terms, both men and women are both "ordered" to a real individuality which is totally integrated into human "collegiality".

Can, then, what is so deeply expressed in masculinity and femininity, namely the mystery of the divinely originated unity-in-diversity of human personhood, be anything other than integrally expressed in the actual origin, nature, structure, psychological and social expression of being male and female?

---

[115] There is an "analogous" image and likeness between God and man in that God is pure Spirit and man is an expression of enfleshed spirit; albeit, however, the very "enfleshed" nature of man, male or female, entails a concrete witness to the interpersonal nature of the Blessed Trinity.

[116] Cf. *Lumen Gentium*, 7.

[117] Cf. *Lumen Gentium*, 65.

Inevitably, then, as the references have already indicated, it is necessary to preface the discussion of the beginning of personhood with a consideration of the opening chapters of Genesis.

Scripture says: 'In the beginning' (Gn 1: 1): Philosophy and Theology in Dialogue: Part III of XII

I wish to preface my discussion of the Scriptural evidence of the beginning of the human person with a general discussion, philosophical and theological, of the question of a beginning to the universe[118]. For the question of the beginning of the human person is asked in the context of the question of the beginning of creation.

The question of a beginning to the universe could be said to involve three categories of discourse or types of human activity: the scientific; the philosophical; and the theological. But because philosophy follows on its own first principles and the verifiable truths of the empirical sciences, it could be said that there are in fact only two categories of questions: the philosophical and the theological: what we can naturally know and what is supernaturally revealed. I wish, then, to comment on *the beginning* of the universe from both of these points of view.

---

[118] Cf. An excellent article by Professor Neil Turok, *The beginning of everything*, on the possible beginning of the universe from a single particle, (*The Daily Telegraph* Weekend, March 14, 1998, pp. 1-2).

Conception: An Icon of the Beginning

A brief philosophical look at the question of a beginning

What kind of proof is required to prove that the universe had a beginning?

If the different kinds of physical evidence converge on the possibility of a beginning, rather like the fracture lines in ice would point to the centre of an impact, would this prove a beginning? In other words, what kind of "event" is the beginning? In the case of my example of the fracture lines which radiate out from a point at which there was an impact, the "place" of that point of impact could have become a hole. Thus, the kind of "event" that a beginning of the universe is, is not necessarily of the same kind as the evidence which convergently points to its existence.

Why is the beginning of the universe different from the activities to which its existence gives rise? A beginning of the universe would be different for the reason that a beginning is the point at which a cause of the universe would be shown to exist; and, indeed, not only a cause of its beginning but a veritable "explanation" for it continuing to exist, where cause to exist and continuing to exist are ordered to one another.

Why is this? "No Thing" *begins* without a cause; and, therefore, what is caused necessarily has a beginning. Indeed, for something *to have no cause,* it must also *have no* beginning. This is because of the impossibility of a thing being its own beginning. For, if a thing was its own beginning, then it would have to be there before it began; but if the thing was there before it began, then it was not the cause of its own beginning but was already in existence. In other words, to paraphrase St. Thomas Aquinas: if there was a point when there was truly *nothing whatsoever* in existence, then it would be impossible for *anything* to come into existence[119]. Therefore the existence of anything is by definition the evidence of there being *something* which always was in existence. That something which always was in existence is called God.

Thus the beginning of the human person has a cause; and, by implication, a cause capable of bringing to exist what is a psychosomatic whole; and, therefore, anything that can only contribute a "part" of the whole cannot be the full cause of the whole. Thus parents, while contributing what is necessary, do not contribute all that is necessary; and, therefore, God drawing on the secondary contribution of the parents-to-be, is the primary cause of human personhood.

Secondly, the beginning of the universe would be a different kind of event from the beginning of, for example, a fire, which can occur within the existence of the universe. This is because a *resemblance* between causes does not preclude a *difference* between causes. Thus a fire may be *caused* by a lighted match, lightning, the sun on a hot day, an animal pushing over a barbecue or a person starting it either deliberately or accidentally. In each case the *effect of the cause is the same, namely the fire*; but it is also true that these causes can be classified by their differences: the physical cause of the sun; the movement of an animal; the deliberate or accidental act of a person. Furthermore, the difference between a cause "within" the universe and a cause "of" the universe is the difference between the cause of created existence and the modification of what is already in existence; and, therefore, the beginning of a human being is both a "modification" of what already exists and a "cause" of existence. Therefore the cause of human being "echoes" the nature of the cause of existence itself; and, as such, the cause of human being entails an action of the Creator.

---

[119] Cf. *Summa Theologiae,* Benziger Brothers, Pt I, Qu 2, art 3, p. 13.

Conception: An Icon of the Beginning

The cause of created existence is from "no-thing" to "some-thing" and, therefore, exceeds human creativity to the extent that human originality "takes" a start from what exists and entails a kind of modification of what it is; whereas, in the case of Divine creativity, the starting point is the divine nature and the "expression" of creaturely existence from the starting point of its prior, non-existence. Similarly, in view of the action of a different kind of being, namely the Divine being, it is also true that human beings can understand it "analogously" but not absolutely: that we can understand the action of God as "like" the action of a human being. Therefore it is possible to "imagine" the creation of the universe or the beginning of human personhood; but, in a sense, as the reality entails an action of God who, *per se*, exceeds created being, to an extent it is not possible to fully comprehend the "event" of creation: either as a whole or of a particular person.

Thirdly, however, even if it is not possible to fully grasp the mystery of divine causation, just as creation is evidence of its occurrence, so is the existence of a person evidence of the action of God; and, therefore, just as, by implication, the universe has a "moment" of beginning, so the human person has a moment of beginning.

In conclusion, then, the actual beginning of the universe, while a question that natural science and philosophy can converge upon, is in fact a question that *requires* the divergent methods of each discipline. This is for the reasons stated earlier: if the cause of the true beginning of the universe requires the existence of something which was always in existence, then that "Agent" is by definition *different* to all other known causes of creaturely existence. *Secondly*, when that "Agent" which has always existed *causes* the beginning of the universe, this event of the beginning of the universe is by definition an *event* which both brings the universe into existence and *reveals a mystery*. The mystery that is revealed is *precisely* the following question: What kind of event is the event of *the universe coming into existence?* This event is the coming into existence of what did not exist before; and, therefore, it *cannot be the making of one thing from another*[120]. Thus the event of the beginning of the universe differs in two fundamental ways from other, similar events: the "Agent-cause" of the event is different; and, because of this first reason, the event itself is different from all temporal types of cause. In the case, however, of the human person, there is the radical integration of two types of cause being brought together in "one" causal act of human personhood: the contributing but subordinate "cause" of spousal love and the transmission of life; and, secondly, the primary but mysterious bringing to exist the whole psychosomatic human person, one in body and soul, from the first instant of conception.

A brief theological look at the question of our beginning

The point of departure of theological science is *different* from both that of the physical sciences and philosophy. But this different point of departure is not a rejection of the true conclusions of these other disciplines, nor of the facts from which these disciplines proceed by way of their response to them. The reason for this was well expressed in 1870, in one of the two documents of the *First Vatican Council* of the Catholic Church. The document on the *Catholic Faith* said: truth does not contradict truth. Nor, it might be added, does theological science reject any method which can assist its own investigations. Thus anything that can be reliably understood or demonstrated as true, embryologically or

---

[120] Cf. CCC, 296.

philosophically, is a relevant consideration to the theological elaboration of the beginning of personhood.

But what is theology? In 1965 the Fathers of the *Second Vatican Council* wrote the *Dogmatic Constitution on Divine Revelation*, otherwise known as *Dei Verbum*. It is necessary to draw attention to the following three, if not four, ideas: that Scripture can be compared to the *Incarnation of the Son of God* because the words of God are expressed in the words of men (cf. 13)[121]. Secondly, the truth they contain is the truth necessary for our salvation (cf. 11)[122]. And, thirdly, that the sacred page is the soul of sacred theology (cf. 24)[123]. Therefore, just as Revelation is to God what doctrine is to Revelation, so faith is to the Word of God[124] what theology is to thinking it through[125].

On the one hand, then, there is a unique contribution of Scripture to this discussion, which follows on the very nature of the word of God being 'expressed in the words of men' (*Dei Verbum*, 13); and, therefore, the word of God entails the possibility of a kind of divine assistance in the very challenge of communicating an understanding of the beginning of human personhood. On the other hand, though, the disciplines of physical science, philosophy and theology, while complementary to one another, entail that each has its own *"way" of investigation*. The corollary of this is that each

---

[121] Cf. *Dei Verbum*, 13.

[122] Cf. *Dei Verbum*, 11.

[123] Cf. *Dei Verbum*, 24.

[124] Cf. The Pontifical Biblical Commission, *The Interpretation of the Bible in the Church*, art 3, p. 97.

[125] Cf Pope John Paul II: 'A faith that does not become culture is a faith which has not been fully received, not thoroughly thought through, not faithfully lived out.' This quotation was quoted on the Advent 1995 newsletter of the *Centre for Faith & Culture*. Cf also *Evangelium Vitae*, 95.

type of work must *acquire the discipline* by which it both defines its own proper object and, *at the same time*, respects that of the others. This would excite discovery and not diminish it, just as a dialogue develops out of a difference that is irreducible, such as the difference between a man and a woman: a difference which purdures and constitutes the *permanent basis of the dialogue of friendship and indeed that of marriage*.

"Physical" science, for example, has observed the "porous" nature of the ovum[126] prior to fertilization which, quite naturally, suggests a kind of image of the created being's "openness" to the act of God entailed in the creation and ensoulment of the human body[127]. Furthermore, creation and ensoulment constitute one indivisible instant of the action of God; indeed, if the soul is the soul of a human body, then not only is it necessary that the "body" be human but that there is a "body" to be ensouled. Physical science, however, actually means human scientists striving to "picture" what is in fact barely visible. Philosophically, then, there is the whole history of the "soul" as a determinant of matter and bringing about a certain kind of living being: plant; animal or human[128]. Theologically, then, there is the relationship, indicated earlier, between the conception and simultaneous ensoulment of Christ and the originating "moment" of human personhood.

---

[126] Cf. *A Child is Born*, photographs by Lennart Nilsson and text by Lars Hamberger, translated by Clare James, London: Doubleday, 1990.

[127] Cf. Francis Etheredge, p. 75, Chapter 1, of *Volume I-Faithful Reason*, the trilogy as a whole is called, *From Truth and truth*, Newcastle upon Tyne: Cambridge Scholars Publishing, 2016

[128] Although the concept of 'form' is "that which determines matter to be what it is"; and, therefore, form determines matter to be what it is more generally than that of what types of life exist.

But, on the other hand, if it is the same God who made reason and faith, then the results of reason and the conclusions of faith can only assist one another in the perception of the "action" of the *Three Persons* in *One God*.

This discussion of the Scriptural evidence of our beginnings will begin with the opening chapters of Genesis. Thus this investigation of conception takes place within the context of "the" beginning. The fact is that Scripture gives two different, indeed *complementary* accounts of creation. Scholars have given these two accounts names: the first is the Priestly account and the second is the Yahwist account.

In the Beginning, God Created (Gn 1: 1): Part IV of XII

The Priestly account says: 'In the beginning God created the heavens and the earth. The earth was without form and void, and darkness was upon the face of the deep; and the Spirit of God was moving over the face of the waters' (Gn 1: 1-2). Thus there is what one might call a divine pause: a moment of the beginning. This could be described as a *theocentric*[129] account of creation. It is an account in which the act of God the Creator is established through, as it were, the solemn repetition of the act of creation.

The Yahwist account says: 'In the day that the Lord God made the earth and the heavens, when no plant of the field was yet in the earth ...' (Gn 2: 4-5). Thus these verses set a context for the creation of man: a context of what was not there *before* the creation of man; with what was there *at* the creation of man; and with what came *after* the creation of man. In other words, this second account is almost

---

[129] Cf. Pope John Paul II, *Original Unity of Man and Woman*, Boston: St. Paul Books and Media, 1981, *Man's Awareness of Being a Person*, General Audience of October 24, 1979, art 2, p. 52.

anthropocentric[130]: it gives the context of the event of creation – but then it is as if the author's additional detail is from the perspective of creation's need of a man 'to till the ground' (Gn 2: 5). In a sense, therefore, the author has established the "cultural" context of the relationship between creation and man: the cultural context of work. The man is "fit" for the work which "creation" requires of him.

The opening sentence of the first, Priestly account, and the first statement of the second, Yahwist account, are equivalent but significantly different. The Priestly account speaks of a beginning and indeed says: "In the beginning"; and. while this is but one Hebrew word, it suggests a style of *conceptual precision* in contrast to the style of *descriptive precision* of the Yahwist's opening words: "In the day that the Lord God made the earth and the heavens." It is to the Priestly account of creation to which it is now necessary to turn; and for two reasons: this account has dwelt on the first moment of creation *and* it has done so with what I have called *conceptual precision*.

The precision of "In the beginning" is continued in the first part of the next sentence where the author says: "The earth was without form and void". This remarkable combination of terms at once asserts the existence of 'the earth' and simultaneously denies any development of it. This is because, if one considers another biblical use of the term form (cf. Ps 139: 16), one can see that 'form' signifies development in *time*. Therefore the earth exists at the first moment of its existence - but at the moment before the development which characteristically unfolds *through* time. In a similar way one can see that 'void' signifies a type of space that is empty (cf. 2 Chron 18: 9 and 1 K 22: 10). In other words, the author has composed his assertion of what exists out of a series of denials concerning the usual

---

[130] *Ibid.*

properties of existence: what exists does not extend in space; and what exists has not unfolded through time. And to these two "negations" are added a third, namely that of 'darkness', such that although the 'face of the deep' exists, it exists in darkness (Gn 1: 2): it cannot be seen. This second sentence of the first chapter of *Genesis* then comes to an end with the phrase: 'and the Spirit of God was moving over the face of the waters.' Now because of this last phrase we are left with more than a conceptual account of the first moment of the existence of the 'earth'. We are left with the impression that God made 'the heavens and the earth' to exist in the presence of God. For while what God has made is undeveloped, non-extensive and invisible, it is nevertheless 'the Spirit of God' which moves over the 'face of the waters' (Gn 1: 2). In other words, the coming to be of creation is *at the same time* creation's coming to be in the presence of the Creator.

There is, then, an inescapable possibility of understanding "creation as a whole" as "analogous" to the creation of the human being in particular; indeed, in Psalm 139, David speaks of the Lord knowing 'every one of ... [the days] that were formed for me, when as yet there was none of them' (verse 16). In other words, there is a very lively philosophical sense of a beginning, whether of creation as a whole or of the creature in particular, that is both real and undeveloped; or, better, a beginning that both exists and entails a development known to God. Similarly, then, to the presence of 'the Spirit of God' at the beginning of creation is the action God at the beginning of human personhood, which implies the active presence of God at the beginning of man (cf. Gn 4: 1; and cf. Ps 139: 16).

Finally, just as one part of Scripture illuminates another, so the Old Testament is renewed, as it were, in the New Testament. Thus the whole theological investigation of *the beginning* takes on a new meaning with the first and second sentences of the *Gospel of St. John*: 'In the beginning was the Word, and the Word was with God, and the Word was God. He was in the beginning with God; all things were made through him, and without him was not anything made that was made' (Jn 1: 1-2). Thus one has to conclude that the mystery of creation is ultimately the act of the God who progressively reveals Himself to be the mystery of the *Blessed Trinity*. In other words, while it is possible for philosophy to conclude to the existence of *God the first cause*, it transcends what can be known by philosophy to conclude to the existence of the Blessed Trinity. Furthermore, and this is what really constitutes the point to which this exposition tends and at which it terminates: if God is love (1 Jn 4: 7), then the acts of God are acts of love. And so *the theological investigation* is in the end a *complementarily different* investigation to all the others: it is the *investigation of love*. In the context of the creation of the human creature, then, it is clear that man and woman are brought to exist in both the presence of the Holy Spirit and the Word of God. On the one hand, then, being created in the presence of the Son of God is, actually, to exist in view of the *Incarnation* such that Christ 'has in a certain way united himself with each man' (*Gaudium et Spes,* 22). On the other hand, just as each man is in a 'certain way' united to Christ so "he" is also united to the possibility of the Holy Spirit 'proceeding' from the Father and the Son; and, therefore, there is a marvellous sense of each man and woman being created, as it were, in view of their salvation in Christ and His Church.

Drawing further on the opening chapters of Genesis for the relationship of Creator to creature

The structure of the Priestly account of creation is almost a pattern of like giving forth to like. In the first instance creation receives existence from God: 'In the beginning God created the heavens and the earth' (Gn 1: 1). In a logical inquiry the first thing that we need to establish is whether or not something exists[131]; and, on the basis of knowing that something exists, one can then inquire as to what kind of thing exists. This suggests that it is God the Creator-Father who gives existence to all that exists; and, in the light of that revelation, the identity of what exists is to be understood in the light of the identity of God. This principle, of understanding creation in the light of God, is explicitly expressed in terms of the creation of the human being: 'So God created man in his own image, in the image of God he created him; male and female he created them' (Gn 1: 27; and cf. Gn 1: 26). Thus the very existence of the human person is itself a work of God; and, indeed, a work characteristic of God: of bringing to exist what did not exist. In view, too, of the interrelationship between the identity of the person and God, there is an essential relationship between knowing God and knowing ourselves (cf. *Gaudium et Spes*, 22).

Secondly, 'God created the heavens and the earth' in such a way that they do not live in the sense of having the breath of life itself and yet seem to exist at the point of an absolute beginning. But creation does not simply exist: it exists in the presence of the 'Spirit of God': a Spirit of God which moves over the face of the waters (Gn 1: 2). Thus, taking into account an alternative translation which says 'there was darkness over the deep, with a divine wind sweeping over the waters' (*NJB*[132], Gn 1: 2), one can almost *see* the

---

[131] *Summa Theologiae*, Benziger Brothers, Pt I, Qu 2, art 2, p. 12.

[132] *The New Jerusalem Bible*, general editor Henry Wansbrough, (London: Darton, Longman & Todd, 1985). When I am comparing translations I will give the initials of the other translation in the biblical reference.

connection between the *moving Spirit of God*, as a kind of agent of movement, and creation both existing and being set in motion by this "activity" of the Spirit of God. Just as a wind *moves the waters over which it moves, so the Spirit of God animates creation*. Thus we contemplate the possibility, almost invisibly present, that the soul's animation of the body is not only "analogous" to the Spirit of God in the Church (cf. *Lumen Gentium*, 7) but that the Spirit of God is "at work" in the soul's animation of the body; and, therefore, the Spirit of God seeks, as it were, the goal of completing the soul's animation of the body through the human being's incorporation into Christ which, ultimately, aims at the transfiguration of the resurrection of the psychosomatically whole human person.

Thus one is brought to consider the mystery of the Holy Spirit

Pope St. John Paul II, in his Encyclical Letter *On the Holy Spirit in the Life of the Church and the World*, otherwise known as *Dominum et Vivificantem*, says the Holy Spirit is "*the Lord, the giver of life*"[133]: a life that is an animation of things[134]: a causing of things to move: a progression from living to "eternal life" itself. Thus, in the beginning, the Spirit of God *causes* creation both to move and to move in the direction of God; and, therefore, the Spirit of God is both uniquely involved in the animation of creation in general and of the human person in particular (cf. Lk 1: 35; and 4: 1). St. John Paul II says elsewhere: 'In the Bible, the primary function of the spirit is not to give

---

[133] Pope John Paul II, *Dominum et Vivificantem*, 1986, translation by the Vatican Polyglot Press) art 1.

[134] Cf. *Dominum et Vivificantem*, 66.

understanding, but to give movement; not to shed light, but to impart dynamism'[135].

After creation itself is brought into existence, and animated by the Spirit of God, the first word of God is: "Let there be light". Therfore, just as the natural power of light is to reveal what exists, so the light of Christ is to reveal the work of His Father (cf. Jn 9: 4-5)[136]. This trace of the Blessed Trinity, as St. Thomas Aquinas[137] calls it, is not to be confused with the conscious intentionality of the human authors of Scripture - *except in so far as it expresses their diverse attempts to communicate the full extent of the mystery of God*. In other words, while it is not supposed that these authors knew of the existence of the Blessed Trinity in the same way that we do, yet it can be supposed that the very fact that their writing is *written through with the trace of this truth* is precisely because of their attempt to communicate the full complexity of the reality of God's work of creation, a work both expressive of God as a whole and of each member of the Blessed Trinity in particular.

The relevance of this to the question of our beginning is that it brings to light the parallel significance of the animation of creation by the Holy Spirit and the animation of the soul by the body[138]. Thus, referring back to the general principle that the opening of the book of Genesis proceeds by way *of the pattern of like giving forth to like,*

---

[135] Pope John Paul II on *The Meaning of "Spirit" in the Old Testament*, General audience of January 3, 1990, p. 152 of Vol III of *A Catechesis on The Creed, The Spirit Giver of Life and Love*, (Boston: Pauline Books & Media, 1996).

[136] Cf. also *Dei Verbum*, 2.

[137] *Summa Theologiae*, Methuen, Pt I, Qu 45, art 7, p. 87; and cf. *The Faith of the Early Fathers*, The Liturgical Press, Vol III, *The Trinity*, extract 1673, p. 78.

[138] Cf. also *Lumen Gentium*, 7.

one can see that the soul stands in relation to the body *like* the Divine-wind is to the waters of creation: as a mover of the body, just as the wind *moves over the water and moves the water it moves over*. Furthermore, from the point of view of the scriptural author, it is this pattern of *like giving forth to like* which prepares the reader for the perception that man, male or female, is created in the image of God. Finally, the *idea* that it is the *breath of God* which is particularly responsible for the man becoming 'a living being' (Gn 2: 7) is an idea that could be said to be a particularly *fundamental perception of the different authors of Scripture* and, moreover, if this is true of man being animated from the beginning, then it is possibly true of each instance that a human being comes into existence.

The creation of man, male and female

> 'So God created man in his own image, in the image of God he created him; male and female he created them' (Gn 1: 27).

The first connection between the *breath of life* and the living creatures (Gn 1: 20 and 24) that move upon the earth (cf. Gn 1: 28), comes at the end of the work of creation when the creatures other than man (cf Gn 1: 29) are given the food of plants: "And to every beast of the earth, and to every bird of the air, and to everything that creeps on the earth, everything that has the breath of life, I have given every green plant for food" (Gn 1: 30). Thus, in so far as man can eat *green plants for food*, he is in an indirect and remote way included in this category of things which has the breath of life in it.

When it comes, then, to the second account of creation, there is already the canonically prior fact that the first use of the 'breath of life' as an expression of what makes a living creature, was its specific application to the animals. So it is not until the second account of creation that Adam is specifically described as brought to life by the breath of life which the Lord God breathed into him: 'In the day that the Lord God made the earth and the heavens, when no plant of the field was yet in the earth ... the Lord God formed man of dust from the ground, and breathed into his nostrils the breath of life; and man became a living being' (Gn 2: 4-7). In a word, then, there is clearly a difference between all the creatures which are animated by breath and the nature of man, who is uniquely animated by the 'breath of life', which was 'breathed into his nostrils' by the 'Lord God'. Thus the second account develops, further, the insight of the first account and shows, more obviously, the interrelationship between the identity of God and the identity of man, in the very dependence of man on the 'breath of life' he received from the Lord God. This foundational event, as it were, communicates the distinctive nature of the creation of each person and the "personal" involvement of God.

The creation of woman differs again from the creation of man: 'So the Lord God caused a deep sleep to fall upon the man, and while he slept [God] took one of his ribs and closed up its place with flesh; and the rib which the Lord God had taken from the man he made into a woman and brought her to the man' (Gn 2: 21-22). This fact clearly parallels the mystery of the Church coming forth from the side of Christ[139]; but it could also pertain to the mystery of the difference between the Son who is generated by the Father and the Holy Spirit who proceeds from the Father[140]. In other words, the author is exploring the parallel, perhaps unbeknown in an explicitly and theologically informed way,

---

[139] Cf. CCC, 766.
[140] Cf. also *Letter to Families*, 6.

of the way that the creation of human being "imitates" the mystery of the Blessed Trinity; or, to put it the other way round, reflecting on the mystery of "human difference", the human author ends up propounding an inspired parallel between the "inner life" of the Blessed Trinity and the creation of man and woman (cf. *Letter to Families*, 6). In one sense, then, the very obvious but overlooked reality of male or female descendents of Adam and Eve (cf. Gn 5: 1-3) is a kind of remote image of the mystery of the inner life of the Blessed Trinity: of "divine person" from or through "divine person"; indeed, the very existence of Adam and Eve is, in a certain sense, the very beginning of making explicit the inner life of the Blessed Trinity that is then "enfleshed" and "incarnated" in the transmission of human life. Thus procreation is an expression of life from Life, of person from Person, of human personhood from the action of God and man.

The origin of man in the context of original sin

God will put enmity between the serpent and the woman, 'and between your seed and her seed' (Gn 3: 15). This is rather striking from the point of view of the fact that while genealogies tend to run through the male line (cf Gn 4: 17 - 5: 32), it is God who refers to a male descendant of the woman (cf. Gn 3: 15) as *her seed*. This gives the impression of an implicit understanding of the woman as *bearing* the *seed of children* just as, it seems, plants and trees are seed bearing (cf. Gn 1: 29): a seed which characteristically brings forth each species 'according to its kind' (Gn 1: 12). Furthermore, this sort of idea is essential to St. Paul's understanding of what kind of body[141] God will give at the

---

[141] Cf. John L. McKenzie, *Dictionary of the Bible*, London: Collier Macmillan Publishers, 1965, p. 101: Body.

resurrection: 'But God gives it a body as he has chosen, and to each kind of seed its own body' (1 Cor. 15: 39). In other words there is a very "realistic" account of the reality of the transmission of human life that is more than indicated in these theologically subtle pages of the beginning of creation; and, as such, one idea "plays" into another by both signifying a parallel and simultaneously exploring a significant difference.

Subsequently, however, we see that as a direct consequence of sin there are a number of changes introduced into the original nature of creation; and, in particular, these changes impact on the "temporality" of man. God addresses the woman: "I will greatly multiply your pain in childbearing; in pain you shall bring forth children ..." (Gn 3: 16); and then God speaks to the man: "you shall eat bread till you return to the ground, for out of it you were taken; you are dust, and to dust you shall return" (Gn 3: 19). In direct contrast to God revealing Adam's "experience" of death and, by implication, Eve's, Adam goes on to say to Eve in a spirit of remarkable optimism: 'The man called his wife's name Eve, because she was the mother of all living' (Gn 3: 20). Furthermore, there yet seemed to be a possibility that the man would live forever if, that is, he remained in the garden and ate of 'the tree of life' (Gn 3: 23) - but then God 'drove' the man out of the garden (Gn 3: 24). In other words, it seems as if there is a "residual" immortality of man which, despite the changes wrought through sin and its anthropological implications, endures; and, even if it will remain unclear for an indefinite period, there is definitely the "open sense" of an immortality to man being retained even after the original sin. Thus, reflecting back on the original creation of man through the 'breath' of God, there is a definite possibility that the text is intended to draw out an "enduring" relationship to God as the "vehicle" through which to understand what has become the event of creation and the history of salvation. In reality, then, even in view of the "coming" of death, the coming into existence of the human person, precisely because of the kind of action of God it entails (cf. Gn 4: 1), implies the beginning of an eternal relationship to God.

The woman's perception of conception: Part V of XII

There appears very early on a tradition of understanding human conception, not as unrelated to the fact of the sexuality of the man and the woman (cf. Gn 4: 1), but as a perception of the fact that human life is conceived 'with the help of the Lord.' In the words of the narrative we read: 'Now Adam knew Eve his wife, and she conceived and bore Cain, saying, "I have gotten a man with the help of the Lord"' (Gn 4: 1; and cf. also 4: 25). In other words, while the narrator says that Adam 'knew' Eve, a knowledge of Eve which in this case is through intercourse[142] with her, Eve's perception is of the fact that *God has helped her to conceive*. This does not mean that she did not realize the connection between intercourse and conception, albeit it is the narrator who explicitly recognizes the connection between Adam and Eve knowing each other and the action of God, but it does give prominence to her perception of the action of God in her child coming to exist within her. In due course, then, the related natural facts begin to emerge and to be identified; and, therefore, the narrator says subsequently: 'Now Abraham and Sarah were old, advanced in age; it had ceased to be with Sarah after the manner of women' (Gn 18: 11). Thus this perception of the woman pertains in a particular

---

[142] Cf. McKenzie, *Dictionary of the Bible*, p. 485: Know, Knowledge.

Conception: An Icon of the Beginning

way to a mystery *inscribed*[143] *within the natural process of human generation*. The mystery of conception, however, as we are beginning to discover, is a mystery which communicates itself through outward signs.

This wisdom of the woman is repeated and deepened in the words of the Mother of seven martyrs: "I do not know how you came into being in my womb. It was not I who gave you life and breath, nor I who set in order the elements within each of you. Therefore the Creator of the world, who shaped the beginning of man and devised the origin of all things, will in his mercy give life and breath back to you again, since you now forget yourselves for the sake of his laws" (2 Mac 7: 22-23). On the one hand, the very context of the intensity of her and her children's passion is that this is a particularly lucid, if not translucent example of what, ordinarily, we are ignorant and what, perhaps, is generally hidden from our sight. But this woman's perception is nevertheless *in the tradition of biblical culture* in such a way that she *confirms* and *develops* the insights of it. For the three things which she does not know correspond, as it were, to the three expressions of the creative act of God which is indicative of the action of the Blessed Trinity from the beginning; and while one does not wish to impute to her the perception of God as the Blessed Trinity, yet one can say her threefold ignorance is more knowledgeable than it first seems.

Her first perception is that she does not know how her son 'came into being' in her womb (2 Mac 7: 22). This echoes the coming into existence of creation itself: a coming into existence which is particularly the work of God the Father; and, just in case we should think we have overestimated what she has said, she later says: "I beseech you, my child, to look at the heaven and the earth and see everything that is in

---

[143] Cf. *Letter to Families*, 9.

them, and recognize that God did not make them out of things that existed. Thus also mankind comes into being' (2 Mac 7: 28). Thus it is clear that she recognizes the "originality" of God's creation of each one of us; but, also, it is clear that the divine originality does draw on "the elements within each of you". In other words, in a very general way perhaps, one might almost say in a scientific way, she recognizes both the "elements" and the "order" which God has drawn upon and brought about in bringing her children to exist. Now the context of this woman's words is the torture and death of her sons. Therefore her thoughts are on the possibility of the power of God to give back to them the life they have given up for him (cf. 2 Mac 7: 23). Thus she is not just thinking about the mystery of their conception from the point of view of what can be naturally known (cf. 2 Mac 7: 22 and 27); rather, she is thinking of conception from the point of view *that these facts of her motherhood* have revealed a great mystery to her: the mystery that at the beginning of each one of us and at the beginning of mankind, *God's act of creation is an act which causes to exist what did not exist.* For it is this *power of God to bring into existence what did not exist*, which is the basis of her confidence that God can give back to her the sons the death of whom she is now witness (cf. 2 Mac 7: 29). In other words, this mother realizes that only a power as great as that which can create out of nothing, is a power which can give back life *after* it is lost through death.

This woman's second perception is that: "It was not I who gave you life and breath ... " (2 Mac 7: 23). Thus again she speaks from within the biblical tradition of the connection between 'life' and 'breath'; and, as such, the power *to animate* with life and breath is the 'divine wind' (*NJB* Gn 1: 1): the Spirit of God. However, it may be that her distinction between *life* and *breath* is in fact a distinction between *two works of the Holy Spirit*. On the one hand, it

Conception: An Icon of the Beginning

could be said, the Holy Spirit is "present" to all creation: a "presence" that is almost a kind of "causal" presence (cf. Gn 1: 2); and, on the other hand, God gives the breath of His Holy Spirit when He gives spiritual life to a human being (cf. Gn 2: 7). It is striking, too, that when the Lord gives life to the dry bones in the vision of the prophet Ezekiel, it is in connection with the breath that he does so: 'I will cause breath to enter you, and you shall live' (Ex 37: 5). In this famous 'prophecy of the resurrection'[144] it is possible to see that the fullest definition of life for the Scriptural author is the life of the resurrection.

Thirdly, she says: nor was it "I who set in order the elements within each of you" (2 Mac 7: 22). In other words, she recognizes a whole process of growth which, once begun, proceeds according to a pre-established and wholly organized goal: the bringing together of all that is necessary to manifest the unique gift of personhood which each one of us is. She has seen that the creation of human life establishes a *pattern* that then unfolds, to use a word which Pope St. John Paul II uses when he says: 'Before creating man, the Creator withdraws as it were into himself, in order to seek the pattern and inspiration in the mystery of his Being, which is already here disclosed as the divine We'[145]. It is this *order* and *pattern* which could be, as it were, the *trace* of the Son: the archetypal human being born of the Virgin Mary. Furthermore, she speaks in such a way as to make one wonder if *she knew* that God created Adam and Eve *at once body and soul, man and woman* (cf 2 Mac 7: 28): in their integral humanness.

---

[144] Cf. Pope St. John Paul II, *A Catechesis on the Creed*, Boston: Pauline Books and Media, 1996, Vol. III, on *The Creative Action of the Divine Spirit*, Gen. aud. Jan 10, 1990, p. 157; hereafter, *A Catechesis on the Creed*.

[145] *Letter to Families*, 6.

In the light of the woman's perception of conception, let us return to the narrator's account of our origin in what is otherwise called *The First Book of Moses*[146], but let us also go on to Jacob, Rachel and Job:
Part VI of XII

The woman's perception of the "help of the Lord" in the conception of a man is complemented by the different perspective of the man; however, the two perspectives are pointing in the same direction and, as it were, focus on the one reality.

'This is the book of the generations of Adam. When God created man, he made him in the likeness of God. Male and female he created them, and he blessed them and named them Man when they were created. When Adam had lived a hundred and thirty years, he became the father of a son in his own likeness, after his image, and named him Seth' (Gn 5: 1-3).

The narrator perceives the history of the family of man through the male line in so far as the genealogy which follows at this point is in terms of a principal son (cf 5: 6-32) and the fact of other sons and daughters (cf 5: 4, 10, 13, 19, 23, 26 and 31); but it is also and quite clearly a perception of *the continuity of the mystery of the beginning,* in that the language in which Adam's son is said to be 'in his own likeness, after his image' is a language which unashamedly repeats, reinforces and reveals the force of the expression that 'God created man in his own image, in the image of God he created him; male and female he created them' (Gn 1: 28).

Finally, in time a man will come to say things in almost the same way as the woman. 'When Rachel saw that she bore

---

[146] RSV Catholic edition, p. 1.

Jacob no children, she envied her sister; and she said to Jacob, "Give me children, or I shall die!" Jacob's anger was kindled against Rachel, and he said, "Am I in the place of God, who has withheld from you the fruit of the womb?"' (Gn 30: 1-2). But in due course, and not without Jacob and Rachel's suffering, God listened to Rachel's desire for a child 'and opened her womb' (Gn 30: 23). Thus Rachel herself comes to see that God has helped her to conceive a child (cf. Gn 30: 23-24). Indeed, more generally, then, we might speak of a reciprocal knowledge of the conception of the person: a mutually enriching combination of different aspects and insights concerning the beginning of each one of us; and, as such, this is an undoubted expression of that grace of inspiration which assisted the Scriptural writers and aided them in their work of communicating the acts of God: the intelligible nature of the act of God in bringing creation and the human person to exist.

Job expresses remarkably "prescient" imagery or accounts of the nascent human reality

If we take Job's reflections on the beginning of his life, we see a very clear process of an "imagined" reality; although, it has to be said, taking him as a "real" father, he may well have observed and reflected on the conception of human life. Job says, following the thread of being in the hands of God (Job 10: 7): 'Thy hands fashioned and made me …. of clay; and wilt thou turn me to dust again? Didst thou not pour me out like milk and curdle me like cheese?' (Job 10: 8-10). In other words, there is an almost "visual" account of what could only be described as a change in the substance of milk through being curdled 'like cheese' proving to be, through modern embryological observations, an almost literal expression of the radically new beginning which occurs in the first instant of fertilization: the change of substance from milk to cheese being just as irreversible as conception itself. To which Job, developing the earlier, almost nascent embryological moments of his beginning, adds: 'Thou didst clothe me with skin and flesh, and knit me together with bones and sinews' (Job 10: 11). Again, then, this almost actual account of early embryological development entailing, in reality, a gradual appearance of the differentiated "clothing" of 'skin and flesh' and, at the same time, the interior structuring, through 'bones and sinews', of Job himself: clothed and knitted together. Indeed, the very expressions, 'clothe me with skin and flesh' and then again, 'knit me together with bones and sinews', not only addresses God as the author of Job's "incarnation" (cf. *Familiaris Consortio*, 11), as it were, in the flesh; but, in addition, Job invites us to an intimation of his becoming visible through the very clothing of 'skin and flesh' and the very knitting of 'bones and sinews'. It is almost as if, then, there is a sense of the existence of Job as "clothed" and "knit" together in the very process of *manifesting* development: of being made manifest through his development.

In addition, then, to the development of the more mature bodily structure, Job says: 'Thou has granted me life and steadfast love; and thy care has preserved my spirit' (Job 10: 12). Thus Job expands more fully on what it is to be a human being, which is both a gift of 'life' and 'steadfast love' and, furthermore, the care that has 'preserved my spirit'. Inescapably, again, there is that echo of three gifts and the three persons of the Blessed Trinity: the Bringer of 'life', 'love' and 'care'. Although with intervening verses, Job goes on to complete the account of his beginning by saying: "Why didst thou bring me forth from the womb?" (Job 10: 18). What being created has brought about, then, is a relationship to God; indeed, it is the relationship to which we turn in search of the meaning of our existence: "Why

Conception: An Icon of the Beginning

didst thou bring me forth from the womb?" Thus, possibly, the widespread malaise about the meaning of life, suicide and depression, may well indicate the degree to which people have overlooked, forgotten and need to rediscover that the meaning of life is to be "read" in a lived relationship to our Creator (cf. *Gaudium et Spes*, 36)[147].

This analysis of Job's own beginning is in the context of his wondering about the very purpose of his life: 'Would that I had died before any eye had seen me .... [and gone] to the land of gloom and chaos, where light is as darkness' (Job 10: 18, 22). Thus Job covers the whole span of life, even if it is overshadowed with his suffering and the pain of his life, and gives us an intimation of the whole of life: from conception to the mystery of death; and, at the same time, the very words that he uses expresses a "dialogical" relationship to his Creator and thus leads to, or already implies, the very listening to the word of the Creator and the very prayer that expresses the awakening of our relationship to Him.

In conclusion, what emerges from this is the overwhelming perception of these people that the conception of a child is as it were *principally an expression of the power of God, precisely because it involves a mystery of creation that is beyond the power of man* (Gn 30: 2).

It is not obvious, however, that these texts point to Jesus Christ except in so far as they recognize the reality of conception; and, in so far as they do, they point to the culmination of the human reality of the *Incarnation* being a real event that fundamentally entails an action of God. Although, as we also know, the *Incarnation* is a unique action of God which almost "recapitulates" the singularity of

---

[147] Cf. An article of 18 pages by Fr. Joseph Tham, "Communicating with Sufferers: Lessons from the Book of Job", published by Oxford University Press, on behalf of *The Journal of Christian Bioethics, Inc.*, 2013 (a copy was supplied by the author).

our original creation: almost as if the personal involvement of Mary reveals even more fully the intimately personal nature of God's creation of each one of us. In other words, whereas Genesis drew upon, as it were, the earth to be formed into Adam, the coming of Christ draws upon the very flesh of the Virgin Mary. Thus the coming of Christ is a personalistic expression of redemption's "remaking" of creation and, ultimately, a re-expression of the personal nature of creation as a whole and the creation of each one of us in particular.

The significance of blood: Part VII of XII

After Cain kills Abel, Abel's blood cries to the Lord from the ground: 'The voice of your brother's blood is crying to me from the ground' (Gn 4: 10). Thus the significance of blood begins to appear, not just as a sign of life but as a sign of a life that endures after death.

Again the theme of the blood of life appears in the commandment to Noah at the end of the flood: 'Only you shall not eat flesh with its life, that is, its blood' (Gn 9: 4). So the idea is sown that there is a distinction between the *body* and its *blood*: a distinction which seems to correspond to the difference between life and death: a distinction which suggests that the blood, which is the life of the body, is in a particular way the *bearer of life*. Whether, however, the distinction between the body and the blood *corresponds* in this concrete sign language, to the distinction between the *body* and the *soul* is a question which remains to be answered. Nevertheless, the fact that the body is "permeated" by blood makes the blood, as it were, a natural image for what brings life to us as a whole and, in particular, entails the central action and activity of the heart in human life; and, at the same time, makes the blood a particularly potent image of the interior life because, of course, it is from the "heart" that comes forth what is in us (cf. Mk 7: 14-23).

On the one hand, then, we have seen that there is a relationship between the ordered elements of the body and the breath of life and then, in this case, there is a relationship of life between the body and the life-blood. Thus this gives rise to the impression that the life of the human being is almost concretely ordered to the natural signs of life: to the body's circulation of the blood and the breath that we breath; and, therefore, in the terms of biblical realism, the life of the person is expressly evident in the signs of human life. Consider, then, in the biblical language drawn from reality, the possibility of a "blood-breath" definition of being alive; and, at the same time, while this is more obviously expressed in the older human being, it is nevertheless clear that there is an implication of the "blood-breath" bearing an inexpressible "life-spirit". In other words, that even the "visible" signs of life are still, actually, the visibilization of an inner determinant of human life; what, in fact, a more philosophical tradition would call the "soul" or "form" of the body: that which makes matter, in this instance, integrally expressive of personal human life.

The significance of this theme is further emphasized by the following three elements. The first element is the prohibition to eat flesh which has not been drained of its blood (cf. Gn 9: 4); and, therefore, there is an injunction to see that blood has a particular significance as regards the life of a creature. The second element as regards the use of blood is that it is used in the religious rites of the people of God[148], which associates it with the *sacredness of life and, at the same time, with the power to save life*, not least of which was when the *blood of the lamb* was put on the lintel of the houses as a sign to the Lord to 'pass over' that house

---

[148] Cf. McKenzie, *Dictionary of the Bible*, p. 99: Blood.

and spare it from the destroying plagues (Ex 12: 13; and cf. also Ex 12: 1-13). The third element and, as it were, its fullest expression, is the fact that it is the body and blood of Christ[149] which are the two great concrete reality-signs of the mystery of our redemption: of the Life that makes possible everlasting life.

While on the one hand, then, there is an immense and growing significance to these reality-images, what continues to escape demonstration is a convincing *Scriptural argument for the existence of the soul that animates the body at conception.* Does the absence of an explicit reference to a soul that animates a body, imply a philosophical problem because of the deficiencies in the Hebrew mentality? On the other hand, then, is there a different kind of perception which, while not entailing the concept, "soul", nevertheless draws on a complementary but subtly different understanding of human origin and personhood?

Where is the creation of the soul in all this? Part VIII of XII

If God has given an immortal soul to Adam, then how is it that Adam's death is of such a kind that in the very description of it there is absolutely no trace of life: no trace of what is called the soul, which gives life to the body and which lives on after death? Indeed the very dust to which Adam will now return (Gn 3: 19) is the very dust that it is now the serpent's punishment to eat (Gn 3: 14).

Whereas in the book of the *Wisdom of Solomon* there is the recognition that God 'created man for incorruption, and made him in the image of his own eternity' (Wis 2: 23) although, as the sacred author goes on to say: 'but through the devil's envy death entered the world, and those who

---

[149] Cf. McKenzie, *Dictionary of the Bible*, pp. 99-100: Blood.

belong to his party experience it' (Wis 2: 24). Further, the *Book of Wisdom* says: 'the souls of the righteous are in the hand of God, and no torment will ever touch them. In the eyes of the foolish they seemed to have died ...' (Wis 3: 1-2).

Therefore, on the one hand the authors of Scripture acknowledge the existence of a soul which lives on after death in the hand of God and, on the other hand, there seems to be no trace of this in the death that awaits Adam: 'In the sweat of your face you shall eat bread till you return to the ground, for out of it you were taken; you are dust, and to dust you shall return' (Gn 3: 19). The whole image of dust, then, conveys what is dried up and incapable of life. In other words, the whole emphasis of "dust" seems to lie in the contrast with the promise of life, implying if not stating the possibility of eternal life (cf. Gn 3: 22-24); and, therefore, the sin of Adam and Eve revokes even the possibility of an immortal, temporal life, never mind an immortal, eternal life. In the book of the *Wisdom of Solomon* the author also says, altogether more positively: 'Wisdom protected the first formed father of the world, when he alone had been created; she delivered him from his transgression, and gave him strength to rule all things' (Wis 10: 1-2).

The soul is, as it were, hidden

Thus I began to realize that the "soul" that I was looking for was the soul as defined philosophically: the soul that animates the body[150]: the soul that is the form of the body[151]: the soul that is the life of the body[152].

---

[150] Cf. *Summa Theologiae*, Methuen, Pt I, Qu 75, art 1, p. 108.
[151] CCC, 365.
[152] Cf. CCC, articles 362 and 365.

The soul as philosophically defined is, more precisely, the *life of the natural body*; and this definition of soul is scarcely evident in the Scripture *in precisely this way*, except by way of a few incidental references made to it by St. Paul. As regards the "soul", then, John McKenzie says: 'The use of the adjective *psychikos* is rare and slightly different. This word signifies the natural as opposed to the spiritual (1 Co 15: 46), the man endowed with natural life but lacking the spirit (1 Cor 2: 14; Jd 19), the body with natural life as opposed to the spiritual body of the resurrection (1 Co 15: 44)'[153]. This precious and priceless piece of scholarship gives the *beginning of a key* to the mystery of the *invisibility*, as it were, of the philosophical concept of the soul in the Scriptures. In other words, this scholarship indicates that the concept of 'human nature' with which the Scripture tends to work is a concept of human nature that is understood from the point of view of the *spiritual life and the spiritual death of the person*. In other words, the Scriptural perception is of an ontological state of life or death. Thus the ontological death[154] of the person is also and paradoxically *the ontological death of the totality of the person, one in soul and body*. Therefore, for the Scripture, there is a state which is as it were the death of the spiritual life of the soul: the state that 'will be held in horror by all humanity' (*NJB* Is 66: 24); and, in addition, it is the state that the Scripture expresses by saying it is what happens to the 'corpses of those who rebelled' (*NJB* Is 66: 24) against

---

[153] McKenzie, *Dictionary of the Bible*, p. 838: Soul.

[154] I am indebted to the *Neocatechumenal Way* for this concept; but I do not know with whom it originated nor if it had an origin elsewhere. Cf. CCC art 403: 'a sin which is the "death of the soul"' (footnote 291 is to the Council of Trent: DS 1512). Cf. also the articles on the Body (p. 100), Life (p. 508), the Curse (p. 166) in McKenzie, *Dictionary of the Bible*. Cf. also the 'curse of destruction' (*NJB* Jos 6: 17) and also Lv 27: 28-29 etc.

God: it is the paradoxical state of the living dead (cf. Num. 16: 30-33)[155]. In other words, in the very implication of the state of the living dead there is an implication of there being a subject: a kind of personal subject who is the one whose life is expressed in the very horror of what happens to 'those who rebelled'. This state of spiritual death is intimated by juxtaposing the following two texts in *The First Book of Moses*, commonly called *Genesis*. On the one hand God curses the serpent and says: "dust you shall eat all the days of your life" (Gn 3: 14); *and,* on the other hand, God curses the ground and says to Adam: "you shall eat bread till you return to the ground, for out of it you were taken; you are dust, and to dust you shall return" (Gn 3: 19).

The emphasis of the biblical author is on the totality of "life" and "death"

What begins to emerge is that the Scriptural author of *Genesis* is communicating the origin of life and death as it *came to be understood at a certain point within the biblical tradition*; but which *yet pertains to a truth which is permanently valid and relevant to our salvation.* Therefore one has to take into account three things: the development of ideas up to and including *the time that Genesis was written*; the fact of the continuing development of that tradition, which among other things led to the differentiation between states after natural death which correspond to the doctrines of at least heaven, purgatory and hell; and, finally, *the basic vision of the author which pertains to a meaning of "life" and "death" which is perhaps unfamiliar to some of us and which can only be appreciated through study.*

---

[155] Cf. McKenzie, *Dictionary of the Bible*, p. 509: Life.

When, therefore, the author of sacred Scripture wrote in the *book of the generations of Adam* (Gn 5: 1), that the 'LORD God formed man of dust from the ground, and breathed into his nostrils the breath of life; and man became a living being' (Gn 2: 8), one has to conclude that the life which Adam received was the wholly undivided life that can only come from God: *that in the very giving of God, God gives a wholly indivisible spiritual life to man which is the complete gift of life, entailing the unity-in-diversity of body and soul.* But so profound is the biblical perception of this spiritual life that the loss of it is the loss of 'life'. Thus, even if man is left in his totality of being one in body and soul, this *natural state* is in fact totally unnatural: it is a terrible state of death.

Finally, however, the giving of the soul by God and the giving of spiritual life by God *becomes, because of the fall of man, the two acts of natural and supernatural conception*: the first of which is what happens with the 'help of the LORD' (Gn 4: 1) when a person is naturally conceived; and the second of which happens with the help of the Lord when a person is supernaturally conceived (cf. Jn 3: 5-6). Thus to be baptized is to be immersed[156] in the new and yet original grace of God given in our Lord and Saviour Jesus Christ[157]: the one in whom we were first created (cf. Jn 1: 1-5) and in whom, therefore, we first came to be (cf. Ac 17: 28).

---

[156] Cf. McKenzie, *Dictionary of the Bible*, p. 79: Baptism.

[157] Cf. *Summa Theologiae*, Methuen, Pt II, Qu 110, art 2, p. 313.

The Opening Chapters of Genesis are an Expression of an Integral Gift of Life: Part IX of XII

St. John Paul II says: 'Sacred Scripture therefore gives us to understand that God has intervened by means of his breath or spirit to make man a living being. In man there is a "breath of life," which comes from the "breathing" of God himself. In man there is a breath or spirit similar to the breath or spirit of God'[158].

But it could be possible to argue that God creates man in three, interrelated ways, in view of the fact that the original and redeemed totality of man is, as St. Paul says, spirit, soul and body (cf. 1 Thess 5: 23). Therefore the original act of creation involves the one act by which these three elements are created "in" one act of creation; and this one act could yet be said to express the one action of each Person of the Blessed Trinity[159]. In other words, the fundamental reality of existing is signified by the totality of the existence of body and soul, which is the flesh[160] (cf. Jn 1: 14)[161]. Thus the work of the Father is to give existence and that of the Holy Spirit is to animate it (cf. Mt 1: 20). What follows, then, is that the form of this unity, of this "embodied soul" is, as it were, the Son through whom all things are made (cf. Jn 1: 3); and, finally, the Holy Spirit establishes the person in a spiritual life of grace which expresses the fact that this person lives *in, and through and by the power* of the Holy Spirit of God (cf. Jn 1: 17).

---

[158] Pope St. John Paul II, *A Catechesis on the Creed*, Vol III, Gen. aud. Jan 10, 1990, pp. 156-157.

[159] Cf. CCC, art 258.

[160] Cf. *Summa Theologiae*, Methuen, Pt III, Qu 5, art 3, p. 483.

[161] Cf. McKenzie, *Dictionary of the Bible*, p. 280: Flesh.

Now it remains to be seen whether one can take this rather clumsy *expression* of a mystery and determine whether or not its elements are present at the beginning of our creation.

Revisiting the act of Creation: time as an "instant" and as a "duration" of development

The "whole man" is almost certainly implied in the second account of the creation of man and woman when God makes them with His hands[162] (cf. Gn 2: 7 and 2: 21-22) which, taking the hands as "figures" of the Son and the Spirit (cf. CCC, 704), more than suggests the action of the Blessed Trinity: *both working together and, through the limitations of that impression, working together in the same and yet a "differentiated" moment of one act of bringing one person to exist*. Alternatively, it could be argued, in not stating the actual use of God's hands the author, while implying them, has retained a degree of "difference" between God and man; and, therefore, while clearly anthropomorphic, the author has resisted absorbing the mystery of God into a "literalism" concerning how He 'formed' Adam and 'made' a rib into Eve. In other words, even in bringing God into intimate contact with the creation of Adam and Eve, the author has retained a sense of the otherness of God as the Creator who 'breathed' ... 'the breath of life' into Adam. By implication, then, the flesh that "passed" into Eve was already infused with what made her "to live"; and, therefore, not only do they "share" a common life but that they are also constituted, equally, "breath-of-God-filled".

Secondly, the totality of what God has made is called 'flesh' (Gn 2: 23) in such a way that it expresses the fullness of what has been given by God; and, at the same time, 'flesh'

---

[162] Cf. CCC, 292.

is used to express the relationship entailed in the first nuptial union: the 'one flesh' (2: 24) of Adam and Eve. It is possible, even, to consider that the repeated use of the word 'flesh' is one way of indicating that both man and woman are integrally ordered to one another: to the reciprocal gift of self. Therefore the 'one 'flesh' of their union is as "natural" as the very existence of their being a man and a woman expresses the body language of self-gift: of the man "being" a gift for the woman and of the woman "being" a gift for the man. Indeed, it is almost as if "personhood" itself is indicative of gift: of a completely gratuitous reality which, as it were, always entails "celebration". This, clearly, however, does not mean that marriage is the only vocation; but, in these foundational texts of Genesis it does work by way of recognizing that "relationship" is a universal characteristic of the human race to which we are all called, whether we marry or remain single. In other words, "relationship" is constitutive of human being.

While man is made out of the ground (Gn 2: 6), the first expression of this does not contradict the good that God's creation is (Gn 1: 31), nor does it preclude the giving to man of the grace which the Church has come to call 'original justice'[163] and which the Scriptures recognized both then (cf. Gn 3: 22) and later in the words: 'God created man for incorruption, and made him in the image of his own eternity ... ' (Wis 2: 23).

Thirdly, the grace which is given to Adam and Eve is a grace which is given to them in their wholeness: of each being a created creature. In other words, Adam and Eve are created *in grace*. Therefore, after the fall, both body and soul are destined to *express* in the death which is a return to the dust (Gn 3: 19) that is now their inheritance, *the effect of this loss precisely as the loss of the life of the flesh*. The corpse

---

[163] CCC, 376.

(cf. Is 66: 24) is now a sign of this ontological death: this death of the very being of what it is to be a living existence: a living *Icon of the Creator*. This explains why the Church has taught that original sin is transmitted through generation, because the living body of man now expresses its participation in the fall of man, just as St. John Paul II reminds us that the body of man will participate in the glory of the resurrection.

Fourthly, one has to recognize that the sacred authors have given us two emphases to the act of creation. The first emphasis involves the impression that the act of creation involves a succession of objects and creatures coming into existence *instantaneously* (cf Gn 1: 1, 3 etc.). The second emphasis is one which develops the implied period of time even in an account of instantaneous acts, some of which involve a secondary act of separating, for example, 'God separated the light from the darkness' (Gn 1: 4 ; but see also 1: 6-7). Thus this type of work can be called creation *through time* (cf. Gn 2: 7). The sacred author has also given us, similarly, two accounts of the creation of man, male and female: both one which is instantaneous and one which is in time. It is possible to argue, therefore, that each contributes to the whole meaning and that, possibly, the overall impression is that *the author or authors have understood as occurring in time what God did instantly*. However, it is also true that God acts *once in the beginning* (cf. Gn 2: 2-3), which signifies that the act of beginning is a new and in a way an unending act, and God *continues to act through time*, which signifies that the act of Creation is also and explicitly an act of parental love: an act which begets the continuous end of creating, redeeming and glorifying the children which are brought into existence.

Finally, the nature of an absolute beginning of creation, of which God is necessarily the one author, does not preclude God *from creating our participation in His act of creation.* This is what Eve expresses when she says: "I have gotten a man with the help of the Lord." This is also what St. Thomas Aquinas means when he says: 'The whole of bodily nature is God's instrument, so there is no reason why a bodily power can't form man's body and his intelligent soul be created in him by God alone'[164].

A second difficulty: An account of making man which is instantaneous and an account which "takes" time

If the general pattern of the two accounts of Genesis is to give an instantaneous beginning to Creation and to creatures and then to show their development through time, then why doesn't the account of the creation show that man was complete in all he is from the first instant of his creation and that what followed on from that fact was his development through time? On the one hand, the first account does give the impression that man and woman were created whole and entire from the first moment of their existence, especially as the text goes on to refer to both work and procreation (cf. Gn 1: 26-28). On the other hand, the second account does not describe man as complete from the first moment of his conception, but at the last moment of his making; and, furthermore, it is not until a dialogue between God and Adam that Eve is drawn and developed from him (cf. Gn 2: 4-24).

Genesis, then, is an account of the making of man from the point of view of God; and, in this respect, if fulfils perfectly the common understanding of Scripture that the act of creating a human being is *principally* an act of God. This is further expressed by the *anthropomorphic presentation of God's act in the second account of the crea-*

---

[164] *Summa Theologiae*, Methuen, Pt I, Qu 118, art 2, p. 163.

tion of man. The "making" of Adam communicates in a readily understandable way the fact that God is, as it were, making man in his own image, much as a sculpture can be made in the image of the artist and, in so doing, the Yahwist account conforms to the theme of the Priestly account: each being reproduces its own likeness. This accords with an ancient[165] account of the creation of man, bearing in mind that the human authors worked through a framework of natural knowledge. For if inspiration is to be real then it has to work with the historical development of the author's imagination: a historical development which, while it does not preclude the perception of what is necessarily permanently true, if true at all, nevertheless expresses a grasp of it which is relative to the development of human knowledge. In other words, one could say on the basis of a previously acknowledged principle of St. Thomas Aquinas, that the author is using an image to aid our human understanding of a mystery[166]. This image of the potter working the clay with his hands[167] would be present in the author's time: an image which in its own way expresses the beginning of human understanding *precisely because* it proceeds from the *physical facts of human experience* to the *supernatural truth* they are seeking to communicate[168]. Thus, in its own way, this image "of a beginning" is about a "concrete" conception of understanding the complementary origin of both man and woman as much as it is about "visualizing" the work of the Creator; indeed, drawing Adam

---

[165] Cf. *A Catechesis on the Creed*, Vol I, on *In Creation God Calls the World into Existence from Nothingness*, Gen. aud. Jan 29, 1986. Cf also E. Loveley, *Creation*, page 417-419 of Vol. IV, NCE.

[166] Copleston, *Aquinas*, pp. 176-177.

[167] Cf. McKenzie, *Dictionary of the Bible*, p. 159: Creation.

[168] Cf. *Summa Theologiae*, Methuen, Pt 1, Qu 84, art 7, p. 131.

Conception: An Icon of the Beginning

from the earth is a kind of statement about his tendency to work the earth and to name it and, at the same time, drawing Eve from Adam is also about the tendency of woman to perceive the relationship to the other as deriving, in a certain way, from her very origin. Clearly, however, in the case of both men and women, there is both the capacity to cooperate in the "common work" of the other and, in addition, the significance of their complementary origin.

Finally, then, Genesis is an attempt to give an account of the relationship between God and man: a relationship which is established and expressed in *God's work of making man*; and, therefore, a fundamental feature of the choice of this method of making man and woman is that "man" is thereby revealed to be *the personal work of the Creator*[169].

The help of Aristotle in understanding the implicit "witness" to the human soul

St. John Paul II says: 'The "Yahwist account does not speak of the "soul". Nevertheless we can easily deduce from it that the life given to man in the act of creation transcends the mere corporeal dimension (that which is proper to animals)'[170].

Now I agree that the Yahwist account does not directly *speak* of the soul and that therefore we must *deduce* from it the nature of the life given to man which *transcends* that of the animals.

However, there seems to be a direct *parallel* between the point of departure for Aristotle's reasoning that the soul is the form of the body and the point of departure for the

---

[169] Pope St. John Paul II, *A Catechesis on the Creed*, Vol. III, Gen. aud. Jan 10, 1990, p. 157.

[170] Pope St. John Paul II, Vol. I, *Man is a Spiritual and Corporeal Being*, Gen. aud. April 16, 1986, p. 277.

author of the book of Genesis on the formation of man. This is not to say that there is a dependence of the one on the other, so much as a resemblance in the human process of their thinking and expression, in that both seem to start from the same sort of consideration of the human act of craftsmanship: of making an object. The sacred author considers the work of the Divine sculptor in the light of human workmanship (cf Job 10: 8-9): clearly echoing or drawing upon the imagery of Adam being 'formed' from the ground (Gn 2: 7). Aristotle considers the work of a carpenter and says that without imparting a material part to the object he is making, yet 'the shape and the form are imparted from him to the material by means of the motion he sets up'; and then, a little later, he says: 'it is his knowledge of his art, and his soul, in which is the form, that move his hands or any other part of him with a motion of some definite kind ... '[171]. While for the sacred author, when a mist had 'watered the whole face of the ground - then the Lord God formed man of dust from the ground' (Gn 2: 6-7). In other words, common to both these accounts is the universal human experience of making objects: of carpentry and modelling; and, secondly, this common human experience is applied to understanding a similar "moment": the philosopher is trying to understand the transmission of human life and the sacred author is trying to understand the beginning of human life.

---

[171] Sir David Ross, *Aristotle*, (London: Methuen & Co Ltd, reprinted 1964), p. 120 (footnote 2: 730 b10-21).

One will proceed, then, by way of applying the philosopher's terminology to the sacred author's *imaginative understanding of the beginning of human life*

In the first place, the philosopher distinguishes between the shaping of the material by the carpenter and the 'form'. Aristotle says of the form that 'it is his knowledge of his art, and his soul, in which is the form'[172]. In other words, it would seem as if the form is the inner "determinant" of the action of the craftsman which determines the "outward shape" which the wood receives. Thus imparting 'the shape and the form' to a material thing is Aristotle's way of saying that the shape of an object is a *translation into material terms* of the intellectual form or understanding that the carpenter has of what he is making: of the matter "receiving" the shape determined by the carpenter. This involves both knowledge of the carpenter's art, *of how to make things*, and his soul, *of what he understands the intelligible structure*[173] *of what he is making to be*. Thus it is *through* action that the carpenter *imparts the form of what it is he is making through the particular and multiple acts of shaping the material and finishing the object*. Through his work, then, *the carpenter has transformed the materials with which he works*.

In the case of the canonical text of Scripture, the second account of the creation of man, which is *descriptively rich*, follows on the first account, which has already said with *conceptual precision*: 'God said "Let us make man in our image, after our likeness; and let them have dominion over ... every creeping thing that creeps upon the earth"' (Gn 1:

---

[172] *Ibid.*
[173] Copleston, *Aquinas*, p. 32.

26). Therefore, when it says that man is to be made in the 'image' and 'likeness' of God, it could be suggested that the second account translates this conceptual vision of man into a descriptive vision of man. Or, alternatively, the second account is at the least influenced by the first account, if not at the time of writing, although this cannot be absolutely excluded as a possibility, then at the time of the sacred author's editing his sources into a whole. Thus the image of God is given to man through the act by which God 'formed man of dust from the ground' (Gn 2: 7); and the likeness of God is given to man when God 'breathed into his nostrils the breath of life; and man became a living being' (Gn 2:7).

It can be said, then, that this distinction of 'image' and 'likeness' mirrors, as it were, the distinction between the *soul as the form of the body* and the *breath of life* being *the spiritual life of the person*. In other words, for the natural philosopher, for what is living to receive a form is for it to be given that by which it is intelligibly animated and animated intelligently. However, *for the author of Scripture*, it is the spiritual life which is *life*; and, therefore, implicit in the possibility of spiritual is the soul that makes it possible. It is understandable, then, that the sacred author did not distinguish more evidently the making of the soul, *precisely because the giving of spiritual life was so profoundly the giving of life that the loss of it results in man's return to the dust from which he came: the "death of dust" being a sign of his ontological death because of sin*. Therefore, for the sacred author, the giving of spiritual life was also and inherently the giving of what makes spiritual life possible: the human soul's animation of the body. In addition, in the very breath of God there is, as it were, a twofold signification or significance. There is the fact that breath does animate and bring to life, like playing a flute transcends the capabilities of the inanimate object; except, however, that the inanimate object is specifically designed to respond to the expression of a person's musical sensitivity. Then there is, also, the breath of God "as" a sign of the direct imparting, as it were, of what God uniquely is and gives: the graced perfection of the gift of human being-in-relation; for, in itself, to possess a "graced perfection" is to be, in other words, in a direct relationship with God, each other and with creation (cf. CCC, 374-384).

Finally, what can perhaps be adduced from the *natural contrast* which arises from the very fact of this anthropomorphic description of the creation of man, as a sculptor would make an artefact, is the fact that what God makes 'becomes a living being' (Gn 2: 7), whereas when man himself does this, all he produces is a 'lifeless product'[174].

A relevant discussion on 'formless matter' (Wis 11: 17)

The expression that God 'created the world from formless matter' (*NJB,* Ws 11: 17) has an undeniably Greek ring about it[175]. But, at the same time, this confirms the general impression of the opening lines of the first account of creation which was analysed earlier, and which led to the view that the sacred author was positing a state of what existed at the beginning, but which existed as undeveloped. Furthermore, this 'formless matter' echoes the description of the initial state of the earth: 'The earth was without form and void, and darkness was upon the face of the deep; and the Spirit of God was moving over the face of the waters' (Gn 1: 2). The *concrete expression* of this state, as it were, which

---

[174] Paul Auvray, *Creation,* translated by W. Jared Wicks, p. 99 of *Dictionary of Biblical Theology,* edited under the direction of Xavier Leon-Dufour, (London: Geoffrey Chapman, reprinted with revisions 1988).

[175] Cf. *New Jerusalem Bible,* footnote m, p. 1061.

most expressed the author's intention was that of the 'waters'. For water will *take* any shape which is given to it in so far as it will take the shape of anything into which it is put; and, what is more, this type of state of matter is *naturally* responsive to the Divine wind which moves over it (cf. Gn 1: 2).

Two questions arise out of these considerations: What is "formless matter"? and whether or not Adam is formed from "first matter"? Firstly, if one accepts the influence of Greek philosophy on the formulation of the concept of 'formless matter', which *mirrors conceptually the description of the state of the earth in the very beginning*, then this raises the question of what kind of existence a state of formless matter is? Clearly 'formless' cannot mean that this type of matter does not express the Creator's intention[176] (cf Wis 11: 24); rather, 'formless matter' is already the concrete embodiment of an intelligible plan of the Creator. Alternatively *first matter* is matter that has neither *received nor been given* either the shape of objects nor the form of living beings. It is, therefore, the existence of a matter which, while it cannot be pure potentiality or it would not exist, yet exists more as the craftsman's material than as the finished artefact that He proposes to make. This 'material' of the earth would be what God first created when He first created 'heaven and earth' (Gn 1: 1); indeed, it almost makes the state of the earth a kind of "opposite" to the mystery of 'the heavens'. Thus the earth is a kind of state that is to be further unfolded or developed in order to express and to reveal what it really is whereas, by contrast, the heavens are definitively formed immediately and, in particular, the 'heaven' or 'heavens" that expresses the presence of God.

The second question is whether or not this *first matter* is what the Lord God used to make Adam - and this has to be

---

[176] Cf. *Causality*, by G. F. Kreyche, p. 344 of Vol III, NCE.

first asked of the account of man's creation itself - or whether man is made out of a *material called the dry land* (Gn 1: 10) which has already been shaped in the sense that it is what emerges from the further action of God: "Let the waters under the heavens be gathered together into one place, and let the dry land appear" (Gn 1: 9).

Now when the author comes to describe the second account of the creation of man, which on its own terms is the first[177] *descriptive* account of the creation of man, the writer seems to refer back to that *state of matter which existed* either on the first or on the third day; from when 'God created the heavens and the earth' (Gn 1: 1) to when 'God called the dry land Earth' (Gn 1: 10). In other words, the *state of the matter which the Lord God used to form man*, was a state of matter which at the least was 'without form' (Gn 1: 2) or, at most, had been differentiated from the seas (*ibid*).

The second account of creation, however, seems to have its own version of time: it seems as if there is a *day of life* (cf. Gn 2: 4f), in which God gives life in its various forms and ways, and a *day of death* (Gn 2: 17), which will follow *only* on the eating of what is forbidden by God for man to eat. In the perspective of the *day of life*, man is made after the absolute beginning of the 'heavens and the earth' (Gn 2: 4), when the earth was capable of plant life but had none in it Gn 2: 5) and when 'no herb of the field had yet sprung up' (*ibid*), although 'a mist went up from the earth and watered the whole face of the ground' (Gn 2: 6). In other words, creation is here portrayed as a beginning in the sense of a day without end: a day that is intended to be *endless*; indeed, this could be said to be parallelled in the original Hebrew

---

[177] I just recall to the reader that my intention is to work with the chronological order of things as established by the canon of the Scripture.

expression, *bereshith*, which is without the definite article 'the' and thus literally reads: In beginning, God created the heavens and the earth'[178]. This could also be said to be parallelled in the first account of creation with respect to the cycle of the week and the day of rest which is without end[179]; however, the *day of life* has its own particular insight in that this is what a true conception is: a beginning without an end.

Therefore, just as both accounts do not place man at the absolute beginning of God's creative activity nor, significantly, do the Fathers of *The First Vatican Council*, who say that God created 'at once' the 'spiritual and the corporeal' orders of creatures, 'and then (*deinde*) the human creature'[180], so it seems plausible to conclude that *the matter* from which God makes man is 'matter' at a stage subsequent to the absolute beginning of creation. This would also allow for the presence in man of elements, minerals and vitamins, which are themselves the product of time, and which therefore would have legitimately pre-existed him as the *ground* out of which he was made. And so while one could not deny the possibility that God made the first man in a way which was *natural to Him as the Creator but miraculous to us the creature*, still the suggestion of Revelation is that *the Creator worked through the time He at the same time created*[181].

---

[178] Cf. Gordon Wenham's discussion of an aspect of this in *Genesis: 1-15*, Word Biblical Commentary: Vol. 1, Waco, Texas: Word Books, Publisher, 1987.

[179] *Creation Account*, by H. J. Sorensen, p. 427 of Vol. IV, NCE.

[180] *Dei Filius*, (art 3002), art 412, page 124 of *The Christian Faith*.

[181] Cf. *Summa Theologiae*, Methuen, Pt I, Qu 46, art 3, p. 89.

Conception: An Icon of the Beginning

The answer to the objection that the Mother of seven martyrs raises, namely that God made man as he made the heavens and the earth, that is *not* out of 'things that existed' (2 Mac 7: 28), could be that man *as man* does not come into existence until he *comes into existence one in body and soul*. But he does not come into existence as one in body and soul until the moment the soul is created one with the body. Thus in that sense man as essentially man is not made out of anything *and* this is a characteristic shared by all 'mankind' (*ibid*).

The mystery of God making the first man and the first woman is one which was without any existing and *prior human* "material"[182], except in the sense of taking up what necessarily pre-existed as "matter". Even so, however, it is necessary to acknowledge that from the point of view of *all* human conception subsequent to that beginning, that there is the antecedent, prior flesh of the contributing human parents. This applies even to Christ to the extent that His flesh is human flesh and of Mary, even if it is not the flesh which arises out of an ordinary human conception; and, as was argued earlier, if Christ is the 'prototype'[183] of all humanity, then this *does* seem to be a theological argument for the making of Adam to reflect *in some way* the making of Christ *in whose image Adam was made*. In other words, in a more general way than the more personalistic drawing on the natural origin of one of Mary's ova, Adam was "formed" from the ground.

Finally, given the expression that man without the Life of God in him will return to the 'ground, for out of it you were taken; you are dust, and to dust you shall return' (Gn 3: 19), it seems likely that the biblical authors understood that *in*

---

[182] Cf. *Summa Theologiae*, Methuen, Pt I, Qu 91, art 2, p. 142.
[183] *Summa Theologiae*, Methuen, Pt I, Qu 44, art 4, p. 85.

some sense, the 'dust' to which man returns is not exactly the same dust from which he came. For this dust to which he returns is a dust *without the moistening of the water from the mist* (cf. Sir 24: 3) *which was present in the dust out of which he was made* (cf Gn 2: 6). In other words, and *through many concrete expressions*, the biblical authors seem to express some awareness of what elsewhere was begetting the beginnings of philosophy and science.

Drawing on this Meditation on Genesis

In conclusion, the type of matter to which the soul *and the spiritual life of the human being are united*, would appear to be that type of matter which, while not necessarily as completely *undeveloped as that in the absolute beginning*, is yet not that either which has been used for any other purpose save that of making dry land.

Secondly, whatever is the type of matter out of which man is made, and I note here that elsewhere in Scripture it is called 'clay' (cf. Job 10: 9; Is 64: 8; Jer 18: 1-6) and thus Scripture itself tends to the view that it is subsequent to the first and 'formless matter' of the earth - this and all matter exists in the presence of the Divine wind which animates it. For while all matter subsequent to this first moment of formless matter is then given to exist in diverse shapes and forms, it does not follow that it ceases to exist in the presence of the animating and Divine wind; indeed, on the basis of the second account of man, it would seem that man is made in such a way that his nature is *perfectly ordered to the reception of that Divine wind as to the very breath of his life*. 'For the Semites, it is not the soul but God who by His Spirit is the source of life: "God breathed in his nostrils a breath (*nesamah*) of life, and man became a living soul (*nephes*)"[184].

In answer to the difficulty with which this particular aspect of the question began, one can say that the *anthropomorphic approach* of the second account of man's creation has the particular merit of allowing for a reasonable comparison between the creation of man as envisaged by the sacred author and the creation of man as we understand it now. For both the creation account and the reality of our human conception *concur* on a process of the formation of man which at least presupposes a pre-existent material, *and one which has not passed through any other process of development*[185], and culminates with the instantaneous *beginning of human life* which is true to the *essential nature of man's conception as one in body and soul*.

Furthermore, if God created what exists in such a way that they are an expression of His goodness, the expression of which requires diversity[186], presupposes unity (cf Gn 1: 31) and is written through with a trace of the Blessed Trinity[187], then it seems to follow that there is at least the possibility that *the unity and the diversity of creation*[188] is a created expression of the being of the Living God: the Blessed Trinity. In which case the creation of man is in a way the exemplary example of this mystery; for man is a unity of

---

[184] Xavier Leon-Dufour, *Soul*, translated by John J. Kilgallen, p. 567 of the *Dictionary of Biblical Theology*.

[185] Cf. J. E. Royce, *Soul, Human, Origin of*, page 471 of Vol XIII, NCE.

[186] Cf. *Summa Theologiae*, Methuen, Pt I, Qu 46, art 3, p. 89.

[187] *Summa Theologiae*, Methuen, Pt I, Qu 45, art 7, p. 87.

[188] Cf. Marc-Francois Lacan, *Unity*, translated by Donald F. Brezine, p. 624 of the *Dictionary of Biblical Theology*.

both 'spirit' and 'body'[189]. This makes clear that Revelation contains a *manifestation* of being that constitutes a definition of being; for the being of creation, if it is an 'image' of the Blessed Trinity, is *manifestly* a *unity-in-diversity*. Therefore creation as a whole and man in particular is, as it were, a *living*[190] *Icon of the Blessed Trinity*.

'Your eyes beheld my unformed substance' (Ps 139: 16):
Part X of XII

This text is especially significant with respect to the whole discussion on the biblical evidence for the beginning of the person, body and soul, from one moment of conception. This is because it not only falls within the general perspective of Scripture so far defined, namely that it perceives God to be *the* formative cause of each and every person, losing sight as it were of the 'human parents in the clear vision of the Divine Creator'[191], but it is also one of the texts which specifically concerns the absolute beginning of human life[192]. I shall consider some general observations on this psalm before examining it in more detail.

---

[189] Cf. *Dei Filius*, (art 3002), art 412, p. 124 of *The Christian Faith*.

[190] Cf. McKenzie, *Dictionary of the Bible*, p. 508: Life.

[191] A. Maclaren, *The Psalms*, p. 387 of Vol. III, (London: Hodder & Stoughton, MDCCCXCIV [1894]), which is part of the series entitled *The Expositor's Bible*, under W. R. Nicoll.

[192] This is 'the verse which Pope St. John Paul II has chosen to head the section of *Evangelium Vitae* between articles 58-63' (p. 283, Chapter Eleven, Francis Etheredge, *Scripture: A Unique Word*, Cambridge Scholars Publishing: Newcastle upon Tyne, 2014).

General Observations on Psalm 139

The writing in this psalm is 'Often regarded as some of the most exquisite poetry in the Psalter, perhaps unsurpassed as a description of the inescapability of God's presence (cf. Amos 9: 2)'[193]; and in the words of another commentator, this psalm is 'beautiful ... but textually difficult'[194]. Psalm 139 is also and elsewhere said to be 'The climax of Old Testament thought on God's omnipresence and foreknowledge'[195]. Indeed, perhaps it is in the very recognition that the Lord's knowledge of us is incomparable that has, as it were, prompted this theme: 'O Lord, thou has searched me and known me!' (Ps 139: 1); and, therefore, the whole psalm is an exposition of the many ways in which we are open to Him: from our origin to our end (Ps 139: 16).

There is some uncertainty as to which category this psalm belongs: lament[196]; thanksgiving[197]; imprecatory psalm[198]; or song of praise[199]; and, therefore, it traverses a

---

[193] J. S. Kselman, SS & M. L. Barre, SS, *Psalms*, p. 550 of *The New Jerome Biblical Commentary*, R. E. Brown SS, et al, (London: Geoffrey Chapman Ltd, 1990).

[194] T. E. Bird, *The Psalms*, p. 472 of *A Catholic Commentary on Holy Scripture*, Dom B. Orchard, et al, (London: Thomas Nelson & Sons Ltd., 1953).

[195] A. H. McNeile, *The Psalms*, page 374 of *A New Commentary on Holy Scripture*, C. Gore et al, (London: Society for Promoting Christian Knowledge, reprinted 1939).

[196] *The New Jerome Biblical Commentary*, Psalms, p. 550.

[197] R. E. Murphy, O. Carm., *Psalms*, p. 600 of *The Jerome Biblical Commentary*, R. Brown SS, et al, (London: Geoffrey Chapman Ltd., 1968).

[198] L. S. McCaw & J. A. Motyer, *The Psalms*, page 538 of the *New Biblical Commentary*, D. Guthrie et al, (Leicester: Inter-Varsity Press, third edition, 1988). The 'Imprecatory Psalms' are when the psalmist seems 'to pray evil against' another:

variety of moods or attitudes and, in that sense, evokes knowledge of the psalmist's heart as much as where he is, the origin of his thought and the mystery of his making. It has a natural structure of four parts and a kind of conclusion which returns it to the theme with which it opens: the Lord's "searching" and "knowing" of the psalmist[200]. The "I-Thou"[201] dialogue of this psalm makes it one of the most personal expressions of an Old Testament[202] author.

If this psalm is in the last of the five books of the Psalter[203], a structure which reputedly echoes the five books of the *Pentateuch*[204], then this raises the question of a kind of *equivalence* between Psalm 139 and the book of *Deuteronomy*[205]; as if to say the Psalmist expresses an *experienced*[206] knowledge of himself in the desert, under the sun: a sun that does not compare to the eyes of the Lord - for the 'eyes of the Lord are ten thousand times brighter than the sun' (Sir 23: 19).

---

https://www.biblegateway.com/resources/asbury-bible-commentary/Imprecatory-Psalms.

[199] *herder's commentary on the psalms* edited by E. Kalt, translated by B. Fritz, OSB, (Westminster, Maryland: The Newman Press, 1961), p. 525.

[200] *New Jerome Biblical Commentary*, Psalms, p. 550.

[201] *Jerome Biblical Commentary*, Psalms, p. 600.

[202] Cf. *Jerome Biblical Commentary*, Psalms, p. 600.

[203] Cf. *New Jerome Biblical Commentary*, Psalms, p. 523: Introduction.

[204] *New Jerusalem Bible*, p. 815: Introduction to the Psalms.

[205] *New Jerusalem Bible*, p. 6-7: Introduction to the Pentateuch.

[206] Cf. L. S. McCaw and J. A. Motyer, *New Biblical Commentary*, D. Guthrie *et al*, Leicester: Inter-Varsity Press, third edition, 1988: The Psalms, p. 537.

Conception: An Icon of the Beginning

This Psalm and the Personal Act of Creation

This introduces us to a particularly relevant theme of this psalm, and of the Scripture as a whole: what is *not* known to man is known to God[207]; and, it could be argued, *what man can know follows on from what God already knows.* Furthermore, and with specific reference to the question of our origin: 'It is because God has created everything that he knows everything'[208]; and indeed other commentators call God's knowledge of the psalmist 'intimate', as it is 'based on the fact that Yahweh created him'[209]. Furthermore, what God knows is also incomparable because 'Before the universe was created, it was known to him; so it was also after it was finished' (Sir 23: 20).

But there is as I say a particular relevance of this psalm to the question of our origin and this is in part because Scripture elsewhere regards this question as *especially mysterious*: 'As you do not know how the spirit comes to the bones in the womb of a woman with child, so you do not know the work of God who makes everything' (Eccles 11: 5); and it is almost impossible to consider this passage without thinking of the more well known one of a similar kind in Ezekiel (37: 5-6), and so to see an enumeration of the two works of the Spirit between them: the giving of natural life and the giving of supernatural life. This could be said to be expressed in the use of two similar phrases in that same passage of Ezekiel: the first is when natural life is given to

---

[207] W. E. Barnes, *The Psalms*, Vol II, (London: Methuen & Co. Ltd., 1931), p. 638.

[208] Artur Weiser, *The Psalms, A Commentary*, translated by Herbert Hartwell, (London: SCM Ltd., 1962), p. 805. This book is part of the *Old Testament Library* series, edited by G. E. Wright *et al.*

[209] *New Jerome Biblical Commentary*, Psalms, p. 550.

the bones: 'Thus says the Lord God to these bones: Behold, I will cause breath to enter you, and you shall live' (Ez 37: 5); and then, following the completion of the work of that first gift of life, which culminates with the creature being covered in skin and thus recognizably human (cf Ez 37: 6), comes the gift of 'breath' *through* which the person will live and know 'that I am the Lord' (Ez 37: 6), which is the gift of supernatural life.

More generally Scripture says that the works of God are beyond the grasp of man (cf Eccles 3: 11), and while this could be the *proportion as it were of the work of God to the time which is available to a man to devote to understanding it* (cf. Eccles 8: 16-17), yet there is a sense that the work of God is in a way beyond the grasp of man *precisely because it is the work of God*. This is in part conveyed by the 'Semitic idiom' which expresses the whole of a thing through the statement of opposites[210], and so the whole of God's work is beyond the grasp of man: 'He has made everything beautiful in its time; also he has put eternity into man's mind, yet so that he cannot find out what God has done from the beginning to the end' (Eccles 3: 11). But on the other hand there is a more specific sense to what is beyond the grasp of man and this follows from a consideration of the context of the latter excerpt, for the fact is that the whole of chapter three refers to *times*: 'a time to be born, and a time to die' (Eccles 3: 2). It is therefore in the context of the different seasons of things that the author draws attention, at the end of this chapter, to the beginning and to the end of man and animals (cf. Eccles 3: 19-21), such that one could almost contrast what man knows, which corresponds to the things *between* the beginning and the end of life (cf Eccles 3: 22), with what God knows, which *includes* the beginning and end of everything (cf. Eccles 3: 11).

---

[210] *Jerome Biblical Commentary*, Psalms, p. 600.

In conclusion of these introductory reflections one might say that God's *actively knowing presence* is at the heart of the origin of man[211] and is therefore *the source of whatever man can know of the theological mystery of his own origin: the mystery that reason thinks through in faith – even if it is possible for reason to begin to ponder the action of God from the starting point of natural evidence*[212].

Particular observations on Psalm 139

The aforementioned interpretation of these lines also allows David[213] to differentiate further between the two types of work which "brought" him to be in such a way as he is brought to be the *possession*[214] of God he is: the divine action of God and the natural processes which are not to be separated from the action of God but are yet not the same thing. For God 'didst form my inward parts, ... didst knit me together in my mother's womb' (Ps 139: 13), could easily be understood as the making of the most inmost part, the human soul, and the knitting it together with the body: *acts which of their nature exceed what can be done by human beings*. This would be the act by which God both creates the soul and at the same time creates it to be the form of the body.

---

[211] Cf. C. A. Briggs and E. G. Briggs, *A Critical and Exegetical Commentary on the Book of Psalms*, Vol. II, (Edinburgh: T & T Clark, 1909), p. 498.

[212] Cf. *Dei Verbum*, 6.

[213] Cf. *New Jerusalem Bible*, p. 954. The question of authorship is strictly beyond the scope of this particular discussion; however, I accept the canonical convention of David's authorship if for no other reason than that of relieving the repetition of 'author', 'psalmist' and other such terms.

What then follows is the second type of the making of man which, while not hidden from God does not involve the same direct action of God: 'my frame was not hidden from thee, when I was being made in secret, intricately wrought in the depths of the earth' (Ps 139: 15). Thus it seems as if God is perceived to be the author of David's life not only because He is as it were the originator and designer of it, but *because God is the originator of man and also the end of man in such a way that man's relationship to God constitutes the very vocation of man himself.* In other words, *both* the development *and* the vocation (cf. Wis 9: 1-4; 10: 16) of man are *works of God* which flow *from* and *through* God's original act of man's creation.

On the one hand, just as the effort of translating the Hebrew word *golmi* very often gives rise to a twin-termed concept such as 'unformed substance' (RSV[215]), 'imperfect substance'[216], and 'imperfect being'[217]; then, on the other hand, this combination of concepts resembles the juxtaposition of ideas in the etymological root of *golmi*, which is that of *unfinished* and *vessel*. Thus this process *in some way* recapitulates the psychological process of the original author as he came to *create an original word*[218] to describe the very beginning of his life; indeed, just as the very words convey an outer beginning to what exists interiorly, so the suffix "i" indicates that this is "my" beginning. In other words, the psalmist is expressing the truth of his beginning as a "personal" act of the Creator. *And*

---

[214] W. E. Barnes, *The Psalms,* Vol. II, (London: Methuen and Co. Ltd., 1932), p. 637.

[215] Catholic edition.

[216] Barnes, *The Psalms,* Vol. II, p. 637.

[217] *herder's commentary on the psalms*, p. 522.

[218] Barnes, *The Psalms,* Vol. II, p. 638.

Conception: An Icon of the Beginning

why create an original word if you are not striving to say something which is in its own way radically new? In addition, this very juxtaposition of the *descriptive facts* 'unfinished' and 'vessel', the first an action of making and the second an object which is being made, does in its own way echo the first account of the beginning of the earth (Gn 1: 2) and the second account of the beginning of man in the book of Genesis (Gn 2: 7).

Psalm 139 echoes Genesis 1 and 2

The Scriptural echo of the first account of the beginning of the earth is what I will call a *conceptual* echo: an echo of the task that confronted the author of the Priestly account of creation in the task that confronted the author of Psalm 139. For each is in its own way an attempt to understand an *unprecedented* beginning: the first is the absolute beginning of everything; and the second is the absolute beginning of a particular person. David could be said to be juxtaposing two pairs of related ideas with a third: the existence of a creature and that creature being undeveloped; and, at the same time, David is considering the unity of a complex nature of human beginning: as both an object of the senses *and* yet a container of something else - an *unfinished vessel*[219]. Furthermore, there is the fact that the object of his thought is the beginning of his *living* human being, his *embryo* (*NJB*, Ps 139: 16), which incidentally has a Greek etymological sense of what can be said 'to swell or teem'[220]. In

---

[219] Cf. McKenzie, *Dictionary of the Bible*, pp. 685-686: Pottery.

[220] *Blackie's Compact Etymological Dictionary*, page 108: Em'bryo; cf. also F. Delitzsch, *Biblical Commentary on the Psalms*, translated by Rev. D. Eaton, (London: Hodder and Stoughton, 1889), pp. 350-351.

other words there is a marvellous sense of the very "beginning" of the psalmist's life: the beginning of intense growth and development.

The concepts which seem to have a particular echo with the beginning of the earth (Gn 1: 2) are that of *unformed* and *substance*. The resemblance is twofold: firstly in the manner of constructing a concept out of the juxtaposition of *discreet* elements; and secondly that the concept so created gives rise to the idea that something both *exists* and at the same time *exists as yet undeveloped through time*. In other words, it is *through* these initial and perceptible "objects" that one sees the origin of what one could call *theological* thought: thought which transcends the empirical facts and *at the same time* expresses an insight into the *signification of those same facts*[221].

The second Scriptural echo is to the second account of creation, particularly the creation of man (Gn 2: 7): 'In the formation of each man there is repeated, according to the view of Scripture, the manner in which the first man was made (Job xxxiii 6, cf. v. 4)'[222]. Delitzsch goes on to say in a footnote to his comments, drawing on Epiphanius: 'that the Hebrew ... [golmi] signifies the peeled grains of spelt or wheat before they are mixed up and baked, the still raw (only bruised, rough-ground) flour-grains - a signification that can now no longer be supported by examples'[223]. The possibility of *golmi* referring, originally, to a *peeled grain* is beyond the scope of this discussion to take further; however, the image of a grain has its own capacity to communicate, especially

---

[221] Cf. Pope John Paul II, *Original Unity of Man and Woman, Meaning of Original Human Experiences*, Gen. aud. December 12, 1979, art 1, pp. 85-86 and the *Nuptial Meaning of the Body*, Gen. aud. January 9, 1980, pp. 106-112.

[222] Delitzsch, *Biblical Commentary on the Psalms*, p. 351.

[223] Ibid., 351-352.

considering a "peeled" grain: one imagines a suggestion of a *bare seed*. In other words, the image gives the impression of something not protected but vulnerable to the "elements"; and, therefore, a very apt image for what in fact naturally "dwells" within the maternal body.

The third Stanza

Another observation on Psalm 139 follows on the structure of the third stanza, which begins with 'For thou didst form my inward parts'[224] (Ps 139: 13) and ends with 'the days that were formed for me, when as yet there was none of them' (Ps 139: 16). The structure of the third stanza perfectly corresponds to the general principle of construction[225] which can be said to underlie the whole psalm. This is because the third stanza gives *the dimensions of man* between which one apprehends the *whole of man*, his beginning and fullness of days. Thus this stanza complements the other *dimensions of the psalmist's life* to which it could be said each stanza of this psalm is devoted. The first stanza is about God knowing his life and speech as intimately as '[e]ven before a word is on my tongue, lo, O Lord, thou knowest it altogether' (Ps 139: 4). The second stanza is about God's illuminating presence leaving nothing hidden, just as 'the darkness is as light with thee' (Ps 139: 12). Thus the third stanza takes up the implications of the first two and shows us that, just as God knows the root of human speech and everything is, as it were, open to His illuminating presence, so He acts at the beginning of life and knows the whole of a man's 'days ... when as yet there was none of them' (Ps 139: 16). Finally, the fourth stanza is about

---

[224] RSV, Catholic Edition, whereas other editions of this psalm give it in several stanzas.

[225] Cf. *Jerome Biblical Commentary*, Psalms, p. 600.

God's just discernment of the evil within us and the path of conversion which completes his creative love of us: 'and lead me in the way everlasting!' (Ps 139: 24). In other words, the whole psalm justifies the claim that it is possible that God 'beheld my unformed substance' (Ps 139: 16) at the very beginning of the life that He Himself had given.

In conclusion, and while I fully admit the incidental purpose of this exegesis to the *fundamental purpose of this psalm*, I nevertheless accept, *precisely because* this is *integral to the psalmist's purpose*, that line sixteen of this psalm is an expression of the mystery of our absolute beginning to be: a beginning to be which is *both* integrally one act of beginning of all that each one of us is, *and at the same time that this act of our beginning is a dynamic act* (cf. Wis 15: 11) *which will unfold through time and unto eternity* (cf. Wis 2: 23). For if this psalm is an unparalleled dialogue of man and God, a dialogue in which man comes to know himself *through* God's knowledge of him, then it is completely fitting that it should contain and express the mystery of human conception that it does.

Other texts on the beginning of life and the action of God which makes the barren fertile – leading to the ultimate question about the conception of Christ

In the context of this discussion on Psalm 139, it is helpful to add other Scriptures to our account of human beginning; for, in general, one account "acts on" another and helps to bring its meaning to light. Thus there is Job who, finding his life full of suffering, dwells on his beginning as indeed does one of his friends and there are some other observations from the *Book of Wisdom*.

Job says: 'Didst thou not pour me out like milk and curdle me like cheese?' (Job 10: 10). Later in the same book Elihu says: 'The spirit of God has made me, and the breath of the Almighty gives me life' (Job 33: 4), which is his basis for claiming a human equality with Job: 'Behold, I am toward God as you are; I too was formed from a piece of clay' (Job 33: 6). Elihu then returns to these thoughts as his reason for a more general conclusion concerning the action of God: 'If he should take back his spirit to himself, and gather to himself his breath, all flesh would perish together, and man would return to dust' (Job 34: 14-15).

In the *Wisdom of Solomon* we read that he was 'mortal, like all men, a descendant of the first-formed child of earth; and in the womb of a mother I was molded[226] into flesh, within the period of ten months, compacted with blood, from the seed of a man and the pleasure of marriage' (Wis 7: 1-2). In other words, given the time in which the author lived, this is a remarkably clear, concise and accurate account of human conception from, as it were, the point of view of natural science. Moreover, he realises that intrinsic to this process is the reception of a soul (cf. Wis 8: 19-20) which, however, is not the same as the earth from which he was taken (cf. Wis 15: 8), because on his death he is 'required to return the soul that was lent him' (Wis 15: 8). Furthermore, the author sums up all that has so far been said in this discussion, and especially that concerning *Genesis, Job, Ecclesiastes* and *Ezekiel*, when he says so succinctly of the man who has devoted his life to making 'a futile god from the same clay - this man who was made of earth a short time before' (Wis 15: 8): 'his life is of less worth than clay, because he failed to know the one who formed him and inspired him with an active soul and breathed into him a living spirit' (Wis 15: 11).

---

[226] The spelling of 'molded' is retained from the translation of the RSV, Catholic Edition, (San Francisco: Ignatius Press, 1966).

Combining traditions: on conception and fertile barrenness

The ultimate question, then, that emerges through the very progress of reflection on the beginning of human life is that, together with the biblical tradition of the action of God that makes the barren fertile (cf. 1 Sam 1: 6 – 2: 11; Lk 1: 36), is the mystery of the conception of Christ. In other words, there are three levels to this biblical reflection on human conception. To begin with, it is natural to ask what is entailed in the act of human conception; and, in view of it involving the action of God (cf. Gn 4: 1), it makes sense that the biblical author draws on insights about the mystery of human beings coming to exist – both from the very beginning of creation and in each subsequent act that a human being comes to exist. Secondly, given that human conception already involves the action of God, there is a whole tradition of this act of God taking up the prayer of the person afflicted by barrenness and, therefore, the act of God "encompassing", as it were, the whole "moment" of the person coming to exist. Finally, in the context of the coming of Christ, the biblical author brings together an implicit history of the act of God in the conception of the human being (cf. Gn 4: 1), the "miraculous" act of God that makes the barren fertile and the virginal conception of Christ which reveals and confirms that 'nothing is impossible to God' (Lk 1: 34-38).

A Patristic Consensus concerning Christ: What is not assumed is not redeemed: Part XI of XII

The Fathers, after and even contemporary with the Apostles, were early Christian commentators on Scripture. Together with Scripture and the Magisterium the Fathers contribute to the influence of Tradition on the development of Church teaching. Without a painstaking process, however, of inserting these extracts from the Fathers into their original context, linking them where possible with the relevant Scriptures upon which they draw, it is nevertheless invaluable to see what kind of consensus emerges concerning their understanding of the conception of Christ's humanity. This section is justified, then, on the basis that an argument from the Fathers is relative to the degree of their consensus concerning the interpretation of Scripture; indeed, as it says in the *Council of Trent*: let 'no one dare to interpret the Scripture in a way contrary to the unanimous consensus of the Fathers'[227]. While these texts are not explicitly commenting on the following Scripture, they are held by this author to be applicable to it: 'the Word became flesh and dwelt among us' (Jn 1: 14). So it is at least necessary to cite a number of their statements, even if this is not an exhaustive list; and, where possible and appropriate, there is a relatively brief comment on each extract: the comment arises more out of the stimulus of the extract than an exact exegesis or explanation of it.

Besides presuming, if not explicitly stating that Christ was virginally conceived by the action of the Holy Spirit, what can be established as an actual bodily fact of our humanity, as integral to it as the development of the nervous system, then this is the true humanity that they understood Christ to assume. Similarly, even if our understanding of conception and embryological development differs in detail to theirs, provided a stage of human growth *can be demonstrated to be a true human stage of development,*

---

[227] *The Council of Trent*, "Decree on Sacred Books and on Traditions to be Received" (1507), in *The Christian Faith in the Doctrinal Documents of the Catholic Church*, edited by J. Neuner

then what follows is what they understood, namely that Christ recapitulated the whole of human life and, therefore, sanctified each integral stage and fact of it – beginning with conception understood to be the first instant of fertilization.

The following selection of extracts is taken from the three volumes of *The Faith of the Early Fathers* selected and translated by William A. Jurgens; and, therefore, the selection will proceed on the basis of progressing through the aforementioned volumes.

St. Athanasius says in his "Letter to Epictetus of Corinth": 'The incorporeal Word appropriated as His own the properties of the body' (6)[228]. Thus the humanity of Christ was both a true humanity and, at the same time, an expression of the 'incorporeal Word'; indeed, in Christ the bodily-less Word was expressed bodily. Slightly further on in the same letter, St. Athanasius goes on to say: 'the Savior having in truth become man, the salvation of the whole man was accomplished' (6). In other words, just as Christ assumed the whole man, so everything characteristic of the whole man was saved; and, therefore, being conceived, albeit differently to the rest of us, nevertheless entails the saving of human conception. How is this possible? As St. Athanasius also says, 'the body of the Lord was a true one - a true one, since it was the same as ours' (6); and, therefore, that unity of human being which flows from and, as it were, expresses conception, was nevertheless a true characteristic of His

---

and J. Dupuis, New York: Alba House, revised edition, 1982: no. 215, p. 75.

[228] This and the following extracts are from *The Faith of the Early Fathers, Volume 1*, selected and translated by William A. Jurgens, Collegeville, Minnesota: The Liturgical Press, 1979; and, therefore, extracts from Volume II will be cited as such and then those from Volume III.

being. In other words, Christ was embryonically formed from the earliest stage of human existence and grew to term like any other human being.

St. Cyril of Jerusalem, in his "Catechetical Lectures", said: 'Neither did he pass through the Virgin as through a channel ... , but was truly made flesh of her, and was truly nourished with her milk ... , and did truly eat as we eat, and truly did drink as we drink' (4, 9). Thus, to the extent that it was understood, St. Cyril expressed the recognition that Christ 'was truly made flesh of her'; and, therefore, that Christ was truly carried and nourished by the Virgin Mary, both within the womb and subsequently. The comprehensive significance of this for our salvation is furthermore expressed in the words: 'Jesus the King, when about to become our Physician, girded Himself around with the apron of humanity; and He healed that which was sick' ("Catechetical Lectures", 12, 1). From the point of view of conception, then, Jesus received a "healed" flesh from the Virgin Mary and not, therefore, the flesh impoverished by the lack of grace transmitted by Adam and Eve. In other words, the Virgin Mary's *Immaculate Conception* made it possible that she gave to Christ a graced ovum free from original sin.

St. Irenaeus, in his work called "Against Heresies", says: 'Therefore He passed through every age, becoming an infant for infants, sanctifying infants; a child for children, sanctifying those who are of that age, and at the same time becoming for them an example of piety, of righteousness, and of submission; a young man for youths, becoming an example for youths and sanctifying them for the Lord. So also He became an old man for old men ...'²²⁹. Again, although without specifying the early stages of human development, it is clear that St. Irenaeus understands that Christ sanctified every stage of human life. Whatever is characteristic of the stages of human life, so Christ sanctified it; and, therefore, infancy is embraced in all its human totality: 'becoming an infant for infants, sanctifying infants'.

Marius Victorinus, in his work entitled, "Against Arius", says: 'The whole man, therefore, was assumed, and having been assumed was also made free. For in him all things were universal: universal flesh, and a universal soul' (3, 3). In this rather unfamiliar language Victorinus suggests that the flesh and soul that Christ received was, in fact, the "typical" flesh and soul of a human being: of a man; and, in so doing, that Christ took them as united at conception and as uniquely expressive of the human person as indeed it is for us. Extrapolating from the idea of a 'universal flesh' and a 'universal soul' one has the impression that the human identity we have received is the human identity He has received; and, therefore, from the moment of the first instant of the mystery of the *Incarnation*, Christ has received the

---

[229] In a dialogue with the author over the dissertation in which this research was originally expressed, the Rev. Dr. R. Conrad asks if Irenaeus' claim that Christ died at 50 invalidates Irenaeus' argument (4/07/01). To which I replied: It would be different if Christ were to omit a stage of development which is foundational to human life and being, than to omit to live as long as others. In the case of the former it would pose a problem with the full humanity of Christ, whereas in the case of the latter it is a question of the transmission of grace to us (cf. *Gaudium et Spes*, 22): that the adulthood of Christ sanctifies adulthood. The dissertation is called, "Can the Relationship between Fact and Moral Norm, as Indicated in *Humanae Vitae*, be further Explained?", submitted in partial fulfilment of the MA in Catholic

whole program of the manifestation of the "Person" that is characteristic of what we receive.

St. Ambrose of Milan, in his "Letter of Ambrose to Sabinus, a Bishop", says: 'Because He came, therefore, to save and redeem the whole man, it follows that He took upon Himself the whole man, and that His humanity was perfect' (48, [al. 32], 5)[230]. Perfect, then, has the meaning of complete. Just as grace builds on nature, so the perfection which Christ received was precisely that He received His humanity as we do: as a gift from God and the woman who was His mother, namely, the Virgin Mary. St. Ambrose also says of Christ in the work called "The Mystery of the Lord's Incarnation": 'He is not one from the Father and another from the Virgin, but the same in one way from the Father and in a different way from the Virgin. Generation is not prejudicial to generation, nor flesh to divinity ... ' (5, 35). Indeed, it may also be that there is an extraordinary work of communication in the *Incarnation*: that it is precisely the infinite God who takes on the utter fragility, locality and apparent insignificance of human flesh – to show that just as the Son of God is made visible so conception is ordained to making visible the person who is conceived. Furthermore, St. Ambrose goes on to say: 'According to the condition of the body He was in the womb ...' (6, 54); and, therefore, both being conceived and carried in the womb are conditions of the body Christ experienced.

Theology (now discontinued) of the Pontifical University of Maynooth and the Maryvale Institute, 2001.

[230] This and the following texts are from *The Faith of the Early Fathers*, Vol. 2, selected and translated by William A. Jurgens, Collegeville, Minnesota: The Liturgical Press, 1979.

St. Gregory of Nazianzus wrote in a "Letter of Gregory to Cledonius the Priest, Against Apollinaris": Christ was shaped 'both divinely and humanly, divinely because without man and humanly because in accord with the law of gestation ...' (101). In Christ being shaped 'humanly ... in accord with the law of gestation' there is a wonderful summary of the hidden 'law of gestation'. Whether it was evident through miscarriage, premature birth or timely delivery, there was more than an intuition of the progressive manifestation of the person – albeit pregnancy itself demonstrated this externally through the gradual changes in the size and shape of the mother's womb. More comprehensively, St. Gregory says: 'That which was not assumed has not been healed; but that which is united to God, the same is saved' (101). Therefore, St. Gregory makes vividly clear that the embryonic Christ-child is united to God; indeed, in terms of the *Incarnation* - the embryonic Christ-child manifests the wholly good assumption of the processes of generation. Thus we are invited to ponder the absolutely amazing vulnerability of the Christ-child being conceived and, as it were, showing forth the deliberate expression of a fact integral to human personhood: that we are invisibly relational from the beginning and that we gradually manifest this more and more fully throughout life – even to the point of helping us to realize that salvation is ordered to the Church just as a child is "conceived-into" the human relationships of the family.

St. Gregory of Nyssa, in his "Refutation of the Views of Apollinaris", says: The 'Godhead ... is prepared to raise up with Itself that which has fallen in accord with the law of human nature, so that while each part continues to exhibit its natural qualities, It heals the nature of bodies by the body, and the nature of souls by the soul' (55: *Jaeger*, pp. 225-226). Raising up that which 'has fallen in accord with the law of nature, so that each part continues to exhibit its natural qualities' really puts me in mind of the enduring good of human nature that God had created; and, therefore, the human being from conception: conceived as it were in relationship to Christ (cf. *Gaudium et Spes*, 22).

In St. Augustine of Hippo's, "Christian Combat", he says: 'Our Lord Jesus Christ ... who came to liberate mankind, in which both males and females are destined to salvation, was not averse to males, for He took the form of a male, nor to females, for of a female He was born' (22, 24)[231]. St. Augustine helps us to see that human personhood is sexed and that the sex of the person is an integral expression of created personhood mirroring, however remotely, the "difference" between the three persons in One God. At the same time, however, as there are generic differences between men and women, nevertheless each man and each woman is a "singular" event.

St. Cyril of Alexandria, in his "Against the Blasphemies of Nestorius", says the following: 'For if He had not been born like us according to the flesh, if He had not communed on an equal basis in what pertains to us, He would not have absolved the nature of man from the crimes contracted in Adam' (1,1). In other words, 'if He had not been born like us' refers to all that accords with nature and expresses what belongs to and shows forth that nature; indeed, although slow and difficult as it is to perceive, it is evident that there is an original nature to human life to which salvation responds as to that which needs healing.

---

[231] This and the final selection of texts are from *The Faith of the Early Fathers*, Vol 3. Selected and translated by William A. Jurgens, Collegeville, Minnesota: The Liturgical Press, 1979.

St. Cyril of Alexandria, in "Against those who do not wish to Confess that the Holy Virgin is the Mother of God", said that Jesus 'came forth from her a man in all that could be externally discerned, while interiorly He was true God' (4). In other words, St. Cyril acknowledges the manhood of Christ to be formed through the motherhood of Mary, just as any child is formed through the relational unfolding of pregnancy.

St. John Damascene, in "The Source of Knowledge", says: 'For the Holy Virgin did not bear mere man but true God ... not passing through her as through a channel, but *homoousios* with us, having taken flesh from her, though subsisting in Himself' (3, 3, 12). Again, without necessarily holding all that we hold in terms of modern embryology and yet not necessarily objecting to what has been learnt of the truth of 'having taken flesh from her', St. John observes that Mary was a true mother; and, indeed, the thought arises that what constitutes the bodily expression of human being is 'from her': that the ovum "determines" as it were the bodily substance of man more, in a sense, than the sperm which completes and animates it. In other words, while the Holy Spirit brings about the *Incarnation* of the Son of God, the interiority of His human identity is as intimately internal as the very conception of His being entailed transcending the necessity of a sperm and yet bringing about an integral humanity: one in body and soul. Ordinarily, then, God creates and ensouls the human body in the inseparably relational moment that sperm and ovum unite and husband and wife become parents of their child; however, in terms of the *Incarnation*, the Holy Spirit expresses the relationship to God the Father in the moment of animating the flesh of the ovum of Mary, bringing about an incomparably ontological completion of the human flesh of Christ.

St. Fulgence of Ruspe, in the "Letter of Fulgence and Fourteen other African Bishops Exiled in Sardinia, to various of their Brethren", says that 'If the Word of God had become flesh in the Virgin in such a way that He had not been of her ... then there would have been no sacrament of a Mediator ... for Christ the Son of God would not have united unconfusedly in Himself the full truth of the human and divine substances' (17, 5). In terms, then, of uniting 'unconfusedly in Himself the full truth of the human and divine substances' it is possible to argue that just as the Son of God is uninterruptedly from the Father, just as light is from light, so the *Incarnation* was an uninterruptedly first instant of Jesus Christ becoming man from the flesh of the Virgin Mary; and, therefore, if this was 'the full truth of the human and divine substances' then it follows that human existence is given to the rest of the human race from the first moment of each person's creation which, in general, is from the first instant of fertilization. St. Fulgence goes on to say: 'God ... was made man to this end, that whatever He had created sound in man, this same creation God might make sound again, assuming it wholly into Himself' (17, 11). In other words, even in view of the different nature of the virginal conception of Christ echoing, in a way, the original conception of Adam and Eve from nothing and the spousal conception of human beings, there remains the fundamental relationship of the immediate creation and ensoulment of each person at conception.

St. Gregory I, says in the "Letter of Pope Gregory I to Bishop Quirius and other Catholic Bishops of Georgia (Asiatic Iberia)": 'just as soon as the Word came into the womb, just then was the Word, the power of His own nature being preserved, made flesh' (11, 52 [*al.* 67]). In other words in terms of the "moment" of the incarnation, as it were, in so far as it was understood, it was understood to be identical to the "moment" of human conception; and, therefore, just as the 'power' of the 'Word came into the womb' and Christ was conceived so the 'power' of the man's sperm begets the beginning of the life of the child in animating the woman's egg.

In his "Moral Teachings Drawn from Job", St. Gregory I also says, speaking of the incarnation: 'in accord with the realities of both natures, the same Virgin would be both handmaid of the Lord and His Mother also ...' (18, 52, 85). In other words, just as the flesh of Christ is true flesh so the motherhood of Mary is a true Motherhood. By implication, then, the reality of the relationship of parents to child, of the moment in which, inseparably, parents and child come to exist, so this moment expresses the inseparability of the parent and child relationship from the moment the child comes to exist.

St. Leo I says, with respect to Christ, in his "Sermons": 'the nature of God and of man were so completely joined in him that the unity thereof could not be impaired by punishment nor disrupted by death. For each substance remained with its own properties ...' (68, 1). Thus it becomes clear, then, that just as parents are forever parents from the moment of the beginning of their child, so the union in Jesus Christ of 'the nature of God and of man' once begun, is for eternity: expressing the insoluble, "parental" love of God for man in the *Incarnation* and *Paschal Mystery* of Jesus Christ.

Leporius says in his "Document of Amendment": 'And thus, from the time when He took flesh, we say that all that was of God passed into the Man, and all that was of man

Conception: An Icon of the Beginning

came into God ...' (3). Salvation, then, beginning with the *Incarnation* and its preparation from the beginning brings man incomparably close to God in the entirety of his being; and, ontologically, founds the possibility of eternal life passing from God Himself to man, male and female, in view of the union of God and man in Jesus Christ. Just, then, as conception brings about a new human person, so conception "mirrors" the conceiving of eternal life springing from the mystery of our incorporation into Christ.

St. Vincent of Lerins (who died before 450[232]) writes in "The Notebooks" that Christ has 'Full humanity ... since, while He has both soul and flesh, it is true flesh, ours, from His mother, and a soul endowed with intelligence, possessing mind and reason' (13, 19). Therefore, just as soul and body are united in Christ, so the whole 'Man is united to God ... in the virginal conception itself' (13, 19). In other words, just as from the beginning of conception itself both soul and body are inseparably expressive of each other, so the union of God and man proceeds from the first instant of the *Incarnation* and permeates the whole relationship between Christ and the human race which follows on it (cf. *Gaudium et Spes*, 22).

St. John Damascene (c. 676 - 749[233]), in an extract from Chapter One of *The Statement of Faith*, says: 'It was you, Lord, who drew me forth from my father's loins [and] ... you [who] formed me in my mother's womb'[234]. On the one

---

[232] St. Vincent of Lérins' date of death is taken from: http://www.newadvent.org/cathen/15439b.htm.

[233] Dates from the website: https://www.franciscanmedia.org/saint-john-damascene/.

[234] I have taken this slightly adapted extract from "The Office of Readings", p. 13* from *The Divine Office*, London: Collins etc., 1974.

hand, then, he clearly identifies the triple cause of his conception to be his father, mother and God; whereby it was God 'who drew me forth from my father's loins' and it was God who 'formed me in my mother's womb'. In other words, there is an impression of the work of God being in, as it were, the transmission of life from his father and its welcoming reception by his mother. This account implies that both the transmission of life through the active nature of the sperm and the reception of that "transmitted life" in the moment of its active reception by the ovum is wholly and entirely a work of God which, nevertheless, draws upon the complementary contributions of father and mother: each contribution of which is already a work of God; and, therefore, there is an activation of the ovum which, in the moment of its activation, ceases to be the work of an ovum's reception of a sperm and "is" the first instant of the coming-to-be of the child[235].

A Critically Rounded Account of the Conceptions of Christ, Mary and Each of Us: Part XII of XII

In this final section of chapter two there is a relatively brief but slightly more wide ranging reflection on the influence of the Fathers and Mother(s) of the Church on our understanding of conception; indeed, the reason for using the possible plural of mother(s) is that while Mary is pre-eminently the Mother of the Church, just as there are many Fathers of the Church so there are many Mothers, notably

---

[235] For a fuller account of this argument, see Chapter 12, pp. 320-233, of Etheredge's, *Scripture: A Unique Word*.

Conception: An Icon of the Beginning

the biblical mothers[236] and many others[237], including a modern Mother, Edith Stein.

Jesus Christ and the Fathers

In terms of Tradition, St. Thomas Aquinas advances an argument for the immediate ensoulment of Christ that is relevant to our present discussion. St. Thomas says: 'The gospel account implies ... [Christ had a human mind] when it talks of his wonder; the incarnation's purpose requires it, since it is through the mind that man sins and receives grace; and the truth of the incarnation demands it, since if Christ took a mindless soul, he would have taken on animal, not human, flesh'[238]. Further on St. Thomas says that 'conception of the body [does not precede] ... animation by a human soul ... in Christ'[239]. In other words, even if St. Thomas would not use this terminology, he thought that

---

[236] Notably Eve (Gn 3: 20), Sarai (Gn 11: 29-31), later called Sarah (Gn 17: 15), Hagar (Gn 16: 1-16), Rachel (Gn 29), Deborah (Judges 4 etc.), Ruth and Naomi, Hannah (1 Sam 1: 2 etc.), Judith, Esther, the martyred mother of seven martyred sons (2 Macc 7: 1-41) and many others.

[237] Notably the canonized women, particularly Saints Catherine of Siena (b. 1347), Teresa of Avila (b. 1515), Therese of Lisieux (b. 1873) and Mother Teresa of Calcutta (b. 1910) and many others.

[238] *Summa Theologiae*, Methuen, Pt III, Qu 5, art 4, p. 483.

[239] *Summa Theologiae*, Methuen, Pt III, Qu 5, art 5, p. 484. The burden of this adapted quotation from St. Thomas is to exclude his contrast between the conception of Christ and his view that in our case 'conception of the body precedes animation by a human soul' as this is a part of the tradition which is, in my view, to be discarded (cf. also the rejection of it by St. Maximus the Confessor [to be discussed subsequently]); and, therefore, the point is to emphasize that St. Thomas held the *Incarnation* of the Son of God to be in the moment of the conception of the whole Christ, one in body and soul.

Christ is conceived one in body and soul from the first instant of fertilization. The same argument, then, can be applied to Mary: that if Mary was not ensouled in the same instant as being conceived "in the flesh" then grace could not embrace her entire being[240], as the presence of grace depends on the presence of the soul; and, therefore, Mary must have been conceived, one in body and soul, from the first instant of fertilization: the same instant her human nature was graced. What can be established, then, about the first instant of Mary's existence, for all the difference of the presence of grace in her, is a reality common to each and every child of Adam and Eve.

More widely, the Tradition of the Church advances a recognition of the general principle that what is not assumed is not redeemed; and, while many more could be cited, the following two Fathers of the Church will be taken as "typical" although each one has his own nuanced way of expressing an insight. St. Gregory of Nazianzus wrote: 'That which was not assumed has not been healed; but that which is united to God, the same is saved[241]'. St. Gregory's expression is almost reformulated in *Gaudium et Spes*, which says of Christ: 'by his incarnation, he, the Son of God, has in a certain way united himself with each man' (22). Thus we are made aware that if 'by his incarnation ... [Christ] has in a certain way united himself with each man', then it follows that this union is not dependent on each man but on God; and, if it is

---

[240] It is worth mentioning, too, that there is another aspect of the tradition that is rejected, namely, that Christ received fallen flesh from Mary; St. Thomas, then, held that since Christ 'took his nature from already sin-laden material [it] makes his purity and freedom from sin all the more marvellous' (*Summa Theologiae*, Methuen, Pt III, Qu 4, art 6, p. 483).

[241] Letter of Gregory to Cledonius the Priest, Against Apollinaris (101), quoted in *The Faith of the Early Fathers*, Vol. 2,

Conception: An Icon of the Beginning

dependent on God, then just as God acts in the first instant of the incarnation then so could being 'united' to Christ be from the first instant of the conception of each one of us. The second Father to quote is St. Irenaeus, who said: Christ 'passed through every age, becoming an infant for infants, sanctifying infants ...'[242]. In other words, if Christ was conceived from the first instant of conception, the same instant that Mary and each one of us was conceived, then it follows that Christ has sanctified each stage of life from the first instant of human life onwards.

Mary and the Fathers

In *Lumen Gentium*, from the same Council of the Church as *Gaudium et Spes*, there is a specific sense in which reflection on Mary, the Mother of the Lord, has come into increasing prominence and, as such, is almost beginning to constitute the basis of a *Marian anthropology of mankind*. What is meant by this? On the one hand the Church says of Mary: 'Mary, in a way, unites in her person and re-echoes the most important doctrines of the faith' (*Lumen Gentium*, 65); and, on the other hand, the Church says of Mary that she is 'Enriched from the first instant of her conception with the splendor of an entirely unique holiness' (*Lumen Gentium*, 56[243]). In other words Mary "expresses" the human person before God in such a way that what is true of

---

passages selected and translated by William A. Jurgens, Collegeville, Minnesota: The Liturgical Press, 1979, p. 41.

[242] Against Heresies (2, 22, 4), quoted in *The Faith of the Early Fathers*, Vol. 1, passages selected and translated by William A. Jurgens, Collegeville, Minnesota: The Liturgical Press, 1970, p. 87.

[243] It is not possible to go into it here, but the dogma of the *Immaculate Conception*, promulgated in 1854 by Pius IX in

Mary's salvation, and all it implies, is true for each one of us. Therefore, if Mary is enriched from the 'first instant of her conception', then that first instant is the first instant that we all come to exist as personal beings.

The conception of each one of us and the Fathers, the Eastern Orthodox and the Mother(s) of the Church

In St. Thomas Aquinas' discussion on the origin of Adam and Eve there is a wonderful grasp of the value of the argument for the creation of the whole person, one in body and soul, from the very beginning; St. Thomas says: 'Adam's body was formed by God immediately, there being no preceding human body that could generate a body of like species to itself'[244]. St.Thomas then goes on to explain further when he says: 'Some have thought that man's body was formed first in priority of time, and that afterwards the soul was infused into the formed body. But it is inconsistent with the perfection of the production of things, that God should have made either the body without the soul, or the soul without the body, since each is a part of human nature. This is especially unfitting as regards the body, for the body depends on the soul, and not the soul on the body'[245]. What is interesting, however, is that St. Thomas does not deploy this same argument, that it is consistent 'with the perfection of the production of things' to create man, one in soul and body, with each act of the transmission of life. In other

---

Ineffabilis Deus, drew upon the teaching of the Fathers of the Church in coming to this conclusion.

[244] St. Thomas Aquinas, *Summa Theologiae*, I, 91, 2; indeed, St. Thomas saw a 'perfection of the production of things' in the creation of Adam (I, 91, 4, Reply Obj. 3, http://www.newadvent.org/summa/1091.htm).

[245] St. Thomas Aquinas, *Summa Theologiae*, I, 92, 4, reply to objection 3: http://www.newadvent.org/summa/1091.htm.

words, owing to the embryological account which St. Thomas drew from Aristotle, namely of a being inadequately developed to receive a soul at conception, he accepted the threefold theory that aimed at human animation: a plant soul; followed by an animal soul; and then finally a rational soul which inherited and replaced the previous plant and animal souls. It is clear, then, as an adequate embryological account of early development shows, the human embryo is equipped from the first instant of fertilization for the reception of the human soul; indeed, to paraphrase St. Thomas, there is no human body without a rational soul animating it.

Thus the Tradition does not entail an unqualified acceptance of everything recorded in the course of Christian history; and, therefore, there has been a steady rejection of St. Thomas Aquinas' theory of delayed ensoulment and a progressive assimilation of modern embryological findings[246]. Nevertheless, St. Thomas embraced such a comprehensive account of Christian and philosophical thought that it is worth considering his understanding of the implication of the delayed ensoulment of a human being; he said: 'foetuses are animal before they are human ... [but] nature, in producing the animal foetus, is aiming at producing a man'[247]. In other words, even with the antiquated biology upon which he is drawing, St. Thomas recognizes that the intention of nature, as it were, is different when it comes to considering the reproduction of an ape and the procreation of a human being. The production of an

---

[246] In Chapter 5, Part II, there is a wonderful exposition of the modern understanding of the conception of human being from the first instant of fertilization (from Professors Aznar and Tudela); and, in principle, the recognition that the sophistication of this moment is of the order that makes it possible to accept an ensouling spiritual life from the first instant of fertilization.

[247] *Summa Theologiae*, Methuen, Pt I, Qu 85, art 4, p. 136.

animated kind of life, such as an ape, is the direct object of what nature produces in the process of an ape reproducing an ape. But the nature of the procreation of a human being entails that 'nature, in producing the animal foetus, is aiming at producing a man'. Thus in the case of procreation, nature is already "orientated", as it were, to 'producing a man'[248]; and, as such, the whole process of what is involved is aimed at a distinctly rational being. Even in St. Thomas' account, then, of the human conception of a child, he understood the whole process to entail a radical orientation to human being; and, by implication, that the radical orientation to human being *entailed differences that were unique to the conception of a person*. Even so, though, it is clear from this book as a whole that the Catholic Church in particular and philosophical thought more generally is still "coming to terms" with the problem of how to account for the radical unity of man, one in soul and body (*Gaudium et Spes*, 14), from conception.

Tradition as a whole, however, is wider, earlier and capable of enriching St. Thomas' understanding of human conception; and, therefore, there are Fathers of the Church who advanced a holistic argument for the conception of each one of us, as it were, in the light of the conception of Christ. Thus Fr. John Saward, drawing on St. Maximus the Confessor, says: 'Apart from the saving novelty of its virginal manner, the conception of Christ is in all respects like ours'[249]; indeed, just as St. Thomas rejected the possibility of

---

[248] Although it has been adapted and developed since, the research for this point was first compiled in a dissertation in partial fulfilment of an MA in Catholic Theology at the Maryvale Institute, entitled: "Can the Relationshps between Fact and Moral Norm, as Indicated in *Humanae Vitae*, be further Explained?", 2001, pp. 70-71. The MA in Catholic Theology is now discontinued.

[249] *Redeemer in the Womb*, Ignatius Press: San Francisco, 1993, p. 12, but see also pp. 8-13.

Conception: An Icon of the Beginning

Christ's divinity being united to an animal type of flesh, so again drawing on St. Maximus, Fr. Saward says that 'if the embryo immediately after fertilization is endowed with only a vegetative soul, then men father plants, not men. But in fact the act of fertilization establishes a human-to-human relationship between father and child; *I* am conceived by my father'[250].

In a document summarizing "An Orthodox View of Abortion", there are numerous citations of the Fathers of the Church and, at the same time, a clearly widespread agreement on the validity and truth of this scholarship amongst the present members of the Church: 'Modern science has borne out the prescient wisdom of the Holy Fathers of the Church, that life begins at conception ... [and] at no other arbitrary or scholastically derived juncture'[251]. Indeed, it could be argued, there is still to resound in the Church the full voice of both lungs of the Church[252] breathing new life into the recognition of each human conception from the first instant of fertilization.

At present, however, it could be said that the influence of the Fathers of the Church and the truth in Tradition is still to make it fullness "heard" in the teaching of the Church on human conception; nevertheless, there is a kind of grace of simplicity about the work of the Fathers which "echoes", as it were, between the following three women. Eve simply says: 'I have gotten a man with the help of God' (Gn 1: 4), where Eve clearly recognizes the fullness of the life she has

---

[250] *Redeemer in the Womb*, p. 10, drawing on the Ambigua 2, 42; 1337B-1340B.

[251] "The *Amicus Curiae* Submitted to the Supreme Court [of America], No. 88-605, 1989", signed by many but in particular: James George Jatras and Paul Farley: http://orthodoxkansas.org/Orthodox_Amicus_Curiae_brief.html

[252] St. John Paul II, *Ut Unum Sint*, 54: 'the Church must breathe with her two lungs'.

conceived as being a man. Mary is sanctified from the first instant of being begotten by the action of God and her parents. Edith Stein, in her philosophy, recognizes the need to recover the sense of the "whole" that each existence expresses.

There is a tendency, then, towards consensus between the tradition concerning the conception of Christ's humanity being from the first instant of fertilization and St. Maximus the Confessor's view that so is ours: 'Apart from the saving novelty of its virginal manner, the conception of Christ is in all respects like ours'[253]. It is this discriminating progress through the variety of arguments in the Tradition that could, indeed, be said to be a part of what the modern Fathers of the Church wrote about in the *Second Vatican Council* when they said: 'The Tradition that comes from the apostles makes progress in the Church, with the help of the Holy Spirit' (*Dei Verbum*, 8). Just, then, as we have glimpsed that the dogma of the *Immaculate Conception* emerged out of disparate views on whether or not Mary was free from original sin, so it is possible that the Holy Spirit will bring us to recognize the "logical necessity" of the following reality: that if Mary is conceived from the first instant of fertilization then so are we. Furthermore, then, just as Christ is conceived from the first instant of fertilization, so we are conceived-in-relation to Him in that same moment (cf. *Gaudium et Spes*, 22); and just as Mary received the fullness of grace from her conception, so we are as it were "in potentia" to the reception of the grace of baptism from the first moment of our conception.

---

[253] *Redeemer in the Womb*, Ignatius Press: San Francisco, 1993, p. 12, but see also pp. 8-13.

Conception: An Icon of the Beginning

Nevertheless, it is still necessary to find a way forward, beginning with the teaching of the Church on conception as it is currently developing[254].

---

[254] I am happy to acknowledge here the stimulus to a final version of Parts XI and and XII of this chapter owing to the proof-reading of these sections by Dr. Anthony Williams.

CHAPTER THREE:
FOREWORD AND BIOGRAPHY

Fr. Michael Baggot, LC

Francis Etheredge

Biography[255]

Fr. Michael Baggot was received into the Catholic Church on the Easter Vigil of 2003, after a high school conversion from agnosticism. He then graduated *summa cum laude* from Christendom College with a B.A. in Philosophy, before working in Rome as a Resident Director for the school's study abroad program. In 2013, he received a Licentiate in Philosophy *summa cum laude* from the *Pontifical Athenaeum Regina Apostolorum* in Rome. In 2017, he received a Baccalaureate in Sacred Theology *summa cum laude* from the same institution.

Prior to entering the seminary, Baggot reported on prominent bioethical issues as a writer for the Toronto-based LifeSiteNews organization. He spent his initial period of seminary formation near Cologne, Germany. He later worked as an assistant for the *Curso de Hispanidad* in Mexico City and as a teacher at Pinecrest Academy in Atlanta, Georgia, before returning to Rome for further studies. He has worked as the Correspondent of the UNESCO Chair in Bioethics and Human Rights since 2011, during which time he has penned articles for the organization's website and for the scholarly journal *Studia Bioethica*. In 2015, he began contributing to the journal of religion and public life *First Things*. In 2016, he began teaching in the Faculty of Philosophy at the Pontifical University *Regina Apostolorum*. In 2016-2017, he also acted as a tutor of the *Sinderesi* program that aids university students in the discernment of contemporary social issues.

He is currently an Adjunct Professor of Theology at Christendom College, Assistant Professor of Bioethics at *Regina Apostolorum*, and the Rome Director of the Catholic Worldview Fellowship program for university students. In

---

[255] Photograph taken by Br. Robert Antonio, LC.

addition to prayer and study, he enjoys singing in the choir, playing basketball, and giving tours of the Eternal City.

Foreword to Chapter 3: What does the Church say "Today" about the Moment of our Beginning?

In his farewell discourse to His disciples, Jesus promises to send them the Spirit of truth who will lead them to all truth (John 16:13). They will therefore not be orphans left to go astray in the winds of false doctrines (John 14:18; Ephesians 4:14). St. Irenaeus noted that early Christians like Clement of Rome had the preaching of the apostles ringing in their ears.[256] Thanks to the apostolic succession to which St. Irenaeus so often appealed, contemporary Christians can still hear the same Gospel teaching ringing in their own ears nearly 2000 years later. The Spirit of truth has guided and protected Christ's Church so that she faithfully speaks the unchanging words of her Master in the ever-changing today of our own technocratic society. In the chapter that follows, Francis Etheredge ably explains how the Church has exercised her mission these past decades regarding the fundamental question of human origins. As the post-biotech revolution world daily demonstrates, errors regarding human origins have deadly consequences in the fields of IVF mass embryo production and destruction, associated embryonic stem cell research, and permissive abortion legislation. Etheredge's compilation and analysis of the Magisterium's various pronouncements reveals the Church's constant preoccupation with protecting human dignity and her ongoing solicitude for highlighting the ethical implications of each new technological development. His work should be of interest to Catholics and non-Catholics alike since he repeatedly notes both the theological and the

---

[256] Cf. Ireanaeus of Lyons, *Adversus Haereses*, III, iii.

philosophical considerations of the Church texts. Etheredge helps us to read the documents with the two eyes of faith and reason in the one unified vision in which they were written.

The author thus notes the Magisterium's reluctance to pronounce definitively on the philosophical question of human ensoulment without neglecting the value of embryology in helping us come to a compelling philosophical conclusion regarding the uniquely important moment of fertilization in a person's beginning and development. While the identification of personhood remains an ongoing philosophical debate, there is widespread agreement in embryology regarding conception as the first moment of a genetically distinct human individual who, under the proper conditions, will develop into a morula, blastocyst, fetus, baby, adolescent, and adult. Given our knowledge of biology, the question raised in *Donum Vitae* arises, how could a human individual not be a person? The strong probability of the personhood of the embryo provides grounds for prudently refraining from acts that at least *might* cause the murder of innocent people. As Etheredge briefly discusses, the subtlest objection to the human individuality of the embryo comes from those who cite monozygotic twinning as evidence that the embryo is not indivisible and therefore not an individual. However, it is important to note that individuality simply requires one to be undivided, not necessarily indivisible. In other words, the embryo is undivided (a unified individual), even if he is capable of division. Such division can be explained as a sort of asexual reproduction in which the second individual arises from the first individual akin to the budding of a hydra or the fragmentation of an incised blackworm. All too many thinkers follow philosopher Norman Ford's landmark 1988 book *When Did I Begin? Conception of the Human Individual in History, Philosophy and Science* in questioning the need to extend protection of innocent life to the first moments of conception.[257] Moreover, many other bioethicists employ a variation of the argument against the individuality of the fertilized egg as grounds for the concept of a "pre-embryo" that can be destroyed for personal or medical purposes. In contrast, the Church has resisted an arbitrary exclusion of some human beings from the equal care and protection. As Pope St. John Paul II noted in his 1989 address to the University of Uppsala quoted in the chapter: "The dignity of the person can be protected only if the person is considered as inviolable from the moment of conception until natural death." Having witnessed and survived two inhuman totalitarian regimes as a young man, the Polish pontiff was profoundly familiar with the dangers implicit in categorizing some members of the human population inferior to others. Academic debates about personhood have influence that extends far beyond the academy into the legislation that protects or threatens the wellbeing of the most vulnerable.

The need for an Adequate Anthropology

The myriad bioethical dilemmas that plague the world flow from the inadequate anthropology to which Pope St. John Paul II devoted much of his sizable intellectual acumen to correcting. In an age in which transhumanists dream of downloading personalities to other bodies or to computer networks, the following chapter does well to remind us of our inescapably bodily dimension as incarnate spirits. We are neither beasts nor angels but enjoy the unique privilege of communicating the invisible and spiritual through the visible and material. Our true selves are not locked away in a

---

[257] Cf. Anthony Fisher, *Catholic Bioethics for a New Millennium*, Cambridge University Press, Cambridge 2012, 101-130 for an extended critique of Ford's work.

machine awaiting an upgrade. Nor are our bodily acts indifferent to the shaping of our interior character. The self-gift that all lovers seek to make to their beloved presupposes a self-possession by which the giver gives freely and not according to the mere dictates of blind passion. Chastity does not therefore suppress vital energy but rather integrates the diversity of our two inseparable dimensions so that we can love more fully and promptly according our state in life and our relationship with the other.

Parents "enter into a unique participation in the creative power of the Lord of life and the providential care of the Lord of all history"

Etheredge also helps us to recall the noble ministry of those called to cooperate with the Creator in the production of a new and unrepeatable human being called to share in the divine life of his Creator in this world and forever in the next. The chapter's synthesis of the spirituality of the married state thus offers a timely antidote to the widespread disparagement of children as obstacles to success. In many developed nations, ambitious young adults are pressured to postpone their longing for marital bliss for the sake of degrees, career advancement, or simply the manifold pleasures promised the autonomous bachelor or bachelorette. In the peak years of female fertility many women suffer the hormonal manipulation of oral contraceptives and the physical and emotion risks of so-called "safe sex." When they finally reach the career stability that allows them to consider settling down to raise children, they sadly find that the combined effects of age, hormonal contraceptives, and possible sexually transmitted diseases have rendered their interest in childbirth a desire difficult if not impossible to realize. We will continue to bemoan declining demographics and broken hearts unless we succeed in living and effectively educating those under our care in the liberating truth of marital spirituality. Without hiding the challenges of self-sacrifice entailed in Gospel authenticity, our testimonies and teachings should be winsome and never burdensome. The same God who designed our human sexuality as a reflection of His own eternal trinitarian mutual self-donation will no doubt continue to pour out the gift of divine life needed to imitate so worthy a model in the loving mutual self-donation of our family life.

To collaborate in the conception of a new human being and to then help form that new being's talents is to enter into a unique participation in the creative power of the Lord of life and the providential care of the Lord of all history. Here, we do well to recall C.S. Lewis's insight in his 1942 sermon "The Weight of Glory" that while even the greatest nations, cultures, and civilizations will pass away, the human being lives on indefinitely.[258] The parent's irreplaceable role in generating new life allows them to contribute new citizens to the heavenly kingdom. Without belittling the worth and importance of pursuing a meaningful profession outside the home, parents should never fall for the lie that would define their societal value only according to such professional accomplishments. The daily diapers, soccer practices, heart-to-heart talks on cultivating the virtues lose none of their transcendent import for not occupying newspaper headlines. We adults of today are deeply affected by how seriously or lightly the adults of yesterday treated the mystery of conception that marked the fragile but real beginning of our human adventures. Much of children's future depends upon who we stand before and receive the mystery of their beginnings.

---

[258] Cf. C.S. Lewis, *The Weight of Glory and Other Addresses*, HarperCollins, New York 2015, 25-46.

God is the ultimate mystery, whose glory exceeds our finite understanding. So too does the reflection of the Creator in the procreative dimension of the conjugal act exceed our full comprehension. The prominence of various technologies of medically assisted reproduction have fooled us into thinking that we have attained full mastery over the gift of human life itself. Rather, as parents quickly learn, children are nothing if not surprising. Parents can and should do all in their power to provide their children with quality education, reliable health care, wholesome friendships, and any other means to assist their child's flourishing. Yet, no matter how well the parents manage to orchestrate the surroundings of their child's growth, these offspring will develop talents, virtues, and vices that cannot be reduced to the mere logical outgrowth of their generators' planning. Parents thus do well to learn from the very beginning of their relationship to receive the gift of new human life as a precious gift of which they have been made stewards and never absolute masters. If parents think themselves the mere producers of a new biological reality, they will be constantly tempted to exercise their absolute dominion over the product of their sexual acts. If instead they embrace their vocation as stewards, they will exercise their parental roles with the utmost responsibility to the One who has commissioned them while respecting the freedom of the offspring likewise accountable to the Lord for the use or abuse of the unique talents given.

"The Church's inexhaustibly rich patrimony of teaching on God's plan for marriage and the family"

It is fitting that Etheredge should offer us a helpful panorama of the Church's contemporary teaching on the beginning of human life as institutions around the world gather to reflect upon the fiftieth anniversary of Pope St. Paul VI's document devoted to the transmission of human life, *Humanae Vitae*. While some thinkers sadly squander their intellectual energies in revisionist efforts that effectively empty the document of its prophetic force, Etheredge chooses the wiser and more fruitful path of explaining the beauty of the document's call for spousal love within the larger context of the Church's inexhaustibly rich patrimony of teaching on God's plan for marriage and the family. In a sad irony that the sage Pope himself foresaw, the so-called sexual revolution has ended not in an exaltation of sexual relations but rather in their banalization and at times even their abandonment. What began as a liberation of sexual experimentation in the fields of Haight-Ashbury or Woodstock has proven a slavery to passions. Once separated from its proper context in the permanent marriage covenant of total mutual self-giving, the sexual act becomes but one of many optional means of personal gratification. Technological developments have facilitated our capacity for such pleasure apart from the sexual act in the explosive growth of the online pornography industry and have enabled us to forego the sexual act in favor of a putatively more efficient means of obtaining its product through the burgeoning IVF industry. The problem is not with the technology but with the deformation of those who misuse such technology. Those looking to form their minds and hearts according to God's plan for human happiness will benefit greatly from reading through the chapter that follows.

Francis Etheredge

"Matrix"

by

Alison Batley, USA[259]

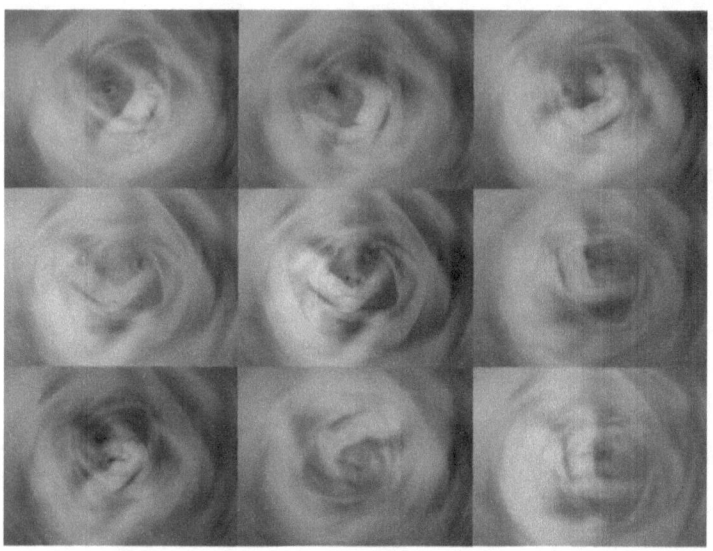

Artist's Statement

'This digital painting entitled Matrix is a celebration of life in full bloom. Each of the nine brilliantly colored images represents a unique person, developing within the protection of the mother's womb. Within this maternal matrix, the vulnerability of each child must be safeguarded to ensure the full blossoming of his or her potential. If this gestational

---

[259] Unesco Chair in Bioethics and Human Rights Art Competition: Reproduced with the Permission of the Director from the 1st Global Art Competition of the Bioethics in Art Collection. This image, in its own way, suggests "coming to see" the presence of the child from conception.

period is approached, with due respect, by parents, doctors, scientists, lawmakers and others, each individual will grow in the security of being treated with justice and human dignity.

Every child should have the opportunity and freedom to flourish within his or her own cultural heritage. Celebration of diversity is illustrated in the vivacious colors amalgamated into the whole by the common good of the structural matrix. At the center of each of the buds, a child's face appears, foreshadowing of the future emergence of this life. Each portrait reveals the body and soul of nine diverse children from various ethnic backgrounds. At conception, the celebration of life has begun and the anticipation of his or her entrance nine months later is awaited with great expectation!'

CHAPTER THREE: WHAT DOES THE CHURCH TEACH "TODAY" ABOUT THE MOMENT OF OUR BEGINNING?

General Introduction to Chapter 3: "Today". It is almost as if part of the work of the Church is clarifying the state of the question concerning the beginning of each one of us. Thus it is clear that there is not, at present, a definitive philosophical answer to the question of when ensoulment occurs: of when God creates the soul in union with the body and thus begets the beginning of human personhood.

It is, however, ingenuous to suppose that soul and body are distinct in the way that body and clothes are distinct. In other words, the bodily human person exists prior to being clothed; and, therefore, the relationship of body to clothes is not one whereby body and clothes are inescapably and inseparably one. One person can choose a variety of clothes and is still the same person. The language, then, of body and soul, can give a false impression of "parts" that are brought together. Nevertheless, this language of "body" and "soul" has a certain usefulness if it is not misunderstood. It is necessary to remember, though, that there is no human bodily life if there is no human soul; human soul and human body are so ordered to one another that one cannot exist except in relationship to the other. Thus death cannot be a complete rupture but is, nevertheless, a real "withdrawal" from the manifestation of life expressed bodily. The human body, then, having come into existence insolubly, is yet subject to the law of sin and death; and, at the same time, "lives" the God-given possibility of being reclaimed in its amazingly integral unity-in-diversity in the moment of the resurrection of the body.

The Church, then, in following the path of life, has gravitated to 'conception' as the first moment of human personhood; and, even if all the difficulties have not been overcome, there is a particular authority to this position in view of her divine-human nature and mission (cf. *Lumen Gentium*, 7-8). At the same time, however, there is a growing need to recognize the threefold nature of what comes together in the dialogue of salvation; and, therefore, while drawing upon Scripture and the Magisterium it is also necessary to turn to Tradition (cf. *Dei Verbum*, 10). While recognizing, however, that this is not an uncritical endorsement of whatever is to be found present in the Tradition, it is nevertheless an integral part of what constitutes the 'one deposit of faith' (*Dei Verbum*, 10). Thus, as will see, there is a kind of "simple"[260] apprehension of the

---

[260] I am indebted to Dr. Mary Anne Urlakis who, in her correspondence with the author, has helped to clarify this point

"conception" of each human being which tends, again, to the view that human conception is from the first instant of fertilization.

Introduction to Chapter 3: Understanding "Today" in the Modern History of the Church.

The central purpose of this chapter is to review what the Church is saying "today" concerning the beginning of human life. Indeed, perhaps it is necessary to consider the verb 'saying', as this is a dynamic and developing dialogue: both drawing on the discoveries of natural truth and the discernment which derives from the mystery of the *word of God* and its fructifying effect in the Church. What is the precise beginning of each of us? The conclusion of this discussion is that *conception*, by definition, *is the integral beginning of the person,* one in body and soul; however, as we shall see, the definition of conception needs, in due course, a certain clarification. What follows, then, is an orderly account of the foundation of this position in the progress of the Church. Even restricting the discussion to relevant principles, pertinent indications as well as explicit statements, there are still numerous documents to review, in brief, beginning with the Second Vatican Council's *Lumen Gentium, Dei Verbum* and *Gaudium et Spes* and proceeding to *Dignitatis Personae*.

A Development of Doctrine: An Ongoing Work?

Whoever thinks that the Church's teaching is a "dead end" does not know the excitement of discovering an area of "ongoing development" in the dogmas and doctrines of the

---

and to show the necessity of explicitly referencing both research and appreciation of the value of the Fathers of the Church.

Catholic Church: developments open to modern science, philosophy and ecumenical collaboration. In general, 'The Tradition that comes from the apostles makes progress in the Church, with the help of the Holy Spirit. There is a growth in insight into the realities and words that are being passed on' (*Dei Verbum*, 8). One among many areas of "progress in the truth" is the 'pondering'[261] of the beginning of human personhood: of the beginning of a being-in-relationship: of the beginning of each and every child. This brief survey of what is relevant to understanding the first instant of the beginning of each child, is both about taking up what has been done and exploring its further development; and, as such, more than encourages us to see that not only is development actually taking place in the teaching of the Church but that she is beginning to come closer to the truth-speaking-reality she is investigating.

Gaudium et Spes, 1965

The 7 December, 1965, saw the publication of the *Second Vatican Council's* document, *Gaudium et Spes*. At the beginning of chapter one the Fathers of the Council ask a question that is particularly pertinent to our time: 'what is man?'[262]. The answer to this question is a balanced exposition of the single vision which nevertheless makes full use of both "eyes": a vision '*centered on man*' and '*centered on God*': a vision which finds its pre-eminent fullness in 'the divine Person of Christ, true God and true man'[263]. The

---

[261] Etheredge, "Chapter 12: Life "from" Life: Introduction", pp. 291-299 of *Scripture: A Unique Word*.

[262] *Gaudium et Spes*, 12.

[263] Pope St. John Paul II, September 2, 1988, quoted on p. 22 of *The Philosophy of Life*, compiled by Fr. Rosario Thomas (Cochiti Lake: *Pro Fratribus* Press, 1989).

basic question, then, of the nature of man cannot but take account of both his origin and his relationship to Jesus Christ.

Gaudium et Spes includes many reflections on the nature of man and gives some doctrinal indications of particular relevance to this investigation of the beginning of each of us. On the subject of *The Essential Nature of Man*, the Fathers of the Council say: 'Man, though made of body and soul, is a unity'[264]; and, as such, it is this 'uni-duality'[265] which almost encapsulates this whole inquiry. The disadvantage, however, of this expression as applied to the individual human person is that the 'duality' is not equivalent to the difference between men and women. In other words, the unity of the human person transcends the "duality" of body and soul to the point where we need to express this in a new way. We need, then, an account of the integral nature of a man, one in body and soul, and a woman, one in body and soul; and, at the same time, a profound recognition of the "identity" and "difference" in male personhood and female personhood.

Nevertheless, 'Man, though made of body and soul, is a unity', naturally raises the possibility of the *origin of this union in the first instant of conception*. The Fathers furthermore say of the soul that its existence is not a 'false

---

[264] *Gaudium et Spes*, 14.

[265] This is actually a phrase used by St. John Paul II in his *Letter to Women* as he explains the interrelationship of man and woman: the 'most natural relationship, which corresponds to the plan of God, is the "unity of the two", a relational "uni-duality", which enables each to experience their interpersonal and reciprocal relationship as a gift which enriches and which confers responsibility' (8).

imagining'[266]. It is possible, then, in the intellectual climate in which we live, to find the whole question of the existence of the soul, not only challenging in its interrelationship with the body but challenging, too, in even recognizing that the soul exists; but, of course, it may be part of the problem that the soul is so insufficiently understood, except as 'the "form" of the body' (CCC, 365), that this is indeed part of the problem of reconciling the soul's existence with the reality of human personhood.

Finally, in the opening words of the section of this document on *Human Activity: Its Fulfilment in the Paschal Mystery*, the Fathers of the Council say: 'The Word of God, through whom all things were made, became man and dwelt among men[267]: a perfect man, he entered world history, taking that history into himself and recapitulating it'[268] [269]. Is it therefore unreasonable to *see within* the idea that Christ *recapitulates world history*, that Christ *recapitulates the history of the individual*? Indeed, is Christ's recapitulation of the history of the individual, the ontological basis of His recapitulation of world history? This suggests, therefore, that *the first instant* of the *Incarnation*, while it did not involve Joseph (cf. Lk 1: 34) and expressed, in the flesh, the eternal personhood of the Son of God, was nevertheless *the conception* of Christ in the ontological unity of His human nature, one in body and soul[270]: a beginning

---

[266] *Gaudium et Spes*, 14; and cf also Pope St. John Paul II, Jan 4, 1986, quoted on page 50 of Fr. Rosario Thomas' *The Philosophy of Life*.

[267] The conciliar footnote says: cf. Jn. 1: 3 and 14.

[268] The conciliar footnote says: cf Eph. 1: 10.

[269] *Gaudium et Spes*, 38.

[270] *Summa Theologiae*, Methuen, Pt III, Qu 6, art 5, p. 484.

which could be said to *recapitulate the beginning of us all*[271].

Humanae Vitae, 1968

In 1968 Pope St. Paul VI published *Humanae Vitae* in which he develops the inheritance of *Gaudium et Spes* in the formulation of '*A total vision of man*': a vision that takes account of 'the whole man and the whole complex of his responsibilities that must be considered, not only what is natural and limited to this earth, but also what is supernatural and eternal'[272].

As regards the origin and conception of human life, St. Paul VI quotes his predecessor, in the statement: "Pope John XXIII, recalled, 'since from its first beginnings [human life] ... calls for the creative action of God'[273]. In other words, the phrase, 'from its first beginnings', could apply both to the very origin of the human race and to the conception of each individual member of the human family. The view that human life, then, 'from its first beginnings ... calls for the creative action of God', rather opens up the possibility of an almost dialogical relationship between spousal union, conception and ensoulment: almost as if the very moment of conception constitutes an irrevocable appeal to the creative action of God: an appeal as natural and irrevocable as the natural act of fertilization: an appeal that the Creator determined to exist as inseparable to the very instant of the

---

[271] On the one hand there is the challenge to respect the Church's tradition concerning the 'Person' of Christ as existing from all eternity, in that He is the Son of God; and, on the other hand, to recognize that His humanity had a concrete beginning, one in body and soul.

[272] *Humanae Vitae*, 7.

[273] St. Paul VI cites: *Mater et Magistra*, n. 194.

first moment of fertilization. Why? Precisely because the relationship to God is as integral to the very nature of human personhood as it is to the relationship of parents to child.

St. Paul VI also says that spousal love is 'above all fully *human*, a compound of sense and spirit' (9); and, as such, is again a manifestation of human personhood which returns us to the unity-in-diversity of the person being one in body and soul. Thus, in other words, the very action of human love is an inseparable expression of the unity-in-diversity of human being; indeed, just as human being is a 'compound of sense and spirit' so is the act of human love a 'compound of sense and spirit'. Thus there is an inescapable relationship, as it were, in which "being is manifest in activity"[274] in such a way that the integrity of human personhood, one in body and soul, is expressed in the integrity of the spousal act expressing a unitary act of 'sense and spirit'. At the same time, however, there is the implied "logic" of the incarnation of the soul (cf. *Familiaris Consortio*, 11) constituting the first instant of human bodily life; and, therefore, the very act of being begotten by God brings about that indivisibility of 'sense and spirit' manifest in human being and activity.

Let me Live, 1974

Pope St. Paul VI went on to authorize, in 1974, the publication of *Let Me Live: the Declaration by the Sacred Congregation of the Faith on Procured Abortion*. It is in footnote nineteen of this document that there are two points of particular relevance to this development of ideas on the beginning of each one of us. On the one hand, 'This declaration expressly leaves aside the question of the moment when the spiritual soul is infused'; and, on the other hand, the question of the moment of the infusion of the soul

---

[274] A scholastic adage.

is a 'philosophical problem ...'[275]. Therefore the following questions arise: even if the 'philosophical problem' of when the soul is united to the body is a question to which this document *does not give an answer*, does the Church nevertheless give a *theological answer to this same problem?* In other words, how clear is the distinction between *these two types of answer to the same question?* Furthermore, then, is there a parallel between the difficulty of arriving at a philosophical answer to the question of whether or not creation had a beginning[276] and the philosophical question of whether or not the soul is one with the body from conception? Just *as Revelation is an assistance in the question of the beginning of Creation*[277]*, is Revelation an assistance in answering the question concerning the beginning of the body-soul union that each human person is?*

When it comes to the beginning of each person's life, however, this document has a number of points to make. To begin with,'From the time that the ovum is fertilized, a life is begun which is neither that of the father nor of the mother, it is rather the life of a new human being with his own growth' (12). In other words, it is perfectly true that the child is an independent entity - not in virtue of being able to grow independently - but in virtue of the very fact that he or she possesses and expresses a life which, although dependent on the mother's life, is nevertheless different from her life. At the same time, though, this dependency of one life on another is a basic characteristic of each human being; and, as such, the characteristics of this dependency change but not the dependency itself: dependency is, as it were, a

---

[275] *Quaestio de abortu*, 18 November, 1974: footnote 19.
[276] Cf. Copleston, *Aquinas*, p. 138.
[277] Cf. Copleston, *Aquinas*, p. 138.

significant word about each of us - a word that speaks to both the nature of our temporal and eternal life.

Thus the very fact that the ovum, or egg, leaves the woman's ovary and travels down the fallopian tube is objective evidence of the independence of the life which, on fertilization, begins an independent existence. Independence, however, is relative to the requisite stage of human development and, more generally, to the *interdependence* which is a part of what unfolds from birth and is characteristic of general human development. The independence of the human embryo, as an existing entity, is already expressed in the activity which manifests the fact that he or she is alive: activity manifests life; and, therefore, fertilization is demonstrated in the formation of the embryonic "wall", the development of intra-embryonic processes, cell multiplication and specialization and, in due course, implantation and the formation of the placenta.

In addition, 'From the time that the ovum is fertilized', indicates that there is a process of fertilization, as it were, in the sense that there is a stage of development from the first instant of fertilization to the completion of that process and the formation of the zygote. The zygote, in this sense, is the initial state of development in which the originally separate nuclei of the egg and the sperm have now undergone the completion of the process which unites them in one nucleus. Thus, developmentally, a stage in the unfolding of the first instant of fertilization has founded further development because, after all, this is a continuous process from the first instant of fertilization until natural death[278]. At the

---

[278] It is necessary to note that even the Warnock Report recognized that there is a seamless process of development: 'there is no particular part of the developmental process that is more important than another; all are part of a continuous process' (Department of Health and Social Security [UK], *Report of the Committee of Inquiry into Human Fertilisation and Embryology*

beginning of this process there is, as it were, a first instant: modern genetic science 'has demonstrated that, from the first instant, there is established the program of what this living being will be: a man, this individual man with his characteristic aspects already well determined' (13). The 'first instant, then, of this process, is a different reality to the completion of any interim stage of development, whether it be the stage of the zygote, pre-implantation, implantation, maturation of the fetus or even birth of the child; and, therefore, it is the 'first instant' that determines the whole, just as it is the lighting of the candle which begins the burning of it: a burning of which is "inter-dependent" with the lighting which set it alight. Just as the light which lit the candle is "inseparably" taken up in the flame of the lighted candle so, in a certain way, the very causing of the person to exist, which is God, establishes an inseparably permanent relationship to that person.

Developmentally, however, what is begun at conception takes time to manifest the full reality of what is "concealed", as it were, in the beginning. What is "concealed" in conception is "revealed" in the growth of the human being-in-relationship: the child. 'Right from fertilization is begun the adventure of a human life, and each of its capacities requires time - a rather lengthy time - to find its place and to be in a position to act' (13). In other words, if it is now

---

(London: Her Majesty's Stationery Office, July 1984), para. 11.19, quoted in Catholic Bishops' Joint Committee on Bio-ethical Issues, *Response to the Warnock Report on Human Fertilization and Embryology* (London: Catholic Media Offices, 1984), 13. In response, the Catholic Bishop's of Great Britain said that 'our society should resolve to protect the life of the human embryo *precisely from the beginning of its continuous development, ie, from conception (fertilization)*' (Catholic Bishops' Committee, *Response to the Warnock Report*, 13). In other words, the very truth of the seamless process of development requires the welcome of each human life from conception.

empirically obvious that 'there is no particular part of the developmental process that is more important than another; all are part of a continuous process'[279], it is even more obvious that the goal of embryological development is the manifestation of the person begun at conception. But, at the same time, this does not alter the visible reality undergoing innumerable changes; indeed, like the growth of any bulb or seed in the ground, the process of unfolding development brings about irrevocable changes and developments, the natural goal of which is the full flowering of the plant. Thus, similarly, the unfolding of embryological development is not a process which changes what exists, as if "biological" development "changes" into "psychological" development; rather, the very developmental process reveals itself to be biologically inscribed psychological development. The child's humanity, in other words, is not just present but fully manifest according to the degree of development. Humanity is intrinsic to the being-in-relationship that a person is and, at the same time, is expressed according to his or her developmental stage of development.

Finally, notwithstanding the difficulties of answering this question in detail, the beginning of each person is manifestly more involved than a biological process of reproduction in that the human being transcends the biological in the very expression of human personhood; and, therefore, the biological beginning of human generation is the expression of a cause which transcends the biological generation of life. Just as an outcome cannot exceed its cause but must be in proportion to it, so the cause of human personhood must be in proportion to the integrity of human being. In other words, just as the existence of the universe cannot exceed the power that brought it to exist, so the human person implies

---

[279] Catholic Bishops' Committee, *Response to the Warnock Report*, 13.

the presence of a power that exceeds the biologically human gametes in the very act of coming to exist. In other words, calling a computer a type of "artificial intelligence" does not bring about the intelligence of a human being. Conversely, claiming that biologically human gametes are a sufficient cause of human personhood does not change the reality that human personhood exceeds the power of biologically human gametes to cause the human person who has come to exist. A cat comes from the biological gametes of cats and expresses a cat nature; however, writing about cats exceeds the biological existence of cats to the point of raising the philosophical problem: What brings to exist what exceeds biological characteristics? What causes the possibility of raising a philosophical problem if the very expression of a philosophical problem exceeds the possibilities of the animal kingdom?

Familiaris Consortio, 1981

Pope St. John Paul II published *Familiaris Consortio* in 1981. In article eleven of this Apostolic Exhortation he says: 'As an incarnate spirit, that is a soul which expresses itself in a body and a body informed by an immortal spirit, man is called to love in his unified totality'[280]. In other words, the *union of the body and the soul* is that of 'a soul which expresses itself in a body' in such a way that the human person is 'an incarnate spirit ...' (11). Thus the question arises: has Pope St. John Paul II implicitly compared the relationship of the unity of the body and the soul, *to the incarnation*, in order to draw out two, if not three features of this reality? Firstly: just as the divinity of Christ is the *ontologically prior archetype, as it were, of the man Christ*, so the soul is *logically* but not ontologically prior to the body

---

[280] *Familiaris Consortio*, 11.

in determining, as it were, the identity of the body. In other words, the human body is, by definition, a human body animated by a human soul; and, even at death, what remains retains a relationship to who the person was and the resurrection of the dead. At the same time, however, can a non-human body "call" for the creation and ensoulment of it (cf. *Humanae Vitae*, 13)? Is it not precisely as a biologically human being that we receive and transmit the gift of humanity? But, nevertheless, the transmission of human life requires a cause of personhood which exceeds the nature of the spousal act. Secondly, it would naturally follow from this that the soul and the body were created "one" in the moment of conception. Thirdly, there is the possibility that the conception of Christ is the implied "model" of human conception, not because the two are identical – but because of Christ recapitulating the whole mystery of human being; for, if Christ Himself is a true human being, one in body and soul, then the unity of His human nature had a beginning just as the unity of each human being has a beginning.

However, even if one cannot say with certainty that these points are implicit in the Pope's language[281], one can at least advert to them as a *theological direction in his thinking: a theological direction in his thinking with philosophical implications.*

---

[281] My three reasons for this reservation are: firstly, I am not reading a translation of his original writing; secondly, the implication to which I refer is not stated explicitly in his text; thirdly, it is possible that this can be true for the reason that God *anticipates* the reality of the whole person: a fact that is prior to how that "totality" is actually realized.

Conception: An Icon of the Beginning

Making explicit the philosophical implications of a theological reality

The *union of the body and the soul* is that of 'a soul which expresses itself in a body' in such a way that the human person is 'an incarnate spirit ...' (11).

The principle of the 'soul' expressing 'itself in a body' entails the possibility of, analogously, a vehicle of meaning: a comparision between a note being born on an instrument or the paint bearing the image of Van Gogh's sunflower. Without the instrument, the note dies; indeed, without the instrument, the note does not even begin. Similarly, the real paint bears the "idea" of the artist which is, precisely, a certain kind of painting. In other words, the painter is as much about how he paints as he is about what he paints; and, bearing that in mind, it is clear that the artist or musician communicates through a specifically chosen media or instrument. In a certain sense, then, we can say that both the paint and the instrument are integral to both the picture and the sound in that without that particular instrument or this particular paint, the picture and the sound would not be what they are. Just as the note has "taken up" the instrument that makes it and the picture has "taken up" the paint that expresses it, so the body is completely integral to the soul's expression of the person.

What is clear, then, is that the "body" in which the "soul" is expressed is a body that would not be what it is without the soul, just as a wax seal would not be what it is without the embossed insignia "stamped" upon it. It is as if the "interiority" that meaning makes possible in a word is indistinguishable from the word itself, just as the word "food" is different from the word "foreign". So it follows that the very "being a body" is always a profoundly personal reality: that a body is always and only the body of Charlotte or Jonathan.

Francis Etheredge

Donum Vitae, 1987

In 1987, Pope St. John Paul II approved the publication of the Congregation for the Doctrine of the Faith's *Instruction on Respect for Human Life in its Origin and on the Dignity of Procreation*, otherwise known as *Donum Vitae*, in which the authors make the following two observations.

On the one hand they say: 'no experimental datum can be in itself sufficient to bring us to the recognition of a spiritual soul; nevertheless, the conclusions of science regarding the human embryo provide a valuable indication for discerning by the use of reason a personal presence at the moment of this first appearance of a human life: how could a human individual not be a human person?'[282] In other words, the very individuality of a human being, the very non-divisibility of the being that has come into existence, expresses the fact that the human being which has come into existence is a human person. This can be taken in two ways: the indivisibility of body and soul is irrevocable and that, therefore, the individual as constituted is a human person.

Secondly, in the case of monozygotic twins, twins which arise from a single embryo, the instant an embryonic cell separates from the whole there is a new individual and therefore another human person has come into existence. In other words, whether the origin of an individual is at conception or, in the case of twinning, subsequently, it is scientifically clear that there is a beginning to the living being; and, as such, this constitutes evidence that points to the existence of a 'personal presence' from the actuality of that moment of beginning[283]. Furthermore, twinning is a

---

[282] *Donum Vitae*, 1. 1.
[283] *Donum Vitae*, 1. 1.

Conception: An Icon of the Beginning

clear illustration of the relationship, already obvious in the development of a single individual, that the body is a personal "parameter" to the expression of human identity. Twinning, in other words, does not confuse the origin of human identity; rather, twinning makes it clear that human identity is expressed in terms of bodily integrity: where the body is, there the soul is, and where both are is the person.

On the other hand the authors of *Donum Vitae* say: 'The Magisterium has not expressly committed itself to an affirmation of a philosophical nature ...'[284]. Therefore, *precisely because of the juxtaposition of these two sentences in Donum Vitae*, one wonders what kind of affirmation it is when in the first of these two sentences it is said that there is 'a personal presence at the moment of this first appearance of a human life ...'. In other words, if the affirmation of a 'personal presence at the moment of this first appearance of a human life' is not an 'affirmation of a philosophical nature' then what is it?

There seem to be two, not necessarily mutually exclusive possibilities to what this juxtaposition of statements actually means. Firstly, does it mean that the Magisterium *is committed* to a theological affirmation of the truth that the person is one in body and soul from conception; and so, *precisely* because of this *prior and theological affirmation, other evidence can be seen more clearly to assist in reason's apprehension of this truth as true?* In other words, this is almost an expression of the possibility of divine assistance in the very statement of an affirmation of a 'personal presence at the moment of this first appearance of a human life'. Secondly, does the juxtaposition of these statements indicate that the Magisterium, while still not wishing to commit itself to a philosophical answer to this question, nevertheless wishes to indicate a philosophical tendency in the thinking

---

[284] *Donum Vitae*, 1. 1.

of this same Magisterium: *a tendency to the philosophical view that the person does exist as one in body and soul from conception?* Moreover, even if this conclusion is not regarded as philosophically proven, yet it has the human characteristic of being "ordered to" and "derived from" the 'conclusions of science regarding the human embryo'.

Thus, when the authors of *Donum Vitae* said that 'no experimental datum can be in itself sufficient to bring us to the recognition of a spiritual soul', they are acknowledging a "discontinuity" between an 'experimental datum' and the 'recognition of a spiritual soul'. In other words, we do not observe the creation and ensouled existence of the soul in the first moment of the body's existence in that this is of a different order to what is susceptible to direct empirical investigation. Nevertheless, owing to the very origin of embryonic human life, it is clear that there is a beginning to that life and, therefore, that life is by definition the life of a human person; even if, positively, it is not possible to demonstrate the existence of a 'personal presence' beyond the empirical evidence of an actual origin to the human embryo. At the same time, however, it is clear that 'personal presence' is more than implied at the beginning of each one of us in that this is what human development makes manifest.

Finally, I exclude the possibility that there is nothing affirmed in this statement concerning the beginning, *precisely because of the words*: 'the conclusions of science regarding the human embryo provide a valuable indication *for discerning* by the use of reason *a personal presence at the moment of this first appearance of a human life* ...'.

Conception: An Icon of the Beginning

Address at the "University of Uppsala", Friday, 9th June, 1989

In 1989 Pope St. John Paul II said that 'The dignity of the person can be protected only if the *person is considered as inviolable* from the moment of conception until natural death'[285]. Furthermore '[u]nless a society treats the human person as inviolable, the formulation of consistent ethical principles becomes impossible, as does the creation of a moral climate which fosters the protection of the weakest members of the human family'[286].

Here, then, we see the implications for human ethics of the inviolability of the human person. In other words, the universality of human ethics begins, as it were, in the recognition of the inviolability of each person; and, therefore, there is no discrimination possible if the foundation of human ethics is, precisely, the nature of each person. In virtue, then, of the very existence of human personhood, each person is radically equal; and, if radically equal in human personhood, radically equal in the human rights entailed in human personhood. In the very existence, then, of human personhood, there is a relationship of equality-in-human-identity; and, therefore, human rights are an expression, as it were, of the "relationship" of kind between all human beings.

Rights, then, are as much an expression of the "relationship" entailed in human being as the very nature of being a human person expresses a relationship to others: of

---

[285] Pope St. John Paul II, June 9, 1989: University of Uppsala, 5, (https://w2.vatican.va/content/john-paul-ii/en/speeches/1989/june/documents/hf_jp-ii_spe_19890609_univ-upsala.html).

[286] Pope St. John Paul II, June 9, 1989: University of Uppsala, 5.

being a father or mother or of being a son or daughter; indeed, human rights are an objectification of that common humanity that is expressed in the very reality of being a human person-in-relationship: of being conceived through the very relationships which bring each one of us to exist.

Even if, then, a human being is deprived of the full development which naturally follows on conception through the spousal act, the very constitution of human being brings about an inseparable and inalienable relationship to human kind; and, as such, each human being radically possesses the right to life, not by choice, permission or other determining factor, but in virtue of the very relationship of origin. Human rights, therefore, are inherently relational and express the universal recognition of the equality of all human beings.

In the Service of Life, 1991

The Pontifical Council for the Family published a text in 1991 entitled *In the service of life*, otherwise known as an *Instrumentum laboris*. The authors make the following three points.

Firstly: 'it is necessary to reaffirm the full anthropological value of the human individual from the moment of fertilization (cf. *Donum Vitae*, Part I, n. 1)'[287]. In other words, the moment of fertilization is the determining "moment" in terms of the gift of each person's humanity; however, that moment of fertilization is "replicated" in the moment that a monozygotic twin is formed. Thus, while the moment of fertilization is the first moment following on the event of the contact between what was an ovum and a sperm but is no longer, by definition of that contact, there are "other" moments which equally specify the foundation of

---

[287] The Pontifical Council for the Family, *In the service of life*, 1991, (*Instrumentum laboris*), (Vatican: Vatican Press, 1992).

human being: the moment of "twinning". Even if, however, this is a difficult moment to identify, the existential reality of a twin defines the actual existence of the person; and, in that sense, the actuality of twinning comes before the conceptual elucidation of it.

Secondly: 'The first moments of the beginning of human life are fundamental in determining the development which follows'[288]. If, in other words, there is a developmental problem and the human embryo does not implant, it follows that if there was the beginning of a human life then there was the loss of a human child; and, therefore, the grief a mother and father experience is intrinsic to that relationship: the grief expressing the relationship that was established in the very coming-to-exist of their child. Conversely, if the problem was of such a nature that there was no actual moment of fertilization, in that whatever happened it did not constitute fertilization, then it follows that a human being was not conceived; however, the evidence of this is scarcely visible except in so far as what develops is clearly different to what follows actual fertilization. In view of any developmental uncertainty, however, there is of necessity the "presumption" of the humanity of the embryo conceived (cf. *Evangelium Vitae*, 60).

Finally: 'We should remember that at the moment of the union of the male and female gametes, all the characteristics of the new human being, including gender are defined'[289]. Thus gender is as much a part of the whole human being as everything that determines the humanity of the human person; and, as such, whatever developmental problems there may be there is, as it were, a genetically determined

---

[288] *In the service of life*, 1991.
[289] *In the service of life*, 1991.

sex: a gender that is replicated throughout the developmental process as cell upon cell communicates the unfolding reality of the son or daughter conceived. Gender, then, is not an additional element of human identity in that it "follows on" human being; rather, it is an integral expression of human personhood from the beginning. Furthermore, the very integral nature of human development, evident in the very presence of a psychological relationship between parents and child, indicates that biological conception entails the presence of an unfolding psychological identity and interpersonal relationships. It is not as if, however, the identity of being a boy or a girl is a genetically determined identity as if genetics and psychology are independent of each other; rather, then, there is an *intra-personal dynamic to the very development of the inward psychological characteristics which are "enfleshed" in the outward physical development.*

Given, then, the profoundly relational nature of God, who "originates" human personhood (cf. *Letter to Families,* 6) in its "uni-duality" (*Letter to Women,* 8), it follows that being male or female is at once a profoundly ontological identity (*Letter to Women,* 7) and, at the same time, a profoundly relational identity. Thus it is not as if the physical determinants of sexual identity are an adequate indication of its depth of meaning; and, therefore, it may yet be necessary to explore the very "roots" of personhood in the mystery of God in order to consider, more fully, both the very existence as well as the amazing complementarity of man and woman.

It is obvious, furthermore, that a non-therapeutic intervention at the moment of fertilization is an intervention in the profoundly vulnerable stages of human development. The clearer it is that the whole process of early development is vulnerable to external and non-therapeutic interference, the clearer it is that there is an inalienable right to this development to proceed unhindered and with whatever assistance is ordinarily required. Thus the natural right of the child to come to term through the completion of pregnancy is, as it were, inscribed within the very structure of human conception and development; and the corollary of this is the child's natural right to the unfolding of the intra-uterine care and the relationship to the child's parents. Obviously, however, this does not automatically entail extraordinary interventions nor does it exclude the well-being of the child in view, for example, of the mother being raped and the need to protect both mother and child from the possibility of harm.

In view, also, of the inherent sensitivity of these early stages, it is especially clear that anything which obscures or interferes with the natural humanity of the human being is an offence against the human person. In other words, any kind of "mixing" of the genetic inheritance of a human and a non-human being is of itself a crime against the humanity of the human person; and, as such, these rights intrinsic to the relational nature of human personhood require enshrinement in international law. On the one hand, then, there is the natural right to the preservation of the integral nature of human personhood; and, on the other hand, there is the right that the natural relationship of each person to the rest of the human race be retained.

Veritatis Splendor, 1993

In what follows it is necessary to consider why it is so difficult to appreciate the wholeness of human being: the wholeness that begins from the first instant of fertilization; and, therefore, it is necessary to look at a number of facets in the culture in which we live, facets that have become splinters and need re-integrating into the whole to which they point. In sum, Pope St. John Paul II's *Veritatis*

Splendor expresses an integrated account[290] of the diverse goods that modern man tends to *disintegrate*[291]. I will therefore indicate what the Pope perceives to be "divorced" or even denied; and, although he advances an integral vision of these diverse elements, I will only refer to a few aspects of what he affirms and reconciles.

It almost seems as if everything that can be opposed has been opposed: some 'individuals or groups want the right *to determine what is good or evil*'[292]. Therefore, in that it is the truth which reveals the moral value of an act[293], then 'truth itself would be considered a creation of freedom'[294]; and, at the same time, modern culture even questions the existence of freedom[295]: as if the very project of showing how free we are ends up in discovering how "unfree" each one of us actually is. Thus there is a tendency to deny 'the very idea of human nature'[296]. On the one hand human nature is almost reduced to some kind of *a*-moral material[297]. But then, on the other hand, it seems that even the evidence of raw material possessing *a nature that is "given"* is like a path lost in the undergrowth of objections to the possibility of a Creator. In other words, instead of

---

[290] This is the work of the very virtue that man, and modern man particularly, tends to reject: chastity (cf. St. John Paul II, Karol Wojtyla, *Love and Responsibility*, translated by H.T. Willetts, [London: Fount, *An Imprint of* Harper Collins *Publishers*, 1982], pp. 140-147).

[291] Cf. *Veritatis Splendor*, 18.

[292] *Veritatis Splendor*, 35.

[293] Cf. *Veritatis Splendor*, 61.

[294] *Veritatis Splendor*, 35.

[295] *Veritatis Splendor*, 33.

[296] *Veritatis Splendor*, 32.

[297] *Veritatis Splendor*, 46.

evaluating the empirical fact of what exists possessing "given" characteristics, the tendency to exploit without reflection the reality of what exists, obscures both the existence of the gift of material and indeed the gift of human nature. The concept of conscience, then, becomes so completely subjective that it is argued that 'one's moral judgment is true merely by the fact that it has its origin in the conscience'[298]; and, therefore, a statement is true, not in virtue of it corresponding to reality, but in virtue of the self-supporting claim that it expresses the author of it. In other words, it is true that a statement can articulate the position of a speaker "perfectly"; however, this does not vindicate the content of the claim itself. In other words, it may be true that Descartes expressed exactly what he thought when he said, "I think, therefore I am". But, implied in that is the fact that unless he existed, he could not have thought at all and, therefore, his thinking is already evidence that he exists and not a proof of it; or, at best, thinking is one of the many ways that existence is manifest in activity. This kind of thought process is evident in the denial that the activity of the human embryo is not a sign of a person's development: as if a person's development can be other than what is actually happening in the course of the growth of an embryo. Clearly, in view of what was said earlier, if what exists is not a human embryo then its activity is not that of a human person; however, it is necessary for this to show itself in such a way that there cannot be the risk of interfering or ending the life of a person.

There is also a kind of "divorce" in the heart of man: his fundamental option for or against God is not expressed in the moral value of his acts because, it is argued, the one is

---

[298] *Veritatis Splendor*, 46.

not ordered to the other[299]. On the one hand there is the denial that human acts are ordered to God and this expresses, clearly, what a particular person thinks. However, if human acts do not possess a particular content or meaning then it is like saying that there is a "disconnect" between person and action: a disconnect that rejects the principle that action manifests being. A denial of the relationship between being and action does not vindicate the claim that there is no relationship between being and action. Therefore, the relationship between being and action that is revealed by its denial is that a person wants to behave as if there is no personal responsibility for an intention and its embodied action; or, and this almost amounts to the same thing, a person denies that an action carries a meaning beyond that deliberately "given" to it. In the event of a child being conceived, then, it is denied that the human embryo is indistinguishable from a "cell mass": as if the truism that there is a "cell mass" describes the ontological reality of the beginning of a human person. In other words, if a human embryo does not unfold the manifestation of being a human person then it is not a human embryo. Thus, if a mass of cells is in reality a cancerous growth then that mass of cells is not a human embryo but a cancerous growth. An object contributes to our concept of it or the concept is not communicating what exists.

There is a false autonomy of earthly realities, such that man wants to use created things without reference to the Creator[300]. This radical separation of "things that belong together" is extended to everything pertaining to faith and morality[301]. Thus there is a denial of the binding moral

---

[299] *Veritatis Splendor*, 65.
[300] *Gaudium et Spes*, 36, and *Veritatis Splendor*, 39.
[301] *Ibid.*

content of Divine Revelation[302] in part, it seems, because the idea of a God-given judgement of what is right and wrong, applicable in all circumstances, to all individuals and at all times, is denied as even possible[303]. In other words, there is a denial of God being God: of the existence of One to whom all is known, foreseen and understood. Thus there is a mentality that what is impossible for man *is now argued, perhaps implicitly, to be impossible even for God.* Thus there is a denial that the authority of the 'Church and her Magisterium'[304] was intended to be effective for the moral life of the people of God. The implications of this mentality for the beginning of human personhood would be that if God cannot express a universal truth in His word or the teaching of His Church then truth cannot be expressed philosophically or as embodied in a concrete reality. It would be denied, therefore, that there is a truth expressed in the beginning of human personhood to be discovered; and, in principle, the whole endeavour of science and philosophy would become a project of "imagining" or thinking thoughts that it would never be possible to judge as true or false.

---

[302] *Veritatis Splendor*, 37.
[303] Cf. *Veritatis Splendor*, 55.
[304] *Veritatis Splendor*, 37.

Francis Etheredge

Conversely, St. John Paul II expresses the realization that reality entails order, diversity, proportion, nature, and the dynamic unity of all these interacting elements, which leaves out nothing acceptable to reason and includes everything acceptable to Christ and His Church.

At the same time, however, owing to the recognition of sin and the reality of the fall from grace, it is also recognized that creation bears both the evidence of its wonderful origin and unimaginable end and, at the same time, the trace of redemption and the work of God to bring the help we need to the very roots of created being and to every aspect of life as it is lived. Thus there is the leaven of grace which cooperates with all that is true, good and beautiful, bringing it to fruition; and, in addition, there is a growing recognition of the trace of natural law[305] and how it contributes to the

---

[305] Two useful works on Natural Law are the following: C. S. Lewis, *The Abolition of Man*, Collins, Fount Paperbacks, 1978 and reprinted since; and, secondly, "In Search of a Universal Ethic: A New Look at Natural Law" (http://www.vatican.va/roman_curia/congregations/cfaith/cti_documents/rc_con_cfaith_doc_20090520_legge-naturale_en.html). Neither of these documents address the "common" experience of mankind concerning the conception of children; however, it may be considered so obvious as not to deserve a mention. In the Scriptures, for example, there are a variety of accounts which attest to an awareness of, simply, a beginning to the life of each one of us. It could be argued that it was not until the "problem" arose as to how to explain the origin of personhood that the "simple" understanding of a beginning was regarded as "too" simple: but perhaps it is now time to recognize the virtue of that simplicity: conception means '[a] beginning' (*The American Heritage College Dictionary*, senior Lexicographer, David A. Jost), p. 228: con-cep-tion: the archaic sense of which is 'A beginning …'. What about the wonderful clarity of the narrator's account and Eve's insight: 'Now Adam knew Eve his wife, and she conceived and bore Cain, saying: "I have gotten a man with the

Conception: An Icon of the Beginning

recognition of the whole, dynamically ordered, unity-in-diversity of human personhood. With respect to natural law, then, St. John Paul II says that the true meaning of the natural law is that 'it refers to man's proper and primordial nature, the "nature of the human person"[306], which is *the person himself in the unity of soul and body, in the unity of his spiritual and biological inclinations and of all the other specific characteristics necessary for the pursuit of his end*'[307]. In other words, although it is possible to express how the different characteristics of the human person come together, in particular '*the unity of soul and body, in the unity of his spiritual and biological inclinations*', it is also necessary to recognize that this implies that there is a beginning to human personhood which is of itself an "ontological moment": a moment in which all that is characteristic of the human person is founded as indivisibly "interior" of the "exterior" of the human being that comes to exist.

It would appear, then, that the natural law is now understood to be a kind of manifestation of the person. The light of the natural law, to which St. Thomas Aquinas referred[308], would now seem to be seen as an expression of the totality of the fact that man is a person. This would imply that all that man is, in whole and in part, has *its constitutive relationship to the natural law which is now understood to be a manifestation of man in his totality, much as the light of the lamp is the "end" to which the body of the lamp and*

---

help of the Lord"'? (Catholic RSV, Gn 4: 1, San Francisco: Ignatius Press, 1966). Note that it is all here: the recognition of the relationship between 'Adam know[ing] Eve' and Eve conceiving, saying: "I have gotten a man with the help of the Lord".

[306] *Gaudium et Spes*, 51.
[307] *Veritatis Splendor*, 50.
[308] Cf. footnote 19 of *Veritatis Splendor*, 12.

all its parts are ordered. The relationship between the bodily and the rational aspects of the human being, therefore, *cannot be understood except as a manifestation of their prior and ontological unity expressed in the fact that the person is a* "unified totality"[309]: "a soul which expresses itself in a body and a body informed by an immortal spirit"[310]. In terms of the "structure", as it were, of human personhood, there is the whole constitution of what makes possible the common pursuit of truth and the dialogue with God. In the section of *Veritatis Splendor* devoted exactly to this question, the Pope says: 'The relationship between man's freedom and God's law is most deeply lived out in the "heart" of the person, in his moral conscience'[311]. Thus the moral conscience is understood as the "heart" of the totality that is called the person. What takes place in the heart is both hidden from the eyes of everyone outside[312] and is a *dialogue of man with himself and with God*[313]. This is a dialogue *in which God's law* reveals to the conscience of man the truth about the moral value of an act; and it is on the basis of this truth, which the conscience of man recognizes but does not originate[314], the person makes a responsible, practical and particular judgement that this is to be done and that is to be avoided[315]. Therefore the relationship between the con-

---

[309] *Veritatis Splendor*, 50.
[310] As found in *Veritatis Splendor*, 50 and quoted from *Familiaris Consortio*, 11.
[311] *Veritatis Splendor*, 54.
[312] *Veritatis Splendor*, 57.
[313] *Veritatis Splendor*, 58.
[314] *Veritatis Splendor*, 60.
[315] *Veritatis Splendor*, 61.

science of man and the truth is that if the conscience is the heart of the person then the truth is its life blood.

What an amazing event, then, that brings about an interior identity which is expressed exteriorly: that the outward expression of the person communicates the existence of an interiority to be communicated; indeed, that it is possible that the interiority of the person is communicable: that not only does there exist an interiority to the exteriority of human personhood but that human identity is evident, expressible and a "dialogical-event" to be communicated. On the one hand, then, this suggests that the intimately interior dialogue of man with God *follows on man's conception by God being at the same time constitutive of a relationship to him*; and, therefore, it makes sense that this relationship begins with the very beginning of conception and includes nothing that belongs to man as man. On the other hand, the very interiority that manifests itself in human communication again draws on the whole person and, similarly, suggests that the first instant of fertilization is the moment from which the whole human being is founded, fruitfully "ignited", as it were, and formed in a "whole" that constitutes the capability of being communicated in its entirety.

What are the implications of how these issues are treated in Veritatis Splendor for a theological understanding of the nature of human conception?

The history of the term "person" does itself seem to be a particular case of the following: 'In fact, *it is only in the mystery of the Word incarnate that light is shed on the mystery of man*'[316]. The development of the term person *passed through, indeed by way* of, the Church's under-

---

[316] *Gaudium et Spes*, 22, cited in *Veritatis Splendor*, 2.

standing of Christ[317]. Therefore this question concerning "the beginning of each one of us" cannot be separated from *Christ*, through whom we come to know the full truth concerning *the faith-fact of the 'imago Dei* present in man ... '[318]. Thus *a fundamental presupposition of the Christian vision of man is what simply follows from the truth of the revealed mystery that man makes present the imago Dei: the image of God.* Just as the *Incarnation* makes present the action of God in bringing the Son of God to be incarnate in the flesh of Mary, so, it could be argued, *the action of God brings the soul to exist and to exist-as-incarnate in the flesh given through the spousal act.*

The *central implication* for the *theological* discussion of the conception of the human being is that the human being is understood within the vision of man being a person, one in body and soul. *Therefore*, if the human being is a person, one in body and soul, then it is possible that the human being is a person from conception. It is possible, however, that this implication derives more from Revelation than from reason in so far as, from the philosophical point of view, the following is still considered to be an open question by the Church: whether the body is animated by the soul from conception or from some subsequent point of development[319]. But this is not to say that a philosophical answer cannot be found, or that theology cannot anticipate, if not assist its answer. It is simply to say that this is the situation at the moment. The Church also says, concerning

---

[317] Henri de Lubac, *On Christian Philosophy*, Communio, Vol. XIX, No 3, (Fall 1992), p. 481. Cf also Pope St. John Paul II, June 9, 1989, quoted on page 42 of *The Philosophy of Life*, compiled by Fr. Rosario Thomas.

[318] *Veritatis Splendor*, 111.

[319] Declaration by the *Sacred Congregation for the Doctrine of the Faith, Let Me Live*: footnote 19, p. 16.

this same point: 'it suffices that this presence of the soul be probable (and one can never prove the contrary) in order that the taking of life involves accepting the risk of killing a man, not only waiting for, but already in possession of his soul'[320]. On the one hand, just as a word of God is inspired from its very origin in the writer, so is the soul ensouled from the very first instant of conception. On the other hand, just as a designer intends his goal from the beginning, so what contributes to it is begun with the end in view. In a certain sense, then, it is possible to say that if the Son of God became man in an instant, whole and entire, then this is the "pattern" of the creation of the human person: in an instant and whole and entire.

In conclusion, *Veritatis Splendor* contributes a theological implication of direct relevance to the following discussion, namely that the embryo is the first developmental stage of being a person; and, finally, it offers a vision of man in his "totality" and, as such, provides a context within which to understand particular aspects of the whole. In other words, the very structure of the intra-personal dialogue between God and each one of us is, in its own way, as concrete an evidence as the inter-personal dialogue between parent and child. The very coming-to-exist of each person through the mysterious action of God in the very fruit of the spousal act of husband and wife is at the same time evidence of what makes possible the very psychosomatic whole of the human being-in-relationship.

---

[320] *Let Me Live*, footnote 19, p. 16.

Francis Etheredge

A Letter to Families, 1994

Part One of the *Letter to Families* is called *The Civilization of Love*[321]. The first sub-heading of Part One is: 'Male and Female He created them.' It is here that St. John Paul II explains the original meaning of what it is for man, male and female, to be created in the image of God. He says: 'Before creating man, the Creator withdraws as it were into himself, in order to seek the pattern and inspiration in the mystery of his Being, which is already here disclosed as the divine "We"'[322]. Indeed, it could be argued, that an expression of the 'the pattern and inspiration in the mystery of his Being' is imitative of the divine Being in three ways. Firstly: there is the creation of the very spousal dialogue which makes human conception the relational coming-to-be of each human person it is. Secondly, the conception of the human person is "triadic": it entails the mysterious cooperation of man, woman and God. Thirdly: that just as each of the Divine persons eternally proceeds within the other, so God brings to exist each human person through the instantaneous ensoulment of the fruit of spousal love; and, just as the "whole" of the Son of God was incarnate from the first instant of becoming "flesh", so each of us is from the first instant whole and wholly immersed in relationships: a child of God and a child of his or her parents.

Extracts from *'The Genealogy of the person'*

The fourth sub-heading in this section is 'The Genealogy of the person'[323] and what follows is a series of brief

---

[321] *Let Me Live*, p. 6.
[322] *Letter to Families*, 6.
[323] *Letter to Families*, p. 9.

extracts which, I hope, illustrate some of the main features of this genealogy. 'Human fatherhood and motherhood are rooted in biology, yet at the same time transcend it'[324]. On the one hand, there is a biological expression of fatherhood and motherhood. But on the other hand, it is equally possible to say that the psychological relationship of mother and father is "incarnate" in the biological union of the gametes through which parenthood comes to be expressed, to exist and to bear fruit in the reality of "their" child.

'Every act of begetting finds its primordial model in the fatherhood of God'[325] (cf. Eph 3: 14-15)[326]. If the 'primordial model' of begetting is 'in the fatherhood of God', then by implication the "begetting" of God is relational: the interrelationships of the Blessed Trinity are the 'primordial model' of man, male and female, and their mission to 'fill the earth' (Gn 1: 28). At the same time, if the first instant of creation is the beginning from which all unfolds, then it follows that the first instant of fertilization is when the human person comes to exist and from which moment the whole manifestation of the person begins. Thus the "first instant of conception" in time is a temporal "imitation" of the eternal relationships between the three persons in one God: the Blessed Trinity.

'When a new person is born of the conjugal union of the two, he brings with him into the world a particular image and likeness of God himself: *the genealogy of the person is inscribed in the very biology of generation*'[327]. On the one hand, the '*biology of generation*' is not adequately described without recognizing that there is a specific '*genealogy of the*

---

[324] *Letter to Families*, 9.
[325] *Letter to Families*, 9.
[326] The Pope quotes this text earlier at art 7, p. 7.
[327] *Letter to Families*, 9.

person': there is a specific expression of biologically human being that is, as it were, uniquely expressive of personhood. The very fact of the kind of hand that a human being has makes possible the touch of love, the consummate performance of the musician, the dexterity of the mechanic, the sensitivity of the surgeon and the comfort of a child. At the same time, the *'genealogy of the person'* also refers to the transmission of family characteristics while, at the same time, opening new horizons owing to the inheritance which is both passed and combined through the gift of the mother and the father; and, it could be said, the new horizon of the child's genetic inheritance belongs, as it were, to the new horizon of the person who has come into existence. On the other hand, the *'genealogy of the person'* refers to the human inheritance endowed by God from the very beginning of creation and renewed with the coming into existence of each new human person and his or her relationships: an inheritance which intrinsically refers back to the originating splendour of the Blessed Trinity. In other words, in the very constitution of the human being there is an "embodied" expression of the *imago Dei* which is, as it were, both historically transmitted from the origin of the human race, and actual in that each person "lives" an original expression of the gift of being made in the image and likeness of God. The very "generation" of each human person, then, is like a transposition into time and flesh of the eternal generation of the Son from the Father and the Spirit from both the Father and the Son. We have scarcely glimpsed the sacredness of human life in view of the mystery of the Blessed Trinity, the death and resurrection of Jesus Christ and the sanctifying help of the Holy Spirit who makes possible our return to the Father's house.

'In affirming that the spouses, as parents, cooperate with God the Creator in conceiving and giving birth to a new human being, we are not speaking merely with reference to the laws of biology'[328]. The 'laws of biology' are, in other words, enfleshing an embodied expression of the mystery of "person" from "person". Indeed, in the very language of the flesh the Creator has expressed a mystery that not only speaks of the origin and goal of human life but of the very reason for the transmission of human life through "procreation": through the inner transformation of the reciprocal spousal gift of egg and sperm. In other words, what is it about the very reality of procreation that expresses the vision of the Creator for the whole human race? What if the very mystery of procreation is that it expresses a kind of unity-in-diversity in the "generating" of flesh from flesh and the "proceeding" of each person by an act of God? In other words, the Blessed Trinity has "written" within the very reality of procreation a profound "witness" to the mystery that God is the "Being-in-Relationship".

We 'wish to emphasize that *God himself is present in human fatherhood and motherhood* quite differently than he is present in all other instances of begetting on earth'[329]. The act of 'begetting' entails a unique presence of 'God himself' in '*human fatherhood and motherhood*'; and, therefore, it is clear that God has chosen the ministry of parenthood (cf. *Humanae Vitae*, 13) to be a participation in His love of us. Just, then, as human parenthood is not just a "moment of begetting" but a ministry which began with marriage (cf. *Humanae Vitae*, 8-9), if not before, and follows on the very nature of human conception, so the perception that '*God himself is present in human fatherhood and motherhood*' opens up the possibility of a radical participation of God's action in human parenthood. In other words, realizing that God is present transforms, in a sense, the

---

[328] *Letter to Families*, 9.
[329] *Letter to Families*, 9.

burden of parenthood into a Christian service; and, whatever the imperfections of parents, it is an essential part of the presence of Christ to take our daily burdens and to transform them into blessings (cf. Mt 11: 29). It is certain, then, that the prayerful parental confession of the problems of parenthood, both sacramentally, in the rite of reconciliation and daily, in the prayer of the heart and the spousal dialogue, is a work of God which brings about the fulfilment of the ministry of parenting: a participation in the work which God does of bringing us to be His sons and daughters.

'God alone is the source of that image and likeness which is proper to the human being, as it was received at Creation. Begetting is the continuation of Creation'[330]. If '[b]egetting is the continuation of Creation', then the Creator is communicating an immense dignity to the creature through involving husband and wife in the conception of their child. In other words, there is in the moment of conception an echo of the very first moment of creation in that a person did not exist who then comes to exist: a new act of creation, as it were, expressed in the flesh of the human embryo. 'God alone', then, 'is the source of that image and likeness which is proper to the human being' as He continues to be the "unoriginate" originator of each human person; and, therefore, each human person is both an embodied expression of the Creator's creativity and, at the same time, a particular "translation" into flesh of the "archetypal" being-in-relationship which is at the origin of human personhood.

'*God willed man from the very beginning, and God wills him in every act of conception and every human birth*. God wills man as a being similar to himself, as a person'[331]. If

---

[330] *Letter to Families*, 9.
[331] *Letter to Families*, 9.

'God wills man as a being similar to himself' then man is a being-in-relationship; and, if man is a "being-in-relationship", then being a man or being a woman are co-fundamental expressions of personhood. If being a man or being a woman are co-fundamental expressions of personhood, then the human race absolutely needs to be 'a relational "uni-duality"' (*Letter to Women*, 8): a dynamic relationship between men and women. In other words, it is completely inadequate to identify the relationship between men and women as complementary: it is complementary for a personal and universal purpose; indeed, the very complementarity that naturally exists *is precisely in order for it to be* dynamically active: men and women are intrinsically and vocationally created and called to develop the dialogue that was frustrated in the very sin of Adam's silence in front of Eve's temptation.

'Inscribed in the personal constitution of every human being is the will of God, who wills that man should be, in a certain sense, an end unto himself'[332]. If, however, the very constitution of the person is orientated to a gift of self, the reciprocal gift of self from which all gifts come, the mystery of the Blessed Trinity, then it follows that the sense in which man is an 'end unto himself' is that each person is a "gift" to himself or herself; and, on the basis of discovering and living the "gift of self", it is possible to discover the vocation inscribed within the very being of the self: that the self is orientated to the gift of self. Each person "receives" the gift of self; and, therefore, there is no greater equality than that each one of us is a gift. Moreover, just as each one of us is a gift, so each person "receives" the possibility of "giving" the gift of self. In other words, the "constitution" of the very being of the human person is a recapitulation of the mystery

---

[332] *Letter to Families*, 9.

of the Blessed Trinity: of being the unoriginate origin of all relationships between "giving" and "receiving".

Finally, the 'dimension of the genealogy of the person which has been revealed by Christ'[333] is that man is destined[334] to reach 'fulfilment precisely *by sharing in God's life*'[335]: the life of the Blessed Trinity[336].

An "Incarnational" understanding of creation discloses the secret of the Blessed Trinity that fulfilment is found in "being-in-relationship"

The structure of this thought is therefore quite clearly expressed in beginning with the mystery of our *conception* in God: a conception expressed in the word of God (cf. Gn 1: 26). Thus the word of God receives *an incarnate* (cf Jn 1: 3; and cf. Gn 1: 27) *expression in the creation of man, male and female*: an identity which is then *transmitted to all the children of Adam and Eve*; and, from within the relationship of Creator to creature, comes the call[337] back to God through the gift of Christ and His Church.

This great movement became a more and more explicit *theological pattern* in the pontificate of St. John Paul II and expressed, as it were, the *programme of it*[338]*: a programme which expressed his apostolic struggle to articulate the Gospel of Life.* In *The Redeemer of Man*,

---

[333] *Letter to Families*, 9.

[334] *Letter to Families*, 9.

[335] *Letter to Families*, 9.

[336] Cf *Letter to Families*, 9.

[337] *Letter to Families*, 9.

[338] Cf. Jesus Colina, *The Key to John Paul II's Thinking*, published in a Special Supplement of the magazine, *Inside the Vatican*, (Rome: Inside the Vatican, 1995), pp. 28-29.

otherwise known as *Redemptor Hominis*, published in 1979, he says: 'man is the primary route that the Church must travel in fulfilling her mission: *he is the primary and fundamental way for the Church*, the way traced out by Christ himself, the way that leads invariably through the mystery of the Incarnation and the Redemption'[339]. This theme finds a particularly concise expression of its Trinitarian orientation in the publication of *As the Third Millennium of the new era draws near*, otherwise known as *Tertio Millennio Adveniente*, published on the 10th of November, 1994, in which St. John Paul II said: 'Paul's presentation of the mystery of the Incarnation contains *the revelation of the mystery of the Trinity and the continuation of the Son's mission in the mission of the Holy Spirit*'[340]. Finally, the *way of the Church through the man in our time* finds a particularly eloquent expression in the *Gospel of Life*.

Evangelium Vitae, The Gospel of Life, 1995

On the 25 March, 1995, on the feast of 'the Annunciation of the Lord'[341], St. John Paul II published *The Gospel of Life*, otherwise known as *Evangelium Vitae*. This Encyclical Letter could be said to have taken up the analysis of the situation expressed *in Veritatis Splendor's* contrast between the tendency to divide what belongs together and the tendency to unite what has been unnaturally divided. On the one hand the *evil* (cf Gn 3: 1) *originating tendency of sin to*

---

[339] Pope St. John Paul II, *Redemptor Hominis*, 14.
[340] Pope St. John Paul II, *Tertio Millennio Adveniente*, 1.
[341] Pope St. John Paul II, *Evangelium Vitae*, 105.

separate what God has united[342] culminates in what the Pope calls the "culture of death"[343]: a culture orientated to the ultimate end of 'eternal punishment' (Mt. 25: 46) - the definitive separation of man from God; and, on the other hand, all of what can be united *through the mystery of the blood of Christ* (cf Heb 12: 22, 24)[344] constitutes the "culture of life"[345]: a culture orientated to the promise of 'eternal life' (Mt 25: 46) - the definitive union of man and God.

This work, in an *almost eschatologically* simple way, provides the perspective within which particular questions concerning man and his origin *are in reality asked*: the one perspective of faith and reason. On the one hand, faith says: 'The blood of Christ, while it reveals the grandeur of the Father's love, *shows how precious man is in God's eyes and how priceless the value of his life*'[346]; and, therefore, '*how priceless*' is the individual life: a pricelessness which contradicts the exploitation of the poor, the extermination of the suffering and the commercialization and experimentation on the gift of a child at conception[347]. On the other hand, faith assists the perception of reason[348] in seeing that "Without the Creator the creature would

---

[342] Cf. G. K. Chesterton, *Aquinas*, (London: Hodder and Stoughton), p. 149.

[343] *Evangelium Vitae*, articles 28 and 95.

[344] Cf *Evangelium Vitae* and the biblical title to the section from articles 25-28.

[345] *Evangelium Vitae*, articles 28 and 95.

[346] *Evangelium Vitae*, 25.

[347] Cf. for example, *The Guardian*:
https://www.theguardian.com/science/2016/jan/13/uk-scientists-ready-to-genetically-modify-human-embryos

[348] Cf *Dei Verbum*, 6.

disappear ... [and that] when God is forgotten the creature itself grows unintelligible"349. In other words, the very beginning of personhood has become incomprehensible as an expression of the personal life that will unfold in a child; and, therefore, it is "commonly" reduced to a "biologistic" understanding of biological material: as if the very humanity of the child has become completely excluded from "sight". But each one of us is a "witness" to the beginning of personhood; and, indeed, a beginning that proceeds uninterruptedly to the manifestation of the person conceived. This is not to say that there are not difficulties and problems; however, it is to say that each one of us has a concrete beginning. If it is in this *one vision of the two eyes of faith and reason* that the *Gospel of Life* is written, then it is in this spirit that it has to be read.

Evangelium Vitae is a wide ranging work in its own right; however, the focus here is on the definition, as it were, of the beginning of the human person350. Man *'is a manifestation of God in the world, a sign of his presence, a trace of his glory* (cf. Gen 1: 26-27; Ps 8: 6)'351. In one sense, then, the very existence of man is evidence of a cause "proportionate" to his being; and, therefore, man 'is a manifestation of God in the world'. However, man himself, in the very mystery of his being, is not only evidence of a "proportionate" cause of his being – but is evidence of the

---

349 *Gaudium et Spes*, 36, quoted in art 22 of *Evangelium Vitae*.

350 Cf. Francis Etheredge: two other discussions of *Evangelium Vitae*. The first discussion is to be found in *Scripture: A Unique Word*, Chapter Eleven, Newcastle upon Tyne: Cambridge Scholars Publishing, 2014. The second discussion is to be found in the trilogy, *Truth from truth, Volume I-Faithful Reason*, Chapter Four, also published by Cambridge Scholars Publishing, but in 2016.

351 *Evangelium Vitae*, 34.

existence of God: 'a manifestation of God'. In other words, the very "being" of man is a 'trace of [H]is glory' and, as such, communicates the answer to the question posed in man's very existence: that man "speaks" of the mystery of the Blessed Trinity. Thus in as many ways as man, male and female, is intelligent, imaginative, personal, relational, free, truthful, complementary, dynamic, different, creative, communicative, communitarian, individual, unique, responsible, authoritative, loving and expressive, "they" expresses "their" God: the Blessed Trinity. These qualities, then, and many more, arise out of where and point to whom – if not to God who has given a witness to Himself in the very majesty, beauty and splendidly wonderful detail of creation?

Nevertheless, taking account of all the difficulties involved, the Church nevertheless teaches that 'from the first moment of its existence, [the person] must be guaranteed that unconditional respect which is morally due to the human being in his or her totality and unity as body and spirit' (*Evangelium Vitae*, 60). In other words, to paraphrase St. John Paul II, the only adequate response to the beginning of the person is love[352]; and, by way of explanation, this response of 'unconditional respect' is 'morally due to the human being in his or her totality and unity as body and spirit'. In other words, the very nature of 'his or her totality and unity as body and spirit' entails a response of 'unconditional respect' which is 'morally due' to the person. This expression, of 'unconditional respect' being 'morally due' to the person, brings us to the unique nature, in a way, of human relationships: that there is a type of response which is fundamental to each one of us: 'the due regulation of our free actions, in which morality consists, is simply their right ordering with a view to the perfecting of

---

[352] Cf. Pope St. John Paul II/Karol Wojtyla, *Love and Responsibility*, p. 41.

our rational nature'353. Thus to speak of 'unconditional respect' being 'morally due' to the person is to recognize what expresses the right response to the human person: a response which expresses the perfection of the relationship between people. '[U]nconditional respect', then, expresses that "transparency" of the person to the good of the "other"; and, at the same time, 'unconditional respect' rightly identifies what befits the relationship of one person to another. It may be possible, however, to go further and to say that 'unconditional respect' entails an awareness, almost a marvelling wonder at the very existence of the other person; and, possibly, an intimation that this other person is "mirroring" the very mystery of personhood itself: a kind of glimpse that "person" translates an invisible into a visible reality.

At the same time, however, there is a response of joy which belongs to the conception of a child (cf. Lk 1: 14, 41-48). While 'respect', then, does refer to the dignity of a human person and, in a certain way, expresses the presence of a mystery, as it were, "showing through"354, joy reveals the "en-rapturous" welcome which truly belongs to the child conceived: a joy that "envelopes" the new beginning in a glow of mysterious gratitude and rejoicing. In other words,

---

353 Joyce, George. "Morality". The Catholic Encyclopedia. Vol. 10. New York: Robert Appleton Company, 1911. 5 Oct. 2016 <http://www.newadvent.org/cathen/10559a.htm>. There is also the view that ethics "follows on" morality as a more scientific examination of it (cf. Cathrein, Victor. "Ethics." The Catholic Encyclopedia. Vol. 5. New York: Robert Appleton Company, 1909. 5 Oct. 2016 <http://www.newadvent.org/cathen/05556a.htm>. I do not want to digress, however, into this subject except by way of saying that morality, as such, appears to be expressive of our humanity in a way that ethics, properly understood, refines and perfects.

354 Cf. *Blackie's Compact Etymological Dictionary*, p. 275: 'Respect ... to look behind, to consider ...'.

joy brings out what can so often be overlooked, namely the whole humanity of the relationship between parent and child, *precisely because "joy" responds to the reality of relationship*; and, paradoxically, even the denial of relationship entails an implicit recognition of the humanity of the child conceived, albeit it communicates this positive truth in its tragic dimensions.

How true it is that in the life of Christ we can find and understand the recapitulation of the history of the person[355]. Just as Christ's life was not without the shadow of the cross, however, even in infancy, so this mystery enfolds all the difficulties that we encounter in the welcome of new life and brings us hope, encouragement and the gift of providential help.

Dignitatis Personae, 2008

'If *Donum vitae,* in order to avoid a statement of an explicitly philosophical nature, did not define the embryo as a person, it nonetheless did indicate that there is an intrinsic connection between the ontological dimension and the specific value of every human life' (*Dignitatis Personae*, 5). At the very least, then, it is clear that without a beginning, there is no possibility of human personhood; and, therefore, it is clear that a beginning is at the very least a real prerequisite for the existence of human personhood[356] – either

---

[355] Cf. *Gaudium et Spes*, 38.

[356] In the case of a child conceived through *in vitro* technology, there is nevertheless a real beginning, albeit a real beginning deprived of the natural human context of the maternal environment of that beginning; and, what is more, just as it is clear that a child is conceived, so it is also clear that God loves the person into existence and not the human method that circumvents what conception requires to communicate: the mystery of unconditionally loved life from love.

because an actual beginning intrinsically entails ensoulment and therefore personhood or because a beginning is intrinsically ordered to a developmentally delayed ensoulment. In other words, even if there is no philosophical certainty that, from the first instant of fertilization, *there is an embryonic human person* – neither is there a philosophical certainty that *there is not a human person present* from the first instant of human fertilization. To paraphrase St. Thomas Aquinas, it is irrelevant from the point of view of the goal of the process of human conception that the soul is not present from the beginning, because in either case the *goal of the process of conception is precisely the manifestation of the ensoulment that constitutes the very body as that of a human being*. In other words, if the whole "goal" of the process of human fertilization is the reality of human personhood, then it follows that the relationship to the soul is either *implied or already actualized*. If the relationship to the soul is implied, then the very first instant of fertilization is indeed already ordered to ensoulment; and, if the human soul is present from the first instant of conception, then human personhood is present in all its fullness. From the point of view of indicating 'that there is an intrinsic connection between the ontological dimension and the specific value of every human life' (*Dignitatis Personae*, 5) it is clear, then, that the very ordering of human conception to ensoulment is what constitutes the irrevocable relationship between the 'ontological dimension' of the new being and 'the specific value of every human life' (5). In other words, it is not possible to separate the ontological significance of a being "ordained" for ensoulment and the value of human life; and, indeed, like the effect of a light which illuminates not only where we are but also the path travelled, it is possible to argue that the beginning of a being "benefits" from even the "implied" value of the goal of it becoming ensouled.

The alternative view, however, is that human personhood is present in all its "ontological" fullness, in the unity of being one in body and soul, from the first instant of conception. The argument that points to the heart of this possibility is that a personal being is personal to the depths and details of what that being is. Just, then, as the new being comes to life, with fertilization as the "event" of the unification of sperm and egg and the formation of an embryonic wall, so that "life" in the very moment of it being the life of the new being is ensouled by God and is, therefore, the life of the embryonic human person. Just as "word" and "meaning" contribute to the expressed reality of a person-in-conversation, and the readiness of an electric current for being turned on is actualized as the switch is thrown, so there does not come into existence a human body but that it is ensouled by God and manifests the human person.

In view, then, of the obvious relationship between conception and the manifestation of "who" is conceived, it follows that it is reasonable to recognize that the first instant of fertilization entails the actual presence of the person[357].

In conclusion, then, there has been a progressive assimilation of the developmental reality of human fertilization which, as such, entails an actual beginning; and, at the same time, there are philosophical problems with the claim of immediate animation or ensoulment, particularly concerning the readiness of the new being to be ensouled.

If the Church has managed to 'avoid a statement of an explicitly philosophical nature' concerning the 'embryo as a person, it nonetheless did indicate that there is an intrinsic connection between the ontological dimension and the specific value of every human life' (*Dignitatis Personae*, 5); and, in the process, the Church has nevertheless formulated

---

[357] Cf. *Donum Vitae*, 1. 1.

her position in philosophical terms: that there is 'an intrinsic connection between the ontological dimension and the specific value of every human life' (*Dignitatis Personae*, 5).

Perhaps part of the problem, then, is recognizing that there are a number of philosophical tasks. The first task is that of assembling the real evidence and reasoning from it. Secondly, if it is true that the embryo is a person, it is necessary to find an expression of that truth that both reflects that evidence and reason's argument from it. In particular, what makes it possible for ensoulment to be from the first instant of fertilization is that the soul as "life" is immediately "integrateable" in the very being of the new entity that is in that moment of ensoulment actually "come" to exist. Finally, there is the possibility that reason may benefit from Revelation, from the word of God, just as St. Thomas Aquinas held that we needed the help of divine Revelation to recognize that God created the universe, so we need the help of Revelation to recognize the existence of the person from the first instant of conception.

In the Foreword to Chapter IV that follows, Sr. Helena Burns, fsp, sketches very briefly but strongly a number of features in the culture in which we live, both positive and negative; and, therefore, she prepares the reader to engage with the whole philosophical challenge to go to the depths of human personhood and to discover, anew, the help of philosophy in the quest to understand the mystery of human conception.

Francis Etheredge

Francis Etheredge

CHAPTER FOUR:
FOREWORD AND BIOGRAPHY

Sr. Helena Burns, FSP

Biography

Sr. Helena Burns, fsp, is a member of the Daughters of St. Paul, an international congregation of Roman Catholic Sisters founded to communicate God's Word through the media. She has an M.A. in Media Literacy Education; a B.A. in theology and philosophy from St. John's University, NYC; studied screenwriting at UCLA and Act One-Hollywood; and holds a Certificate in Pastoral Youth Ministry. Sr. Helena is also studying at the Theology of the Body Institute, PA. She is a movie reviewer for Life Teen & The Catholic Channel-- Sirius XM. She wrote and directed a documentary on the life of Blessed James Alberione: www.MediaApostle.com and is a co-producer on www.The40Film.com (40 years since Roe v. Wade: abortion in the USA). She has written a Theology of the Body curriculum: www.tinyurl.com/TOBtraining and her daily book for young women is "He Speaks to You": www.tinyurl.com/DailyBook. She is also a regional vocation directress for the Daughters of St. Paul.

Sr. Helena gives Media Literacy & Theology of the Body workshops & courses to youth & adults all over Canada and the U.S., and believes that media can be a primary tool for sharing God's love and salvation. (She is a dual citizen, Canada/USA: an international woman of mystery.) Her blog is www.HellBurns.com

Foreword: Human Conception in the Context of our Culture

Before I came to faith, philosophy was my sure guide. I loved the way you could reason to the soundness and truth of things and really pin veracity down. Philosophy didn't make me Catholic, but it now helps to keep me Catholic because the Catholic Church loves philosophy, science and any other kind of truth-seeking and gathering. Good philosophy (starting with the ancient Greeks) keeps me Catholic because, as my philosophical minds sees it, the alternatives to the Catholic Faith are religions that are often inconsistent even within themselves and unable to do anything but conform to the zeitgeist, and bad philosophies that fall short of truth or despair of truth. We are reaping the bitter fruits of these faulty lines of thinking, acting and living in today's ever darker globalist culture of death.

Human Beginnings: a Response of Reverence, Wonder and Joy

The "moment" of human beginnings is a fascinating topic, and one that, it would seem, should be approached with reverence, wonder and joy. When technicians first began uniting animal sperm and eggs in the lab, they were able to observe a small burst of light at each animal conception. Human conception in the Petri dish produces a much larger light burst. Sadly, awe at human beginnings (conception) is often not the case, more and more. There is either a cold, materialist, atheistic, scientism-inspired, clinical analysis/praxis (never rejoining the full human

Conception: An Icon of the Beginning

experience), a consumer product experience (IVF, surrogacy) or worse (embryonic stem cell research/experimentation).

British scientist, Robert Edwards, who helped produce the first IVF (*in vitro* fertilization) baby on July 25, 1978 (exactly ten years to the day after *Humanae Vitae* was promulgated), told the *London Times* in 2003: "I wanted to find out exactly who was in charge, whether it was God Himself or whether it was scientists in the laboratory. It was us." Yes, and no. Human beings are derivative. It's like the story about God and the devil. The devil told God he could make a human just as well as God could. "Fine," said God. God went first. He bent down, scooped up some dirt and fashioned a man. "Your turn," said God. But as the devil followed suit and grabbed a fistful of dirt, God said: "No. Get your own dirt." In the case of IVF, God humbly obeys man playing God and infuses a human soul at the fertilization of the egg.

Science updates the Church's teaching on the sacredness of human life

Those who are pro-abortion often point to St. Thomas Aquinas' ignorance of modern science (er, he lived before the advent of modern science) as an example of "the Catholic Church not always being pro-life." They will say things such as: "Aquinas thought the soul only came into the embryo at forty days or when the baby 'quickened' [the mum could feel the baby kick]." Two responses here: a) the pro-abort is then admitting that modern science tells us that life begins at conception b) science (modern or otherwise) does not dictate to or supersede God's Revelation. Although Aquinas drew from Aristotle (and other pagans or non-Christians), he didn't do so in isolation or uncritically. The Church--along with the rest of humanity--may not have known exactly when and how a new human person is conceived and develops until modern science discovered these things, but She always knew that human life in the womb is sacred. The Bible, Old and New Testaments are filled with talk of the respect owed to the sanctuary of the womb, the woman and the new life therein. The greatest example, of course, is the Annunciation and the Visitation (both in the Gospel of Luke, chapter 1). The Holy House of Loreto (the Virgin Mary's house that was miraculously transported to Italy from Nazareth in the thirteenth century) has an inscription (from an apparition and message of the Mother of God): "Here the Word was made flesh!" The Didache (the teaching of the Apostles) rejected abortion from the first century. Regardless of what "stage" life is at in the womb, it was understood to be new human life and the Church never approved ending that life.

Modern science and good philosophy contradict the delayed "Personhood Theory"

Modern science is very clear that human life begins at conception. A new human being (or "beings" in the case of identical twins or multiples) with brand-new, for-the-first-time-on-earth, unique DNA. When running for President of the United States, Barack Obama quipped (when put on the spot as to when life begins): "That's above my pay grade," he was either astonishingly ignorant of basic science or engaging in gross dissembling. For anyone keeping up at all with the arguments for abortion these days, very few will even try to appeal to "it's not a baby yet." Instead, we have the horrific "personhood theory" in place today, promoted by utilitarian philosophers such as the notorious Peter Singer.

"Personhood theory" gets around science's blatant proclamation that human life begins at conception, so it's "reasoned" (or rather equivocated) thus: "Sure, it's alive.

Sure, it's a human being. But it's not a human *person* yet. And only persons have rights, so this living human being does not have the right to life." When queried when "it" actually becomes a human person, these philosophers can't tell ya, *because they're still struggling to define even an adult human person themselves and do not agree among themselves and have wildly varying answers that break with anything any civilization has ever held about the human being-person.* In other words, civilization has always believed that a human being is a human person. Human body? Made of human stuff? Then you are a human being. Here are some of these outre philosophers squishy ideas about what *might* make a human being a human person: Consciousness? (which they also can't define) Memory? A deep level of self-awareness? Productiveness? Happiness? Meaningful relationships? A certain quality of life? Peter Singer has stated that he's not sure if a three year old is a person yet.

"Personhood theory" is the ultimate (or ultimate to date) in evil thinking about the human person: dividing body and soul, matter and spirit, physical and spiritual. "Personhood" is now something defined, bestowed and revoked by philosophers: A human being is not a human person. It is only a human person when "they" say it is. Preposterous and no one will buy it? Not at all. It has already been sold. Philosophy informs bio-ethics which informs policy (very hands-on policy in hospitals when an immediate decision must be made about your loved one's health/life/death). Philosophy/ethics also inform laws and the courts and doctors and lawyers and judges and let's not forget: education. At all levels: from what little Suzy and Johnny are taught in nursery school to what Suzy PhD and Johnny MBA will be taught is Gospel truth, cross-curriculum and throughout their entire academic careers. Therefore: #PlannedParenthoodSellsBabyParts. "Personhood theory" is the semantics of wickedness, or as an English judge trying a Nazi war criminal called such murderous views of the human person: sheer "blackheartedness."

Not a potential person but a person with potential

How about this: the newly conceived human being is *not* a potential person, but a person with a lot of potential? Or, as Karol Wojtyla puts it so much more eloquently: "When a human being is conceived, a new spirit is conceived simultaneously, united in substance with the body, which begins to exist in embryo in the mother's womb. *If it were not so it would be impossible to understand how the embryo could subsequently develop into a human being, a human person*"[358]. An oak seedling doesn't grow into a maple or a non-oak. It is what it is.

---

[358] *Love and Responsibility*, p. 55, Wojtyla, Ignatius Press, San Francisco.

Chapter Four: How Does Philosophy Help Us to Understand the "Moment" of Human Beginning?

General Introduction to Chapter 4: Philosophical and Theological Dialogue. This chapter draws explicitly on *philosophy* for the inseparably complementary understanding of what a soul is and how, therefore, it can be understood to be one with the body from conception. Thus it seems as if it were possible to consider an analogy of differences that yet constitute an inseparable whole: the *biblical* soul and the *philosophical* body of concepts are what *together constitute theology*. Can one any more separate this discussion on the soul from its biblical roots than one can separate it from the philosophical context *through* which it has developed? In other words, philosophy and Revelation seem to *mutually condition* each other in a way that is analogous to what is said of the relationship between the body and the soul[359]; and thus they do so in a way that does not destroy the *logical and ontological priority of Revelation to reason*[360], which is also analogous to the *logical and ontological priority of the unity of man to the "plurality" of his being*[361]. Therefore does the unity of a *biblically philosophical* or a *philosophically biblical*

---

[359] N. A. Luyten, *Soul-Body Relationship*, p. 472 of Vol XIII, NCE.

[360] Cf. I. C. Brady, *Soul, Human, 2. Patristic and Medieval Writers, Nemesius*, pp. 453-454 of Vol XIII, NCE.

[361] P. B. T. Bilaniuk, *Soul, Human, 5. Theology*, p. 462 of Vol XIII, NCE.

theology furnish an analogy with the unity of the person, one in soul and body?

While there is truth[362], which is by definition constant, it is also true that our knowledge of it develops in relation to what is contingent. In other words, as St. Thomas Aquinas suggests, it is not necessary to decide what is still insufficiently determined by the evidence[363]. By implycation, then, the recognition of relevant evidence on the beginning of human being can both *refashion* one's existing understanding of it *or* extend it to the point of obtaining the *resolution* of an acknowledged difficulty - *but in neither case will what is true cease to be true nor will truth contradict truth*[364]. In other words, the accumulation of relevant evidence can be as decisive to the development of human understanding as the possession of the requisite principles. Therefore, it could be said, the development of understanding is in proportion as it were to the availability of the relevant evidence and the *remembrance*[365] of what is already known.

---

[362] Cf. *Summa Theologiae*, Benziger Brothers, Pt I, Qu 2, art 1, p. 11: to claim it is true that there is no truth is to demonstrate that it exists.

[363] Cf. Copleston, *Aquinas*, p. 72 and *Summa Theologiae*, Methuen, Pt I, Qu 32, art 1, p. 71.

[364] Vatican I, *Dei Filius*, art 3017 on *Faith and reason cannot contradict each other*, p. 46 of *The Christian Faith*.

[365] It can be noted at this point, if not discussed, how 'memory' has become a significant term in the modern discussion of a variety of things, as if to say that a modern weakness lies in precisely *not remembering the past and not using the memory generally*. Cf. A. Kenny, *Aquinas*, which is part of the *Past Masters* series, Gen. ed. K. Thomas, (Oxford: Oxford University Press, 1980), pp. 28-30, where he observes a general, but not altogether complete lack of the use of the work of St. Thomas Aquinas. Cf. also Pope St. John Paul II, *Catechesi Tradendae*, 55.

Conception: An Icon of the Beginning

Finally, just as a *theological* idea like that of the person[366] drew on the Greek word for mask, *prosopon*, helping to fashion an understanding of the unitary nature of Christ and the mystery of the Blessed Trinity, so Revelation may assist us with a definition of human being which may complement the philosophical terminology necessary to the explanation of human conception. These definitions, referring as they do to the reality of human life and thought, express a fruit of that profound mystery of the activity of the Holy Spirit in the culture of man[367], which so prepares that culture that it not only contributes to the *incarnational inculturation of the Gospel*, but in some way contributes something necessary, while subordinate to it, just as the body contributes something necessary while subordinate to the soul. In other words, all truth, whether *natural* and of reason, *or supernatural*[368] and of Revelation, has its own *intrinsic relationship* to the Spirit of truth. Thus, in the end, there is a constant dialogue between the truth of Revelation and the truth as disclosed through natural reflection. In any meditation on conception, therefore, which draws on God's act of creation as revealed through reason and Revelation, there is a necessary "osmosis" of meaning as we endeavour to pass to the reality "prior" to both Revelation and reflection: the reality of conception established by the original act of the Creator.

Introduction to Chapter 4: Being and Beginning. This chapter is, more directly and explicitly than the rest of the book, an exposition of the principle: *Where the body*

---

[366] Cf. Henri de Lubac, "On Christian Philosophy", p. 481.

[367] *Ad Gentes Divinitus*, 9.

[368] Cf. *Dei Filius* art 3015 of Vatican Council I, p. 45 of *The Christian Faith*.

lives, there the soul is, and where both are is the person. Thus, even if the rest of the book is a necessary complement to this chapter, entailing as it does an introduction to analogy, to Scripture and to the teaching of the Magisterium, nevertheless this chapter is the one in which the ideas which have arisen elsewhere are pursued more systematically; and, in one sense, it is in the very progress that is necessary to understanding the reality to which, ultimately, our terms refer, that there emerges a synthetic understanding of conception. In other words the formulation of the principle concerning the relationship of *bodily life to the presence of the soul* arises out of the pursuit of the parts and expresses, in a sense, the whole to which the parts constantly refer.

The structure of this chapter, then, emerges out of a series of questions which, almost without end, proceed through a process of examining the meaning if not the origin of a variety of terms; and, in one sense, there has to be a "closure" to the discussion which, like any investigation, spreads out and brings into view an innumerable number of further questions. At the same time, however, the progress of this investigation is not exactly linear; and, in so far as it can, it brings together an increasingly complex consideration of the many-faceted reality of meaning: of expressed embodied meaning. In other words, there is, as it were, a constant "passing" from what "is" in its integral fullness to what can be expressed; and, conversely, there is the task of a fuller exposition of the parts which need to be synthesized: a synthesis that is always "prefigured" as "gift" in the "object" to be investigated. In other words, the reality to be investigated pre-exists the investigator; and, in the case of human conception, its actual existence "anticipates" its exposition. What begins must have a definite moment of its beginning: a beginning which entails the whole of what it is. Thus, as obvious as it is, each of us "witnesses" the beginning entailed in the very fact of our existence; and, therefore, however difficult or problematic this is, there is the possibility of "disclosing" what expresses the reality of that beginning.

CHAPTER FOUR: PART I: A DEFINITION OF BEING

Introduction to Chapter 4: Part I: Being. If being is that which exists, in some form or other, like the being of an inanimate object, fish or human being, then being falls into two categories: the created being of all that exists as created and the uncreated Being of God. What, then, is the relationship between the being of what has been created and the Being of the Creator? Is the relationship of God to creature completely unrecognizable: as if the child bears no relationship to the parents? Indeed, did God "impose" a completely "different" structure upon creaturely being to what is characteristic of Himself? These questions, as difficult as they are to answer adequately, are nevertheless asked and answered.

The tendency inherent in this work is to imagine that the true self-love of God is an unselfish love that seeks to share the goodness of His own Being with all that exists; and, therefore, in seeking to understand the relationship between created and uncreated Being, it makes sense to recognize, if at all possible, the trace of uncreated Being as it is expressed in creaturely being. In other words, even if it is necessary to begin with a certain assumption of the relationship between the being of creation and the Being of the Creator, the credibility of that relationship increases with the depth and beauty of its elucidation. Just, then, as a child has a certain resemblance to the parents, so does creation have a certain resemblance to the Creator; and, just as the child is a personal expression of the relationship to the parents, so creation's resemblance to the Creator is an intimate signature, as it were, in the being of all that exists as created.

If, then, the being of all that exists expresses the unity-in-diversity of the Blessed Trinity, then just as creation "embodies" a "structural imprint" of the Blessed Trinity, *so each one of us is an icon of the beginning*; and, if relationship is essential to there being three persons in one God, then all created being embodies and expresses the mystery of relationships: *ad extra*, *ad intra*, and throughout the whole of creation.

Proceeding to a Definition of Being: Unity-in-Diversity

While it can be said, then, that philosophy is investigating the question of the nature of being, it can be observed that this investigation falls into the two, complementary investigations characteristic of its two points of departure: Revelation and philosophy. The investigation of Revelation in some way proceeds *through the biblical data* on the fact of the creation of man, with *the implication that each created existent* somehow *mirrors* the mystery of the whole. The philosophical investigation, which in some cases is inescapably influenced by the development of *theologically originated expressions*, such as "person", is by contrast an increasingly subtle extrapolation of distinctions and relationships which *follow on the rational appreciation of what actually exists*.

It appears, therefore, that the question of the *definition of being* is one of those fundamental questions to which the interaction of *Revelation* and *reason* can be so particularly useful.

Conception: An Icon of the Beginning

A point of departure in the Being of Christ

My first thoughts on this subject could well have begun with a comment made by the late Rev. Dr. John Redford in his *Introducing Theology*, when he says in the section on *Faith and Reason*: 'de Lubac could argue, in Christ there are two orders of being, Christ's divine and human natures. But these do not exist separately, only together in one person the Word made flesh'[369]. In terms of a modern reflection on the being of Christ, it is clear that His 'Being [is] completely derived from the 'Thou' of the Father and lived for the 'you' of men'[370]. Thus, the argument runs, the fullest expression of human being is that which imitates the being of Christ and thus we have, as it were, an account of the *Mariological* nature of human being: 'to be human most fundamentally is to receive — from God and from all others in God: the primary and deepest activity of a human being is to receive, to bring within, which is to say to interiorize, the relation to God and to all men in God which establishes us in being'[371]. Thus this theological conception of the archetypal structure of human being could well be one of the *modern discernments* of what has been traditionally called the trace of the Blessed Trinity in the work of creation, particularly in the creation of human being.

---

[369] Fr. J. Redford, *Introducing Theology*, A Course Book for the Distance Learning Degree in Theology, (Birmingham: Maryvale Institute, 1990), page 160.

[370] David L. Schindler, *Is America bourgeois?*, Communio, Vol XIV, No. 3, (Fall 1987), part II of his article particularly, pages 267-271. Thus on page 267 Schindler cites a quotation from Cardinal Ratzinger's book, *Introduction to Christianity*, New York: Crossroads, 1969, p. 154. The title of this issue of *Communio* is *On the Soul*.

[371] Schindler, *Is America bourgeois?*, Communio, p. 270.

It could be said, then, that bringing together the 'ideas of relation and unity'[372] anticipates the definition of being which is employed here, namely that being is a *unity-in-diversity (cf. Gaudium et Spes, 24)*.

A point of departure in the Being of the Blessed Trinity

It seems as if Pope St. John Paul II is suggesting, in support of his vision of the nature of the family as he develops it in *Familiaris Consortio,* that God has made His own Being the 'image' of the being of creation (11). But because of the other general principle that God's *Being* is what it is to be a *diverse unity*, then it seems that the existence of corporeality in creation is fundamental to God's creation of a diversity in creaturely being.

Now the question arises as to whether one can take the template of the Blessed Trinity and apply it, as it were, to human being in such a way as to see whether or not it yields, *for the individual human being*, a metaphysical parallel between the structure of the human individual and the mystery of the Being of the Blessed Trinity.

What then are the conceptual requirements that an image of human being, which is in the image of the Divine Being, must fulfil?

The conceptual requirements are twofold: there must be something which expresses the indivisible unity of the human being; and secondly, this being must itself be a unified totality of irreducibly diverse elements[373]. The first

---

372 Schindler, *Is America bourgeois?, Communio*, p. 269.

373 Perhaps a surprising confirmation of this idea comes from Cardinal Ratzinger's book, *'In the Beginning'*, where, on p. 52, he

follows from the reality that God is One and the second follows from the reality that: '*The divine persons are really distinct from one another*'374.

A template of human being

The diversity inherent to human being, of body and soul, makes the 'unified totality'375 of the human person; and, as such, this makes the human being expressive of *the unity and diversity that is God*. This diversity of "body and soul", however, cannot be considered a dualism. Therefore the "unity" of body and soul, even if subject to the unnatural rupture of death, must be radical: a wholly "inhering" of one "in" the other; and, as a consequence, the soul gives life and expression to the human person according to the capacity of the body to receive and to express it. What we have, then, is a unity-in-diversity of the human race: male and female; and, within the radical unity of each person, an inescapable unity-in-diversity of individualized personhood.

Thus the "term" of unity is the person; and the "terms" of diversity are the body and the soul. Therefore, from the point of view of a trinitarian definition of human being, both conditions are fulfilled. For the person is the unified totality of body and soul; and, in addition, the body and the soul are

---

quotes Jacques Monod to the effect: 'all things in the universe cannot be derived from one another with ineluctable necessity.' He then goes on to say something with which I can only agree if what he means is that there cannot be a formula based on the unity of things to the exclusion of this irreducible diversity. The Cardinal continues: 'There is no single all-embracing formula from which everything necessarily derives.' The work from which the Cardinal draws these thoughts of Jaques Monod is from pp. 56ff., 179-79 of: 'J Monod, *Zufall und Notwendigkeit. Philosophische Fragen der modernen Biologie* (Munich, 1973).'

374 CCC, 255.

irreducibly different: the body is corporeal and the soul is spiritual[376]. The body is the "outward" expression of its "inner" determination by the soul; and, conversely, the body "informs" the "inner" determination by the soul just as a material "conditions" the expression of an idea embodied in it. Thus, as St. John Paul II said: 'As an incarnate spirit, that is a soul which expresses itself in a body and a body informed by an immortal spirit, man is called to love in his unified totality' (11). In other words, the very fact that man is a "bioethical whole" implies that human activity is an indivisible expression of the whole of human being.

Finally, then, one comes to the question with which one began: what is being? On the one hand the being of an entity is its unified totality; and, therefore, what exists when it exists is *a unity-in-diversity*. On the other hand, if the entity is a created being, it *participates in the mystery of its Maker*. Thus, if God is a mystery, and created being is made in the image of the mystery that God is, then it follows that created being must in some way *confront us with what it at the same time communicates: the mystery of the Blessed Trinity*.

An imaginative synthesis: 'the burning coal' (Is 6: 6)

It is through the mystery of the *Incarnation* that God reveals the *unity-in-diversity* fundamental to the nature of creation and redemption[377], because that *unity-in-diversity* is fundamental to the *Creator, Redeemer* and *Sanctifier* of man, the Blessed Trinity.

---

[375] *Familiaris Consortio*, 11.
[376] CCC, 362.
[377] Cf. T. E. Clarke, *Created Actuation by Uncreated Act*, pp. 416-417 of Vol. IV, NCE.

Recalling, then, the value of an imaginative apprehension of what we understand of human being: What kind of image would express the different facts and insights that now contribute to one's understanding, however limited, of the nature of human life as *biblically perceived?* In *The Book of Isaiah* (Is 6: 6) there is the image of the 'burning coal'; and, as such, it has the possibility of signifying both Christ *and* ourselves. It signifies Christ because it has the power to forgive sin (cf. Is 6: 7); and it signifies man because it signifies what does not have life in itself but which receives its life from the 'altar' from which it was taken (Is 6: 6). In other words, and in view of the distinction that the Scripture constantly makes between *the life of the Spirit* and *the death of dust,* it seems more and more obvious that what is *created to exist is created to exist in the life of Christ.* Therefore, just as Christ in His total humanity, in His body and soul, in *His flesh,* is alive with the Life of the Spirit of God (cf Mt 1: 20), then all this is expressed in this image: of what is dead and cold without the fire of the Holy Spirit[378] and yet what is alive and full of life *with* the fire of the Holy Spirit. Almost by way of confirmation, this image has been used by the 'Greek Fathers to describe the mystery of man's divinisation in the Incarnation and indwelling'[379].

The expression of the relationship between "grace" and "human nature" and "soul" and "body" in philosophical terms

The image of the 'burning coal' is now understood to be an imaginative equivalent to an intellectual expression which

---

[378] Cf. CCC, 696.
[379] T. E. Clarke, *Created Actuation by Uncreated Act,* p. 417 of Vol. IV, NCE.

would parallel[380] the union of body and soul with the union of God and man in our Lord Jesus Christ: 'God is conceived as communicating Himself to created reality, which He immediately actuates and unites with Himself; the term of this self-communication is a created, supernatural actuation of the creature's obediential potency by God, the uncreated Act'[381]. The metaphysical principle, which translates the *burning union* between man and God, is the polar principle of act and potency[382]: 'God makes Himself, analogously, the act of a created potency'[383]. In other words, having created in human nature a "natural" desire for God, it is God Himself who makes the fulfilment of this desire possible.

Now the work of St. Thomas Aquinas, to which these terms refer, is that the soul is "in act" with respect to the body's potentiality[384]. St. Thomas viewed it as a general characteristic of matter[385] that it existed in potentiality; and, therefore, the soul is that which makes this particular matter into this particular being[386]: a human being. Thus the soul is said to be the act of the body: that which, being what it is, made the matter to become what it could not become of itself. But because the matter *individuates*[387] the

---

[380] Clarke, *Created Actuation by Uncreated Act*, p. 416 of Vol. IV, NCE.

[381] Clarke, *Created Actuation by Uncreated Act*, p. 416 of Vol. IV, NCE.

[382] Cf. J. Bobik, *Soul*, p. 448 of Vol. XIII, NCE.

[383] Bobik, *Soul*, of Vol. XIII, NCE.

[384] Cf. J. Bobik, *Soul, Human, 4. Philosophical Analysis*, p. 462 of Vol. XIII, NCE.

[385] Cf. *Summa Theologiae*, Methuen, Pt I, Qu 47, art 1, p. 89.

[386] Cf. J. Bobik, *Soul, Human, 4. Philosophical Analysis*, p. 461 of Vol. XIII, NCE.

[387] Copleston, *Aquinas*, pp. 91 and 156.

soul and so participates *reciprocally in the making of the whole*, the matter is not an accident which inheres in the substance of the soul[388], like the white of a wall; rather, the soul and the body are *together the one existence of the person*: a unity so profound that it 'has ontological priority before the real and irreducible plurality of his being'[389]. In other words, the actual unity of a being derives, as it were, from the first moment of its existence being an integral expression of all that constitutes it; and, in the case of human being, this implies an act of existence in which "body" and "soul" are one indivisible whole: a human body coming to exist in the moment of its animation by a human soul. At the same time, however, we know that the biological constituents are constituted as "human" in virtue of their being a spousal gift: the egg from the woman and the sperm from the man; and, therefore, the human soul "fulfils" the human potential of the human gametes. Thus, although it is true that the human soul "constitutes" the "inner" identity of the human being, it is also true that it does so in its capacity to realize the potential of the biological constituents of human being.

Just as the act of God by which a human person comes to exist establishes a relationship between God and that person so, analogously, the coal needs the fire to transform a potentiality for the help of God into an actual presence of God's help. In other words, God not only brings a human being to exist, one in body and soul but, at the same time, communicates the possibility of being the "end" of human being just as certainly as God is the cause of the beginning-to-be-a-human-being. If, put negatively, we inherit original sin, an original "deprivation" of what perfected human being

---

[388] Cf. P. Bilaniuk, *Soul, Human*, 5. *Theology*, p. 462 of Vol. XIII, NCE.

[389] Bilaniuk, *Soul, Human*, Vol. XIII, NCE.

in the beginning, namely grace, put positively we retain a thirst, as it were, for the very waters of baptism which will begin to bring us to the eternal life to which we are "determined" by the very love out of which we were created.

The soul as "life" and the "activity" of the soul

St. Thomas Aquinas draws the distinction between the life of the soul and the activity of the soul; for if the soul were itself in activity 'then we would be in non-stop activity all our life long'[390].

This can be explained very briefly by saying that just as the constant activity of the sun does not mean that there is no darkness, so it does not follow that if the nature of being is to be active, that all activity is the same: to rest is an "activity". Further, just as the sun is one source of energy and yet many different things grow, so if *activity is fundamental to being*, it seems to follow that that would result in one kind of activity informing everything else, which is the *desire for God*[391], and yet this leads to the manifest variety of human acts. Therefore, perhaps activity is like light: it has one fundamental and unitary expression of *being white* which can nevertheless be broken down into the colours of the spectrum *and then mixed to produce more colours*, while nevertheless it all *follows* on the nature of *white* light.

The very presence, then, of a vocational "return" to God from whom existence is received, is expressed more fully as the whole identity, development and multifaceted relationships of each one of us unfold and find expression. In other words, the presence of a vocational "return" to God

---

[390] *Summa Theologiae*, Methuen, Pt 1, Qu 77, art 1, p. 118.

[391] *Summa Theologiae*, Methuen, Pt II, Qu 1, art 8: 'God is the ultimate goal of all' p. 174.

"encompasses" the unfolding of the whole humanity it helps to express.

How widely can the principle of unity-in-diversity be applied?

The Fathers of the *Second Vatican Council* were concerned with the 'parallel between the union existing among the divine persons and the union of the sons of God in truth and love' (*Gaudium et Spes*, 24) and not the nature of creation as a whole or of individual human being in particular.

It may be true that the parallel 'between the union existing among the divine persons and the union of the sons of God in truth and love' is itself the fullest expression of the parallel between man and God. Nevertheless, the parallel between man and God does imply a *presupposition*, as it were, of a parallel *between the being of creation as a whole and the Being of the Creator*: a parallel that was established at creation and "suffered" the disfiguration of the fall. Thus it follows that the relationship of the whole of creation to the Creator will be finally restored at the end of time when, as St. Paul says, creation will be freed from its subjection to futility; and, therefore, creation being in the 'image and likeness' of God will shine through the restoration of all things in Christ. In particular, then, it will be transparent how man, male and female, is in the image and likeness of God; and, therefore, how this image and likeness is expressed in the detailed word of human being beginning, as it were, with the mystery of human conception. Meanwhile, however, it is necessary to trace, as it were, the contours of what will be radiantly evident at the end of time: the general contours that manifest the expression of the Blessed Trinity in the reality of human being.

Three conclusions on the nature of being

What this seems to culminate in is that the nature of the beginning, whether of the beginning of creation or the beginning of an individual human being, is a mystery in that it is an act of God. In so far, however, as we can learn about this act of God through reason's reflection on Revelation, this mystery *brings about the real beginning of created being, the activity of which will be both manifestly*[392] *unitary and diverse.*

There seem to be three implications to the conclusion of an act of God that "replicates" the mystery of divine Being in the very act of creation: the first concerns the beginning of creation; the second concerns the beginning of each one of us; and the third concerns a *theological answer* to a philosophical question.

The first implication: the beginning of creation

The first implication to recognizing an original act of God at the beginning of creation is the question: *Is this an argument against evolution?* Evolution is here understood as an uninterrupted "progression" from inanimate matter to animate beings. At the same time, though, there may be characteristics of living beings which, owing to environmental changes and dietary influences do become dominant and, as such, vary from place to place. In the sense that created being, *however*, does not have to evolve to be different, this could be an argument against the evolution of different kinds of creaturely being. Thus, if this is true, differences in created being will be radically evident from the

---

[392] Copleston, *Aquinas*, p. 158: 'activity follows, that is manifests, being *(operatio sequitur esse)* ...'.

beginning of creation *and* evident in the activities of each and every created being.

The inherent unity of the whole of creation and the particular unity of each part of it is something that creation will possess as intrinsic to it from *the very beginning to exist*. The being of creation cannot acquire the fact that it is a particular expression of what it is to be a unity-in-diversity: it will be this from the beginning of its being *or not at all*. What is interesting is that the very language of Scripture denotes a twofold order, as it were, of the 'heavens and the earth' (Gn 1: 1); and, in Hebrew, the term 'heavens' is masculine (*hashamayim*) and the term 'earth' is feminine (*haaretz*). More widely, there are the invisible, heavenly beings of the angels and indeed heaven itself and then there is the whole, visible, created order; and, therefore, even in terms of the "natural" variety of creatures, there are the "visible" and the "invisible".

In general, then, human beings exist in the context of the rest of creation in that from the first instant of their existence they are a visible expression of an invisible principle, a man-person or a woman-person and, at the same time, they possess and express a personal life and capacity for a wide variety of relationships, creativity and moral perfectibility.

The second implication: human being

The second implication of this is that human being will manifest, in the diverse activities of which men and women are capable, the fundamental mystery of their own being. Each one of us is a person: one in body and soul; and that this is, just as with creation as a whole, a fundamental fact of each of us. Thus, if it is true, it will *have to be true from the beginning of each one of us or not at all*. And this is so for the same reason as that expressed above, namely, it cannot be true that we are both a *unity-in-diversity* in the sense I have defined, that is from the beginning of our being, *and* we become a unity in diversity following the union of a soul with a pre-existing body.

Therefore, for the theological reason of a being which is a unity-in-diversity, expressing in a more perfect way *the image of God*, I have to conclude that the human being is a person: is one in body and soul from conception. Thus, in a certain way, if creation began as a unity-in-diversity and if each one of us did too, then *each one of us is an icon of the beginning*.

The third implication: answering the philosophical problems of uniformity or irreconcilable diversity

The third implication is that this vision of being is, as it were, an answer to a problem as posed by philosophy. There seems to be a tendency in a particular kind of rationalism to resolve everything into one type of being, as it were, somewhat like an evolutionary theory would endeavour to do if it begins with an original big bang and proceeds to uninterruptedly differentiate itself into every kind of existing species and individual. *Or* there is a countertendency to resolve things into *relatively unrelated* differences, such as the difference between a particular conception of spirit and matter which expresses an *alienation between the two*[393]: as if "matter" is uniquely evil and spirit is uncompromisingly good. Or there is an apparently unresolvable *metaphysical*

---

[393] Cf. P. L. Quinn, *Manichaeism*, page 519 of *The Oxford Companion to Philosophy*, ed. T. Honderich, (Oxford: Oxford University Press, 1995). Cf also Heino Sonnemans, *Soul, afterlife, salvation*, page 251 of *Communio*, Vol XIV, No 3, (Fall 1987).

Conception: An Icon of the Beginning

parallelism[394] of a physical body and a non-physical spirit that is, contradictorily, resolved by a non-physical spirit being located in a particular place within a physical body. Or, alternatively, a mental state is "identical" to a brain state. A third way, however, which is to perceive differences as existing within a unifying relationship would appear to be intuitively perceived in the following symbol: 'the Chinese Yin-Yang symbol, which sees male and female as harmony, stands at the place where one would expect conflicts and proposals for a resolution of the relationship between the sexes'[395].

On the one hand, then, it would seem that the doctrine of the Blessed Trinity is the source through which these sometimes conflicting tendencies *to unity* and *to diversity* can be reconciled; and, on the other hand, any *natural precursors* to the Christian perception of being can be purified of what is an *obstacle* to assist us in the *living reconciliation of our undeniable differences.*

Finally, while this meditation on the nature of created being was not perhaps the particular 'horizons closed to human reason' (*Gaudium et Spes,* 24) envisaged by the Fathers of the *Second Vatican Council*, nevertheless the

---

[394] Cf. J. Cottingham, *Cartesianism*, p. 123 and A. Belsey, *Matter*, p. 539 of *The Oxford Companion to Philosophy*, editor T. Honderlich, (Oxford: Oxford University Press, 1995). Cf. also Schindler, "*Is America bourgeois?*", p. 275.

[395] E. Moltmann-Wendel, *I am My Body*, translated from the German by John Bowden, (London: SCM Press Ltd, 1994), p. 8. While the context of this quotation is that Elisabeth goes on to express a disappointment concerning this symbol: 'Hasn't brutal physical oppression of women taken place under this old symbol? Here we have open questions to a world-view which hardly touches on reality and real bodies and yet inspires many people.' Cf. also Kwong-loi Shun, *Chinese Philosophy*, p. 131 of *The Oxford Companion to Philosophy*.

principle of created being expressing a characteristic unity-in-diversity does seem to be a fruit of their reflection.

CHAPTER FOUR: PART II: DEFINING WHAT EXISTS

Introduction to Chapter 4: Part II: Questions have answers. A book like this is autobiographical to the extent that it explores how to understand the following question: Did we begin body and soul at conception or did the body begin before the soul and was it, therefore, subsequently ensouled? The conclusion to which this research leads is summed up by the following principle: *where the body lives, there the soul is, and where both are is the person.*

But just as one term is inseparably connected to others and to the reality to which they refer, so questions are inseparably connected to each other and to the cultural context in which they exist. Thus it is that this question about the origin of human life is accepted within the context of the tradition out of which it has arisen[396]. The question of the *moment* of the *animation of human being, of the moment from which a human being exists,* would not be a meaningful question, would not even exist as a question in the same way, if there did not exist a "soul" and a "body" and "life" and "death". In other words, this is about seeking a coherent understanding of "soul" and "body" and how it applies to an outstanding question: When does the soul animate the body? In a certain way, then, there is presupposed a natural "flow" between what exists and the concepts which refer to the "whole" of what exists; however,

---

[396] Cf. *Let Me Live,* footnote 19, p. 16.

Conception: An Icon of the Beginning

as what exists is prior to understanding it, concepts and their interrelationships are capable of refinement in the light of further evidence. Thus thinking through these terminological steps has clarified and informed the very "working definition" of the terms which this work records in coming to recognize a first instant to the existence of a human being.

At the same time, however, as there is a kind of "passing" into words of the world in which we live or, better, expressing in "words" the "word" born within what exists, there is also the "argument" about the truth of what exists. The "soul", as a principle of life, distinguishes what is animate from what is inanimate: a distinction that can designate life, activity, movement, growth, power to reproduce or procreate and the wider capacities of estimating the relationship between need and environment, expressing an understanding of reality, appreciating friendship and loving God. In other words, even if the existence of a soul is denied, there is still the challenge of addressing what differentiates what is living from what is non-living and what is living in general from human personhood in particular and his or her capacity for relationship and communication which clearly exceeds the capabilities of inorganic or organic matter.

Accepting, albeit critically, a tradition out of which and within which to work, is an acceptance which is a fundamental part of conversion to the existence of God: a *fact* inseparable from a *meaning* which *forms us in reality*. Not only is it possible to suffer agonies of uncertainty and to be plagued by impossibly interminable questions but this *state, which in some way arises out of the denial of reality*, seems to be particularly evident in our society and, indeed, one might say, in the very weakness of humans beings who are subject to original sin. Our dialogue with reality is therefore analogous to our dialogue with one another[397] and *can only* proceed to the extent that one agrees with what reason and Revelation tell us to be the true nature of what exists. Truth is not the creation of man but of the Person (cf. Jn 14: 6) who goes before him in everything that he does[398]. Just as creation is not the work of man but the work of God who gives to man a participation in it, so God gives to man a participation in His work of *making known the truth: as if natural truth is ordered to divine truth*[399]. In other words, just as the work of making known the natural truth is ordered to the work of making known the revealed truth, so God gives us a participation in their discovery and dissemination.

If, then, there is a virtue that is especially required of an investigator of reality it would be the *humility to listen*; and, therefore, if there is any merit in what is written here, it is only because of a graced reception of it. Even so, however, there is a need to question how faithfully what is received accounts for what exists. If, therefore, the very language of "soul" and "body" poses a problem it is because it needs a more "integral" account of the person as a whole. "Body" and "soul" need to be complemented or re-expressed to communicate the amazing *unity-in-diversity of the psychosomatic being of the person*.

What follows is first of all an attempt to define the terms which are fundamental to the aforementioned principle, "where the body lives, there the soul is, and where both are is the person", and, in the process, to give an account of the facts and difficulties which occasioned it.

---

[397] Cf. *Summa Theologiae*, Methuen, Pt I, Qu 32, art 1, p. 71.

[398] Cf. H. de Lubac, *Abbyssus abyssum invocat*, p. 295 of Vol XIV, No 3, *Communio*, (Fall 1987).

[399] Cf. Hans Urs von Balthasar, *Theo-Logic: On the work as a whole*, pp. 623-624 of Vol XX, No 4, *Communio*, (Winter 1993).

Conception: An Icon of the Beginning

A Working Definition of Terms

This is an attempt to indicate the main roads which run through the little part of the reality-map with which this book is concerned. Alternatively it is an attempt to indicate the general structure in the cross-section of a tree, taken as it were at the point between the roots and the trunk. At the same time, however, there is a definite focus on the moment that each one of us begins to exist.

God

On the one hand it is God who defines the term "unity"; and on the other hand it is God who defines the term "diversity". The mystery of the Blessed Trinity could be said, therefore, to be *the defining Reality which at the same time transcends all definition*[400]. God is *the ever-existing mystery* in which the propositions of faith[401] and reason terminate[402], just as the being of the Blessed Trinity is the *transcendent origin of the design inherent in all His creation*[403]. It is already clear, then, from what has been said, that the Blessed Trinity is the absolute origin of all creation; and, therefore, what exists-as-created communicates in the very fact of existing an intelligible word of the Creator. In particular, then, what is the intelligible word that

---

[400] Cf. CCC, articles 39-43.

[401] Cf. CCC, 170.

[402] Cf. CCC, 36. Cf. also Cardinal Ratzinger, "Transmission of the Faith and the Sources of the Faith", a lecture reproduced by the *Apostolate of Catholic Truth*, Preston, England, p. 19.

[403] Cf. *Letter to Families*, 6.

conception communicates about the mystery of the Creator? In brief, the very meaning of the word conception entails the concept of beginning and, therefore, communicates the very opposite of the nature of God as the Being without beginning. At the same time, however, that very contrast brings us to consider the "eternal idea" that God has cherished of each person; and, simultaneously, that the conception of each person through spousal communion, communicates the communion of love out of which each of us comes to exist.

Therefore God is both that which no greater can be thought[404] in that all thought about what exists rests on God, as it were, as its foundation; *and,* at the same time, God is *intelligible* to thought in that all thoughts that really communicate the reality of what exists-as-created, communicate the "transparency" between what exists-as-created and the Creator. Conception, then, at once a real "beginning" of the human person, manifests the eternal nature of God's love of us in the very fact of giving us a beginning; but, like a mirror that reflects our origin, the very nature of the creative act of God "implicates" the Blessed Trinity in the human reality that each of us wholly expresses a unique instantiation of being a unity-in-diversity.

PERSON

The term "person" refers to the reality of personal being that expresses the identity of Christ, who is at once the

---

[404] Cf. *Summa Theologiae*, Benziger Brothers, Pt I, Qu 2, art 1, p. 11. I am using this definition of God without entering into the question of its use as a proof of the existence of God.

Conception: An Icon of the Beginning

divine Son of God *and* the human son of a woman[405]. This both gives and draws out a *profoundly relational sense to the reality of the person*. Christ Himself is *from the Father*, as the very name of the Son indicates, and He is at the same time the Person *through whom* we receive the Holy Spirit[406], just as a human being cannot but come into existence as the son or daughter of his or her parents[407], "from" the father and "through" the mother[408].

The pivotal place of "person" in the mystery of Christ raises the question of whether or not the sacrament of baptism is in fact an ontological completion of man, just as the "union" of God and man in Christ is, as it were, the fullest expression of what it is to be a man. This would be because man, who is *ordered by God's original design of him to communion with Him,* is thereby "completed" by his relationship to God being sacramentally begun. In other words the Blessed Trinity is three Persons in one God and we

---

[405] Cf. *The General Council of Chalcedon, Symbol of Chalcedon,* art 302, pp. 154-155 of *The Christian Faith.*

[406] CCC, 248.

[407] Cf. Antonio Sicari, "Mary, Peter and John: Figures of the Church", *Communio,* Vol. XIX, No. 2, (Summer, 1992), p. 192.

[408] It is possible to speak of "from" the father in the sense of the sperm is alive and transmits life and "through" the mother in the sense that the child is conceived by an animation of the mother's gift of the ovum or egg; and, together with an act of God, life is both transmitted and given to be the life of the person conceived: a child of God and of the parents (cf. Chapter 12 of *Scripture: A Unique Word*, for a more detailed discussion of this). At the same time it is not possible to enter into the meaning of artificial procreation except by way of saying that God gives human personhood – even if human beings do not respect the truth integral to cooperating with the truth of love's loving and unfolding that spousal love in parenthood.

are called to enter into the *personal communion*[409] *with God which constitutes the Church*: a personal communion which Christ anticipates on His incarnation as He 'has in a certain way united himself with each man'[410]. This call to communion with Christ is not something incidental to our being[411], as it is the very object of its design: the final end[412] intended from the beginning[413]; and, if to begin is to beget the whole and *the end is integral to the beginning*, then the beginning orientates man's relationship to God. This has, as it were, the horizontal dimension which is expressed in the *diversely complementary humanity of each one of us being either a man or a woman*[414]; and, more generally, this reality encompasses the multitude of relationships which constitute the family of man. Therefore *to be a person* is what applies to us as an individual and to us in community; for we are called to be what we are[415]: a community of persons[416].

St. Augustine saw that each Person of the Blessed Trinity was a 'subsistent relation'[417]. It could be said, then, that the

---

[409] Cf. M. Dorenkemper, "Person" (In Theology), p. 168 of Vol XI, NCE.

[410] *Gaudium et Spes*, 22.

[411] Cf. L. W. Geddes & W. A. Wallace, "Person" (In Philosophy), p. 168 of Vol XI, NCE.

[412] *A Catholic Dictionary*, by William E. Addis and Thomas A. Arnold and revised with additions by T. B. Scannell, (London: Virtue and Company Ltd., ninth edition, 1916) p. 73: Beatitude.

[413] Cf. B. M. Ashley, *Teleology*, p. 979 of Vol XIII, NCE.

[414] Cf. *Letter to Women*, 7.

[415] Cf. *Familiaris Consortio*, 17.

[416] Cf. *Familiaris Consortio*, 18.

[417] M. Dorenkemper, "Person" (In Theology), p. 169 of Vol XI, NCE.

relationality of the term person corresponds to the mystery of the fact that each person of the Blessed Trinity is, as it were, ever open to the life of the others[418]. This fundamental relationality of being is developed by David Schindler in the threefold proposition of being *from, in* and *for*[419]: a conception of human being which is "modelled" on Christ. This relationality is also evident in W. Norris Clarke's view that '*To be* is to be *substance-in-relation*'[420]; and, finally, it was this same author who, after quoting from St. Thomas Aquinas that 'Person is that which is most perfect in all of nature'[421], went on to say that 'the person is not something added on to being as a special delimitation; it is simply what being *is* when allowed to be at its fullest'[422]. This helps us to see, then, that the whole of human being-in-relationship, entailing all that constitutes his or her psychosomatic integrity, expresses human personhood. In other words, being a human person expresses the wholeness of what we are. In that the whole defines, identifies and determines the nature of the parts, each of us is an entirely "personalized" being; and, if a personalized being, then a

---

[418] Cf. Francis Etheredge, "A Reflection on the Language of the Body", *Communio*, (Summer, 1997), Vol. XXIV, No. 2, p. 407; and cf. *Mystici Corporis*, 27.

[419] D. L. Schindler, "The Person: Philosophy, Theology, and Receptivity", *Communio*, Vol. XXI, No. 1, (Spring, 1994), p. 176. Cf also Schindler, "Is America Bourgeois?", p. 270.

[420] W. N. Clarke, "Person, Being and St. Thomas", *Communio*, Vol. XIX, No. 4, (Winter, 1992), p. 609.

[421] Clarke, "Person, Being and St. Thomas", p. 601, footnote 1: *Summa Theologiae*, I, q. 29, art. 3.

[422] Clarke, "Person, Being and St. Thomas", p. 601, footnote 1: *Summa Theologiae*, I, q. 29, art. 3. Cf. also J. Lotz, "Being", p. 84 of the *Encyclopedia of Theology*, ed. K. Rahner, (Tunbridge Wells: Burns & Oates, reprinted 1986).

personalized being from the beginning of his or her existence, identity and relationships.

Definitions and use of the term person

The very origin of the term Person, moreover, seems to indicate something relational in that '*an actor's mask*'[423] is worn both to communicate a part and to conceal the person of the actor. Or, conversely, a mask communicates the concealment of a person precisely in order to communicate a part; for, in the very nature of performing a play there is, as it were, only a partial communication of the whole human being: a kind of animated "still life". Another use of the term person signifies what is uniquely individual: 'Cicero used the term "persona" to designate the totality of ways in which each individual human differed from every other'[424]. It is not possible, however, to investigate the connection between person and the 'incommunicability'[425] of personal being, except by way of indicating that it refers to the person that each one of us is to the "otherness" of the other, although not as 'Other'[426] as God is to man. At the same time, however, as a relationship to the other is always drawing us towards another, it is always drawing us out of ourselves; and, in the case of God, being drawn out of ourselves is also to be revealed to be communicable in our relationships. Thus

---

[423] *Blackie's Compact Etymological Dictionary*, p. 239: Person. Cf. also M. Dorenkemper, "Person" (In Theology), p. 168 of Vol XI, NCE.

[424] K. L. Schmitz, "Concrete Presence", p. 312, and footnote 23 (*De Officiis*, I, pp. 107 ff.), of *Communio*, Vol XIV, No 3, (Fall 1987).

[425] Cf. T. E. Clarke, "Incommunicable", p. 427 of Vol VII, NCE.

[426] Cf. McKenzie, *Dictionary of the Bible*, p. 365: Holy.

incommunicability is a kind of polar requirement of being called to communion[427] through reciprocal communication; and, therefore, to be conceived, capable of communication, shows conception to be both a call to communication and, as it were, a communication "to-be-communicated".

Boethius defined a person as '*an individual substance of a rational nature*'[428]. He used the term '*substance*' in the definition to exclude that type of being which is called accidental[429]. The difference between accidental and substantial being is that accidental being *inheres* in substantial being[430]; and, therefore, accidental being refers to those things which cannot exist in themselves but only in another, whereas substantial being is that which exists in itself and is called subsistent[431]. In other words, the surface colours, textures and shapes, their inward structures and indeed all the dynamically developmental changes of the human being, all constitute the "accidents" of the "substance" of embryonic human personhood. The changing accidents, as it were, make transparently evident the identity of the substantial being. Thus changeable "accidents" evidence the constancy of change throughout the process of the personal nature of the substantial being-in-relation becoming transparently evident. In other words, 'I have gotten a man with the help of the Lord' (Gn 4: 1): a child.

At the same time, however, what Eve says goes beyond what Boethius has explicitly stated in that Eve, however simply, recognizes she has 'gotten a man with the help of the

---

[427] McKenzie, *Dictionary of the Bible*, p. 428.

[428] *Summa Theologiae*, Methuen, Pt I, Qu 29, art 1, p. 68.

[429] L. Geddes & W. Wallace, "Person" (In Philosophy), p. 166 of Vol. XI, NCE.

[430] R. E. McCall, *Substance*, p. 767 of Vol XIII, NCE.

[431] T. U. Mullaney, *Subsistence*, page 763 of Vol XIII, NCE.

Lord' (Gn 4: 1). In other words, Eve recognizes the nature of the relationship between the action of God, and therefore God Himself, and conceiving a child; and, at the same time, she recognizes that she has conceived a child that has a relationship to her and, in terms of the biblical context of the fact that 'Adam knew Eve his wife, and she conceived' (Gn 4: 1), she has conceived a child in-relationship to Adam, who is her husband and the child's father. In other words, integral to Eve's perception of conceiving a child is the whole sense of relationship which is integral to coming to exist as a human being: a being-in-relationship. Even when, however, it is recognized that "relationship" is fundamental to human being, it is not "obvious" that this is constitutive of human being: 'We human beings are vulnerable to many kinds of afflictions and most of us are at some time afflicted by serious ills. How we cope is only in small part up to us. It is most often to others that we owe our survival, let alone our flourishing, as we encounter bodily illness and injury, inadequate nutrition, mental defect and disturbance, and human aggression and neglect'[432]. Therefore we need to draw on the "origin" of the term person.

God is the definitive meaning of the term[433] Person in that God is the Blessed Trinity: the three Persons in one God. Therefore the mystery of God is implicated in the

---

[432] The authors look as if they are paraphrasing A. McIntyre, "MacIntyre, A. (2004). Tras la *virtud*. (2ª ed.). (A. Valcárcel, Trad.). Barcelona: Crítica, p. 15", but then go on to draw on Boethius' definition of a person and overlook the relational nature of it, in: 'Enrique Burguete and Manuel Zunin: "The Status of Person of the Human Embryo": http://www.bioethicsobservatory.org/2018/12/category-person-human embryo/28674?utm_source=wysija&utm_medium=email&utm_campaign=bioethics+72.'

[433] Cf. Ratzinger, "Transmission of the Faith and the Sources of the Faith", p. 19.

mystery of man[434], which is expressed both biblically and philosophically when the *Catechism of the Catholic Church* says: 'The human person, created in the image of God, is a being at once corporeal and spiritual'[435]. Indeed, it could be said, the being that is at once 'corporeal and spiritual' mirrors the fact that creation makes the Creator visible, just as the 'corporeal' makes the 'spiritual' visible. Thus the developmental reality of human personhood communicates, incrementally and progressively, "the face" of the personal being conceived at conception.

If the person is the whole human being, one in body and soul[436], then in a way it is wholly appropriate that Mary expresses as it were the *created sign* of this openness to life in her openness to Christ. Thus when Hans Urs von Balthasar speaks of Mary's 'unreserved openness to God'[437], he seems to bring together - or to see as undivided in the first place - the bodily and spiritual dimensions of the one *attitude of the person to God: her corporeal root and spiritual crown*. In other words, the bodily expression of human personhood participates fully in the relational nature of being a "person"; and, therefore, Mary's motherhood "completely expresses the embodied", relational nature of human personhood. In the reality of Mary's motherhood of the Son of God, we glimpse the embodied nature of human relationships: that Mary is herself an outward sign of the spousal union of her parents and the action of God and, in turn, Mary communicates the divine conception of the

---

[434] Cf. *Gaudium et Spes*, 22.

[435] CCC, 362.

[436] *Summa Theologiae*, Methuen, Pt I, Qu 29, art 1, p. 68.

[437] Hans Urs von Balthasar, *Commentary*, p. 175 of what is published as Pope St. John Paul II, *God's Yes to Man*, (San Francisco: Ignatius Press, 1988).

concretization of the covenant between God and man in Jesus Christ.

Person and action

'A person discloses himself in his actions, and the better we know a person, the better we understand his actions'[438]. The actions of a person are of an interrelated, interpenetrating, threefold order. The first order of the acts of a person are those which flow from the totality of human personhood and are 'acts of a man' in a primary sense[439]. Eating is an action which, superficially, could be considered to be an "animal act". But because eating involves decisions about cooperation, skill, quantity, quality and company[440], eating is also a 'human act'[441] in that it entails the moral life[442]: it is an act of the person. Thus, even more so in the case of the act of procreation, the whole personal structure of spousal love makes the act intrinsically moral, drawing as it does on its inherent characteristics of attitude, function, rhythm, meaning, emotion and openness to the full reality of spousal love. Thus, intrinsic to both eating and procreation, are the determinants of human acts which flow from man's heart and will determine the moral goodness or evil of man's

---

[438] CCC, 236.

[439] Copleston, *Aquinas*, p. 184 (where Aquinas distinguishes between 'reflex acts' which are 'acts of a man' and acts which proceed from 'reason and will' and are called 'human acts'); but also cf. p. 193 etc.

[440] And many other characteristics e.g. training etc.

[441] Copleston, *Aquinas*, p. 184, but also p. 193 etc.

[442] Cf. *Summa Theologiae*, Methuen, Pt II, Qu 94, art 2, p. 287.

whole being[443]; and, in that sense, it is the totality of human being that is implicated, drawn upon and expressed in particular human actions. Furthermore, then, these acts will also involve a fundamental actuation[444] of the vocation to love, whether that of virginity[445] or that of marriage[446], and as such reveal the profundity of the 'image' in which he is made - for man is made in the image of God who is love (1 Jn 4: 8).

On the one hand, then, there are acts which are intrinsically expressive of the whole human being: integrally human acts; and, as such, entail a depth which arises out of the very nature of the fullness of our humanity. On the other hand, there are activities of a functional nature which are human in that they express the orchestration of the whole being to the manifestation of integrally human acts. In other words, the inherent activities of digestion, distribution of energy, cell growth and repair, are integrally human actions in the service of the fullness of our humanity. The moral being of man, male or female, entails the whole humanity of the human being-in-relation; and, therefore, the wholeness of human being is taken up into human action: into integrally human acts.

Christ and human action

What seems to emerge from all this is that the person of Christ is at once the subject of his Divine and human natures in the sense that he is the *unifying subject of all the*

---

[443] Cf. *Veritatis Splendor*, 71.

[444] Copleston, *Aquinas*, p. 186.

[445] Virginity, in this sense, can be understood to be voluntary, consecrated or arising out of a reason which effectively means a person lives a type of single life.

[446] *Familiaris Consortio*, 11.

relationships of which he is an expression, whether as God-man, a human being one in body and soul or interpersonally united to all (cf. *Gaudium et Spes*, 22). Therefore a definition of what it is to be a person must take account of this absolute abundance of relationships which is at the heart of human being. Whatever it is, then, that makes it possible for man to be a person, in terms of the *metaphysical structure of his being*, it must be such as to express *how this mystery is manifested in the reality of his total being*. It is for this reason that it is of especial relevance that Pope St. John Paul II employs the term 'incarnation' in his definition of the relationship of soul to body: 'As an incarnate spirit, that is a soul which expresses itself in a body and a body informed by an immortal spirit, man is called to love in his unified totality'[447]. In the conception of Christ, all that He is in His humanity is at the service of all that He is in His divinity; and, therefore, human conception shows that the whole bodily being of the human person exists to serve the manifestation of the human spirit.

By contrast, immorality could be defined as acting "fragmentally". Human action which is dominated by a part of human reality is not an expression of the whole of human personhood; and, therefore, the actions which undermine our humanity are acts which, in an intrinsic and significant way, are a radically incomplete expression of being a person.

---

[447] *Familiaris Consortio*, 11.

Conception: An Icon of the Beginning

Action manifests being[448]: being is made manifest in action – development manifests what began at conception

The word *manifestation*[449] keeps turning up in this and similar connections and, because of this, one begins to think that creation is fundamentally ordered to the *manifestation of the Creator*. Even the very word existence appears to have a root meaning which is that for something to exist is for that something to manifest itself[450]: to be evidently present.

Pope St. John Paul II says that the body *expresses the person*[451]. This seems to be an articulation of the doctrine that reveals the body *to be* an expression of the person in that the body's act of existence[452] is at the same time the act by which a person exists as a whole human being. In other words, the act of God by which a person comes to exist is an act of God which at the same time *constitutes* the "parts" in their substantial unity, one in body and soul. Therefore the person is one in being, while both body and soul. If one considers the totality of what it is to be a person, from the point of view of the undivided[453] individual, one in body and soul, then inevitably one expects not just a *participation of the body in what it is to a person* – but that the human

---

[448] A scholastic maxim.

[449] Cf. *Evangelium Vitae*, 34; E. Hardwick, "Matter", (Theology of), p. 483 of Vol IX, NCE; *Original Unity of Man and Woman*, 4, of the Gen. aud. of January 9, 1980, p. 109: Adam seems to exclaim of Eve 'here is *a body that expresses the "person"!*'; and *Dei Verbum*, 4; and cf. also 1 Jn 1: 2.

[450] Cf. C. Fabro, "Existence", p. 720 of Vol V, NCE.

[451] *Original Unity of Man and Woman*, 4, of the Gen. aud. of January 9, 1980, p. 109.

[452] Cf. C. Fabro, "Existence", p. 723 of Vol V, NCE.

[453] L. M. Corvez, "Individuality", p. 474 of Vol VII, NCE.

person is radically bodily: bodily in the sense of making the "soul" visible. In other words, it is as if the body is, as it were, the very "expression" of the soul; and, therefore, the whole dynamic of bodily expression is personal. It is "in" and "through" the living body that a human person is a being-in-relation and, at the same time, a real presence in the present. Furthermore, the "body" is essential to the person because it is in virtue of the difference between the body and the soul that the *human person as a whole manifests the unity-in-diversity that God is*; but, just as the unity of God is not compromised or sundered by the mystery of being three persons in one God, so, analogously, the unity of human being is more profoundly understood to be an expression of human personhood "in" and "through" the body.

If this is true then it would follow that the person is one in being from conception. If the conception of the body and the creation of the soul were *two different* "moments", then not only would this be contrary to the natural meaning of a beginning[454], but that it would also and inevitably introduce the problem of successive souls[455] and, at the same time, a distinction between the original act of the body and the original act of the human soul.

A perfect act of unifying existence would, therefore, be one that was so from the natural moment of the beginning of what from then on is an *inseparable* whole of being a person; however, although the act of existence of a person is one act for both body and soul, the unity is at the same time capable of suffering a "separation": the separation of death. Thus any radical division of these parts is "unnatural" to the

---

[454] Cf. P. B. T. Bilaniuk, "Creationism", p. 429 of Vol IV, NCE.
[455] Cf. *Summa Theologiae*, Methuen, Pt I, Qu 118, articles 1-2, pp. 162-163.

unity so constituted[456] and is indeed a mystery in its own right[457]: a mystery, however, that is ordered to the mystery of the resurrection[458]. For man was made for 'incorruption' (Wis 2: 23), but it was 'through the devil's envy death entered the world' (Wis 2: 24).

Thus there seems to be an inseparable connection between the doctrine of the human person and the doctrine of form[459] and matter. In other words, the structural principle of being that an object is constituted by what determines it to be what it is and what expresses that which it is determined to be, is at the same time what is "behind" the specific instance of man being one, in body and soul (cf. *Gaudium et Spes*, 14).

THE BODY IS MALE OR FEMALE

The unity that man is, is a person: a human person is 'a being at once corporeal and spiritual'[460]. Just as each man is a person and each woman is a person, so the reality of human being entails relationality. Therefore personhood is expressed in terms of human sexual identity. In other words, human being is a "relational" reality and the relational nature of human personhood is expressed *precisely* in the very differentiated nature of being a man or a woman.

It is therefore fundamental to the term person that relationality is not considered of secondary significance to

---

[456] Cf. *Summa Theologiae*, Methuen, Pt I, Qu 76, art 1, p. 113.

[457] *Gaudium et Spes*, 18.

[458] Cf. Copleston, *Aquinas*, p. 162: C. G., 4, 79.

[459] L. W. Geddes & W. A. Wallace, "Person" (In Philosophy), p. 167 of Vol. XI, NCE.

[460] CCC, 362.

being a person; and, as this discussion develops, it becomes increasingly clear that the body is, as it were, *fundamentally appropriate to being a human person,* precisely because each is orientated *to the other.* The man is fundamentally orientated to the woman and the woman is fundamentally orientated to the man. In other words, it is practically impossible to define a man and a woman, as a man and as a woman, except in terms which relate to and at the same time are not identical with, bodily difference and complementarity; and it is precisely this which reveals the depth of significance which lies in the body and, as it were, constitutes the terms of reference for a theology of the body open to life. Indeed it is almost as if the body is itself open to life with respect to receiving the life of the soul that it does. But, lest we think of the body as pre-existing the moment of its reception of the soul, there is in effect no "soul" and "receiving body"; rather, there is a body on "reception" of the soul that animates it with a human, personal life.

Each human person is a specific manifestation of the Being that is pre-eminently personal[461], namely, God; indeed, for God to be is for God to be *Three Persons in One God.* Therefore to talk about a theology of the body is also to talk about the body in the context of it being *integral* to how God chose to reveal Himself to man. The *Incarnation* of the Son of God is, therefore, of significance on three counts. Firstly: because God became man in order to redeem each human person. But secondly and, as it were, inseparably to the purpose of the Son of God becoming man, God revealed the body to be intrinsically incorporated into the Revelation His Son Jesus Christ is: 'who is himself the sum total of Revelation'[462]. Thirdly, then, the Son of God revealed the

---

[461] Cf. Lotz, "Being", Rahner's *Encyclopedia of Theology,* p. 84.

[462] *Dei Verbum,* 2.

personal nature of Being God. This is *precisely* because the Son of God became a man and in so doing united Himself in a certain way to each human person[463]. Therefore the Son of God "took on" human relationality in order to express both the mystery of divine personhood and, at the same time, to enter into the "inter-personal" nature of all human relationships.

As *Gaudium et Spes* also says: 'In reality it is only in the mystery of the Word made flesh that the mystery of man truly becomes clear'[464]. In other words there is a significance *for us* that Christ became a man, lived, worked and was crucified *as a man,* and rose from the dead, *as a man,* and ascended to heaven *as a man*; and, at the same time there is a significance for us that Wisdom is she (Wis 7: 22), the Church is she who came out of the side of Christ like Eve was made out of the rib of Adam, and that Mary is the perfect type of the Church[465]. Therefore the "sign" of the man and the woman is a participation in the iconography of creation[466] through which God reveals what it is to be the Blessed Trinity[467].

The act of creation is a personal act

The personal nature of the act of creation follows on from the fact of God being what it is to be *Three Persons in One God*. This almost constitutes a reason for saying that evolution has to be shown to fulfil the criteria, as it were, *of manifesting a personal act of God*. This is not to confuse

---

[463] *Gaudium et Spes*, 22.
[464] *Gaudium et Spes*, 22.
[465] Cf. *Lumen Gentium*, 65.
[466] Cf. *Letter to Women*, 11.
[467] Cf. *Letter to Families*, 6.

one kind of evidence with another, or one kind of discipline with another, so much as to recognize that just as the facts of human procreation reveal the intimately personal character of conjugal union, so evolutionary theory would need to suggest a similarly intimate account of our origin which is appropriate to it being a personal act of the Creator (Gn 2: 7; 2: 21-22; Job 10: 8-12; Ps 139). In other words the very nature of the act through which a human being comes into existence has inscribed within it indications with respect to our beginning to be, both individually and in the very beginning, which are in accord with being a person. Thus the conjugal conception of children has inscribed within it an intimacy which asks God: *Is my existence the fruit of an act of love between the Divine persons?* This is not meant in some confused literal meaning of divine creativity - but in the depths of the mystery out of which God created all and each of us: out of the very depths that are expressed in the words of St. John that 'God is love' (1 Jn 4: 8).

The transmission of life at the origin of bodily expressed personhood

The sexual gametes, the sperm and the egg, are already a highly organized form of a first, fundamental matter of life. This is because the egg and the sperm express the biologically transmissible flesh from the man and the woman; indeed, the gametes are formed in the process of the unfolding development of the man and the woman. Furthermore, the gametes are both formed from early on in the development of the man and the woman and, at the same time, they live and mature[468] *precisely as being capable of*

---

[468] *A Child is Born*, photographs by Lennart Nilsson and text by Lars Hamberger, translated by Clare James, (London: Doubleday, 1990), pp. 11 and 24 particularly. Incidentally the text

Conception: An Icon of the Beginning

being drawn, irreversibly, into the transmission of human life.

These sexual gametes are each a type of corporeal flesh in their own profoundly different and complementary way. The sperm is biologically lean, active and, literally, a minute fraction of the egg's size: possibly the proportion of a knotted piece of cotton to a ball of wool; and the egg is ripe, large, and receptive, literally, to the possibility of an entering sperm. For the surface of the egg is, actually, a multitude of openings: a kind of open weave which, on fertilization, closes. In other words it could be said that the egg is fundamentally open to the life of the sperm: the whole being of the sperm and the whole being of the egg *is for union*; even if, in the process of unification, there are aspects of what constitutes the gametes in their separateness, which are not brought together[469].

While there is a reciprocal corporeality of both the egg and the sperm, there is clearly a fundamental and complementary difference: the sperm transmits its own life to the egg and, in so doing, is incorporated into the egg. In other words, the egg founds the beginning of the body and the sperm transmits-an-animated-life which, on reception, begets the conception of the child. This is particularly clear at the moment of union. The sperm which succeeds in animating the body of the egg, through entering one of the many openings which, literally, open in the surface of the egg, is the sperm which has brought life to the egg: a life which, as philosophically defined, is the beginning of the life of the human body as constituted by the very act of the sperm animating the egg. In other words the absolute

---

on p. 24 only addresses itself specifically to the early development of the 'immature sperm cells or *spermatogonia*' and so see p. 122, too.

moment at which, philosophically speaking, human life begins, is the moment of the animation of the egg by the sperm; and it is this same moment which is, as it were, the moment of the response of the egg. The moment of the response of the egg consists in it simultaneously incorporating *the* sperm *and* enclosing itself; that is, both *taking in,* as it were, the animating characteristic of the sperm and, *in conformity with this,* forming a spatio-temporal skin. A manifestly different fact has now come into existence; this manifestly different fact is the beginning of another human being: a human embryo.

What the sexual gametes are ordered to is both the transmission of human life and, in and through the transmission of human life, to becoming themselves "one body": the bodily beginning of the person, which as the beginning of the body is itself ordered, as it were, to the immediate reception of the spiritual soul. In other words, while analytically one can "see" the possibility of three distinct "forms" of life – material, biologically psycho-social and spiritual - at no point do they all exist independently of one another; and, therefore, they exist *as one* entity when the one act of existence establishes *their union-in-diversity*. But, following their union, these three forms of life exist *ordinarily* as *one life*: the one life of the now existing person. The heat, the wax out of which the seal is made and the impression which the seal makes in it, are analytically three things - but one in the irreversible moment of coming to exist.

---

469 For example, the sperm loses its tail and the ovum excretes chromosomes.

Conception: An Icon of the Beginning

A personal being: human being in relation

Embryologically and philosophically, the moment of personal beginning is the animation of the ovum; and, because of this, there exists a beginning that goes beyond the individual nature of the sexual gametes. Conception is the philosophical beginning of human personhood in that, scientifically, there is an actual change in both the sperm and the ovum on "fusion"; and, in so far as philosophy is a response to the evidence, the evidence to which conception points is that there is a radical "newness" to the human embryo: a radical newness which manifests in being a particular man or woman. Being a man or a woman expresses the natural variety of personhood; and, in so doing, shows us that "person" and "sex" are reciprocally expressive of the human being-in-relation. In other words, just as psychological development expresses biological development, so being a man and being a woman expresses a "personalised" sexuality: a sexuality that is as inseparable to human identity as the body that "visibilizes" the soul.

Being a man or a woman is an anatomical, physiological and psychological expression of the one human reality; and, therefore, to be a man or a woman is an expression of the whole human being. Just as thought is "embodied" in the gardener's fingers, wonder is in the face of the scientist, intelligence is in the activity of the artist, just as emotion is expressed through the physiological changes that communicate psychological reactions, just as the person as a whole "lives" the reality of discovery, excitement and the heart of an embrace that holds the other, so a human being is a male person or a female person. Indeed, it could be said, male and female are psycho-physiological person-types, each expressing a complementary "way of being a person". The radical individuality of each one of us, however, transforms each "way of being a person" such that each man and each woman is an irreplaceable member of the social dynamic we need: "to be" the help to each other to become the society that benefits us all[470].

If a man needs a contemplative grasp of the whole to offset his tendency to specialization, then perhaps a woman needs an active pursuit to develop particular abilities; however, just as the man remains preoccupied by a work-goal, even as he considers what constitutes the whole of life, so a woman's activity expresses the priority of relationships even as she pursues a specific course of action.

MATTER

Dr. Francis Clark raised the question of 'the secret of the Creator': how 'the material universe ... receives created existence from the creative action, how it stands out from nothingness, or how it continues to draw its substantial being from the Source of all being'[471]. This confronts the philosopher with a mystery which is useful from the point of view of sharpening his perception of the implications to the visible, extra-mental, existence of things.

St. Thomas Aquinas says: 'matter as such is formless and adaptable to any form'[472]; and, as such, this 'first matter' exists as a conceptual abstraction. This *matter* 'is the termini of a substantial change'; it is the substrata which is first one kind of entity and then another, in accord with whether it

---

[470] The discussion about gender tends to be polarized between biology and society as if psychology does not manifest physiology and physiology does not manifest psychology.

[471] F. Clark SJ, *A 'New Theology' of the Real Presence*, (London: CTS [Do 396], 1967), pp. 13-14.

[472] *Summa Theologiae*, Benziger Brothers, Pt I, Qu 47, art 1, p. 89.

had one type of form or another[473]. In other words, in order to explain the process of change whereby one type of substance becomes another, it was supposed that there was an "abstractable" principle of being called "first matter" which, as it was said, took one form and then another in order to make first bread and then the Eucharist: the Body and Blood of Jesus Christ. Although, then, this "first matter" never existed in its own right, it was posited in order to explain change; and, therefore, change was a change in the form which determined 'first matter' to be a particular substance; and, therefore, bread was a determination of 'first matter' in such a way that, on consecration, the 'first matter' that was determined to be bread was now, in virtue of the power of God, determined to be the Body and Blood of Jesus Christ.

Signate, concrete or actual "matter"

Matter which constitutes a being as 'undivided in itself and divided from all other beings'[474] is matter which makes a universal form to be a particular object or creature and, as such, this is matter which exists as quantified[475]. Thus a human being exists as determined to be "who" she or he is by a particular human soul, or form, which individuates the living matter which comes to exist simultaneously to fertilization. In other words, *in the moment of fertilization*, the form which determines the sperm to be a sperm and an egg to be an egg "receives a new determination" such that on the body coming to exist as a human body so, simul-

---

[473] A. Kenny, *Aquinas*, part of the *Past Masters* series, Gen. Ed. K. Thomas, (Oxford: Oxford University Press, 1980), p. 39.
[474] J. R. Rosenberg, "Individuation", p. 475 of Vol. VII, NCE.
[475] J. R. Rosenberg, "Individuation", (cf. De ente 2; and De nat. mat. 3), p. 477 of Vol. VII, NCE.

taneously, that body is animated by a particular human soul. Thus the person, one in body and soul, comes to exist in the first instant of human fertilization.

At the same time, however, one of the great problems of this "abstract" type of account is that it does not convey the reality of human being: that "matter" in the human person is specifically expressive of being a girl or a boy. In other words, just as a real orange is what it is by appearance, flesh and skin, so the reality of being a human being is a very explicit expression of the flesh of human personhood[476].

The matter, on reflection, that constitutes the orange can be represented by a list of formula, arrangements of atoms in molecules and a range of colours and textures; but, nevertheless, the "matter" of the orange is characteristic throughout, whether it takes the form of segments, stringy tissue between segments, or skin. Each type of "matter" has its characteristic colours, structures and textures. "Matter" has taste, smell and a multitude of characteristics that fall under the terms of soft, smooth or textured. In actual fact, then, the more "matter" is considered in its actual existence, the clearer it is that it belongs to the orange and indeed expresses what the orange is. In other words, is it possible to say that this is an orange without reference to the whole of its reality?

An orange, however, is the fruit of a particular tree and, therefore, tree and fruit are an organic expression of each other; and, at the same time, just as the fruit has its many

---

[476] The real distress which arises out of ambiguous sexual differentiation cannot be answered in a general way except by saying that it entails a profoundly sensitive assessment of the person who needs help (cf. for example, "The Medicalization of Sexuality",

(https://www.upra.org/convegno/medicalization-of-sexuality/). Thus these questions, as applied to a particular individual, need addressing on a one to one basis.

Conception: An Icon of the Beginning

characteristics, so does the tree. Actual "matter" can be expressed "abstractly" in the philosophical concepts of the orange tree "substance" which exists throughout all changes and the various "accidents" which communicate this to us in terms of colour, shape and changes in texture. Alternatively, but in another type of abstraction, it is possible to analyse the fruit in terms of its nutritional "ingredients", such as vitamins, minerals and fibre. Indeed, any account of the fruit and tree is an abstraction from the reality of the real fruit and tree. In other words, the real challenge is always to "reconnect" the words with the actual reality; indeed, in one sense, to see them as "indivisible".

When it comes, then, to considering the reality of the human person, from which thought proceeds as from the real human being-in-relation, while it is possible to "abstract" one aspect of the human person from another, the challenge of human personhood is to remain "present" to each one of us as an integral whole; and, therefore, even if there is a tendency to the "polarization" of points of view, which contrasts the "biological" and "social" elements of personal identity, the real person is a psychological whole: a dynamic bio-psychologically-social whole.

"Matter", ultimately, expresses the personal nature of a being-in-relation. Even if a "person" loses a number of his or her limbs or organs through injury or illness, there is a sense in which the person is, as it were, imprinted in the whole: the whole bodily expression of the person communicating identity, activity and experience. Just as a person communicates emotion, thought, intention and the experience of life, so the lived experience of life "impacts" on the whole person; and, even if it is possible to speak of a broken leg or hurt feelings, the reality of a human response entails the whole being of the person and, in addition, the time it takes for the whole experience to be consciously expressed. If, then, the "whole" that we are is both a gift and a task, then it is a gift and a task from conception.

'First matter' and 'formless matter'

There is a resemblance between the concept of 'first matter' which, when quantified, is called signate matter[477] and the 'formless matter' (Wis 11: 17) of Scripture.

To begin with, however, there is the difficulty of comparing insights not fundamental to the truth necessary for our salvation[478]; but, having said that, understanding matter could be said to be related to a truth relevant to our salvation. The human person, being bodily, entails an understanding of "matter" relevant to grasping the truth of being one in body and soul (*Gaudium et Spes*, 14). We are seeking to explore the unity inherent to each and every act of creation, particularly the creation of man, male and female: an inherent unity that does not preclude development, just as the conception of the whole person entails the developmental manifestation of him or her. In addition, it is difficult to obtain a precise sense of each of these concepts: the Aristotelian-medieval concept of 'first matter' and the biblical concept of 'formless matter'; but, nevertheless, comparing and contrasting these concepts may help to illuminate each of them.

The concept of *first matter* is like a principle of being and, in so far as it exists as quantified, it does so in view of being structured by a form; and, therefore, both 'first matter' and 'form' are like polarities of being which, together, make the actual existence of a whole entity. The *formless matter* of the earth, at the first instant of its creation (Gn 1: 2), could

---

[477] J. Rosenberg, "Individuation", (cf. De ente 2), p. 477 of Vol. VII, NCE.

[478] *Dei Verbum*, 11.

well be a formless matter of a similar kind to that of a concrete *first matter*; however, on the basis that 'first matter' does not actually exist as un-in-formed, the first expression of created matter as 'formless matter' could be said to be the most *primitive* existence of created matter. 'Formless matter', then, is not here to be understood as "matter" without a "form" or that which determines what it is; rather, the Scriptural 'formless matter' is matter in its 'simplest' and 'first' expression of what would be called the 'corporeal substantial form'[479] of matter. In other words, scripturally, 'formless matter' is not the conceptual equivalent of 'first matter'; rather, 'formless matter' is a kind of "state" or "energy" or the existence of matter without a recognizable shape. Nevertheless, as 'formless matter' exists before it is "shaped", it has a kind of analogous existence to 'first matter'; but, in the understanding of the author of Genesis, the contrast is more between what exists as undeveloped than what exists as without which it cannot really exist. The concept of 'first matter' with which St. Thomas Aquinas works is that form gives matter its actuality. It would, therefore, be a contradiction to say that *formless matter* can actually exist[480], without a determining form, except with such existence as ideas exist; and, therefore, biblical *formless matter* is not so much what does not embody the "idea" of God as that it is a type of matter in its simplest, most undeveloped state. Thus, biblical 'formless matter' (Gn 1: 2) is not so much the contradiction of existing without 'form' as the beginning to what will be developed further by the Word and action of God.

Thus the concept of *form* used at the beginning of Scripture is one of shape, even in the negative sense of an

---

[479] F. J. Collingwood, "Form", p. 1013 of Vol V, NCE.
[480] Kenny, *Aquinas*, p. 42: (S I 66 I).

entity being shapeless, in that this corresponds to the literal sense of form as used by the Yahwist author in the second account of creation: 'then the Lord God formed man of dust from the ground' (cf Gn 2: 7). Clearly, forming 'man of dust from the ground' is about giving visible realization to a divine idea; and, at the same time, using the 'dust from the ground' to make visible that divine idea, even if it is not explained how 'dust' can be shaped. The 'dust from the ground', then, receives from God more than an outward form of a man in that 'dust' clearly has to undergo a transformation to "hold" a shape. In other words, while this could be an effect of translating the Hebrew word, there does seem to be an implication that the action of God is as much transforming the 'dust of the ground' as it is giving 'form' or shape to it.

In other contexts, too, it can also be said that the concept of "form" is extended to the formation of the whole man. In the book of Wisdom, while God has 'made all things' by His word (Wis 9: 1) man is a particular work of wisdom: 'and by thy wisdom hast formed man, to have dominion over the creatures thou has made' (Wis 9: 2). In other words, in the very forming of man there was a fashioning of what makes it possible for them (cf. Gn 5: 2) to have 'dominion over the creatures thou has made' (Wis 9: 2). Similarly, in Psalm 139, the biblical author, possibly David, uses form as a point of contrast: 'For thou didst form my inward parts' (Ps 139: 13) which, at the very least, refers to the organs but could, possibly, refer to attitudes and gifts of personality; and then again, referring to the more mysterious moment of being first conceived, the author says of God: 'Thy eyes beheld my unformed substance' (Ps 139: 16) which, considering the context, could refer to the beginning of human existence. Indeed, is there a parallel between the 'unformed substance' (Ps 139: 16) of a man and 'the earth [which] was without form and void' (Gn 1: 2)? Is one "beginning" echoed or echoing another? Is this one of the ways that the biblical beginning of the person is an "icon" of the biblical beginning of creation?

Genesis: 'First matter' or 'formless matter'?

Returning to the first account of creation, then, matter could be said to be 'formless' in terms of the following three, interrelated ideas. There is a first state, as it were, of pure energy; and, in so far as pure energy exists in time and space then it is "determined" to be what it is by the fact that it "embodies" an idea of God. Or, to put the same possibility in philosophical terms, the pure energy exists as a primal state of matter which does, by definition, embody a 'form'. Thus, in the terminology of form and 'first matter', this pure energy is a state of matter which is differentiated by a particular form. Or there is a second state of matter in which the *form of energy that matter already is* has been further specified into the particular elements of creation: the sun (Gn 1: 3); the firmament (Gn 1: 7); the making of the dry land called 'Earth' and 'the waters that were gathered together he called Seas' (Gn 1: 10). Or there is a third possibility, namely, that matter is referred to as 'formless' as a part of the interpretative wisdom of the writer who, drawing on an amazing analogy, has imagined a first state of matter which God then develops, as it were, in the process of creation.

The first state, if it can be said to have a real existence, would in some sense be comparable to the moment of an impact where the elasticity of energy is, as it were, *prior* to its collapse into particles. This idea comes from the following consideration: in 'order to "divide" a small particle, a very strong pulse of energy must be used, since the wave length of the pulse must be smaller than the diameter of the particle. (...) The resulting splinters from a high-energy collision, then, are elementary particles, and some of these can be of the same type as the original particle'[481]. This raises the question of a state, however transitory, of energy changing its material configuration; and, therefore, that quasi-real intermediary state of one form of matter to another is almost and analogously comparable to 'water' (Gn 1: 2).

An alternative concept of matter which could apply at this first moment of creation is matter as it is resolved into its fundamental entities which are called in their particularity the 'particle-with-field'[482], but which are not as yet the particular thing of a star. A particle-with-field is defined as an 'entity having localized particlelike interactions with matter, but subject to a non-localized field or wave-type law of propagation in configuration space'[483].

In conclusion, the outcome of the comparison between the 'first matter' of the philosophers and the 'formless matter' of Scripture, is that both are understood to be the material 'substrates' of what exist. "First matter", however, is a component of the real thing and only exists, as it were, in the actual existence of an object; and, therefore, 'first matter' only exists as determined by a 'form' to be actual 'signate matter': the matter that individuates or "embodies" a particular 'form' in an individual object. Scripture's 'formless matter' or earth 'without form' (CathRSV, Gn 1: 2) could be, however, an imaginative account of a step in a chronological process of creation; and, as such, may or may not exist as a

---

[481] P. A. Heelan, "Philosophical Considerations" (of Elementary Particles), p. 262 of Vol V, NCE.

[482] P. A. Heelan, "Philosophical Considerations" (of Elementary Particles), p. 261 of Vol V, NCE.

[483] P. A. Heelan, "Philosophical Considerations" (of Elementary Particles), p. 262 of Vol V, NCE.

discreet type of matter in its own right but, if it did, it would nevertheless be what the earth was when it began to exist.

In a sense, however, these subtle difference of terminology, while seemingly remote, constitute a necessary background to understanding more precisely the "principles of being" as they are understood of the human person. Thus 'form' and 'matter' are the more general, philosophical principles, of which 'soul' and 'body' are specific instances.

Nevertheless, in the course of considering the comparison between philosophy's 'first matter' and Scripture's 'formless matter' it is clear that there is a subtlety to both Scripture and philosophy that points to the challenge of created existence. Thus the very existence of these ideas suggest that the actual object of our enquiry, whether creation in general or the human person in particular, is "a contemplation of the deep": that the question of what matter is in general and what "humanized" matter is in particular touches upon the very mystery of the created universe itself. Matter, more widely then, is an "image" of eternity: a kind of endlessly reverberating relationship between the immense and the infinitely small and significant. Just as science discloses the "logic" of interrelationships, art the meaning of an "object-word" in the communicating structure of the universe, artificial intelligence its capacity to be "built up", music melts the distinction between waves and words, so writing differentiates the thoughts expressed in a million-billion-trillion "moments" of interaction. While, at the same time, the very presence of the universe is "personalized" in the mystery of the human being-in-relation: the man or woman; and, in the "moment" of love, the wholeness of human life springs afresh from the hands of the Creator.

Francis Etheredge

Continuity and discontinuity in the order of being

It would appear, however, that there is both a continuity and a discontinuity in the subsequent development of creation and the variety of created creatures. On the one hand there is a fundamental continuity in the materiality of all corporeal bodies. The continuity, therefore, is from the 'particle-with-field', through the atom, the activities of the elements (cf. Wis 7: 17)[484], molecular compounds, types of material structure[485] and mixtures[486], organisms, plants and animals, *to* the human body. This is evident in that the physical structure of the universe is both coherent and interactive. On the other hand there is a discontinuity which is expressed in the distinction between seamless matter and the human soul. Although, however, the human soul, of itself, transcends the capabilities of both physical matter and organically organised material bodies, yet at the same time, this human body is *ordered* to the soul as to the "form" of the body. In other words, the human body, although it does not exist until it is ensouled by a human soul, is not any kind of body and is uniquely ordered to the reception and expression of a human soul; and, therefore, the potentiality of the human body's power of expressing the human soul is a reality that makes the whole human person possible. It is not, then, that the human body pre-exists the soul or that the soul "brings about changes" which belong to the bodily transmission of human life. Rather, the very transmission of human life "founds" the reality to be "personalized" as God

---

[484] Cf. E. H. Maly, "Elements of this World", p. 263 of Vol V NCE.

[485] Cf. K. F. Herzfeld, "Matter, Structure of", pp. 479 and 483 of Vol IX, NCE.

[486] Cf. M. J. Albinak, "Substance, Chemical", pp. 770-771 of Vol XIII, NCE.

simultaneously completes the inner identity which is outwardly expressed in the beginning of a human being's existence.

The discontinuity, as it were, between the whole human person and the biological life to be ensouled is evidenced, as it were, at particular points on what would otherwise be an uninterrupted continuity of matter. Thus there seem to be "life-leaps", particularly with respect to the virus and the cellular or living body, whether microscopic or directly observable to the senses as a plant or an animal. The virus, for example, cannot itself be a form of life which is an intermediary to the inorganic and the organic, as it requires a living cell in which to reproduce. For, if the virus cannot reproduce outside the cell, then the cell must pre-exist the virus if the virus is to reproduce[487] in it; and if the cell must pre-exist for the virus to reproduce in it, then how can the virus be said to be, developmentally, an intermediary stage in the hierarchical development of life when, in fact, the cell is fundamental to the virus' possibility of existing? If the cell, in other words, did not co-exist at the "time" of the virus, then how could the virus exist? In other words, the existence of the virus and the cell are not so much chronological points in a sequence of time in which first the virus and then the cell existed; but, instead, virus and cell need to exist simultaneously, as in the fall of dominoes, the presence of two stones in a mosaic or a parasite and its host.

---

[487] A. M. Hofstetter, "Biogenesis", p. 564 of Vol II, NCE; cf. also H. A. Bender, "Life, In Biological Science", p. 737 of Vol VIII, NCE; and H. A. Bender, "Cell Theory of Life", p. 381 of Vol III, NCE.

What kind of act is an act of creation? Another kind of discontinuity: the discontinuity between Creator and creation. But, at the same time, there is a constructive complementarity between different dimensions of created existence

The idea that two parts make a whole, which can communicate what the parts cannot individually, is a principle of design expressed in the very first line of *The First Book of Moses*: 'In the beginning God created the heavens [a masculine noun in Hebrew, *shamayim*] and the earth [a feminine noun in Hebrew, *eretz*]' (Gn 1: 1). At the same time, the principle of a "complementary difference", is repeated and elaborated as the text unfolds: 'male and female he created them' (Gn 1: 27); and, in a certain way, this echoes and is enriched by the "plurality" of the names of God: God (a masculine plural, *Elohim*, which takes a singular verb) who brings to exist what did not exist (Gn 1: 1) and the Spirit of God (*Ruach Elohim*) who animates what is brought into existence (Gn 1: 2). A third instance of a "complementary difference" is that of the 'breath' that animates Adam (Gn 2: 7) and the ground from which he is formed' (Gn 2: 7). The fact of these differences, however, is not necessarily because one "pole" of the complementary pair is in a causal relationship to another, so much as that what is different is simultaneously[488] created because both are "necessary" to the whole design. In the case of the breath of God, which was complementary to the earthen Adam fashioned from the ground, the breath of God does in fact bring Adam to life. In other words, to be complementary does not mean to be identical but different; but, in addition, not "different" as in unrelated but different as in "contributing" to the whole. Indeed, complementarity can

---

[488] *Dei Filius*, art 3002, p. 124 of *The Christian Faith*.

also mean that there is a causal relationship between, in this instance, the divine breath of God and Adam becoming a living being (in Hebrew, *nefesh*). Thus, although it was God who both formed Adam from the ground and blew the breath of life into him, yet Adam was formed from the ground and the "life-giving" and complementarily different breath of God that filled him.

All in all, then, just as a theme of complementarity runs throughout the nature of what is created and, indeed, between the "presences" of God in the act of creating and animating creation, so there is also reflected in creation the profound discontinuity between God and creature and between being created and being the Creator. Thus, it could be said, that just as there is "discontinuity" between creature and Creator, there is a kind of "discontinuity" between what is complementary. Perhaps, more deeply, there is both a "continuity" and a "discontinuity" between the very "presences" of God: between God who brings existence and the Spirit of God who animates what is brought to exist. Just as the breath of life is necessary to animate the earthen ground out of which the lifeless Adam is formed, so the breath of life does not come from the ground but from God Himself (cf. Gn 2: 7). Similarly, just as the breath of God cannot be radically "dissimilar" to the flesh it animates, in that both together bring about the "one" human person, then neither are the different "presences" of God radically different to one another except in so far as "difference" is encompassed by "complementarity".

Discontinuity as a Principle of Design

There is a discontinuity, then, between non-living matter and that which moves, grows and reproduces; and, simultaneously, that dissimilarity is within the "framework" of a viable compatibility. Plants absorb water and other nutrients from the soil; and, although animals drink water they also benefit from the nutrients absorbed and engendered in plants and other living creatures.

The living body, then, can be as simple as one cell[489] or as complex as the biological manifestation of human personhood. A fundamental definition of an organism is that it is 'made up of different parts (or organs) that are instruments, or tools, of the whole'[490]. The cell is a basic unit of life and from it comes life like itself[491]. Thus "like from like" is a general principle that also applies in the material order - just as particles "react" with each other and produce other particles, so do cells reproduce themselves as cells[492]. The cell, however, is not a uniform entity like an element of a particular type; rather, the cell is a "microcosm" of the body, possessing parts subordinate to the whole. The governing activity of the nucleus of the cell, both its general activities and the process of its own division and replication[493], makes it difficult if not impossible to envisage the formation of the nucleus from parts which are naturally subordinate to it. It would be like a grain of dust "evolving" into a seed.

This is not to deny the usefulness of the term evolution to denote that to which it more obviously and easily applies: the persistence of a characteristic in an environment which favours the survival of a creature; for example, light-coloured butterflies or moths being picked off by predators in woods darkened by soot and thus the darker coloured

---

[489] I presuppose the normal activities characteristic of cellular life, as here and elsewhere it is not my intention to definitively define every aspect of these subjects.

[490] A. M. Hofstetter, "Organism", p. 757 of Vol X, NCE.

[491] A. M. Hofstetter, "Biogenesis", p. 564 of Vol II, NCE.

[492] A. Wolsky, "Embryology", p. 300 of Vol V, NCE.

[493] J. J. Callaghan, "Cell Division", p. 374 of Vol III, NCE.

creatures flourishing. These facts, which cannot really be called evolution in the sense of one creature changing into another, are nevertheless real and require an explanation; however, the power of the explanation is that it accounts for the facts, not that it can be extrapolated to an explanation of the origin of life. More generally, then, "evolution" can be analogously understood as applying to the dynamic and positive development of each individual and the cumulative development of human culture. But, on reflection, considering the development of an individual, or of human culture as a whole, is not so much a comparison based on the radical evolution of one type of creature from another; rather, what "evolution" signifies here, is that the progress is natural, coherent and progressive. The problem, however, with applying the word "evolution" to either an individual person or culture as a whole is that it has a certain connotation of an inevitably good development; and, therefore, in the case of either the individual, or human culture as a whole, it presumes an uncritical assumption that change is always an improvement: that it is always and inevitably bringing about a greater good.

It is interesting to note, too, that scientists are themselves open to consider the existence of animals which feed off other animals as "prior" to the animals which feed off the produce of the ground; although the animals which feed off the plants would have seemed to such scientists to belong to an earlier point in the evolution of life forms[494]. Therefore, for example, it now seems as if it is thought that the cow came after the lion, whereas before they would have thought that the lion would have come after the cow[495]. In

---

[494] H. A. Bender, "Life, In Biological Science", p. 737 of Vol VIII, NCE.

[495] This is not a review of evolutionary theories and, therefore, suffice it to take a summary of Pope St. John Paul II on

other words, if the evidence is unclear about which animal came "first", maybe this is more of an indication that "both" animals fit into a wider account of what exists.

Thus there is the reality of the possibility that an animal could be part of a "picture" which was composed of a general design which was first executed in an act of the simultaneous creation of the principal, complementary differences between the elements of creation: 'God created the heavens and the earth' (Gn 1: 1). Subsequently, then, it is indeed likely that there was a separate creation of individually created species, each with their own dynamic of development and each with their place in a hierarchy of created beings. In other words, if one is going to understand the created order as the expression of a unique creativity, it is necessary to consider it as a whole. At the same time, however, this is not so much biblical exegesis as a discussion of biblical ideas.

First there are the fundamental but complementary differences that have been established in the original act of creation; and, either in the same moment or following it, there is the creation of the individual identity of different creatures in "their habitat". It would then follow that the biblical principle of like from like (Gn 1: 12), which appears to be the principle by which everything is both reproduced and man is "pro-created" (Gn 1: 26-27), would account for the relative development of each aspect of creation or type of creature created. Nevertheless, however, there is that

---

this subject. On the one hand 'The message described "the theory of evolution" as "more than a hypothesis,"'; but, on the other hand, St. John Paul II acknowledged that the soul or human spirit could not emerge 'from the forces of living matter or ... [be] a mere epiphenomenon of this matter' (excerpts from the October 22, 1996, Message on Evolution to the Pontifical Academy of Sciences) (quoted on p. 462 of George Weigel's, *The End and the Beginning: Pope John Paul II – The Victory of Freedom, the Last Years, the Legacy,* Doubleday: London *et al,* 2010).

extraordinary continuity between all that lives, as there was between the material dimensionality of what exists, albeit there is the classic division of the manifestation of "life" into its vegetative, animal and rational forms[496].

If, then, the whole corporeality of the created human being can be sub-divided into an active and "living" physical materiality, a truly biological expression of life and rational soul, how is one to understand the integration of these "elements" in the totality of the whole person?

In conclusion, continuity and discontinuity are, *together*, a helpful account of the work of the Creator. On the one hand there is neither a uniform continuity of materialism, which contradicts the very existence and possibility of intelligent communication; and, on the other hand, nor is there an equally impossible discontinuity, to the point of the utter and mutual un-intelligibility, between the biological and the rational. In other words, "continuity" and "discontinuity" express, together, the reality which exists.

THE HUMAN BODY

It could be said that there are seven characteristics which enter deeply into the constitution of the human, bodily expression of the life of the person.

The first is a spatio-temporal integrity which is a manifestation of a true indivisibility unto itself and a true distinction from other creatures[497]. This does not exclude

---

[496] Cf. *Summa Theologiae*, Methuen, Pt I, Qu 118, art 2, p. 162.

[497] L. M. Corvez, "Individuality", p. 474 of Vol VII, NCE.

the possibility of twins[498]. While the spatio-temporal integrity of twins may be obscured, in so far as two individuals exist, whether conjoined or not, there will be an identifiable identity to each twin. Furthermore, a true spatio-temporal integrity does not exclude the differentiation of parts, within the whole, including organs and functional systems, such as the skeleto-muscular and nervous systems, all of which are, together with everything else, an expression of the person. Nor does the spatio-temporal integrity of the human being exclude injury, recovery, or loss of a part that nevertheless does not prevent the whole from functioning[499]. In other words, the spatio-temporal nature of the human person is neither rigidly expressed nor indefinitely extended; but, on the other hand, it has both general features and, in the case of shared organs and other developmental problems, real challenges to the health of individuals. There is, then, a radical newness in the expression of each person's individuality which, at the same time, expresses a common human nature – but a particularly individualized human nature that expresses a real human being. Relationship to others, through both inheritance and the actual, day to day relationship(s) of parents to child is, therefore, an embodied reality: a reality founded and expressed in the very transmission of life.

The second characteristic is the germ cell. There are three types of germ cells, from which all subsequent development proceeds; these are: an inner (endoderm layer); a middle (mesoderm layer); and an outer (ectoderm layer)[500]. This use of the name 'germ cell' is not to be

---

[498] *Life Before Birth, Reflections on the Embryo Debate,* by Robert Edwards, (London: Hutchinson, 1989), p. 52.

[499] By contrast, then, the loss of the heart would be the loss of a part that frustrates the function of the whole.

[500] "Cell type": https://en.wikipedia.org/wiki/Cell_type.

confused with reproductive cells. Reproductive cells are also called 'germ cells', of which the two types are sperm and ovum. The three types of cells, endoderm, mesoderm and ectoderm, from which unfold the full development of the human body, are part of the overwhelming evidence which increases, almost daily, to show us that there is both a specific beginning and an uninterrupted development of the human person[501].

The third characteristic is the distinction between reproductive and tissue cells[502] which, if it exists early enough[503], militates against the idea that one generation can pass a modification of the species to a subsequent generation. In other words, even if there is modification in the parent's generation, unless it is a modification "encoded" in the reproductive cells it will not be passed on; and, therefore, as there is an early developmental distinction between reproductive and tissue cells, what is acquired subsequent to that distinction cannot be passed on in the transmission of life.

The fourth characteristic is that the sex of each individual is determined at conception[504]. The sex of the child is a recapitulation of the origin of human beings as

---

[501] An observation made by the Warnock Report was that "there is no particular part of the developmental process that is more important than another; all are part of a continuous process" (Department of Health and Social Security [UK], *Report of the Committee of Inquiry into Human Fertilization and Embryology*, London: Her Majesty's Stationery Office, July 1984), para. 11.19, quoted in the Catholic Bishops' Joint Committee on Bio-ethical Issues, *Response to the Warnock Report on Human Fertilization and Embryology* (London: Catholic Media Offices, 1984), 13.

[502] A. Wolsky, "Embryology", p. 300 of Vol V, NCE.

[503] Cf. Nilsson and Hamberger, *A Child is Born*, pp. 122-123.

[504] Nilsson and Hamberger, *A Child is Born*, p. 122; cf. also Pope St. John Paul II, *Mulieris Dignitatem*, 1.

male and female and, at the same time, an intrinsic part of what St. John Paul II calls the *genealogy of the person*[505]. The sex of the human person, however, is an integral fact of the human being. On a general level, relationship is expressed in the very fact of human difference; and, in that sense, male or female are co-equally fundamental "verbs" of human personhood. Human individuality, however, entails that each man, or each woman, is a unique expression of the fact of sexual differentiation; and, therefore, each man or each woman is a "new" expression in terms of the reality of differentiated human personhood.

The fifth characteristic is the homeostatic balance and repair of the whole[506]: two clear indications of a subordination of parts to a whole[507].

On the one hand, then, the psychosomatic unity of the human person functions as a whole; and, not just as a whole, but as a personal whole: expressive of an objectifiably directional subjectivity. In other words, there is an inner relationship between the interiority of the person and its communicability; and, therefore, there is an external "witness" to the interior life of each one of us. Even if, then, a person "manufactures" what is internally experienced, the very fact of a communicable account of an interior life is nevertheless evidence of a transcendent presence which makes communication of the psychosomatic whole possible: a presence which transcends the physiological but is able, at the same time, to express its psychological interiority. The expressed life is, as it were, possible because of a marvellously implicit functioning of the personal, psycho-somatic whole; and, at the same time, this "implicit"

---

[505] Cf. *Letter to Families*, 9.
[506] A. M. Hofstetter, "Organism", p. 758 of Vol X, NCE.
[507] A. M. Hofstetter, "Organism", p. 757 of Vol X, NCE.

inclination to self-expression can be both obstructed and enhanced.

On the other hand, the very goal of articulating the interiority of the person is both what enables and assists the "ordering" of the parts to the whole; for, in its own way, this drives the development of the nervous, muscular and emotional maturation of the person. Thus a developmental problem of finding education meaningless is also indicative of the necessity of addressing the pursuit of the purpose of life; and, conversely, dysfunctional bodily development has an impact on the expressibility of the interior life of a person. In recent years, then, there has been a wonderful computer facilitation of communication with those with impaired powers of expression.

The sixth characteristic is the dynamic order of biological development[508] which proceeds from the beginning in anticipation of its end[509]: a clear indication of the fact that the development of the human body is simultaneously a manifestation of the person. The classic observation, that a process that concludes to an end beyond its own capability to envisage, is a process directed by another; and, in this case, that other is no other than God. The human person, then, founded in the existential moment of conception, is the outworking of a goal-directed-activity as obviously beyond its power to be self-generating as the human being's relationship to the universe: the human race benefits from a universe that it obviously could no more create than a human being can bring himself or herself to exist.

---

[508] A. Wolsky, "Embryology", p. 300 of Vol V, NCE; and cf. H. E. Wachowski, "Biology, II", p. 573 of Vol II, NCE.

[509] Cf. B. M. Ashley, "Teleology", pp. 979-980 of Vol XIII, NCE; and cf. *Aristotle's Poetics*, pp. 27-28 of translated by I. Bywater and included in an anthology of writing on *Aesthetics*, ed.

The final characteristic is that an organism which is ordered to the end of a human soul is an organism which is fundamentally fitted to be an *organ or instrument of the human soul*. A particular feature of how the human body fulfils its ordination to this end is the brain: 'while the exercise of intellectual abilities is non-bodily[,] it has a bodily vehicle, namely the brain'[510]; and, inherently ordered to the psychosomatic whole, are the interrelationships of the movement of the musculo-skeletal system to the will, of physiology and endocrinology to emotion and of the heart[511] of man, which is his conscience, to what is true, right and good.

The body as ordered to the soul is concisely expressed in the etymological root of the Hebrew word, *golmi*, the word from which comes the translation: 'my unformed substance' (Ps 139: 16); the word *golmi* is also rendered as my 'unfinished vessel'[512]. Therefore the relationship of the body to the soul is *"concretely"* expressed in terms of an exteriority which bears an interiority to which it is intrinsically ordered.

PARTS OF A WHOLE

The relationship of parts to a whole is at work on a number of levels: the level of microscopic matter and the

---

J. Stolnitz, and part of the series *Sources in Philosophy*, (New York: MacMillan Publishing Co., Inc, 1965).

[510] *Linacre Centre Papers, Prolongation of life, Paper 1, The principle of respect for human life*, p. 18, (London: The Linacre Centre, 1978).

[511] Cf. *Veritatis Splendor*, 54.

[512] F. Brown *et al, A Hebrew and English Lexicon of the Old Testament,* (Oxford: University Press, 1939), p. 166.

structure of the cosmos as a whole. On the one hand there is the internal unity of all that exists[513], which is comparable to the parts which go to make up an arrow. In other words, just as an arrow does not determine its own shape, composition or colour, an atom does not determine the properties that enable it to bond, interact and manifest at the level of molecule and material, the characteristics of a solid, liquid or gas, chemical compound or contribution to the health of an organism. On the other hand the end of the whole universe, which is also the ultimate end of each and every part of it, is directed to an end it is incapable of determining for itself[514]. In other words, just as the very coherence between the parts of the universe is a "witness" beyond itself to the possibility of a Creator, so the Creator, therefore, would be both "beginning" and "end" of the whole movement of time and its purpose of being the "opportunity" for each one of us encountering God.

The problem, then, of an "evolutionary order" is that the end would have to be present in the beginning, just as the genetic determinants of human development are present from conception; and, therefore, a real evolution of one level of existence to another would have to entail that the last was, as it were, present in the first. In other words, just as the person manifests the presence of the soul from conception, so the "souls" of human beings would have to be present from the beginning of time: a beginning that can no more account for their presence than it can for its own. Alternatively, if the presence of the human soul is denied, then how is it that all matter is not equally "intelligent"? In other words, just as Adam compared himself to what exists

---

[513] Cf. J. H. Wright, "Universe, Order of", p. 457 of Vol XIV, NCE.

[514] Cf. *Summa Theologiae*, Benziger Brothers, Pt I, Qu 2, art 3, pp. 13-14.

and recognized his "difference", so we can examine the variety of life around us and conclude, with Adam and with Aristotle, that our very consciousness of ourselves is a "witness" to being different: a difference we do not invent but which "speaks" of what is uniquely expressed in each one of us.

The interrelationships between the head and the rest of the human body, just as with each 'bodily organ'[515] and the cells which comprise it, just as with the diverse processes and material constituents of each part of each cell, are again an interrelated system of parts to wholes which, in a developmental sense, are in their turn individually and cumulatively necessary to the development of the human being as a whole.

Similarly, the structure of society and the society of the Church[516] are yet other and different *organs* of the family of man which is at the same time, properly understood, the one family of God[517].

A hierarchical or a chronological order?

While it is possible, however, to order hierarchically the variety of what exists, inorganic matter to simple, one-celled organism, it does not follow that this hierarchical order is also the chronological order of their sequential development: of matter to creature, of one creature from and to another. It may be, for instance, that each type of being[518], such as

---

[515] M. J. Fairbanks, "Organicism", p. 756 of Vol X, NCE.

[516] Cf. *Lumen Gentium*, 8.

[517] *Populorum Progressio*, articles 76-80: 4. Development is the New Name for Peace.

[518] R. M. McInerny, "Being", p. 230 of Vol II, NCE: 'Being is the first concept the human mind forms ... on the basis of sense

plant, animal and human being, has an analogous but different order of development: analogous because they have one Maker; but a different order of development, according to the different degree of participation in both creation and its relationship to the Creator. This idea resembles a type of what is called *creationism*[519]. However, this is a type of creationism that would not wish to exclude the possibility that the 'formless matter' (Wis 11: 17), which the Creator had first made, is a formless matter which that same Creator subsequently, and in the course of time, instantiates with the shape and form characteristic of each existent aspect of the universe and the species that inhabit it.

Thus matter in its fundamental or first informed state is plastic and of such a kind that it is natural for it to be fashioned into the variety of what exists, to conceive of it as that which God first made (cf. Gn 1: 2; Wis 11: 17) and out of which He then made everything that takes either a shape, a living form (Gn 1: 20-21) or the spiritual soul-form of man. This is a common beginning of both biblical and philosophical thought[520]. Beginning with matter, whether living or not, being an expression of an idea, leads to two, if not three ways in which unity can be understood[521]. The first type of unity is that which comes from there being One Creator of all that exists, which would exclude sin being made by God. There is a second type of unity, which comes from the material out of which all that is corporeal, is made. But there is also a third type of unity which, in a sense,

---

experience of the things of this world is of something there, what is, being ...'.

[519] Cf. P. B. T. Bilaniuk, "Creationism", p. 428 of Vol IV, NCE.

[520] Cf. Sir David Ross, *Aristotle*, (London: Methuen and Co. Ltd., reprinted 1964), p. 120; and cf. J. A. Oesterle, "Art (Philosophy)", p. 867 of Vol I, NCE.

[521] E. McMullin, "Matter", p. 474 of Vol IX, NCE.

belongs both to each part of creation and to creation as a whole: this is the unity rooted in the particular existence of what is created. In other words, while matter has characteristics which are shared, as it were, throughout the universe as a whole, it is nevertheless expressed in discreet objects. However, discreet objects, which can include sand, water, rock, gas and light, are only relatively "separate" to one another because, in an integral sense basic to their very existence, they "manifest" the "matter" of the universe. There is, then, a kind of radical originality in the way that the matter of the universe is manifest in an amazing variety of forms.

Living creatures, too, possess a unifying wholeness which, in a sense, is more localized to the planet earth, although expressed in terms of the matter common to the entire universe; and, as such, a living plant, although it undergoes many outward changes, nevertheless expresses the reality of being a plant of both a general and a specific type. In plants, then, the leaf can respond to light, energizing it for growth, movement and reproduction; and, at the same time, plants express characteristics which are "local" to the soil and other conditions of their existence. Animals, too, grow through a variety of stages but, in general, come to the conclusion of being a particular bacteria, insect, bird, fish, mammal or lizard, generally developing from the germ or otherwise nascent beginning of the particular creature. While, then, there are many stages in the development of a particular species, it does not follow that all species stand to one another as stages of development in the "one" species of living creature. In other words, while it is possible to observe the successive changes a plant undergoes in the course of flowering, it is also possible to witness the gradualness of these changes – both in a single plant but also across the staggered development of many plants. At the same time, however, these gradual changes are goal oriented: they express the life-cycle of that particular plant.

Were a botanist, therefore, to arrange several plants in a row, according to shape, size and colour and claim, because of it, each one was a stage in the development of the next one, it would clearly be impossible to prove; for, in the case of each plant, each plant would complete its own life-cycle without, as it were, passing through the actual life of another plant. In other words, when it is claimed that a small horse is the ancestor of a big horse, each of which are complete and organically different animals, there is no sense in which the small horse is a "stage" in the development of the big horse. Each type of horse has a completely different developmental programme unfolding from the beginning. Neither horse can increase or decrease its own size, given that it receives what it transmits genetically, anymore than a tennis ball can be a stage in the development of the rugby ball. Thus, in reality, what is proposed in the way of evolutionary development is more an expression of the "imagination" of the proponent than the evidence of sequential development. Indeed, one of the most staggering "absences" of evidence, when it comes to evolutionary theory, are all the transitional forms which are naturally a part of the organic development of a particular plant or animal. In other words, no plant or animal is going to change incrementally except in ways that are considered to be the natural variation of species; and, therefore, the whole problem with evolutionary theory is that "it" has, as it were, no sense of the whole identity that governs the progress, from conception until adulthood, of each species[522]. For evolutionary theory to be "plausible", there-

---

[522] Cf. Fr. Kenneth Baker, SJ, "The Presuppositions of Darwinism", Editorial, October 2011: http://www.hprweb.com/2011/10/presuppositions-of-darwinism/.

fore, there needs to be an "oversight" that is either intrinsic to the whole process or, alternatively, an oversight that acts as an "extrinsic" cause to the whole process.

THE ESSENCE OF WHAT EXISTS

Understanding what exists is sometimes called understanding the essence of what exists. The essence of what exists is that which can be defined[523]; and, therefore, it is the understanding that 'reads within (*intus legit*) by grasping the essence of the thing'[524].

In a second but related sense, what exists and its essence are "two parts" of a metaphysical whole, entailing a distinction within the one, 'finite' reality[525], which does not divide it from itself. For if the essence discloses what exists, then it follows, on the basis of the distinction between *matter* and *form*, that essence must necessarily involve both 'first matter' and form[526]. Therefore, depending what kind of form this first matter "receives" will determine what, *essentially*, it is that exists. Accordingly, 'first matter' that "receives" the form or soul of a plant is a plant, that which "receives" the form or soul of an animal is an animal and that which "receives" the form or soul of a human being is a

---

[523] Copleston, *Aquinas*, p. 97: 'It is clear that essence is that which is signified by the definition of a thing' (*De ente et essentia*, 2).

[524] F. E. Crowe, "Understanding" (Intellectus), p. 391 of Vol. XIV, NCE: the reference is to (*In 6 eth.* 5. 1179).

[525] Cf. Copleston, *Aquinas*, p. 97.

[526] Copleston, *Aquinas*, p. 97: F. C. Copleston actually says, while quoting St. Thomas Aquinas, "In the case of material things 'the word *essence* signifies that which is composed of matter and form'" (*De ente et essentia*, 2).

human being. In the case of plants and animals, however, the "reception" of a plant or an animal soul is integral to the fertilization of animal and plant life; and, therefore, the concept of 'first matter' being in "receipt" of an animal or plant soul is as a result of an analysis of plant and animal being, not an account of its real transmission. Fertilization, then, in the case of a plant and animal being, brings the complete being into existence; and, therefore, there is no "cause" beyond the cause of plant and animal fertilization.

The coming into existence of a human being, however, entails a cause proportionate to human personhood: a cause that exceeds the "causal" power of what brings about plant and animal life. In a sense, the causal "limits" of the transmission of human life are evident in the nature of the sexual gametes, the ovum and the sperm; and, as such, they constitute the necessary biological constituents of what, together with a human soul, will constitute human life. On the death or decay of either sperm or ovum, however, there is not the loss of a human person. It would seem, then, that there is a moment which is really like the ensoulment of 'first matter', except that "in reality" the human biological constituents of ovum and sperm are dynamically ordered to union with each other and with a human soul. In other words, then, the reality of the human flesh of both ovum and sperm is not that they are an indifferent, indistinct or undifferentiated 'first matter'. The relationship of human soul to the first instant of bodily existence is, therefore, a relationship in which the human soul is brought to exist in the very first moment of that person's human existence; and, indeed, the very individuality of the human being is intimately expressed in the prior-until-conception "ingredients" of ovum and sperm. The human soul is not an "*ad extra*" to the human being's existence: the human soul's existence, taking as it does the first instant of the unification of the gametes in the transmission of human life, is therefore integral to the first instant of the whole human being's psychosomatic existence; nor, conversely, are "prior-until-conception" sperm and ovum extraneous to the human being who comes to exist at the first instant of fertilization. A cause, then, not only proportionate to causing the existence of the human soul from nothing – but causing it to exist in union with the first instant of the conception of a human being, is a *Cause* which is unique in its very sensitivity to the reality of human life and in possession of the power necessary to bring it about. In other words, this cause "echoes" and "recapitulates" the cause of creation and is, therefore, God. God, then, is *the Cause* of the "whole" of human being in that the actual, expressed essence of being one in *body* and *soul* is an event that totally depends on the power of God.

Existence and essence are ordered to one another in such a way that they are 'two constitutive and really distinct principles, related as potency and act'[527]. Thus it would seem that the existence of a created being is the act[528] by which an essence exists: an essence is *ordered* to that existence as that which will develop from it and be expressed by it. At the same time, however, to be "in act" is also to denote what determines the being of what exists; and, therefore, as the 'form' determines what exists, so the 'form' stands to what exists as that which determines its potentiality: the nature that will unfold in the activity that fulfils it. Thus the activities which unfold the life of a plant are, generally, nutrition, growth and reproduction; and, therefore, the plant 'form' or 'soul', being that which determines the 'first matter' to be a plant, determines the potential that will be fulfilled through its concrete activity. In

---

[527] C. Fabro, "Existence", p. 723 of Vol. V, NCE.
[528] Cf. C. Fabro, "Existence", p. 723 of Vol. V, NCE.

the case of the human soul, however, its existence and expression is implicit to the very first instant of human fertilization; and, in view of the radical expressibility of the human person, the presence of the person requires the maturing of the developmental processes that make "him" or "her" visible.

These general considerations, however, are "abstracted" from what really exists and what really exists are whole beings: beings which, in the case of a union of 'form' and 'first matter', entail actual "flesh". The actual flesh of a particular plant, animal or human being is called 'signate matter'[529]: the particular "flesh" of this animal, this plant or this human being. As we know, then, more generally, the actual matter of plant, animal and human being is redolent with all the intricacies of the reality of inherited "matter"; and, at the same time, at the beginning of a human being there is a radically new combination of inherited characteristics and, therefore, there is a really new "moment" in the first instant of human fertilization.

---

[529] St. Thomas Aquinas, *Summa Theologiae*, Pt. I, Qu. 119, "The Propagation of Man as to the Body",
http://www.newadvent.org/summa/1119.htm.

Chapter Four: Part III: Form; Matter; Cause; Unity; and Personhood

There are three sections to Part III, "Exploring Ideas of 'Form'" (IIIi); "Metaphysics ... the Underlying Principles of what Exists" (IIIii); and "A Preliminary Discussion of the Personalisation of Matter" (IIIiii).

Chapter Four: Part IIIi: Exploring Ideas of 'Form'. This section begins to establish, if possible, the original sense in which 'form' was used, the better to understand its application in the following expression: 'The unity of soul and body is so profound that one has to consider the soul to be the "form" of the body'[530].

The starting point for this brief consideration of the origin and development of the concept of 'form' is one which is common to both biblical and philosophical thought[531]: the form which is understood as the shape which an object possesses at the end of a process of change[532]. Bringing about a change in the shape of an object is also known under the name of the 'formal cause' of that change; and, therefore, the 'formal cause' of a change in an object's appearance is when that object comes to possess a new shape or 'determination'[533]. In this initial stage of meaning, the term form is obviously related to sight, and it is sight which is commonly used to signify understanding. Thus there is a parallel development between the concept of understanding

---

[530] CCC, 365.

[531] Ross, *Aristotle*, p. 122; Gn 2: 7; Job 10: 8; Ps 139: 13; Wis 9: 2; Wis 15: 11 and many others.

[532] V. E. Smith, "Matter and Form", p. 485 of Vol IX, NCE.

[533] G. F. Kreyche, "Causality", p. 344 of Vol III, NCE.

as a kind of seeing and the concept of form as that which is "received" in this kind of seeing534.

In a very compact statement all this is summarized in the following way: form is from 'the Latin *forma*, a term signifying figure or shape or "that which is seen" and 'it came to signify the intrinsic determinant of quantity from which figure or shape results, and then to mean the intrinsic determinant of anything that is determinable'535. In other words, the external form of an object is to sight what the internal "form" of an object is to understanding. This *progression* from an external sense impression of an object to an understanding of the *internal nature* of that same object is a progression which is a characteristic common to both biblical and philosophical thought; it is, therefore, a progression natural to man.

Ideas as Embodied Form

The resemblance between the Greek word ☐☐☐☐s and the English word *idea* seems to have some etymological and linguistic justification536. This resemblance proceeds by way of Plato who argued to the existence of what St. Thomas Aquinas later assimilated to the following: objects of the divine thought which he called 'the eternal exemplars

---

534 Ysabel de Andia, "The eyes of the soul", p. 230 of *Communio*, Vol. XIV, No 3, (Fall 1987).

535 W. A. Wallace, "Form", p. 1031 of Vol V, NCE.

536 Cf. J. F. Piefer, "Idea", p. 337 of Vol VII, NCE, C. Fabro, "Existence", p. 723 of Vol V, NCE; and *A Greek-English Lexicon*, H. G. Liddell et al, (Oxford: At the University Press, M. DCCC. XLIX), p. 364: eidos: IV. '*the form* of matter, as opp. to the substance, Arist. Ausc. Phys. 2. 1, 9., 4.'; and, finally, Kenny, *Aquinas*, p. 69.

according to which all things are made'[537]. Thus one begins to see a relationship between what is made and an idea. This relationship, because it is predicated of God's act of creation on the analogy between that act of creation and the human activity of making things, gives rise to the following analogical understanding of God's act of creation: it is the *incarnation* or *embodiment of an idea*. In other words, just as the maker of an object has an idea which does not leave his mind but which nevertheless becomes *embodied* in an object, so God brings objects into existence without imparting Himself to them as if they were some kind of emanation of His substance. Clearly, while the *Incarnation* of the Son of God is the great mystery of the Christian Faith in which God does "embody" Himself in creation, the creative principle of the "incarnation" as an expression of God "manifesting" His vision of what is to exist is operative at a more general level in the act of creation.

For man, then, the *idea of what he will make* is the 'germ' of a process by which what did not exist 'extramentally'[538] comes to exist in a process of interactive externalization; and, in this sense, it could be said that his idea is ordered to the intention[539] of it being realized in an extramental object[540]. But not only is the "idea" the germ of the process but it is also and inseparably the end to which the process of making is directed; indeed, it could be said, the "idea" directs the very process by which it comes about that the idea is *realized in an extramental object*. Thus there

---

[537] J. F. Piefer, "Idea", p. 338 of Vol VII, NCE; C. Fabro, "Existence", p. 723 of Vol V, NCE.

[538] Cf. R. M. McInerny, "Being", p. 230 of Vol II, NCE; C. Fabro, "Existence", p. 723 of Vol V, NCE.

[539] Cf. Kenny, *Aquinas*, p. 80.

[540] J. F. Piefer, "Idea", p. 338 of Vol VII, NCE.

Conception: An Icon of the Beginning

arise the following relationships: that the idea of what to make is to the material out of which it is to be made, as form is to material, as what is complete as an objective to what can complete it as an artefact, as "idea" as act to "material" as potency or possibility of being transformed into an artefact.

Therefore an artefact can only have one form in the sense that it can only be the realization of one idea[541]. For 'form' in this sense is precisely what takes account of what constitutes the "whole"; and, therefore, from the 'form' is derived the objective oneness of what exists. 'Form', in this sense, is already an ordering of parts to a whole. Thus if the object is a bookshelf then the joints, the size, the shape and the number of actual shelves, the wall fixings and the finish *are all implied in the subordination of parts to a whole*. In other words, while many things go to make up a whole; the whole is by definition *one object*; and, moreover, it is that "one thingness" which is designated by the word 'form'. Thus there can be no more fundamental expression of the unity of what has come to exist as an extramental fact than that of saying what the 'form' of an object is. For the 'form' of an object defines the unity of that object so fundamentally that it can be said to be what that object is; and the definition of what an object is as inseparable from that object as the essence of a thing is to its existence. Therefore it can be said that the "germ" of the idea is now "incarnated" in the object in the nature of the relationship of 'form' to 'matter' in what has come to exist; and, because of this, there can be no actual distinction between what that object is and its existence as an actual thing.

Even if, however, an object has one "defining form" that expresses what it is, namely that the object is a bookshelf, it is clearly the case that there are many "sub-objects" which

---

[541] Cf. Kenny, *Aquinas*, p. 47.

are naturally a part of what brings the bookshelf to exist. Screws, glue or joints in the wood can all occur in a multitude of applications; but, nevertheless, as a part of this object, this bookshelf, their "significance", as it were, is subsumed in the whole of which they are parts. Therefore, while each discreet item has its own "form", the "form" of the screw, whether posidrive or slotted, the form of each shelf and side, the form of the brackets that fasten it to the wall, the "form" of the whole object is not many "forms" but one in which the others are parts that express the integrity of the whole.

'Form' as a universal and 'form' as a particular

In the case of human beings, let us consider the visible and the invisible determinants of the human reality. On the one hand the idea that is incarnated or embodied is a particular instance of a universal identity called humanity[542]; and, therefore, in this sense the 'form' of the human being is what constitutes the unity of this being as human. On the other hand, however, the idea that is incarnated is also a particular "idea" of a particular person and, in that sense, both the soul-form of the body and the body itself, together and inseparably, constitute the *definitively and actually unique totality of the whole person*. Therefore, while it can be said that the 'positive principle present in a subject at the end of a change is called form'[543], the *end* to which this is ordered and to which the soul is the *one* to the *many* of the body[544], is the *incarnate-creation* of the whole

---

[542] Kenny, *Aquinas*, page 48.
[543] V. E. Smith, "Matter and Form", p. 485 of Vol IX, NCE.
[544] Cf. Kenny, *Aquinas*, page 39.

person-idea: the whole person, one in body and soul, that God loves into existence!

Furthermore, the change of the material substrate of wood into the form of a shelf is at once a modification of what exists and an instance of bringing a new entity to exist. What is continuous with what existed before is the material substrate of the wood; and what is discontinuous and newly existing is the shelf which is at once the union of 'form' and that material substrate of wood. In this process of change, however, it is possible to recognize that the wood remains wood and does not become metal; and, therefore, while wood and metal may well be used together, there is no alteration of the basic materials so much as a new configuration of their existence and use. This change, then, may well be called an "accidental" change. This is not to be confused with the meaning of accident or a chance change; but, rather, in this instance the change is not a change of substance: the wood remains wood and the metal screws remain metal screws.

The point of these considerations is to show how basic is the perception that matter is *ordered to form*: first to form as to the "exterior" shape of matter and then to form as to the inner determinant of that external shape. The parts of a whole are, already, expressing an inner determination which already makes them what they are: screw; wooden shelf; support; but, in the case of the bookshelf as a whole, even the parts participate in an "inner determination" of the whole: the inner determination of a set of "exterior" parts is, precisely, the conceptual whole which brought them to exist. The "idea" of the craftsman, which is now embodied in the work which manifests the bookshelf, is what orders the parts to the whole: even the "random" effects of scratches, saw marks or other "unintended" but incorporated changes.

If this kind of understanding is "analogously" applied to the creation of a human being as we normally understand it to occur, it can be said that there is a new kind of change: a substantial change: a change that is almost as radical as that from non-existence to existence. The termini of the substantial change, at the heart of human conception, are the human sexual gametes up to and including the moment before their unification *and* the moment of fertilization or activation of the egg by the sperm in which God brings to exist a particular human soul. This change takes an 'indivisible' instant[545] in which there is no process of time and which is effectively the *one* "action" of both man and God: a single act which brings to exist the *one* existential beginning of a particular human being. In other words, 'form' is to 'body' what the *unity of an object is to its parts*, and this in the following two respects. On the one hand, from the point of view of defining what gives unity to the parts in terms of what now exists, which in this case is an instance of the embodied human form or soul, there is what is called the human person. On the other hand, from the point of view that what now exists as body and soul *exists* as one human person, it is the very presence of the soul in the body that constitutes the very identity of the body as a human body and the core-body-soul-unity of human personhood. Thus, reverting to the terminology of substantial change, there is a substantial change in the very first instant of human fertilization in which "matter" is now "ensouled"; and, in the process, whereby what had existed were the sexually transmitted, biological precursors to human life, of ovum and sperm, there now exists the outward, bodily expression of the life of a particular human being. In other words, in the very act of God that brings the human being to exist, there is a substantial change in the biological ingredients of human life. While before the moment of ensoulment there were biological bearers of

---

[545] J. M. Quinn, "Instant", p. 546 of Vol VII, NCE.

human inheritance, "in" the moment of ensoulment the biological bearers of human inheritance "are" now one in bearing the reality of human personhood: the biological is now inscribed with the psychological and the corresponding psychosomatic whole is begun.

Furthermore, there is still the continuity of the *human flesh* which now exists as a true human body *with* the human flesh of the sexual gametes which, together and with respect to their mutual and complementary difference, now constitute the *bodily beginning of the person whose body it is*. Thus the person is the totality of God's idea which is realized through the unique unification, by a true act of man, woman and God, of the following three dimensions of human being: the contribution of husband and wife being both complementarily different to each other but, with respect to the action of God, equally "passive" to the act of God which "ensouls" and effects human personhood. There is the historical flesh of man as created from the beginning by God and transmitted through the generations in the flesh of the sexual gametes. Thus there is the particular expression of the bearing of an historical inheritance in the actuality of a sperm and an egg which unite at conception. Finally, there is the human soul, which God in that same instant of conception, *creates in such a way that it is expressed in human flesh*. Thus God creates the soul as one with the body; the reciprocal unity of which is the complete[546] realization of the idea of the human being which God saw to create.

The cause and type of human form

In the case, however, of the human form, the whole human being is a fruit of "inner-determinants" that are

---

[546] Cf. J. D. Robert, "Act", p. 90 of Vol I, NCE.

radically integrated. Although it is true that there are organ transplants, whether from another human being or grown, in a new way owing to advances in biotechnology, the psychosomatic whole of the human being entails a radical integration of the physico-biological, psycho-social and spiritual "dimensions" of the human person. In other words, it is not so much that the human being is an onion, strata or compilation of ingredients as that the whole human being is an integrated expression of an inwardness which is expressed outwardly and an "outwardness" which internally renews an "inwardness". There is a kind of "thermal presence", like the movement of plasma in the sun, in which the expression and communication of meaning arises, as it were, in relationship to all that exists: both all that exists inwardly and all that exists outwardly – as if the very breath of life reverberates from the beginning of each one of us "in turn".

Our constitution, then, in all its dynamically stable fluidity, can be understood on the basis that there are various types of cause which are all orchestrated under the impulse of one "person-idea": the one person-idea which, as it were, is overarching and determining the whole identity of the human person. Just as there are many factors, dimensions and features which come together in the one "person-idea" which is embodied in each one of us, so there are many causes which are subsumed in the one "act" and "combination" of causes which bring each person to exist. Just as inheritance, biological gametes and an act of God come together in the first instant of fertilization, so the voluntary nature of human existence enters into a dialogue of grace and human relationships in the course of human development.

Conception: An Icon of the Beginning

The cause[547] of human personhood

There are, then, a variety of generic causes, in terms of which it is possible to discuss the origin of a particular person: the material, agent or efficient, formal and final cause of human being. In the case of the first, *material cause*, of human being, it is necessary to consider the multi-levelled nature of the biological gametes. On the one hand it is an awesome consideration to note that the physics and chemistry characteristic of the universe as a whole is integrated into the living nature of the sperm and the ovum; albeit at the "moment" of conception there is an "instantaneous passing" from the sperm being active and the ovum or egg being dormant – to the mystery of the embryonic beginning of the child. In other words, from the very depths of the nature of the universe as expressed in terms of particle dynamics, the very moment of human fertilization takes all that is biologically constituted and transmits, in a whole variety of ways, both an activating stream of calcium ions and the very presence of the sperm head, having shed its biological helmet, in one of the openings in the ovum wall. In the very "moment" of the transmission of "calcium ionic activity" from sperm to ovum,

---

[547] Generally, the possibility that one event is not "caused" by another but is a product of the mind perceiving it (cf. Hume [David]: Cf. Francis Aveling: "Cause." *The Catholic Encyclopedia*. Vol. 3. New York: Robert Appleton Company, 1908. 22 May 2017, http://www.newadvent.org/cathen/03459a.htm, transcribed for New Advent by Rick McCarty), suffers from a number of problems. Firstly, there is an insufficient understanding of the variety and reality of causes. Secondly, there is no contradiction between "cause" being both what is understood by a person and understood to be true of an extra-mental (or other kind of event). Thirdly, the possibility of being mistaken or "inventive" about an actual "cause" does not invalidate the real possibility that there may well be a cause still to be discovered.

the ovum wall closes around the sperm head and so constitutes the first instant of an individual human being in its signal, nascent state of "beginningness": a singular event internally completed by God's ensoulment of the individual person[548]. In other words, "material cause" is here principally understood as the contribution made by the very "flesh" itself: that which is of the human species contributes to the human species; and, in principle, just as a plant cannot become other than a plant and an animal other than an animal, the sexual gametes, as such, cannot contribute the life of a person which is not within them to communicate. In other words, the biological gametes require that which makes them capable, in the moment that the sperm fertilizes the egg, of communicating the life of a person; and, in that sense, human fertilization entails, requires and communicates an act of God which constitutes an integrally ensouled beginning of human personhood.

At the level, however, of the "material cause"[549], once the human being has come into existence it is possible to identify the "biological entity" as manifesting the outward expression of the inwardly determining "life" of the person. On the one hand, then, there is the "material cause" of human being as enfleshed. Thus there is given the general structure of human being as male or female, entailing the bodily expression of each psychological reality and, at the same time, expressing an upright posture, one head, two arms, hands and a torso, lower body, two legs and feet. In other words, although there are occasional problems with the transmission of this "flesh of humanity", there is clearly

---

[548] Cf. Francis Etheredge, "The Mysterious Instant of Conception", *The National Catholic Bioethical Quarterly* of America, Vol. 12, No. 3, Autumn 2012.

[549] Cf. Aveling: "Cause", *The Catholic Encyclopedia*. Vol. 3, 1908.

Conception: An Icon of the Beginning

an "inner", inheritable determinant of human flesh. But, on the other hand, there is the soul as "formal cause"[550]: the "human soul" as causing the human flesh to be the flesh of a particular human being. 'Form' is thus understood as the inner determinant of any determinable entity[551].

What brings about the "effect" of the existence of a human being is known as the "efficient cause"[552], namely that the object comes to possess a new shape or determination, which is called its 'formal cause'[553]. In other words, the biological entities of sperm and ovum or egg are, on coming together, ensouled by God; and, therefore, God is the efficient cause of both the soul and the psychosomatic whole of the human being, one in body and soul. Nevertheless, ordinarily the mother and father "to be" contribute, through an act of spousal love, the possibility of the coming-to-be of a child through ovum and sperm coming together; and, therefore, the "parents-to-be" are, truly, co-creators with the Creator: true procreators of their child. At the same time, though, the sexual gametes, the egg and the sperm, are the biological precursors which, on coming together, interact, such that the sperm is, in a sense, the efficient cause of the animation of what was the ovum and what is now the human embryo. However, it also necessary to refer to the ovum as the "co-efficient" cause of the human embryo because of its comparatively massive mass; indeed, without the ovum being ready to transform on reception of the sperm, there would be no human being. Nevertheless, as

---

[550] Cf. Aveling: "Cause", *The Catholic Encyclopedia*, Vol. 3, 1908.

[551] F. J. Collingwood, "Form", p. 1013 of Vol V, NCE.

[552] Cf. Aveling: "Cause", *The Catholic Encyclopedia*, Vol. 3, 1908.

[553] Cf. G. F. Kreyche, "Causality", p. 344 of Vol III, NCE.

God is the Author of human life from both its original and proximate beginnings, including its capacity to transmit the biological precursors of human being, God is also the "remote", efficient cause, of the bodily expression of human personhood.

Form is also understood as orientated to the end of matter, which is also and otherwise known as its 'final cause'[554]: an end which is the personal 'manifestation of the glory of God'[555]. Given, however, that the whole psychosomatic being of the human person, as man or woman, is orientated to being-in-relationship to others, it follows that the "final cause" of all created being is to be "in-relationship" to God and to others. The 'final cause' is here understood, then, as that for the sake of which God acts at all[556]: relationship as both true to human existence and salvation as "rescuing" us from what obstructs our relationship to God and to each other.

"Form", then, is that which *unifyingly informs* the one act of existence of which the body is the material manifestation; and, in this sense, the form is both what determines the whole to be what it is, a human being, *and is the principal origin of activity*[557]. Thus it could be said that a form is "proportionate" to that which it informs. On the one hand the form of an active being *is necessarily a principle that informs a principle of activity*; and, therefore, in the case of human being, the dynamic principle of human growth is "informed" of the very "identity" that that human

---

[554] Cf. G. F. Kreyche, "Causality", p. 344 of Vol III, NCE.

[555] Cf. E. G. Hardwick, "Matter, Theology of", p. 483 of Vol IX, NCE; cf. also *Dei Verbum*, 4.

[556] Cf. Aveling: "Cause," *The Catholic Encyclopedia*, Vol. 3, 1908.

[557] Cf. *Summa Theologiae*, Methuen, Pt I, Qu 77, art 1, p. 118.

growth will manifest. Whereas, in the case of a stationary object such as a statue, the *formal cause* of that statue, the shape it is to express, does not possess this potential to activity[558] with respect to the act which determines what it is, nor does the object it informs possess a potential to be activated in this way. The shape the stone has been given, then, does not of itself bring about a change in the stone; neither does the stone "take" the shape upon itself. In other words, a statue is "unveiled" in the stone it is made; and, at the same time, the stone retains the shape it has been given. In terms, then, of any subsequent change in the sculpture, this arises out of the weathering or deterioration of the sculpture due to "local" changes in temperature, weather or weaknesses in the material.

It is therefore possible to speak more specifically of the *human form*, too, in the sense of the materiality of the human being: the form of the human body in the equivalent sense to that of the marble out of which the sculpture is made[559]. It is with respect to the nature of the personal expressiveness of the human body that it could be said that the parts of the body which transmit the *flesh of a human creature* are of especial significance. Thus 'Pius XII rejected the transplant of sex glands from an animal to a man as being immoral. The reason (not given by Pius XII) is that it seems such a transplant cannot be accomplished without serious modifications of a physical and psychic order'[560].

Finally, it is as a kind of accumulation of these meanings that one can say that the soul is the form of the body, albeit in the particular sense of the dynamic unity of the human being that man is. Secondly, the body is ordered to the soul

---

[558] Cf. *Summa Theologiae*, Methuen, Pt I, Qu 77, art 1, p. 118.
[559] Cf. G. F. Kreyche, "Causality", p. 344 of Vol III, NCE.
[560] J. Paquin, "Organic Transplants", p. 756 of Vol X, NCE.

as to the end[561] which is at once a transcendental fulfilment[562] of it; and, therefore, it is to the human person as a whole that God has 'given' the vocation to love Jesus Christ (cf. 1 Jn 3: 32), which is elsewhere put in terms of first love God and then your neighbour as yourself (Mk 12: 29-31).

The body, then, is ordered to the soul as to the end[563] which is at once a transcendental fulfilment[564] of it: the end of being a person who is loved and called to love. There is, however, more than an element of mystery entailed in the full unfolding of human identity. On the one hand there is the originating divine gift of begetting the "whole" of human being and, as it were, the density of human identity; but, on the other hand, there is the transformation of the human being expressed in the resurrection appearances of Christ: the complete spiritualization of the whole human person. It is as if, in other words, there is a deeper depth to the dense dimensions of human being, a kind of "transfiguration", expressing the fullest personalization of matter that begun at conception.

Soul, particularly the human soul

St. Thomas Aquinas says that 'the first thing we must know of anything is ... whether it exists'[565].

---

[561] *Summa Theologiae*, Methuen, Pt I, Qu 76, art 5, p. 116.
[562] Cf. J. Bobik, "Entelechy", p. 445 of Vol 5, NCE.
[563] *Summa Theologiae*, Methuen, Pt I, Qu 76, art 5, p. 116.
[564] Cf. J. Bobik, "Entelechy", p. 445 of Vol 5, NCE.
[565] *Summa Theologiae*, Benziger Brothers, Part I, Qu 2, art. 2, p. 12.

Conception: An Icon of the Beginning

On the one hand, if there *was nothing* in existence then there would *be nothing* to think about. In the first place, therefore, is the fact of what exists.

On the other hand, if I did not exist then there would be no activity of mine to manifest my existence[566]. Indeed, it would be impossible for me to raise the question of my existence, because this is already a manifestation of the fact that I exist. In other words, whether it is the existence of "the world" or of myself, it is existence that comes first[567]. While Descartes thought, "I think, therefore I am", the very activity of his thinking presupposed the fact of his existence. Although his thinking was, as that manifestation of his existence with which he was concerned, *the activity* which led him to the *conclusion* that he did in fact exist. But then the problem is that, "I think", is already known, not directly, but because I am thinking about what to write; and, therefore, "I think" is known "co-equally" with thinking about writing, gardening or eating[568]. What makes possible, both "thinking" and "thinking about all that exists"? There is, then, the fact that I am transcending the limits of an animal's existence and activity; and, at the same time, there is the psychosomatic whole which makes the questioning possible.

The more one considers the nature of an individual existence, the more possible it seems to assert that the individual's existence implies, in every respect, the existence of everything else. I understand this to be parallelled in physics by the claim that each thing in existence requires the existence of everything else; in addition, and from the point

---

[566] Cf. Copleston, *Aquinas*, p. 158.

[567] Pope St. John Paul II, *Crossing the Threshold of Hope*, translated by Jenny McPhee and Martha McPhee, (London: Jonathan Cape, 1994), p. 38.

[568] Cf. Copleston, *Aquinas*, p. 160.

of view of biology, one can see that even the existence of a single celled creature is an existence, as it were, in the context of the whole of which it is a part. Thus it is necessary, when considering what makes possible the expressiveness of the human being, to take account of all that the human being is.

The reasoning which Descartes followed is nevertheless useful because it demonstrates the difference between the human being and an inanimate object, plant or animal. The act of Descartes' *reasoning* to his own existence, irrespective of what it does or does not prove, is an act which both transcends 'the power of matter'[569] and follows on the fact that he is alive[570]. This is because understanding the evidence is itself an act which exceeds what physically exists; and, therefore, the act of understanding is itself evidence of what is not identical with our physical existence[571]. Therefore our understanding is itself evidence of the existence of "something" to which this activity is natural[572]; and, what that something is, is precisely the purpose of these paragraphs: the identification of what makes a thoughtful question possible. Thus the life of a man expresses a power which transcends that of matter; and, if there is a power which transcends matter, then there is that which possesses that power as natural to it[573]. But, at the same time, the 'soul' is related to the body as 'form'[574] is to matter. Therefore, it is the human soul which, transcending the bodily matter it embodies, enables the activities that

---

[569] Copleston, *Aquinas*, p. 158.
[570] Copleston, *Aquinas*, p. 159.
[571] Cf. Copleston, *Aquinas*, p. 158.
[572] Cf. Copleston, *Aquinas*, p. 27.
[573] Cf. *Aquinas*, pp. 158-161.
[574] Cf. CCC, 365.

Conception: An Icon of the Beginning

transcend matter to be "taken up". In other words, expressed in the human power of touch is a sensibility which goes beyond the power of sensation; and, therefore, the lover, the artist or the musician communicate meanings that transcend the power of touch. In the words of St. John Paul II: the human person is 'an incarnate spirit, that is a soul which expresses itself in a body'[575]. In the celebrated expression of tradition, the soul is 'the "form" of the body'[576].

The contrasting terms[577] of soul and body are of such a kind as to seem a particular instance of a fundamental characteristic of human thought and the reality from which it proceeds: the resolution of reality into *dual unities*. On the one hand, in the case of this particular 'dual unity'[578] of *soul* and *body*, what appears to exist is precisely the necessary difference between what exists as actual and what exists as potential. The soul exists as that which is the actual determinant of what kind of being the particular matter is as a result of being informed by it. Thus the soul as soul "causes" the particular matter it informs to be what it is and is said, therefore, to be in act[579]. The signate matter, which is the actual matter of the body, exists as that which has individuated a universal form. At the same time, then, the pre-ensouled matter, in this case the sperm and the egg,

---

[575] *Familiaris Consortio*, 11.

[576] CCC, 365.

[577] Cf. A. Belsey, "matter", p. 539 of *The Oxford Companion to Philosophy*, ed. T. Honderich, (Oxford: Oxford University Press, 1995).

[578] Bishop, now Cardinal Angelo Scola, Conference Paper: "The Nuptial Mystery at the Heart of the Church", Oxford Catholic Chaplaincy, 21st March, 1998, p. 9.

[579] W. N. Clarke, "Potency", p. 633 of Vol XI, NCE.

exists "in-potentiality"[580] to the ensouling "act" of the soul: the human soul that completes the determination of the pre-ensouled matter in becoming a human body. Thus a plant soul brings about a plant body, an animal soul brings about an animal body and a human soul brings about a human body.

On reflection, however, although there are three "kinds" of soul, namely plant, animal and human, there is no reason to suppose that the objective reality of each one is anything but individual. In other words, just as each plant is a new plant, each animal is a new creature, so each human being is, in one sense, radically individual: individual to the root of personal being. This individuality, then, is both real because of the uniqueness of the inheritable identity and because of the uniqueness of the human soul that ensouls it; but, at the same time, the being which exists is a "human being-in-relation", a child and, therefore, relationship is as "integral" to personhood as individuality.

The particularity of the soul: especially the human soul

One of the problems, then, with a general account of the relationship between "soul" and "body" is the sense, possibly deriving from Plato's "ideal form" being a template of all "forms" of the same kind, is that there is a kind of "universal" form of the human soul which is actually undifferentiated and "fits" all bodies. But what if, in the reality of the soul being immediately created by God[581], there is not an "undifferentiated" soul that is differentiated by its union with matter but, rather, God creates a particular soul that is "simply embodied" in matter? If, then, it is not so

---

[580] W. N. Clarke, "Potency", p. 633 of Vol XI, NCE.
[581] CCC, 366.

much that matter is pure potentiality, except in the general sense that matter does not determine what form it will receive; rather, the "biological matter" expressive of the transmission of human life is already a "biological matter" that is the precursor to ensoulment by God. Thus it can be said that the body and the soul 'mutually condition'[582] one another and thus reciprocally contribute their complimentary difference to the totality of what it is to be a human being.

The difference between act and potentiality is fundamental to the possibility that an entity can both undergo change and remain what it is[583]. In other words, the coming into existence of the psychosomatic whole of human personhood, of the soul being one with the body, is that this constitutes the "act" of God which established the person in act: the reality of who and what exists that then unfolds the person's potentiality. The *Catechism of the Catholic Church* says that 'it is because of its spiritual soul that the body made of matter becomes a living, human body; spirit and matter, in man, are not two natures united, but rather their union forms a single nature'[584]. In view, however, of the evidence concerning the transmission of human life, that the sperm is an active agent in this process, it follows that the 'matter becomes a living, human body' in the sense that before it was neither a human body nor, therefore, a 'living' expression of a particular human person. Nevertheless, as the human sperm is already "biologically living matter", it is clear that the human soul establishes human identity as a whole and, accordingly, re-expresses

---

[582] N. A. Luyten, "Soul-Body Relationship", p. 472 of Vol XIII, NCE.

[583] W. N. Clarke, "Potency", p. 633 of Vol XI, NCE.

[584] CCC, 365.

"biologically living matter" as the bodily expression of personal human life. In other words, in the moment of conception, the soul is inseparably the life of the body: the life of the body is a personal life: the body expresses the life of the person.

The 'spiritual soul' is created immediately by God[585]. The human soul is not the product of a prior process[586] nor, as it is spiritual, is it made out of what is prior to its own existence. Therefore the spiritual soul is not "produced" by the parents[587]; but, by the will of God, the human soul is created by God, at conception, both to be immortal[588] and of one being with the body. Conceptually, then, it is possible to distinguish "body" and "soul" as the "inward" and "outward" expression of human being. Nevertheless, it is true that bodily death challenges our understanding of the unity of the human being in that it is also true that the human soul is not destroyed at death nor is its union with the body completely "uprooted" in that, if it can be integral to the resurrection of the body[589] it must, in some sense, "retain" its relationship to the body. In other words, the union of "body" and "soul" must lie, as it were, in the act of personal existence which was established at conception; but, even so, it is nevertheless a work in itself to understand the nature of human death: both profoundly "unnatural" and perplexing.

The soul is that which '*animates* or makes alive'[590] the body. But, in addition, if the soul is also what co-constitutes

---

[585] CCC, 366.
[586] Cf. Pope Pius XII, *Humani Generis*, 36.
[587] CCC, 366.
[588] CCC, 366.
[589] Cf. Copleston, *Aquinas*, pp. 161-162.
[590] *Summa Theologiae*, Methuen, Pt I, Qu 75, art 1, p. 108.

Conception: An Icon of the Beginning

the human body, then the human body only exists on being ensouled. The soul, however, is a co-constituent of the human body as the very flesh of the sexual gametes, both ovum and sperm, are integral to the transmission of human life; and, therefore, the flesh of the human gametes is, therefore, co-constitutional of the enfleshed being of the human person. Just as, for example, plastic can be moulded but does not conduct electricity, so the human gametes are uniquely "equipped", in the first instant of conception, "to receive, to bear and to unfold" the presence of the internally determining principle of the human soul.

The principal activities of the soul

On ensoulment, the two principal activities in which life shows itself are 'awareness and movement'[591]: 'movement' is demonstrated from the very beginning in that the ovum-sperm unity is now expressed in the enclosed embryonic human being: a "walled" enclosure. The 'awareness' of the embryonic being is, as it were, the awareness necessary to the initial stage of life and entails all the processes *intrinsic* to nascent life, beginning with his or her passage to the uterus or womb of his or her mother. But, as with all that lives, each capacity requires developmental time to show itself present and active; and, therefore, just as there will be no adult plant if the fledgling plant is uprooted, so there will be no expression of consciousness if the development of nascent human life is interrupted. To use a different analogy, two people can exist too far from each other to communicate but, in that they exist, they co-exist in different places. When, then, the road, rail and telecommunications systems make communication between these two people possible, the transport and email systems did not bring either of them

---

[591] *Summa Theologiae*, Methuen, Pt I, Qu 75, art 1, p. 108.

into existence - but it did help to manifest their existence to one another. Similarly the child, on being conceived, comes into existence in the presence of the mother and, through communication, there is a gradual recognition of the presence of the other; and, indeed, even if the mother's consciousness comes before the child's consciousness of the mother, that very fact implies the existence and growing communicability of the presence of the child: a communicability drawn or reciprocally driven by the very ontological existence of their relationship.

Like and unlike life

The life to which this definition applies is at least the life which is common to all organic bodies or organisms[592]. In its way, the development of human life shows "plant like" characteristics as the embryo takes root in the lining of the womb and grows. At the same time, as animated human life proceeds, so movement in the sense of cellular differentiation and growth makes possible the expression of the movement of limbs, digits and other expressions of human activity. Life, as we know, varies fundamentally as the form or soul is plant, animal or human; but, in the unique nature of early human development, there are clearly successive stages of the manifestation of human consciousness. Nevertheless, just as the adult plant cannot exist if the seedling is uprooted and dies, neither can the adult human being manifest the whole identity of the human person if the embryo's development is arrested, frustrated or ended; for, just as limbs are necessary for walking and running, so the cerebral and nervous system's development is necessary to the expression of human 'awareness'. Thus, although there is an "external" likeness of plant and animal development to

---

[592] A. E. Manier, "Life", p. 734 of Vol VIII, NCE.

that of human development, just as animal exceeds plant development and manifests a different kind of life, so human development exceeds both plant and animal development and demonstrates the presence of the person from conception.

The activities of life are characteristically of two kinds: the first is called immanent and effects the perfection of the agent itself, namely the thing that acts; and the second is called transient and the effects of which terminate outside the agent[593]. Again, in general, it can be said that plants change in the course of becoming what they are; and, as such, a number of these changes express the "immanent" growth of the plant: its internal structure, size, odour, colour and possibility of reproducing. But, in the very fact of the plant's growth, there are effects which "terminate" outside the agent: its attractability to insects, pollination and being food for animals. Clearly, however, in the case of the "immanent" or "external terminus" of activity, the animal goes beyond the plant. On the one hand, the dog can recognize the person who cares for it and can accomplish, with training, sniffing out explosives, drugs and the scent of a missing person. Other animals, less domesticated, fulfil their own developmental potential and mature from infancy to adulthood; and, at the same time, they accomplish tasks more natural to them, but which entail the completion of an external work. Thus beavers make dams, spiders make webs and birds either use or make nests. On the other hand human beings acquire self-knowledge, often through a lifetime's searching in the light of experience, relationships and activities, including the power of the word of God to enlighten and the help of other people. At the same time, there are many activities which entail an "external" completion of a subjective process: the union of husband

---

[593] A. E. Manier, "Life", p. 734 of Vol VIII, NCE.

and wife and the procreation of a child; the decorating and improvement of a home and the growth of a garden. In each case, however, there is an almost inseparable development of psychological experience and insight and the completion, however temporarily, of the stages of a relationship and different aspects of an external work. In other words, while it is possible to contrast what is an "immanent" change within us with what "terminates" with an external work, in reality the two are as ongoing as time and eternity permit.

God, the Being alone capable of bringing what does not exist to exist, is directly the agent or efficient cause of the existence of the soul. God, however, does not make the soul out of His own substance. The substantial form[594], which is what the soul is, is created from nothing in the same sense that the heavens and the earth were created out of nothing: not as in the sense of nothing as some kind of something - but in the sense of no-thing absolutely. Thus the soul, or substantial form, is not created out of anything: whether that "anything" pre-existed the soul's coming into existence or not. In other words, the 'substantial form', as being that which determines the biological matter to be a human person, contrasts with an 'accidental form'[595]: a modification of what exists which, as acquired, depends upon the existence of the substantial form. Thus the change which is intrinsic to ensoulment, namely man being one in body and soul, is a substantial change and underlies the whole process through which the actual potential of the person is realized. The changes, then, which follow on the substantial unity of human being, like the acquisition of knowledge, practical skill or the effects of diet, are

---

[594] Francis Aveling, "Form", *The Catholic Encyclopedia*, Vol. 6, New York: Robert Appleton Company, 1909, accessed 25 May 2017, <http://www.newadvent.org/cathen/06137b.htm>.

[595] Aveling, "Form", *The Catholic Encyclopedia*, Vol. 6, 1909.

"modifications" of what exists and, in that sense, they are called "accidental" – not that they are acquired by chance but because they are acquired.

METAPHYSICS: UNDERSTANDING THE UNDERLYING PRINCIPLES OF WHAT EXISTS

Chapter Four: Part IIIii: Metaphysics. If metaphysical ideas, like 'form' and 'first matter', 'soul' and 'body', 'essence' and 'existence', seem particularly difficult to understand, it is because, in part, they are "abstracted" out of the particularities of human experience, what exists and, what is more, they have a long, historical lineage. Thus it is necessary to "visit" these ideas with a view both to their original cultural context and development and, at the same time, to the possibility of their further refinement and applicability. At the same time, a number of these ideas are embedded in their culture and, as it were, need to be understood as "bearing" a meaning that is coloured by a world view which is not necessarily valid; and, therefore, the validity of the relationship of "form" and "matter" is independent of the concept of an "eternal matter" that is modified by its reception of a particular form. Thirdly, in particular instances there has to be an assessment of the understanding of concrete facts which, bearing both the limited knowledge of their time and the intrinsic difficulty of the subject of *the beginning* of a human life and *the end* of a human life, entail a kind of intrinsic revizability as there is an increasing appreciation of their complexity, mystery and actual occurrence.

These factors are crucial. Because if there is to be a solution to the complexity of these ideas it is, in part, to come from the new evidence that the development of science has made available; but at the same time it will not reject or be inconsistent with what is valid *in the tradition*. If, however, what was grasped was true, or even *tending,* as it were, to the truth, because of the thoroughness with which what were thought to be facts were discussed, then it follows that it is necessary to discern among what we receive that which is enduringly relevant and what is not. Bearing in mind that a number of these philosophical ideas are derived from what remains the case, because they refer to the existence of what is stable as well as to what changes and the relationship between them, *precisely because* it is not the evidence that changes but our understanding of it. Therefore, even if our understanding of what endures and alters does change, it will not change in an arbitrary direction, as it were, but in the direction *dictated by the evidence and the truth which expresses it*. In other words, some of the complexity and the difficulty will remain because of the *subject itself*.

Thus the beginning and the end of a person's life are intrinsically difficult moments to conceptualize. Some of the enduring difficulties will be *relative* to the *uncertainty* with which something is known at a particular time; and, as such, there are on-going insights about the actual, evidential moment of conception and the actual death of a person. Something could be known for certain, too, even if the facts that express it are, at the time, uncertain. Thus it is known for certain, *philosophically,* that 'form' is as necessary to understanding what an object or creature is *as it is that there is some kind of matter that it informs*[596]. What precisely "constitutes" the psychosomatic whole of conception, while remaining enduringly credible in view of the dissolution of death, constantly challenges our capacity to understand and to conceptualize adequately. Never-

---

[596]Cf, SuTh, Pt I, Qu 2, art. 1, page 11.

theless, for all the difficulties of study and reflection, there is the simple fact: I was not and now I am; you were not and now you are; we were not and now we are. As regards death, the departure of the living presence of the person does not preclude the possibility of his or her return; indeed, resuscitation, although not resurrection, implies the future possibility of a kind of recovery of the relationship between his or her soul and his or her body; and, therefore, death does not abolish the relationship between soul and body so much as to evidence an enduring "existential" whole of which they are an expression.

Revisiting 'first matter' and 'form'

At first sight it did not seem to follow that 'first matter' is necessary to understanding what "soul" and "body" are; but, more generally, 'first matter' is that which is 'informed' by a type of living soul. Thus, from a general metaphysical point of view, it would seem that 'first matter' is as necessary as 'form', in that the 'form' is what determines 'first matter' to be a shelf or a garden gate; but, as we know, a shelf or a gate receives a "secondary" shaping to that of being wood. In other words, 'first matter' expresses a more fundamental feature of created being than that of shaping wood; for, in terms of the use of wood in a design, wood is already a type of what has been determined to be what it is. 'First matter', then, is the indeterminacy of matter to determine itself and, in an almost common sense way, 'form' accounts for the variety of ways that matter actually exists. Another way of putting it is that 'first matter', understood as pure potentiality, becomes a specific object or creature owing to the existence of 'form': of that which determines matter to be an object or a creature.

Furthermore, when the wood of a living tree ceases to be trunk and branches and becomes a table, 'first matter' seems to give a convincing account of what was first 'informed' as a living tree and which has now been 'informed' as a table. In other words, there is both the constancy of the existence of wood and there is a change in the state and use of that wood: from living to dead and from a natural form to a piece of furniture. 'First matter', however, is not just about a change of shape or use of what is, in effect, the same piece of wood being first used as a fence post and then being re-used as a table leg. The relationship of 'first matter' to 'form' is integral to the existence of an original object; and, therefore, the principles of being an object at all, entail 'first matter' and 'form' as intrinsic to the very existence of an object. Thus the definition or identity of matter from the least to the most sophisticated natural object, whether in part or as a whole, is due to the union of 'first matter' and 'form'. In other words, if the 'first matter' is integral to the whole, like a plant and its seeds, then although the matter "embodied" in it can increase by absorption and growth, there is nevertheless an integral whole which is, for example, grass; and, in the beginning of its existence, there is a union of 'first matter' and 'plant form' that constitutes the living entity called grass, although there are innumerable varieties of grass and, as such, grass itself is a simplification. Even so, of the three types of animating form or forms that constitute living creatures - plant, animal or human forms - plant form is nevertheless one of the three kinds of life that exist and, as such, constitutes a valid "type". In other words, then, as it becomes clear that matter, of itself, *cannot understand itself,* then the human soul necessarily brings to fruition the potentialities of human, biological matter, to be the vehicle of human self-expression. Thus there develops the terms of an enfleshed identity: each one of us is a concrete expression of a particular individual who is nevertheless an inseparable "part" of the whole human family. Our relationships, like pieces of a puzzle, are an inseparable part of the whole human family; and, therefore, if a "person-piece" is "missing", then there is a "person shaped relationship" implied in the remaining pattern.

Understanding that the living body is composed of "matter and form" is not to be confused with a reductionist understanding that human beings are "physical matter". On the one hand it is true that human beings are an enfleshed, psychosomatic and relational whole; and, on the other hand, the function of the imagination in the investigation and communication of meaning transcends the very limitations of matter itself. Thus, in its own way, the existence of the "human imagination" is a proof of there being that which transcends matter in the constitution of the human person. If our perception was wholly the perception of what exists then there would be no apprehension of the possibilities that are generally "present" to the imagination; and, therefore, human imagination entails human personhood bearing within it the power of going beyond a "passive" perception of what exists. Imagination, then, is here understood as going beyond the receptive formation of the "whole impression" of what is derived from the synthesis of psychosomatic perception; and, as such, communicates the stimulus to thinking which arises out of what exists: as if perception itself is more like the "shelling" of what exists and the release of "idea-spores".

Returning to "first matter" and the integral nature of human existence

If, then, another explanation to that of 'first matter' can be found to explain the substantial change that occurs at conception, then it can only enhance and further elucidate our understanding of the beginning of life rather than lead to the contradiction of what has already been rightly understood. Nevertheless, I have to admit, the coherence of this concept, which comes to us through Aristotle and St. Thomas Aquinas, is as it were so consistently and insistently arguing for itself[597] by the very fact of its extraordinary coherence and intelligibility that it no longer seems possible for me to "imagine" an alternative as conceptually and extramentally *realistic as this one*. Moreover, the very possibility that human biological matter undergoes a substantial change at the "moment" of ensoulment so roots the human being in the indivisible existence of being "one" in "body and soul" (*Gaudium et Spes*, 14) that it makes complete sense that there is an integral human development which is at the same time the ongoing manifestation of the presence of the person.

The intelligibility of our existence is what St. Thomas Aquinas calls its form: the 'intelligible structure'[598] which informs and makes real 'first matter': 'first matter' cannot exist without 'form'[599]. Secondly, first matter is not without a materiality that is necessary to it if it is to individuate the soul. For if matter was pure potentiality then it would be without the actual individuality necessary to individuate the soul. St. Thomas Aquinas called this matter 'signet matter'. Thirdly, however, it is necessary to conceive of an integral inter-relationship of 'form' and 'first matter'; indeed, indirectly, it is a part of this whole investigation to "imagine" the oneness of being one in body and soul. In one sense, the embryonic human child is the archetypal image of his or her own identity: the biologically expressed mystery of a human being-in-relation.

---

[597] Cf. *Dignitatis Humanae*, 1.

[598] Copleston, *Aquinas*, p. 105; cf. also F. J. Collingwood, "Form", pp. 1015 of Vol V, NCE.

[599] Copleston, *Aquinas*, p. 95.

Conception: An Icon of the Beginning

The idea of *first matter* belongs to a conceptual order that begins with pure potentiality and ends with pure act. The first does not exist except with such existence as a possibility to exist has, which cannot but exist except in God, first of all, and in us in so far as we can conceive of things before they come to be in relation to what already exists. The last member of this series is God. God, however, as the fullness of being, is not a part of the series in the same way that everything else is. God, *precisely as the efficient cause of all that exists*, is the origin of all good possibilities[600] and potentialities[601] *and, at the same time, God is the being par excellence that is*[602].

Further, 'first matter', informed by a form is that which makes possible the continuity of a creature's existence; indeed, 'form' in this sense is a principle of identity: it is the constant that constantly informs all that changes. Just as the DNA and genetic code determine the absorption, use and developmental incorporation of the nutritional ingredients, so the 'form' that informs the 'first matter' of human being determines it to be a human person. On the one hand, one form is succeeded by another[603]. The biological identity of the sperm and ovum are succeeded, on conception, by the integral identity of the human embryo; and, therefore, just as there is the new entity of the human

---

[600] The essence of a thing is the kind of thing that exists; and on p. 98 of *Aquinas,* F.C. Copleston says, "In a sense the essence pre-existed in God as a divine 'idea'."

[601] Copleston, *Aquinas,* p. 94: 'That which can be and is not is said to exist in potency, while that which is is said to exist in act' (*De principiis naturae,* in first sentence).

[602] Copleston, *Aquinas,* p. 95.

[603] Cf, Agneta Sutton, *Prenatal Diagnosis: Confronting the Ethical Issues,* (London: The Linacre Centre for the Study of the Ethics of Health Care, 1990), pp. 85-91, but particularly p. 90.

embryo, so this expresses the mystery of the 'soul' animating the body: the 'soul' being the 'form' that succeeds the 'form' of the living sperm. On the other hand, at death the 'form' or 'soul' that departs shows its unifyingly animating nature by what happens to the remaining body: the corpse is not only lifeless but disintegrates. Therefore 'first matter' is in a way required by this understanding of life because, if it did not "exist" and was not informed on death, then the loss of the soul at death would, as it were, be the loss of the existence of what remains, because what materially exists exists precisely as informed 'first matter'. Thus it is the inorganic form[604], characteristic of all that exists as "corpse", that informs the 'first matter' after the departure of the human soul and is expressed, as it were, in the progressive deterioration of the body. In other words, it is as if the inorganic form is precisely that and is, therefore, radically different from the biological form of the sperm and the ovum and, even more so, radically different from the ensouled embryo. The corpse, then, in the very expression of death, is in a radically different existential state to that of life: the body decomposes precisely as an expression of the "ceased-to-be" living unity of the whole body. Conversely, it can be argued, the presence of a 'form' contributes to the degree of unity according to the nature it possesses: an inorganic 'form' unifies what is non-living; an organic 'form' unifies what is living; and a human 'form' or soul unifies a human being.

Thus material things are made up of, as it were, both 'form' and 'first matter' in such a way that neither of these "principles" has an existence apart from the other[605]. It is

---

[604] This point possibly dates back to a conversation or an observation made by the Rev. Dr. Richard Conrad, OP, while lecturing at the Maryvale Institute, Birmingham, England.

[605] Cf. Copleston, *Aquinas*, pp. 86-7 and on p. 87 he quotes Aquinas: 'Matter cannot be said to be; it is the substance itself

the 'form' and the 'first matter' that together make the substance of what is material or corporal[606]; and this combination of "principles" constitutes what is called secondary matter: the actually existing particular human being.

Accidental and Substantial Being: What Exists and the Changes it undergoes

This "whole-that-exists", however, is capable of modification. The modifications of which it is capable are an expression of what are called 'accidental forms': modifications such as when a person's hair changes colour, a meal is digested or there is a change in body size[607]. An alteration in the "whole of what a being is" is called a change in its substantial being; and, as such, it is due to a change of 'form'. Thus becoming a human person entails a change of substantial being; and, therefore, the change from the sexual gametes of sperm and egg, to human embryo is a change in the being of what exists: a change from biological to personal being. Alterations, however, which are due to a change in the 'accidental form' of an object are alterations which inhere in the substantial being of what exists. A change in the colour of an apple, whether because it has ripened or been bruised, does not bring about a change in what the apple is: the object is still a ripe or bruised apple.

Therefore it is the 'form' that makes a "whole" out of its "combination" with 'first matter'; and, as a "whole", that union is what brings the substantial being to exist - the human being: that which remains constant throughout all

---

which exists' (*C. G.*, 2, 54). Secondly, the question of human death, of the separation of the body-soul, is a question in its own right.

[606] Cf. Copleston, *Aquinas*, p. 87.

[607] W. A. Wallace, "Hylomorphism", p. 284 of Vol VII, NCE.

changes. It is the substantial being which is fundamentally both constant and capable of consistent change[608], in that the relationship of what is constant to what is changing is that between substance and accident[609]. The accident is an accident 'of'[610] the substance. A change in the accident is not a change of the 'form' with which the signet-first matter is united, but is a change in the object *which is in conformity with the kind of changes commensurate to the 'inherent form' of its existence*. Therefore the growth of a human embryo is the growth of the "substantial being" of the child, where substance denotes the constancy of the integral subject of the changes. In other words, all the "accidental" changes of size, shape, general appearance, mobility and bodily size, function to manifest the identity that the substantial being of the child expresses: the particular human person that the child is.

The range of created existence constitutes a kind of scale of being: from the physicality of the universe, to plants, animals and human beings and, finally, to angels[611]. God as uncreated does not exist in a scale of created being. How we define what exists must take account of where, exactly, it falls in this order of existing things. What exists, therefore, does not exist simply as matter informed by different kinds of form, such that plants and angels are one kind of matter informed by different kinds of form. The situation, according to St. Thomas Aquinas, is that while an animal has a form that informs it and makes it to be what it is, an angel is, as it

---

[608] Cf. Copleston, *Aquinas*, pp. 82-3.

[609] Cf. Copleston, *Aquinas*, p. 81.

[610] Kenny, *Aquinas*, p. 36.

[611] *Summa Theologiae*, Methuen, Pt. I, Qu 50, art. 1, p. 94. Clearly I accept the argument that 'without created intelligences the universe would be incomplete.' Secondly, I do not set aside the testimony of Scripture and Tradition.

were, a pure form: it is an intelligent being that by definition is without a material body. Therefore, while this distinction between 'first matter' and 'form' applies to many kinds of existences, it does not apply to all; and, for the purposes of this discussion it is to that type of being to which it does apply, that this discussion will restrict itself.

One or three types of 'form' in human being?

Now in the case of man St. Thomas[612] is prepared to consider the following two possibilities. The first is that man is one from conception. The second possibility is that there is a successive giving of three types of soul to man, each replacing the other at the appropriate stage of development and each higher soul containing the powers of the soul it replaces but, in addition, the powers that derive from the higher 'form' or soul. In terms of this second, threefold schema, there are three, successive souls. The first soul is the vegetative soul which makes the embryo able to nourish itself. The second, sensitive soul has the power of the first and brings with its own power which makes the embryo able to sense. Finally, the body is given its rational soul, which has both the power to nourish itself and to sense, and is in addition able to understand[613]. Thus the conclusion of this process is not that man has three types of soul, but that at the end of this process he has one soul which has the power of all three.

While I have assumed for the purposes of this discussion that the 'soul' is to the 'body' what 'form' is to 'matter', it is perhaps more accurate to return to the original wording of the *Catechism of the Catholic Church*, which says: 'The unity

---

[612] St. Thomas will here stand for St. Thomas Aquinas.

[613] *Summa Theologiae*, Methuen, Pt I, Qu 118, art 2, pp. 162-163.

of soul and body is so profound that one has to consider the soul to be the 'form' of the body: i.e., it is because of its spiritual soul that the body made of matter becomes a living, human body; spirit and matter, in man, are not two natures united, but rather their union forms a single nature'[614] [615].

The progress of a "relationship"

What is clear, however, from modern embryology, is that there is a distinctive integrity to the human embryo which, on coming into existence from the union of sperm and egg, comes into existence with the nutritive and sensitive powers already present; and, according to the degree of development which each needs to become manifest, their further manifestation is "time" dependent. Thus, just as the nutritional and sensitive powers of the embryo require a "time" dependent degree of development, so the power of reason requires a requisite degree of development; however, the child is a "whole" and, therefore, it is not so much that each power needs time to become "visible" as that the whole process is about manifesting the existence of the human person conceived from the beginning. Therefore, as being-in-relationship is fundamental to human personhood, the whole programme of development could be revized to entail the unfolding of the mother-child relationship and, on the basis of this relationship, the father-child and sibling relationships. In other words, the whole conception and implantation of the human embryo is not just an "isolated" developmental process it is, rather, the on-going process of the manifestation of identity-through-relationship. In other

---

[614] CCC, 365.
[615] Cf. also Kenny, *Aquinas*, p. 48; *Summa Theologiae*, Methuen, Pt II, Qu 50, art 1, p. 226.

words, the mother looks forward to meeting the child whose development she has become progressively more perceptive.

Are 'forms' intelligent?

This raises the general question as to whether all *forms* are, as it were, types of intelligence? This is possible, if what is meant by intelligence *is that which is capable of organizing, or ordering, of itself.* In other words, if the nutritive soul makes possible the existence of a creature capable of growth and the sensitive soul makes possible a creature capable of sensation, then it would follow that these "souls" brought a new, organized degree of development which, in their fullness, would bring about plant and animal life.

The dictionary adverts to a sense of the verb *to organise* that brings out the basic connection, as it were, between organization and matter: 'to make organic, to make into living tissue'[616]. This has two further elements: firstly, *to organize* is a verb: it is an activity; indeed one could say that the soul's power to organize is, in this sense, a principle of activity. The kind of soul that matter "receives" gives a goal to the development of the creature.

Activity and "intelligent" or goal directed activity

If a thing is not active itself, however, how can it be a source of activity? If a flame is not burning, it is neither a flame nor can it light a piece of paper. However, it could be that a better stating point is that of heat: a hot piece of metal can cause paper to burn even if the metal is not burning

---

[616] *The Oxford Paperback Dictionary*, compiled by Joyce M. Hawkins, (Oxford: Oxford University Press, third edition, 1988), p. 571; and cf. also organ etc, p. 570.

itself. Therefore there can be a principle of activity that is *both in act itself and,* being in act itself, *it is a source of activity.* In other words, the soul of a being is both present and, in being present, constitutes the goal of that being realizing the 'form' it possesses. Thus the very presence of the soul-form of a plant not only defines its nature as a plant but constitutes the developmental goal of the whole plant-being.

Activity, however, is one of the fundamental expressions of life: indeed life could be defined at its simplest level as that which moves[617]. For although we frequently make the distinction between what moves and does not move, between the life of things that move and are therefore called animals, *or animated,* and inert matter or what is called *inanimate,* we now understand matter to be in constant motion. Therefore it is necessary to make the distinction that activity in itself, to be like matter in "constant" motion, is very different to the possession of a living soul. To be in constant motion and at the same time to be in relationship to other particles is what defines an electron; but, by contrast, the "soul" of a plant determines not just activity but activity according to the realization of directional growth: of a plant becoming what it is. Matter, then, in its simplest state, may well be "active"; but it is an activity which accords with its "present" nature of existing-in-relationship with other particles.

It was precisely on whether or not a thing can be active and a source of activity that St. Thomas Aquinas argues the following objection: if the basic principle or soul of a creature was itself active, then we would be ceaselessly active[618]. For modern physics, matter is almost in constant

---

[617] Cf. *Summa Theologiae,* Methuen, Pt I, Qu 75, art 1, p. 108.
[618] *Summa Theologiae,* Methuen, Pt I, Qu 77, art 1, p. 118.

motion; and while it is not the same thing, Cardinal Newman argued something like it: to live is to change and so to become perfect is to change often. Therefore *there is a sense in which, if it is true of inorganic matter, to be relatively active is what it is to be what it is*; but, in this instance, to be relatively active is to be so within the framework of being inorganic matter. Thus to be "relatively active" is for metal to grow warm and to cool down as ambient temperatures change but, even with extreme temperature changes, change does not entail changes that accord with an intrinsic principle of development. Metal, in other words, does not of itself grow roots, reproduce or possess that by which it becomes more fully itself: a dynamic nature that changes in order to mature and to manifest a constant identity.

By contrast, if to be is to be alive in the sense of to be active and changing, then inorganic matter and plant life are inherently different. Thus there may be a sense in which St. Thomas is distinguishing the soul as that which exists to determine what kind of being a particular creature is and, at the same time, that the very presence of a plant, animal or rational soul, is also a determinant of the "goal" of each particular being. In the case of human being, then, the origin of voluntary developments is, as it were, a fruit of the involuntary developments which originate with conception; but, nevertheless, there is a sense in which man is what he is by definition of his soul, even if what defines him is also the goal to which he tends, both involuntarily and voluntarily. Therefore St. Thomas refers to the soul's substance and to its potential: to what it is and to what it can become through what it does; the soul determines the body to be a human being, and the soul is the source of the potential activities of the human being[619].

---

[619] *Summa Theologiae*, Methuen, Pt I, Qu 77, art 1, p. 118.

Francis Etheredge

Levels of activity and the coherence of the whole

A created being, to be recognized as being in "act", is to be recognized as existing as what it is; and that, in the case of a living being, to possessing a dynamic activity which is orientated towards the goal of manifesting what it is. Activity, therefore, follows "act"[620], in that activity occurs at different levels and is ordered in such a way that a lower level of activity facilitates a higher level; but, more generally, activity manifests what exists in act: what exists in act is the identity of the created being expressed in its very existence.

Thus the activity of a particle leads to, indeed constitutes, as it were, the order of complexity called the atom – precisely *because* it is the same activity of a particle which is both internal to itself and externally interactive, such that it is the same *energy of relationship* which both makes it what it is in itself *and* forms its relational patterns with other objects. Therefore, at the level of the particle, it makes sense to think of it as constantly in motion because it is an active entity. However, in the order that arises out of this initial activity, that is, in proportion, almost, as it is found in relationship to other objects, stability is realized; and, therefore, while a particle's activity may well continue, the molecule or interconnected mass of molecules that obtains from their coming together, generates a stable identity.

If this were not so then there would be no relation between what an object is, what it does and the relationships it forms. Therefore it is precisely this relation of activity to the being of matter that both reveals and confirms the

---

[620] There is an adage, "activity manifests being"; and, in a certain sense, then, "act" refers to the real existence that founds the possibility of development. If a flame is burning, it can light

existence of a principle underlying material relationships. It is this internally and interactively ordering principle that regulates matter and is itself, as it were, the first law of life[621], because it is itself one of the most general characteristic of all life, namely to exist is to be in dynamic relationships.

But just as what cannot be in motion cannot be in motion without *going somewhere, so what exists is ordered to an end*. The end to which all things are ordered is twofold: the internal unity of all that exists[622]; and, secondly, the end to which the whole is ordered, namely God. Just as an arrow cannot shoot itself, nor make itself, so neither can a planet order its own internal parts nor determine the end to which it is directed. Therefore, while it has been argued that life is intelligent to the degree that its existence is inherently ordered, and this order is evident, as it were, at the different levels of complexification[623], such that the molecule is not the particle but is necessarily ordered to it, so this *intelligence* is not the intelligence of the designer, but the *naturally occurring intelligent activity that testifies to the existence of the Intelligent Designer*[624].

With respect, however, to the preoccupation of these sections, it would seem that *'form'* is generally analogous to intelligence in that it does express an organization of matter which is comparable to the *expression of a person's*

---

other fuel; and, therefore, the fire can grow; but if there is no flame, nothing burns and there is no growth.

[621] Cf. B. F. Brown, "Natural Law", p. 251 of Vol III, NCE.

[622] Cf. J. H. Wright, "Universe, Order of", p. 457 of Vol. XIV, NCE.

[623] This idea is indebted to Teilhard de Chardin, although I hold it in a sense that does not *necessarily imply evolution*.

[624] *Summa Theologiae*, Benziger Brothers, Pt 1, Qu 2, art. 3, pp. 13-14.

intelligence, rooted as it is in the soul and expressed as it is through the body.

What if, however, 'first matter' is a metaphysical possibility because of Aristotle's conception of matter being eternal; and, therefore, 'first matter' is a "hypothetical" state that explains the fact that there can be multiple expressions of a single type of 'form' informing 'first matter'? Or, as in the case of human life, there can be a sucession of 'forms' which, in succeeding one another, require there to be a state of matter which makes this possibility possible?

Why, for example, could matter not come into existence as it is, with its propensity to form discrete objects being actualized; and, therefore, just as a magnet draws to itself what it can attract, so "matter" would come together in the natural variety of atoms, elements and molecules? At the same time, however, there may be other factors that come into play in the making of various elements and molecules, such as temperature, density and proximity to other kinds of atoms and molecules. Indeed, it is possible for there to be a "law of matter" that explains the distance and mass of the sun, earth and moon, their actual relationships to one another and the physical characteristics of each one of them; and, therefore, it is almost as if what already exists is evidence of an arrangement, however it is obtained, that is exactly what benefits the ecological nature of the earth. On the one hand, then, if the arrangement of the immediate vicinity of our solar system is an expression of a certain kind of "physical law", then that itself requires an explanation. On the other hand, if the arrangement of the immediate vicinity of the solar system is not the expression of a "physical law", then it follows, just as surely as the potter who makes a clay pot, that there is a divine Craftsman who has ordered the universe as we know it. Order, then, cannot arise by "chance"; whereas "chance" can exist in the context of order.

This question takes us, then, into the more controversial area of what is not only possible but what, in a sense, is the scope of real possibilities for how what exists comes to exist. It is possible to conceive of the beginning of inorganic and organic matter as a kind of "production process" on the basis of a 'form', like a pattern, being capable of informing 'first matter' in multiple moments of bringing about the existence of all kinds of objects and creatures. This does, however, presuppose the eternal existence of matter; and, at the same time, it implies an almost mechanical production of what exists: a useful "analogy" but an inadequate account of the unity of an object or creature. In other words, given the adequacy of the transmission of plant and animal life, it is therefore coherently possible for both of these kinds of life to come into existence whole and entire through the very nature of the propagation of their species or kinds. Thus there is not the "natural" combination of 'form' and 'first matter' so much as the propagation of one kind of life from the antecedent or "parent" of the species. At the same time, however, there is, as it were, "a quantum leap" between inorganic matter and plant, between plant and animal and between animal and human life. It is not self-evident, then, that there is an "ascent" from inorganic to human life except in the sense that it is possible to "abstractly" order everything that exists into a kind of "hierarchy of being".

In the section that follows there are a few observations on the discussion so far and the theory of evolution.

Francis Etheredge

A Preliminary Discussion on the Personalization of Matter

Chapter Four: Part IIIiii: The Personalization of Matter. What of the presupposition, as Aristotle thought, of a succession of souls: plant; animal; and rational; and, on this basis, a kind of philosophical analogy with the possibility of evolution? It does not follow, however, that this order proceeds, as it were, from the simplest to the most complex. Thus evolution is not self-evident. This is because there are differences between creatures which are so fundamental that the evidence requires a different principle of operation in the one and in the other. Thus the difference between an animal and a human being is of such a kind that one must, while recognizing common characteristics to both kinds of life, recognize that different kinds of life entail different kinds of 'form' which animate 'first matter'. Therefore one could speak of an evolution from the simple to the complex only if it did not imply the evolution of animal life into human life, precisely because animal life and human life are, considered precisely as forms of life, fundamentally different.

The adaptability, for example, of the hands of a human being are an expression of the versatility of human gifts, which range from the musician to the sculptor, the builder to the writer, the baker to the painter; indeed, the whole human body bears the possibility of tracing the most sensitive expressions of love, speech and action that make it the direct expression of the human person. By contrast, the hands of an animal, while sensitive and capable of a range of movements, are limited in the very limitedness of the particular animal and its characteristics. In other words, it is not so much that the "bodies" of a human being and an animal are "successive" steps in an evolutionary process as that they are, as a whole, expressive of a different kind of nature: the animal is immersed in its reality; whereas the human being expresses a flexibility of intention and action which creates out of almost every situation a modification of the world.

This is not a denial of the existence of common characteristics to these *forms of life*; indeed, in general, it is the very existence of these common characteristics that stimulates this discussion. But it does confine the possibility of evolution to the evolution of the body of a creature whose existence does not exceed, of itself, the capacities of such a process - unless, as in the case of man, it were to lead to, but not include, the possession of a rational soul[625]. Otherwise one is asserting, in an unfounded way, the general principle that a process can *manifest* what it did not possess as a prior actuality. In other words, if matter inherently possesses the actuality necessary to becoming the total human being, then the whole human being is by definition already *present*. But if all matter possessed what is entailed in being human, then all matter would be human and, therefore, capable of what human beings are capable. In other words, all matter would be actually human but, like the human embryo, dependent on development to demonstrate what was already nascently present. This is obviously not the case as matter, of itself, does not possess the power to understand. Therefore the theory of evolution *implies, for it own coherence, the necessity* of an account of the origin of human understanding as distinct from the development of the body that communicates the presence of that intelligent grasp of what exists.

---

[625] *Humani Generis*, 36.

Animation and the "levels of matter"

If the soul is by definition the determining 'form' of the body, then this raises the following question: In what sense, if any, is the soul the *life* of the body? This is because it is *precisely* as a form that the soul is what it is, namely, that which *animates* the body. But if the soul being the life of the body is self-evident, *then why has it been so difficult to explain it to the point where it can be said the question is answered?*[626] In other words, how can the soul be the 'form' of the body when *the time it animates the body is so uncertain?*[627] Although, it has to be said, the uncertainty of determining the time of animation does not alter the fact that there is a particular time; indeed, the very fact of human life testifies to a "moment" of animation: of the beginning of a personal human life. The uncertainty, however, has even given rise to the idea of delayed animation, that is, of there being first a vegetative soul, then an animal soul and then, finally, a rational soul with all the powers of the previous souls?[628]

The human soul is the life of the body

Perhaps the answer is that the human soul is *precisely* the life of the body. Thus it is necessary to *define the body* if one is going to say *that* the soul is the life of the body. Human life, expressed in the soul being the life of the body, is not synonymous with the fundamental characteristics that

---

[626] Cf. *Donum Vitae*, 1; and cf. also *Let Me Live*, p. 8 and footnote 20, the latter of which is on page16.

[627] Cf. R. Edwards, *Life Before Birth, Reflections on the Embryo Debate*, (London: Hutchinson, 1989), pp. 49-54.

[628] *Summa Theologiae*, Methuen, Pt I, Qu 118, articles 1-2, pp. 162-3.

all matter possesses in virtue of its very existence. In other words, the movements which occur as characteristic of all existing matter, the movements of the particles in the atoms which are basic to all physical matter, are nevertheless present in matter as it exists. The human soul is, therefore, not necessary to the structure of matter as inorganic; however, having said that, the structuring of matter as organic, entails inorganic matter expressing, derivatively, the human person.

Thus there is the question of the "humanization" of matter in its bodily expression of the person. The corpse-as-physical-matter possesses the "action" and "reaction" which belongs to a life-less corpse and constitutes the process of its corruption and disintegration. If the human soul animated the very physics of matter itself, then at death there would not only be the end of the body's life, but the end of the fundamental activity of all its matter. The corpse, then, would not only be an expression of the loss of human life, it would also, in some indefinable way, express the complete disintegration of matter itself. Matter has an integrity, as it were, which both precedes and follows its animation by a human soul. Sperm and egg, however, are different from the "matter" of a corpse. Thus the animation by the human soul at conception is of a kind of organically living matter, whereas on the soul's departure, the corpse is a kind of inorganic matter. In other words, the soul is the life of the living body.

The "personalization" of matter

The implication, then, is that the soul's animation of the body, which constituted conception, changes radically the nature of the matter expressing the human person; and, while this does not "personalize" absolutely every "passing" molecule or atom, it does imply that there is a new relationship to what materially exists as both "permanently" and "transitorially" necessary to human life and the soul it expresses. The sperm, prior to conception, bears a real significance in relation to the possibility of contributing to the transmission of human life and, as it were, "participates" in the significance of human flesh. The corpse, however, having actually been the expression of a specific human life and, in that sense, having being brought into an ontological union with the soul of the person, bears an irreversible relationship to the "whole" of that person's human being. Even if death is a radical separation of body and soul it does not follow, bearing in mind the ontological unity of the human being, that the corpse does not retain a kind of passive tendency to the resurrection which only God can actualize.

The relation of the human soul to the existence of the human sperm: animated, biologically human matter

Beside, then, the sub-atomic movements of matter and the molecular decomposition of the corpse there is the movement of the sperm; this is something which, from the point of view of the soul's animation of the body, is *already in movement* and is already "biologically" *alive*. Therefore the sperm is something which the soul as immediately created by God does not need to animate, except in the sense the sperm is of the living man, as indeed the egg is of the living woman, and thus in that sense the human gametes arise out of human life: men and women transmit life. The sperm is by definition of its movement, a true *transmission*[629] *of a biologically human type of life*. In other words there *is* a characteristically human type of biological life, transmitted through the man, in the form of

---

[629] Cf. *Humanae Vitae*, 1.

the life of the sperm which, by definition, is realised fully when the sperm animates the egg. The animated sperm is again an existing entity in activity, which with all its characteristics which the soul, as immediately created by God does not have to animate. Therefore, while it is true that a man's sperm would not exist if *the man* did not, and in that sense the sperm is dependent on his existence *precisely as a man,* it is also true that *as a type of life* it is precisely in the sperm's capacity *to transmit life that its own particular* function lies. In other words what is unique about the sperm lies in it being *the living germ of human life.* This, however, gives a second component to the structure of human life, which, while not discontinuous with the first is already different from it and could be called *the biological expression of human life.*

The choice of a third *form of life* is guided by three things. Firstly, what appears to be the aforementioned *natural distinctions,* as it were, in the different kinds of activity fundamental to life. Secondly, that St. Thomas Aquinas saw the possibility of three component forms of life constituting the human being, albeit that the three *informed matter* each in turn, and each one subsequent to the first included the capacity of the previous one, culminating in the final one of the rational soul. St. Thomas defined the rational soul as non-corporeal[630], immaterial and indeed spiritual[631]. A third form of life would be by definition what the first two *could not of their nature give,* such that *it could be called the spiritual principle of human life*; and nature is here defined as the inherent parameter to growth entailed in a particular form of life.

---

[630] Copleston, *Aquinas*, p. 159: C.G., 2, 49.
[631] Copleston, *Aquinas*, p. 160-1.

Francis Etheredge

A working definition of human being

A working definition of the human being, then, *that fits the facts*, is that a human being is a unitary expression of the following three, diverse forms of life: the physical; the biological; and the spiritual. However, lest it be construed that the physically inorganic type of matter is first, the biologically animated type of life is second and the spiritually animated, rational life is third, in some kind of "time" sequence, these three dimensions of human life are here understood to be like recognising the existence of a "three dimensional" box. In other words, "the physical, the biological and the spiritual", are not so much discrete "kinds" as the three "dimensions" of the whole reality that constitutes the one human being-in-relation. In the event, however, of the actuality of human life, the *Catholic Church* has traditionally accepted the distinction between the spiritual and the corporeal as constituting the two orders of created reality which are, in man, one[632]. Therefore this threefold analysis of the human being does not propose a third division, as such, so much as looks at what is called corporeal in the light of modern science and as applied to the task of a philosophical understanding of what it is to be a human being.

Therefore the human being could be said to be composed[633] of *three, philosophically discernible dimensions,* almost as if the human being is like a rope platted from these three strands. The human being expresses, at its simplest level, the unity inherent in its diversity; and, at the

---

[632] Cf. *Dei Filius*, art 3002, p. 124 of *The Christian Faith*.
[633] Cf. *Dei Filius*, art 3002, p. 124 of *The Christian Faith*.

same time, the human person is both an *intra*-personal and an *inter*-personal[634] reality.

In contrast, however, to this claim is the "psychological" dimension. In other words, just as the physical is taken up in the biological, so the psychological is, as it were, the "middle ground" between the spiritual and the biological. Thus there could be an alternative three dimensional account of the human being-in-relation: biological identity and its relationship to others; the psychologically reciprocal relationship to others; and the relationship of our prayer to spiritual communion with God and other people. The biological entails the "plant" type activities of absorption, growth and reproduction. The psychological entails the biological root of emotional reactions and intellectual activities of thought, order and creativity. The spiritual, drawing on both the biologically psychological and the psychologically cognitive activities of thinking and willing, yet are seamlessly integrated with the pursuit of truth, love and a dialogue with God.

If these are both real and, therefore, philosophically sustainable accounts of a unity of diverse "dimensions" of life, then its theological significance is *that the human being is fashioned out of a "Trinitarian" background and,* in St. Augustine's expression, bears a particular kind of "trace" of the Blessed Trinity's unity-in-diversity[635]: a kind of "Trinitarian" watermark which the Creator left "in" the whole of creation.

---

[634] Cf. Sicari, *Mary, Peter and John*, p. 192: 'The coming to be of a human being cannot happen, it cannot even be thought, without the coming to be of intra-human relations, first of all the relations between the child and its parents which serves to introduce other relations.'

[635] Gerard McCann, *Theology of the Trinity: A Course Book for the Distance Learning Degree in Theology*, (Birmingham: Maryvale Institute, 1994), p. 67.

Francis Etheredge

One or many 'substantial forms' to the human being?

Where 'form' is here understood to be that which determines the existence of a particular kind of life. A 'substantial form', therefore, is one which would ordinarily define a discreet, separate type of substance. In other words, the 'substantial form' of the human being would be that which does not cease to exist, even when union with the visible reality of the human being ceases at death[636].

A number of these different sections have touched upon the ancient question of "the one and the many", which took a particular turn with the advent of the Aristotelian-Thomistic doctrine of 'form' and signet 'first matter'. In other words, is the person determined by one or many substantial forms? This question brings together the following seven considerations.

Firstly, earlier sections of this discussion distinguish three dimensions of human existence: the first is the "simplest" and constitutes the activity of atomic and sub-atomic particles; the second is the biologically living and active sperm and the corresponding egg; and the third is the spiritual soul. Fundamental to this differentiation of these three "dimensions" is the argument that each "one" is determined to be what it is *precisely* by the kind of 'form' it has: an inorganic 'form' determines physical matter to be what it is; a human, "biological" form, determines there to be a sperm or an egg; and a human form, namely the human soul, determines there to be a human being.

Secondly, the two types of 'form' with which one is particularly concerned here are the corporeal and the

---

[636] Death has to be defined, definitively, as the cessation of life; and, as such, has to take into account the experience of

spiritual: the first characteristically animates an animal and the second a human being.

Thirdly, there is the animal's being, a union of flesh and substantial form, the characteristics of which are 'educible' from the biological gametes of the male and female animal. On the one hand, to say that the animal is 'educible' from the biological gametes is to suggest that the 'form' or 'sensitive soul' of the animal emerged from the potentiality of matter[637]; but, if the biological gametes of the lion and lioness, for example, are already alive, then they are already transmitting a biological type of life which does not require the emergence of what was potentially present. The potentiality of the gametes to becoming an animal offspring on the fertilization of the egg by a sperm is, as it were, coherent with the biological life of the animal gametes. Thus the corporeal 'sperm' and 'ovum' are the antecedent organically living matter of each animal which comes to exist. In other words, the animal as a being does not exceed the capability of biological life, although it does exceed the capability of physical matter and vegetative life. The 'eduction'[638] of the 'sensitive form' of an animal is not, therefore, an explanation of how animals reproduce so much as a possible explanation about how animals came to exist in the first place; although, even then, it is not clear how

---

resuscitation where, for a certain period, death apparently "was taking place" and then was "reversed" with the recovery of life.

[637] Cf. *Summa Theologiae*, Part I, Question 90, Article 2: 'The production of act from the potentiality of matter is nothing else but something becoming actually that previously it was in potentiality. But since the rational soul does not depend in its existence on corporeal matter, and is subsistent, and exceeds the capacity of corporeal matter, as we have seen (I:75:2), it is not educed from the potentiality of matter'
(http://www.newadvent.org/summa/1090.htm).

[638] V. E. Smith, "Matter and Form", p. 487 of Vol IX, NCE.

inorganic matter possesses the "potentiality" to be made into an organic being. On the other hand, if eduction is like the assembling of an aircraft from a kit, then eduction involves the taking of the real potentiality of the whole from the collection of the predetermined parts; and, at the very least, involves an agent which assembles the parts into the whole.

Or, if "eduction" is related to "education"[639], then to draw out the potential to be a writer is to make manifest what is already, as it were, in some kind of actual existence as a "psychological talent or possibility". The kind of creature that a lion is, however, does not require an act of God to reproduce as, according to its kind, male and female possess the prerequisites necessary to the transmission of animal life. The creation of a human being, however, does require an act of God which is integral to the moment of human conception.

Fourthly, the 'substantial form' of the human being is not a 'form' which can be transmitted by the parents of the child; it is a human 'soul' which is beyond the capability of human biological matter to transmit. In other words, the union of egg and sperm is "in potentiality" to the reception of the human soul; and, therefore, the first instant of the human embryo's existence is the first instant of human ensoulment. Just as a note arises from the flute on contact with the musician's breath, so the potentiality of the flute for music is actualized by the breath which came to it but which could not come from it. At the same time, however, unless the flute was "designed" to be actuated by a human breath, then the flute would not be "in potentiality" to the inspiration expressed in music.

Similarly, the human gametes are ordered to the reception of the soul on their "unifying" transmission of human life - but not until the first instant of the sperm and

---

[639] http://www.yourdictionary.com/educe.

egg's union is the human life in existence. Human being is therefore ensouled in the very first instant he or she comes to exist. In other words, just as the flute cannot play itself, neither can "one part" of the sexual gametes bear the soul; and, as such, the "pre-condition" of human ensoulment is the "whole" of human being: the whole of human being is from the first instant of the animating union of sperm and egg. The human soul is, as it were, ordered to the whole human being and not to a particular part of it; and, as such, ensoulment both expresses and brings about the integrity of being a human being: a human person: a being-in-relation.

The coming into existence of the substantial form of the body, which is the soul of the body, is therefore an instance of what is called substantial change: a change beyond the capability of the subject. Just as a flute cannot "breath" a note into itself neither can the first instant of the human embryo exist without the action of God ensouling it. This change, both irreversible and beyond the power of the subject itself, is called a substantial change; it a change of the 'form' of the matter whereby it can be said that one kind of 'form' replaces another. While substantial change is a change of 'form', which determines what exists, the actual 'first matter' remains constant to this instantaneous change. The "termini" of substantial change are the human gametes and the human person. In other words, there is first the biological order of human life in its separated condition of sperm and egg. The sperm and egg, while ordered to the reception of a human soul on the first instant of their union, are not yet in possession of the soul as "they" are not yet "one". Thus, in a certain sense, the sexual gametes can be said to be in a state of 'privation'[640] with respect to what

---

[640] D. A. Callus, "Forms, Unicity and Plurality of", p. 1024 of Vol V, NCE.

"they" are going to become on union and through the substantial change of being ensouled by God.

The second terminus of this substantial change is that at fertilization, owing to the simultaneous creation and ensoulment of a human soul, the new "whole" is a human person. It should be noted, however, that from the point of view of the traditional use of this terminology the second terminus of this substantial change, the creation and ensoulment of the human soul, entails the coming to be of the substantial form itself[641].

The fifth consideration is the difference between the coming into existence of the person as one in body and soul at conception *and* the mystery of death as the separation of what is inseparable as it came into existence *as indissolubly one*[642]. The beginning of human life involves a substantial change of the following kind: there was no person and then, at fertilization, a person came into existence through God's creation and unification of soul and body. The death of a person, however, involves another kind of change in that the person does not go out of existence in the same sense in which the person came into existence. In other words conception involves the coming into existence of what did not literally exist, namely, the person, whereas death, while a separation of body and soul, is the separation of what is both ontologically "one" and ordered to a subsequent resurrection of the body. Thus death is a change in what *continues to exist*.

A sixth point of relevance is that our baptism makes us a member of the body of Christ, just as our conception makes us a member of the family of man; indeed, it may be possible to say that becoming a member of the body of Christ is

---

[641] V. E. Smith, "Matter and Form", p. 485 of Vol IX, NCE.
[642] V. E. Smith, "Matter and Form", p. 485 of Vol IX, NCE.

"predisposed" on becoming a member of the human race. Our baptism is ordered to Christ's *Incarnation and Paschal Mystery* as to the redemptive "gift" that makes possible both the giving and the receiving of baptismal grace[643]. Furthermore, the ordered community of peoples in which the Church consists, both horizontally in terms of each other and vertically in terms of the divine Persons, is a unity which follows on the true and prior acts of God. At the same time, however, just as the community of the Church involves the "prior" acts of God, yet these acts of God entail truly human and grace "informed" acts of men and women. In other words, the indissoluble union of man and God in Christ is "recapitulated" in the history of salvation and the saving mystery of the Church. The Church expresses this in her own words when she says: God 'has shared with us his Spirit who, being one and the same in head and members, gives life to, unifies and moves the whole body. Consequently, his work could be compared by the Fathers to the function that the principle of life, the soul, fulfils in the human body'[644]. The Church, and indeed before the existence of the Church, the mystery of the Blessed Trinity "through" which the mystery of the Church exists, is a mystery of what could be called in a technical sense the mystery of "substantial communion": an "ontological" unity-in-diversity of peoples.

A final factor is the faith-fact that the damned and the blessed are the two contrasting and definitive "end" states of the change which makes us either good or evil: the substantial union of the blessed and the "substantial" separation[645] of the damned: the former is as necessary to

---

[643] Cf. *Gaudium et Spes*, 22.
[644] *Lumen Gentium*, 7.
[645] Pope St. John Paul II, *Salvifici Doloris*, 18.

life and happiness as the latter is suffering the painful deprivation of love's "relational" fulfilment.

These considerations come together in the following two possibilities, each of which, with respect to human beings, presupposes the necessity of the union of 'form' and 'first matter': either there is one or many substantial form(s) per creature

An answer to this question begins with noting what constitutes a creature to be what it is, namely, what kind of 'form' has come into existence. In other words, the 'form' or soul of a human being is what *determines* the 'first matter' to become the 'signate matter' of a particular person. While there are as many 'forms' as there are different objects, creatures and beings, if 'form' is what determines there to be "one" identity of that being then it follows that there can only be "one form" *per* being. Physical matter, plant life, an animal, a human being or an angel are all different kinds of being; and, therefore, in each case it is one kind of form which brings each kind of being to exist. The point is, then, that it is each type of form that in each case *radically determines the being that exists.*

Passive receptivity or reciprocal co-constituents of human being?

While, therefore, in the case of the human being it is the human person which God brings into existence, it is nevertheless true that each person has the *form* which is the common characteristic of that category of being, namely, the human soul; and, in view of what we know about human development, each human being has the common characteristics of the inherited "flesh" of a human being. It is from this perspective that one can see that St. Thomas

Aquinas argues that each created object, creature or person *can only have one substantial form*[646]; for each created object, creature or person can only be "one being". If, therefore, it were to be possible for a creature to be one kind of being, then another, as with the suggested sequence of human development from a plant, through animal to the human stage of development, then each radically different level of being would require a different type of 'form'. What is more, in view of the wholly different kind of being that each of them is, whether it be a plant, animal or human being, it follows that to envisage a "successive" kind of ensoulment of one to another suggests a degree of "passivity" in the "matter-to-be-ensouled" which does not correspond to its actual existence. In other words, the possibility of a succession of "ensoulments", from plant to animal to human, would entail not only just a "plant" type of ensoulment but a "plant to human type of ensoulment". In addition, because the "biological entity" to be "ensouled" by different types of soul is actually, by definition of its origin, human, it follows that ensoulment is a reciprocal reality: the "flesh that forms the human embryo" co-determining, in the first instant of fertilization, the whole human being in the same instant that God ensouls him or her.

By contrast, then, successive souls and their complicated changes constitute an incoherently complicated process which, however briefly, passes through radically different types of being. Instead, then, of conceiving of a unitary being, we end up constrained to think in terms of a number of "transitional forms" which require a "moment" of transition to the one which follows until the whole process comes to rest at the creature having become a human being. It makes more sense, then, to consider that just as there is a

---

[646] D. A. Callus, "Forms, Unicity and Plurality of", p. 1025 of Vol. V, NCE.

real transmission of human flesh constitutive of human life, so there is a reciprocal simplicity in God ensouling the human being with the soul of the human person.

The reciprocal insights of "life" and "death"

The second part of an answer to the question of whether there is one or many 'forms' constitutive of human being is that the substantial change from non-being to being, which in this case is the conception of a person, is a radically different change to that of the death and subsequent resurrection of that same person. In the first type of change, a person *comes into existence* from diverse 'elements'; whereas in the second type of change there is a change in the state in the already existing person. It is interesting to note that the first type of change can be described as a move from the "many" to the "one", and that the second type of change can be described as a reversion of the "one" to the "many"[647]. However, on the basis of the previous distinction between non-being to being *and* the life and death of that same person, it is the initial substantial change of the "many" to "one" which is literally true, whereas the second change, of the "one" to the "many", is only true relative to the continuation of what is already in existence but which is now undergoing a separation in view of a further re-unification at the resurrection of the body.

It is therefore useful to consider the respective insights concerning the beginning and the end of life. At the moment before the beginning of a person there is an existing "germ" of bodily life which is called the sperm and the corresponding human egg: each sperm and egg are, as it were, reciprocally ordered to each other. Thus there is in existence at the moment before the person begins to be,

---

[647] Cf. Kenny, *Aquinas*, p. 39.

what can be called the *transmitting germ of bodily human life* and there is in existence the human egg, with all its equally necessary and characteristically different contributions to the beginning of human bodily life. However, in contrast to what happens at the beginning of human life, there is what happens at the end of the life once begun: *the body dies*. In other words the elements which were distinguishable as the basis of human bodily life at the moment before fertilization, are now no longer distinguishable after conception, as separate to the life of the whole person which came into existence at conception.

If, therefore, there were two substantial forms at conception, namely that of bodily life and that of spiritual life, then at death, when the spiritual substantial form departed from the body, it would leave *a living human body behind*[648]. But in so far as what is left is not living in the spiritual or biological sense it can be concluded that the act of conception was an act which *insolubly united the biological and spiritual life of the person at conception*. On the one hand we can assert that there is a "germ" of bodily human life before conception; and, on the other hand, from conception onwards, bodily human life is *the life of the person* conceived. Just as the germ of human life is expressed in the biological gamete, the sperm, which is organized to this end, so it can be said that the "matter", out of which the body is made, is integral to the life and death of the person. In other words the nature of conception has radically integrated every part of what constitutes the whole of the person whose beginning it is. The nature of the relationship of the body and soul at death, however, remains a challenging mystery. Nevertheless, the very persistence of the personalization of the body at death, evidenced by the

---

[648] Cf. *Summa Theologiae*, Methuen, Pt III, Qu 5, art 4, p. 483.

possibility of resuscitation, points to a real "rootedness" of the soul's relationship to the body; indeed, resuscitation expresses the inseparable relationship between the life of the body and the life of the person.

Conception or eduction?

The third part of an answer to the question about whether or not human personhood is an expression of one or many substantial forms is the following, related question: What can be "educed" from the unity of conception? Educed, then, seems to mean that which can be drawn from a particular substance; and, in that sense, it is similar to thinking of education as the drawing out of a student's talent. "Eduction", then, does not bring to exist what did not exist, so much as to draw out what is present.

In the case of an animal, what can be educed from the reproductive cells is beyond what was present in either seed or egg but, at the same time, does not go beyond the 'form' of life characteristic of it. In other words, biologically sensate life, such as that of a dog, develops from the fertilization of the female dog; and, therefore, although the puppy is educed from the moment of conception, prior to which it was not present, the animal does not go beyond the capacity of the gametes to transmit and to "reproduce" the life of a dog. In the case of a human being, however, the personal nature of the creature that comes to exist exceeds the "power" of the human gametes to transmit it; and, therefore, the conception of a human being implies and entails an "ensouling" act of God. Otherwise, according to the logic of "eduction", human sexual gametes would need to possess the nascent presence of the person; and, therefore, there would need to be the presence of the person in the gametes. A person, however, is a wholly completed entity. Even if it takes time to manifest the personal reality of the human being begun at conception, he or she cannot be present in the sperm or the egg: the sperm and the egg are not, by definition, constitutive in their "separateness" of the whole human body. On the conception of a human being, however, the union of sperm and egg begets the beginning of the human being and defines the outward identity of the ensouled personal being. What was present before that moment of conception was a human egg and a human sperm; but, at precisely the instant of conception, a new personal form of life comes to exist.

It is now more obvious to us, however, that even in the case of human being there is a continuity of "substrate" between the moment before conception, the moment of conception and the moment following conception. The continuity of "substrate", however, does not mean the identity of the substrate "before" and "after" conception. Indeed, although conception could be said to be an activation of that substrate, on the unification of sperm and egg, nevertheless the nature of human conception as entailing the presence of a human soul changes the activation of the substrate into the activation of the development of the whole person. It therefore seems that the natural activity of the biological order which "transmits life" at conception, is that which the soul as "act" completes *and which the soul as a source of activity actuates.* The soul as "act", then, brings to exist the whole human person; and, in bringing to exist the whole human person, the soul as personalizing the human being begins to be, to express itself and to act in the process of human development.

Thus it could be said to be significant that at *precisely* the point that God creates the *soul which brings to exist and animates the human body*, there is the "outward sign" of the moment of fertilization which is, in its own right, the "natural end" of the complex of factors contributing to the conception of the human person. In other words, one can easily and without effort apply the analogy of the nature of a sacrament to the beginning of the human person: there is an outward sign of an inward act of God; and that outward sign corresponds, in the natural meaning of what it signifies, to the work of God within[649].

It could be argued, then, that it was for want of this perception of the precise moment of fertilization, *or understanding its precise content*, that there was no clear reason, historically, for assigning a particular "moment" to the beginning of the person. Just as a sacramental action has an "outward sign" so it would seem perfectly natural that the action of God which completes and begins the creation of the person is an action which "constitutes" the natural beginning of the person. Thus it could be said that if one had to compare the point of natural conception with the point of implantation[650], with respect to which one of these or any other "moments" were the more natural outward sign of the inward act of God which begins the life of the person, then quite simply one would have to conclude that the first moment of natural conception is the moment of ensoulment: the moment of the "inward" act of ensoulment by God.

In conclusion, if there is one substantial form that determines what a being is, then there are three implications that flow from this principle.

The first implication is that the corpse of a human being was *determined, as of the conception of the person, to be what it was, namely, the body of a human being.*

---

[649] Cf. *Inter insigniores*, art 5, p. 339 of *Vatican Collection: Volume 2: Vatican Council II: More Post Conciliar Documents*, Gen. Ed., Austin Flannery, New York: Costello Publishing Company, 1982: "Sacramental signs", says St. Thomas, "represent what they signify by natural resemblance" (footnote 19 on p. 345: 'In IV Sent., dist. 25, q. 2, quaestiuncula 1a ad 4um').

[650] Cf. *Let Me Live*, footnote 19, p. 16.

The second implication is that the body exists as ordered *by*, *to* and *for* the particular soul which *determined it in life*. In other words it is as if the relationship of the *body* to the soul is that of the human word of Scripture to the Holy Spirit which inspired it. Just as the word of man could not *be* the Word of God if it were not for the inspiration of the Holy Spirit, so the body could not be a human body if it were not for the soul through which it came to be what it is. The corpse is, therefore, not so much a sign of the "absence" of the soul, which in some sense it is, so much as a sign of the passing of the personal life which it expressed and which it will "re-express" on the transfiguring restoration of the resurrection of the body.

The third implication is that there seems to emerge a pattern of "relations": of intra-human and divine relations and inter-personal human and divine relations. In other words, the question of the unity or the plurality of substantial forms with respect to the human being, is a question which has to be asked and answered in the context of the full mystery concerning man. The biological life and the singular substantial form established by God at conception, and which constitutes the being so created as human, is co-extensive with the fact that the person now exists and thus in some sense exists in Christ; this is because Christ, in the incarnation, 'has, in a certain way, united himself with each man' (*Gaudium et Spes*, 22). There is, also, the act by which Christ makes it possible for us to exist in Him as to the beginning of our ultimate end of union with God, which is our baptism: a kind of "actuation" of the relationship established in the "incarnation". Thus there follows the call to conversion by which our baptism is brought to its definitive "end" of communion with God and the saints in the glory of heaven.

It therefore seems no longer a matter of a substantial form which establishes us in our human singularity, although this is true and significant, so much as it establishes us simultaneously in the whole plurality of human relationships. On the one hand the substantial form enables the expression of the personal nature of the relationships established in the moment of conception; and, on the other hand, the natural relationships found the baptismal-completion and communion with God and our neighbour. The baptismal-communion completion of human being can be called a created mystery which "imitates" and "participates" in the "substantial communion" of the three Persons in one God. The act of baptism by which God establishes the beginning of our salvation in Christ is an act which *ontologically presupposes* the being-in-relation that we are, but then goes on to *establish the beginning of a transfigured ontology: being a new creature in relation to Christ and His Churh* (2 Cor 5: 17).

If, then, an object is what it is according to the nature of the 'form' which informs it, then the human being is transformed by the grace of the Holy Spirit informing human nature to the extent that God gives to each of us. It could be said, therefore, that it is the 'form' of the Holy Spirit which makes what is diverse, one, to the extent that all of these diverse elements are unified in the holiness of God: a hierarchical and yet communal Church of the holiness of God. It is through the holiness of God that the Church of Christ could be said to be made perfect by the same Spirit which unifies and activates it as the soul does the body.

Finally, with respect to the precise question with which this section began, the act by which the whole human person comes to exist is both a true human act and a true act of God; and, therefore, their union constitutes the basis of the *indissoluble, ontological reality,* of the resurrection of the body. But this act of existence *falls*, as it were, at death into the "ruptured" distinction between the corpse and the spiritual soul. Thus, in the end, the separation of death is with respect to the one act of existence *at the root of human being*. Therefore the corpse *expresses the corporeality* which follows from that one act of existence, when and only when, the body is divorced from its animating soul; and the soul expresses the *spirituality of the 'form'* which inseparably flows from that one act of existence as from its unifyingly integrated origin.

CHAPTER FOUR: PART IV: AN ANALOGY

Chapter Four: Part IV of V: The Whole Person. The child is ontologically "whole"[651] in the "moment" of God's ensouling action and is "in act", being that which he or she is from conception; and, therefore, that which the child does is an expression of that which he or she is: a child in the process of a development that increasingly manifests the person he or she is.

An analogy

The washing machine is made up of a kind of three dimensionality: the physical matter; the mechanical parts; and the "brains". The physical matter, the mechanical parts and indeed the circuits of the "computer controls" are indeed the "corporeality" of the washing machine. It will not work, however, unless it is activated, unless it is switched on. In

---

[651] This emphasis on the "whole" person is definitely influenced by phenomenology (e.g. cf. Alasdair Macintyre's, *Edith Stein: A Philosophical Prologue,* London: Continuum, 2006, p. 39: 'But what is presented to me in experience is the whole, a whole composed of parts, and not just a series of auditory sense-impressions'. Thus, although this is referring to the perceptual whole of 'a song, a house, a cabbage, a landscape' (*ibid*), the same applies to the making of a whole.

this poor comparison, electricity is as necessary to the completion of the machine as that completion is the washing machine ready to run. In other words, the switched on washing machine is "in act"; and, therefore, possesses the active potential to be switched on to run.

It is also interesting to note that an "automatic" machine necessarily goes beyond the capability of both simple matter and that of a manual machine. In going beyond the "simple" matter, and the simpler type of mechanism, the "automatic" washing machine incorporates these "simpler" elements by subordinating them to the electrically activated "governing" computer programme. However, it is also true that while "motorising" a machine can entail a relatively modest modification of it, the change to computerization is a more fundamental design change and entails a whole restructuring of the machine. By comparison, then, a change from an animal kind of creature to a human kind of creature is more than a quantum leap and entails a whole restructuring of the being; and, by implication, the human being is "conceived" as a different kind of being from the beginning. Just, then, as a modification can imply a slight change, whereas a computerization entails a wholesale redesign of the machine, so the redesign of a machine is a new beginning and not just an alteration in what had pre-existed it.

A goal-governed process

It could be said that the making of the washing machine, which presupposes pre-formed parts, is a process governed by the goal of the design, from computer functions to the casing. In other words, from beginning to end, from bolt to computer code, the design is what determines the place of every part in the whole. Although, therefore, it is the electricity which animates the machine, it is the "idea", first

Conception: An Icon of the Beginning

translated into a design, a building plan and then embodied in an artifact, which *determines what this object is to be*: an automatic washing machine. The function, the user-friendly controls and appearance and the materials out of which it is being made, guide every aspect of its construction. Thus it is the "idea" which can be said to be the "end" which is envisaged from the beginning: the "end" of a button-operated washing clothes machine. The "end" to which all else is ordered is divided into the following elements: the beginning of the design, which includes the building program; the materials, which include the animating principle; and, finally, the "switched on" programme in which it is all actively embodied, actually washing clothes.

The idea as "germ" of the goal

The "idea" is, therefore, the totality of everything; and, at its simplest, it could be called the "germ" of the object. The materials which condition the design could be distinguished in various ways. The main distinction, however, is between what will power the whole and what will be put to work: the electricity and what the electricity will "drive". Some parts of the machine, like the casing, will not be working parts except in a structural sense; however, they are unified in the whole, not by the fact as to whether or not they are "working parts" but by the "function" expressed in them by the designer's realization of the initial idea. Even the basic materials are taken up into the design, principally because the design presupposes their properties and how, therefore, they can be incorporated into the whole. The point, however, is that whether it is the multitude of different kinds of materials, the smallest part, the relationship between the power and what it drives, it is the idea, embodied in the unifying design, which has informed and integrated everything into a whole. Thus the whole is called, not by the name of any part, but by a name which communicates what the object is as a whole: a washing machine. Even if individual parts are identified in themselves, everything in which the washing machine consists is now identified in relation to the whole of which each is a part.

The "design-form" and the "concrete" object: a constant relationship in an ongoing process of change

It is the design, then, together with what expresses it, which are the two complementary and yet different constituents of the whole washing machine "idea". The design is therefore the 'form' of the washing machine and the concrete object is the signet first matter. It will be noted that the matter out of which the washing machine is made is not an "abstract" non-thing, but a concrete reality which contributes its necessary characteristics to the whole; it can rightly be said, therefore, that the design and the matter "mutually condition" each other in the realization of the idea of which each is a radically inseparable expression.

It is the design which forms and informs the whole washing machine; and it is this 'composite' which is called 'secondary matter': the actually existing object which integrally embodies the 'design-form'. The change in the material substrate has an end or point of rest: the end of this process of change is when the material substrate comes to possess the full form of the object it is expressing; and, therefore, from the beginning of the process there is a kind of "form changing" which takes up all the parts, bit by bit, into the whole washing machine. In other words, throughout the whole process of designing and building the washing machine, including feedback and modifications, the whole process is governed by the whole object-to-be-completed; and, in a certain way, then, it is not just that the "germ" and "goal" are governed by the design of a washing machine –

Conception: An Icon of the Beginning

but that every step in between is a manifestation of the progress between "germ" and "goal". The "design-to-be-accomplished", then, is not just a beginning and an end; but, rather, an ever-present determinant of the whole process of development.

The "termini" of the process of change

The termini of the changes that the washing machine undergoes, until its completion, are the idea which inspires the design and the switched on washing machine which expresses its completion. The termini of the materials are the "many" parts, their different dimensions, requirements and interrelationships and the "one": the working washing machine as a whole. The material, expressed as a 'privation', is the material prior to it receiving the 'form' as a whole or in part[652]. Thus, in a certain sense, beyond the verbalization, initial sketches or even models, the beginning of the realization of the design-idea is the concrete change in the material as it embodies the 'form' of a part of what brings the concrete washing machine to exist. The material which is changed and ordered by the 'design-idea' stands as 'potential' to 'act': as a potential part to the existence of the washing machine being ready to use. It is the design which completes, unifies and actuates the potential of these materials: a potential which is, however, an actuality to the extent that the properties of the material are real and existent. In other words, although the materials are "in potentia" to the washing machine, they actually possess qualities as rubber, metal or circuitry which make them "fit for purpose" already; and, if already formed into specified pipes, nuts and bolts or other pieces, then they are even

---

[652] Cf. S. Marc Cohen, "Aristotle on Change", https://faculty.washington.edu/smcohen/320/archange.htm.

further along the line of being ready to be incorporated into the developing object.

Time and change

The 'instant' of indivisible time, in which change could be said to occur, is the moment in which the washing machine is switched on. This is the moment in which everything the object is intended to be is actually present. This first moment of completion is simultaneously ordered to a second, namely, the running of the washing machine to the end of the washing cycle. The running of the washing machine is that to which everything else is definitively ordered. The running of the washing machine is, however, ordered to time. Thus it is running when, having been switched on, it progresses the programme of actions which fulfil what it is to wash clothes. The instant that the washing machine is switched on is the instant that the created whole is in "act" and in readiness to be "active".

Assuming that this is the first time that the washing machine has ever been switched on, this is the first time that the idea is completely and perfectly realized: the idea expressed in the dynamic unity of the "design-form" and its "material" expression. The washing machine now exists in the sense of the kind of being it is; and, as the ancient adage goes, this being manifests itself in its natural and characteristic activity. In other words, while time and process are involved, there is a concrete moment when the washing machine expresses what it is; and that concrete "instant" is when it is switched on: when the whole-that-it-is activates for the first time. It is in this 'instant', therefore, in which the act of its existence is expressed: the act of existence in which the whole washing machine is both established and expressed.

Conception: An Icon of the Beginning

The agent-builder and the limitations of the analogy

On reflection, one of the principal differences between the conception of a human being and the design of a product is that the conception of a human being is the fruit of a personal, spousal act. Thus there is, as it were, a "visible" transmission of the humanity of the parents to their child: the "whole" of whom is complete from the first instant of fertilization. At the same time as the dynamic whole is present from that first instant, it is human growth which makes visible the invisible presence of the person. In other words, the growth of the individual makes the personal presence from conception visible through the increasing recognizability of "who" is present.

It is now necessary to consider a number of weaknesses in this analogy

The fact that the "agent-builder" is external to the washing machine is one of the many reasons why this analogy is only partially applicable to the inner reality of human conception it has been modelling. However, even an "agent-builder" has its place in the analogy because it makes abundantly clear that there has to be an active designer-builder who knows how to translate the "germ" of an idea into an incarnate reality. This designer-builder is God.

A human designer-builder makes use of many preformed materials, processes and types of collaboration in the course of realizing his or her design. It does not detract from the work of the designer-builder that parts are brought together from different places and production lines; on the contrary, it brings out the social nature of creativity and work. In the case of the creativity of God, there is a marvellous "integrity" to the "whole" work of creation being *one* work and one work of the Blessed Trinity; and, at the same time, there is the immense individuality of each person, the relationships between people and the common reality of each one of us being a member of the human race. More particularly, there is the cooperation between the spouses and God. In the nature of human pro-creation, there are the ovum or egg and sperm: each of which has matured to the stage of being "ready" for the unification that makes possible the transmission of human life; and, at the same time, on conception there is the "womb-welcome" of the embryonic human child, who then develops until birth and beyond.

Secondly, the analogy makes explicit that the washing machine 'idea' has an origin 'internal' to the designer-builder and is as much a part of what can be investigated as any other part of the process. In terms of human experience, then, it is possible to consider the labour-time intensive process of washing, the limitations of rinsing and pressing out the water; and, conversely, the "new" application of an increasingly sophisticated technology and its wide ranging applicability to domestic work.

In the case of the Creator, however, the investigation of that interior process is quite simply dependent on the extent to which the Creator reveals what "inspired" the "idea" of human beings in the first place. The text of Scripture makes it clear that, ultimately, the inspiration of man, male and female, is the mysterious Being of the Blessed Trinity (cf. Gn 1: 26-27[653]). One can only humanly "enter into" what that means to the extent that the analogy of actual human pro-creativity permits. The co-creation of human life is an instance of the human experience of life from life: of new life proceeding in imitation of a life which already exists, while at the same time that new life is "different" from "who" already exists. Furthermore, there is the whole origin of the desire for children as it exists in the heart, as it were, of the

---

[653] Cf. also Pope St. John Paul II, *Letter to Families*, 6.

Conception: An Icon of the Beginning

husband and wife; and, in that respect, there is the possibility of an echo of the divine reality in the human reality: of love leading to life. It is possible, too, that the whole psycho-physiological reality of the manifestation of parenthood, of becoming a mother and father, is also open to investigation in that it is integral to their humanity.

Thirdly, just as metal transcends raw materials, the pressed shape the sheet metal, the mechanism, the individual parts, and the circuits and their activating electricity transcend the mechanism, so the programme transcends the computer which is programmed, such that it can be said that the design transcends the material out of which it is made and through which it is expressed. So, then, does the human person's imagination transcend the materials which express the "idea" of the designer. So the person transcends the objects that he or she has made. So, then, does the Creator transcend His creation. Yet, just as the "idea" of the engineer "accompanies" the whole design process and influences each part of it in the course of producing the whole washing machine, so the Creator's transcendence of creation is not a "distance" of Creator "from" creation, rather it is an "immanent" presence "in" creation. If the design-form was not inwardly present to the material-corporeality it is determining, then there would be no washing machine, just as if the designer-builder did not switch the machine on then the 'idea' would not be realized in a complete artifact.

The act which unifies everything, is the act which "switches the washing machine on"; and, therefore, switching the machine on transcends the machine but is "immanent" to it. The sign that the washing machine is on is the sign which indicates that the electricity is now in the body of the machine. This is signified by a light coming on as the switch is put on. In other words there is an external and concrete act which completes the incarnation of the idea in the artifact; and, moreover, this external and concrete act is as necessary to that completion as the switching on is to the washing machine being on.

Just as switching on a washing machine is a completion of it and is evident in its activity, so a person's existence begins at the first instant of an ensouling fertilization and is outwardly "signified" by the activation of the egg by the sperm and is evident in the formation of the embryonic wall. This is the act by which man, woman and God co-create and complete the act by which the person begins. What we cannot "see", however, is the soul completing the body, just as we cannot see the design's embodiment in the whole washing machine as separate to the whole object; but, conversely, just as we can see that the whole object expresses a design, so we can see that the human person is a whole being-in-relation and not an amorphous agglomeration of parts. Similarly, just as we can see the switch go down and the lights come on, so we can "see" the act of fertilization, the animation of the egg by the sperm and the manifestation of the person whose development shows the person to have been present from the beginning. It is fertilization, this "act of activation", which is the evidence of the actual beginning of the person. Fertilization is, therefore, an act of activation which *is* the observable beginning of the person. Fertilization is the "external" reality-sign of the "internal" act of God; and, therefore, in the instant of ensoulment there is the first instant of human embryonic life.

Two implications to all this: the relation of the design-form to the material object and the fact that the whole cannot but exist in relation to its maker

The first implication of this discussion is how the design-form gives "life" to a material object when it is so "different" from it. This can only be explained from the point of view that the design-form gives "life" to a material object when it is actually embodied in it. In other words, just as there can be no actual washing machine if there is no "embodied design-form", so neither can there be an actual washing machine if there is no "material embodying that design-form". But further, just as the design-form and the material are only definitively united at the moment the washing machine is switched on, so the union of soul and body are not and cannot be what they are to each other until the moment of fertilization. Just, then, as there is a specific contribution of the sperm and ovum to the new family individual of the human race, so there is a progressive determination of the parts that contribute to the whole washing machine.

The second implication to this is the implication of relationship. In other words, just as the washing machine does not originate its own idea, design itself, build or switch itself on, so the person cannot begin to be without an antecedent cause. Therefore the relationship between the washing machine and its antecedent cause comes into existence as completely as the factors which contribute to that existence are made one at the moment the machine is "switched on". Thus the relationship which co-constitutes the beginning of the person, and yet is not that beginning, is the fruit of the reciprocal spousal gift of self and the mystery of that first instant in which the person begins to exist. This evidence of relationship is of two kinds. There is the positive existence of the person conceived, which is the *relational* fact of the embryo's existence and the total "signification" of that fact; or the tragic quality of the reactions of men and women to the death of their child, either because of a miscarriage or an abortion[654].

---

[654] Cf. D. Alton with A. Holmes, *Whose Choice Anyway?, The Right to Life*, Holmes, (Basingstoke: Marshall Pickering, 1988) pp.

CHAPTER FOUR: PART V:
FACTS, DIFFICULTIES AND A WAY FORWARD

Facts and difficulties

A question is related to what exists; and, therefore, an answer is related to what *inspired the question*. This is a brief attempt to indicate the various stimuli and sources to which the principle, "*where the body lives, there the soul is, and where both are is the human person*" is an answering response.

If the loss of the soul is *by definition* the end of human life, then the beginning of human life is *necessarily concomitant on the coming into existence of the soul?* How can a human *life* come to an end by the departure of "something", if that "something" did not also constitute its first moment of life? How could there have been human life at all if there was not from the beginning of it that which is the life of the body? Therefore what is the nature of that

---

84-5. Cf. R. Winter, *Choose Life, A Christian Perspective on Abortion and Embryo Experiments,* (Basingstoke: Marshall Pickering, 1988), p. 46. Cf. Philip G. Ney, and his research assistant, Adele Rose Wickett, BSN, *British Victims of Abortion, Occasional Paper, Mental Health and Abortion: Review and Analysis,* (Summer 1991, Issue 2), pp. 1-8. Cf also but in a different way the following: S. Vanauken, *A Severe Mercy,* (London: Bantam Books, 4th printing 1981), pp. 169-171. This autobiography of a marriage is a beautiful book in its own right. The author admits his wife *may* have come out of the coma herself (p. 170); but when she does he says: 'She came wholly out of the coma - against all predictions - came out of it with a memory of happiness' (p. 171). Cf. also, Francis Etheredge, "Philosophy is about Real Questions: Why the Pain if there is No One There?" (http://www.hprweb.com/2016/06/philosophy-is-about-real-questions-why-the-pain-if-there-is-no-one-there/).

beginning to human life such that death is the separation of what belongs together?

The life of the human embryo is another human life[655] to that of the child's parents and, once this life has begun, *'there is no particular part of the developmental process that is more important than another; all are part of a continuous process...'*[656]. In other words it is *precisely* because, from the beginning, the child's development is continuous[657] that this fact itself leads on to the conclusion that a person's life is seamless and, therefore, the mystery of a beginning is the time to consider the coming into existence of a soul and not at any subsequent stage of development.

Twins: A new beginning

Fertilization, however, is not the only point at which another life begins. Identical twins are twins who come into existence, as twins, when a single embryo divides and each of them obtains a bodily expression of their individuality. The second twin, however, does not receive its soul from the first twin. There was, until twinning, only one body and therefore only one soul, as the soul is by definition the life of the body[658]. Thus the second twin receives its soul from God *on the coming into existence of its own body*. In other words, *where the body lives, there the soul is*, irrespective of how that body came into existence.

The body of the first twin is animated by a soul in such a way that not only can the normal process of cell division

---

[655] Bishops' Response to the Warnock Report, p. 12.

[656] Bishops' Response to the Warnock Report, p. 13, which itself quotes from *The Warnock Report*, para 11. 19.

[657] Bishops' Response to the Warnock Report, p. 13.

[658] Cf. CCC, 366.

occur, but that the body of the second twin can come from the body of the first twin without the soul of the first twin animating the body of the second twin. What makes this possible is indeed the precise characteristics of this early stage of the child's development. For it is *precisely* at this early stage of development that the very nature of human growth, which proceeds by way of cell division, duplication and differentiation, is also the *reason why it is possible for one human being to be, in a sense, begotten of another*. Thus, it would seem, there is a "window" when twinning arises, as it were, completely; however, as development proceeds, so it is possible that twinning beyond that "window" is, possibly, less complete and there are various kinds of conjoined twins.

The truth of a principle and the remaining questions

It is necessary to distinguish between the embryological, philosophical and theological evidence for the truth of the principle, *where the body lives, there the soul is, and where both are is the human person,* and the need for further clarification. It is obvious, for example, that until it is possible to say more definitively what the actual[659] and the contributing[660] causes of a twin are, and whether or not they are operative at conception, or subsequently, or both, then it is difficult to discuss the relevant and contributory factors. However, it is already possible to say that no sooner does the body of the twin exist, then so does the soul of the

---

[659] Cf. G. F. Kreyche, "Causality", p. 344 of Vol III, NCE: an agent or efficient cause is the person who acts directly to bring about an effect.

[660] Cf. *Summa Theologiae*, Methuen, Pt I, Qu 118, art 2, p. 163: a contributing, instrumental cause, would be that which helps

twin; and, therefore, irrespective of the unknown factors, the separating of embryonic stem cells raises the really tragic possibility of people unknowingly "multiplying" persons.

A related question arises, namely, if this principle is true, what can one predict on the basis of it? For instance, if a living body must necessarily exist the moment a human soul animates it, can one exclude the possibility that both identical twins exist at conception, *precisely* because there is only one body and therefore there can only be one soul animating it? In other words, is it possible that a mechanism could be involved from conception, such as whether or not a second sperm attached itself to the egg after a first one had done so, but that this "mechanism" didn't become operative until a certain point in the early development of the already existing child? Thus, through a delayed mechanism, there would be one child conceived who, in the course of development, separated into two, equally developing, children.

But it is possible, too, for another, and as yet unkown external factor to be involved, which may or may not require a preceding and predisposing cause. In other words, if it can be stated unequivocally that the embryo first formed at conception is one embryo, then it can be said, also unequivocally, that the twin *must necessarily* come into existence at a later stage. Thus the truth of the existing principle is verified, *precisely* in its power to inform the investigation, as distinct, even, from the point at which the results of the investigation confirm it. Conversely, it could be argued, if this principle is true, *where the body lives, there the soul is,* then even if identical twins are simultaneously conceived at conception, then there *will be the physical existence of these two at conception.* Now if the definition of

---

to bring about the effect of the efficient cause; for example, a saw helps a woodman to bring about the cutting up of wood.

an embryo is that it is a *one cell body*[661], then it must follow that there cannot be, intrinsically, other than one human being in existence at that point. Therefore, whatever the process by which the subsequent twin comes into existence, it must be at a time subsequent to when the first one did; and, therefore, there must be a point at which a division in the developing process brings about, simultaneously, two distinct individuals. In a sense, conjoined twins confirm this speculation because they show, albeit in virtue of their incomplete separation, the bodily requirement of personal individuality. In other words, that even if there is an incomplete separation of embryonic cells, provided that there is what constitutes the integrity of the body, there is the presence of another human being.

The possible death of a first child, leading to the twins being the second and third child from a single conception

Another and related question is whether or not the first child dies and there comes into existence, at the moment of twinning, two different children to that of the first one. For it to be said, however, that a death has occurred, there must be a dead body. But there is not a discarded body. Therefore what has taken place has not involved a death, even the death of the first embryo being consumed by the twins to which he or she gave rise. Thus, whatever the process by which the twin comes into existence, it is one which involves the continuation of the life of the first child.

---

[661] Edwards, *Life Before Birth, Reflections on the Embryo Debate*, p. 52.

Conception: An Icon of the Beginning

The possibility of twins being "recombined"

Another unanswered question pertains to the possibility of an embryo dividing to the point of bringing into existence twins and then recombining[662].

This question requires a factual base to determine, initially, just that: What are the facts? Nevertheless, it is possible to assert that if the beginning of the union of the egg and the sperm is what conception is, then at least the following question would seem to require investigation: Is there a similar act of beginning which begins the twinning, as begins the existence of the individual from the union of egg and sperm? For unless there is an actual beginning of a twin, which by definition is another ontological individual, then there may not be a true beginning of another twin "who" is then recombined. In other words, it is not just a matter of determining whether or not there is a cellular development, which is redefined in the process of further development; it is, rather, a matter of establishing a degree of ontological integrity which, in reality, is the beginning of a human being. It may be the case, however, that in an on-going process of development it is almost impossible to say that a discreet individual has come into existence and died.

Further discussion of this point would require, I think, further information on this point; however, given that a person has a beginning, it does not seem unreasonable to say the following: that where the body of an individual begins to live, there the soul is, and where both are there the person is. Thus the task is to establish whether or not the body of an individual has come to exist; and, as such, this is a question

---

[662] I acknowledge a debt to the whole series of articles on this question. The one referred to is by Oliver Pratt, "A case for research: The embryo debate: 1", published in *The Tablet*, (London, 24 February, 1990, p. 240).

to be decided, irrespective of whether the body begins to be and to live as a result of procreation, twinning or an a-sexual beginning[663].

Conjoined twins imply a real "moment of beginning" when each of the two people comes to exist

One can say, therefore, *that the bodily person* of a twin comes into existence *at the moment of the beginning* of what constitutes *another bodily existence to that of the first*. While developmentally all sorts of changes might occur, such as an incomplete separation of the two twins, what cannot occur without the death of one of them, once they have begun to be, is that one of them simply ceases to be. In other words, bearing in mind that one child can end up inside another one, *determining whether or not twins have formed and then recombined is quite different to determining that "cells" have separated and recombined.* For if a true twin has formed, then either one has died or there was not a true twin; and if a true twin has not occurred, then what has happened is either a part of the normal process of development, *and its variations,* or it is an abnormality of some other kind. But, and this is the point, if another twin comes to be and then ceases to be, then whatever form that ceasing to be takes, it is nevertheless a death. Therefore it must be possible to recognize *that a dead body* exists.

Finally, what is evident from the existence of conjoined monozygotic twins, which are the result of the partial division and therefore the incomplete separation of a single

---

[663] Cf. Teresa Iglesias, *IVF and JUSTICE, Moral, Social and Legal Issues related to Human in vitro Fertilisation*, (London: The Linacre Centre for Health Care Ethics, 1990), p. 11.

embryo[664], is that *the complete physical separation of the twins is not a precondition for the coming into being of two people: of twins.* In other words, it is *the beginning* of what constitutes the reality of the existence of twins which constitutes the moment of the existence of each of the two being ontologically complete; and, therefore, even if there is a degree of "shared" bodily existence, the reality is that each one of them is equally body and soul. Therefore it is again obvious that the soul is created at the beginning of being a twin and that, if the physical separation does not complete what has begun, nevertheless *two people exist from the moment of that beginning.* The crucial fact, from the point of view of answering the question *"when did I begin",* is not when is that process complete - but *when did it begin? Conception, whether of an individual or of twins, is about the moment of beginning!*

> *A final question to which I want to turn is the following one: How are we to understand what constitutes the necessary and sufficient basis of the living body? What definition of body, then, is expressed in the following statement? Where the body lives, there the soul is, and where both are, is the human person.*

The same requirement applies to this aspect of the investigation, as indeed to all these technical questions, namely, that of an adequate data base to the discussion. However, at this point all I want to ask is the following: What constitutes the physical expression of the person? Clearly the answer follows from observing what *can be held*

---

[664] Cf. *Gray's Anatomy,* editors Williams, Warwick, Dyson and Bannister, (Edinburgh: Churchill Livingstone, 1989), *Twinning,* p. 158. This is not the place to discuss different theories

in common by "unseparated" twins and what *must be distinct* if it is to be truly said that this is a case of twins who are incompletely separated. But, in general, it can be said that the complete integrity of the individual is the good to which *nature tends because of the intention, inherent to it, of the Creator*.

In conclusion there is a radical beginning to each life, which recapitulates the creation from nothing of the beginning of creation, and there is the incarnation of each soul, on coming *into existence*, such that it cannot be said to have been in existence *before* the union of egg and sperm. The soul, then, comes into existence at the moment of that beginning we call conception; and, in that moment, the soul comes into existence as the 'form' of that body: as that which determines there to be the bodily expression of a personal life.

Secondly, the absolute individuality of the soul is mirrored in the unique inheritance, as it were, of the body. Traditional philosophy held the individuation of the soul to be because of the body, whereby the "matter" of the body differentiates, as it were, the identity of the soul. The phenomenon of genetically identical twins, twins who arise out of the early division of a single embryo, indicate that the human soul is also "individual" and contributes to determining the identity of the person. If the soul *only* determined *life* and not identity then identical twins would be identical persons. For, in the case of identical twins, it is the same 'material' which individuates each soul.

---

of twinning because the question is about establishing the fact of its beginning.

Conception: An Icon of the Beginning

A Way Forward: The possibility of "common" knowledge

Finally, considering the widely divergent views on the nature of the human embryo, is common knowledge possible? In the first place, the very existence of the human embryo is a fact presupposed by differing perceptions. For even the possibility of a public delusion concerning the reality of a human embryo presupposes *the reality of the human embryo* that made the delusion possible. Thought, in this type of case, follows on the existence of *an object*, even if what is thought is mistaken, a deliberate misrepresentation of what in fact does exist or, as in the case of true fiction, the thought is an imaginative development of what does in fact exist. Therefore, while the difficulties of knowing what does exist seem to exceed the possibility of obtaining common knowledge of it, nevertheless *it is the common fact of the human embryo's existence* which constitutes both the necessary presupposition of our common knowledge *and, therefore, furnishes the necessary determinants of the reality to be known.*

On the one hand, then, it is in the very fact of *what exists* that there is to be found the rule of thought as regards what it is. In that *scientific thought particularly* is both a response to *and* an investigation of what exists, where what exists also, in virtue of its existence, manifests its existence in activity; and it is both the being and *activity*, in this case of the human embryo, which continually calls, as it were, for the right formulation of what this extramental entity is[665].

---

[665] Cf. Copleston, *Aquinas*, p. 47: "In a rather cryptic passage Aquinas states that truth is 'a resultant of the activity of the mind, when the mind's judgement is about the thing as it is. Truth is known by the mind according as the mind reflects on its act, not only as knowing its act but also as knowing the relation of

On the other hand, *precisely because* we are different to one another and that, because of this, we will see and express what we see through our individual *selves, a fact each of us has in common,* does not of itself make common knowledge impossible. For even if our individuality does make common knowledge difficult, not only is our relationship to reality a common objective but so is there a common reality to which we objectively seek to relate.

Existence, then, implies communicability. In other words, intelligibility *follows on, is commensurate with, the fact of our existence*[666].

---

conformity between the act and the thing (*proportionem eius ad rem*). .... (*De veritate*, 1, 9)."

[666] Cf. Clarke, "Person, Being and St. Thomas", *Communio*, pp. 603-604..

Conception: An Icon of the Beginning

"Baby is the Best Healing Gift"

by

Isao Kurihara[667]

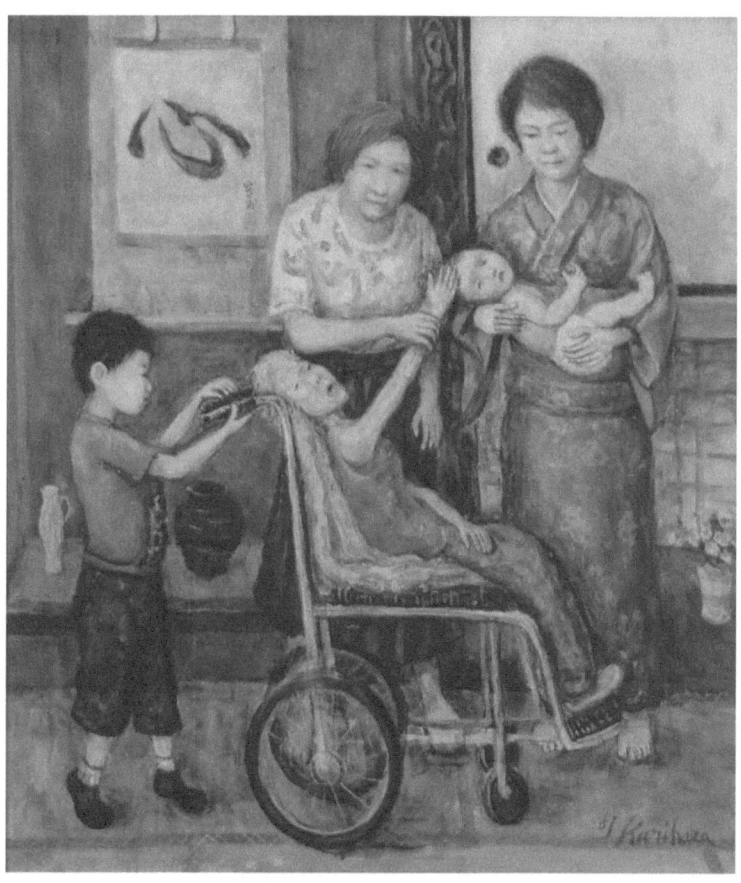

---

[667] Unesco Chair in Bioethics and Human Rights Art Competition: Reproduced with the Permission of the Director from the 2015 Bioethics in Art Collection.

Francis Etheredge

Artist's Statement

'In a traditional Japanese room, there is a Tatami (straw mat) in a Tokoma (decorated corner).
A Kakejiku (hanging scroll painting or calligraphy) is often hung on the wall in the Tokonoma.
In this painting, the KOKORO character depicted on the kakejiku means "heart" for the whole Japanese room is filled with healing. The newborn baby is the splendid present to the great-grandmother, not only for this family, but the baby is a gift to all mankind. As the world population is on [the] decrease, one has to ask, "Is this because love disappears?" A heart of love and a healthy body are the most important factors, perpetuated through healing.
A heart of love and a healthy body are the most important factors, perpetuated through healing.'

CHAPTER FIVE: FOREWORD AND BIOGRAPHY

Kathleen Sweeney

Biography

Kathleen Curran Sweeney holds a Master's degree in Theological Studies in Marriage and Family from the John Paul II Institute in Washington, DC, an M.A. in History from the University of Washington, and a B.A. from Seattle University. She has worked for several years in the pro-life arena, producing educational materials on life issues for the *National Right to Life Committee* in Washington, DC. She has published articles on pro-life topics, bioethics, theology, education, and history. She is a member of St. Agnes Church in the Catholic Diocese of Arlington, Virginia and of the Fellowship of Catholic Scholars. She and her husband (William, d. 2013) are parents of a grown son and daughter.

"The Trinitarian Structure of the World's Reality"

The very precise examination of the beginning of human life that Francis Etheredge presents provides a service to the embryonic child and to the society whose duty it is to respect and protect human life. His focus on the situation for the frozen embryo brings clarity to one of the most perplexing ethical dilemmas of our society. The text of two scientists,

Justo Aznar, MD, PhD, and Julio Tudela, Pharm PhD, "When Does the Human Being Begin" in Part II of this chapter, provides biological detail in support of Etheredge's assertion that the human child begins at the moment of conception of the one-cell human embryo.

To better understand the critical nature of this issue, it is necessary to awaken an awareness of the Trinitarian structure of the world's reality, the ground of existence, nature and the origin of human personhood. Hans Urs von Balthasar has said that the creation of the world unfolds in some sense within the act of the Father's begetting of the Son. The Trinity of Father, Son and Holy Spirit are united in the common work of Creation which reflects the diversity and unity within the Trinity. Thus the universe is one whole, from its instantaneous beginning in God's word, and unfolds in a multiplicity that is interconnected. God creates out of pure unnecessary love, so that love is embedded in the origin and structure of our universe. The human being is created as an Image of God, and the conception of a child is an image of the Father's begetting of the Son and originates in it. The purpose of each child conceived is to become another Christ-bearing person. Etheredge has elucidated this foundation carefully, but much of our society ignores this fundamental reality, and, as a result, initiates serious problems which it does not know how to face. A social order that directly denies God's purpose in creating the world rebels against the order of the world based on the Father's love, the Son's mission, and the gift of the Holy Spirit, and is grievously offending God.

A Child is the Outward Expression of Spousal Love

That existence is good is reflected in the acceptance of the child conceived, welcoming a new human being who is distinct from the parents. The unity of the family and the difference of each member images the Trinity, a unity of distinct Persons acting together in love. Love and being (existence) are united and the difference of the other is confirmed as good, a gift, contributing to the rich diversity of the world. In human begetting, a father and mother give themselves fully to each other in love and receive each other's love. When God chooses to create a new human life as the outward expression of the fruitfulness of their love, a child is conceived. It is critical that the child be conceived in this embrace of love rather than in an impersonal laboratory that leaves the child vulnerable to utilitarian values. Etheredge describes human conception as God "hovering" over the sexual unity of man and woman to bring forth new life, just as the Holy Spirit "hovered upon the face of the waters" at the creation of the universe. In other words, the soul created by God from nothing recapitulates the act of creation of the world from nothing. Sexual unity and difference collaborate with God's divine fruitfulness. The one-flesh union of a man and woman is spiritual as well as organic. Thus, its fruitfulness originates from the Spirit, and God creates the spiritual soul bringing forth an organic-spiritual human being. This structure grounded in Trinitarian life is the source of human society and [is] meant to be the orientation of human love in the unity and diversity of man, woman and child. The tender self-forgetful love between husband and wife in total gift of each other, bringing forth a family, bears witness to the world of the kind of love God has for his creatures.

We draw upon Reason and Revelation

Etheredge addresses in considerable detail the question of delayed ensoulment which has been proposed in the past. He carefully describes the instantaneous nature of human conception at the moment of fertilization, both in scientific terms and with the light shone on this by Revelation. A beautiful reflection on the Immaculate Conception demonstrates how impossible it would be for Mary to have a body at any instant without her sinless soul. The Incarnation of Christ also sheds light on the necessity of instantaneous conception of the ensouled body of the human being. This understanding of the integral unity of body and soul is a critical concept for human anthropology. Another contribution to this reflection is consideration of Christ's instantaneous changing of bread and wine into His Body and Blood, further confirming the instantaneous nature of a change of substance.

"Whoever Welcomes one such Child in My Name, Welcomes Me"

Etheredge also makes the important point that the human person is in a relationship to the other from its beginning as a human embryo, to father and mother and to God. Jesus said, "Whoever welcomes one such child in my name, welcomes me." As Balthasar has said, "a child therefore is not merely a distant analogy for the Son of God;" a child is in some way intimately identified with Christ Himself, the Child who is eternally "in the Father's bosom," (Unless You Become Like this Little Child). The child is not some "pre-ethical" being, as though without its own unique spirit, whether in a mother's womb or outside it. Balthasar points out that neither father nor mother would pretend that their contribution has given the child its spirit, its freedom, its immediacy with God, the idea that God has of him, the intention therefore that God wishes to realize with him. Each child is a critical part of Christ's mission and we ignore this at our peril (see Lk 17:2). When God creates the soul of a child at conception, whether in a petri dish or in a woman's womb, He desires that this child become part of His Family through Christ. Christ suffered so that this redemption may occur and that He may bring this child back to the Father. This reality is forgotten in a society that has lost sight of the purpose of human life and the sacredness of human fertility and sexual relations. This is a concrete embodied life to whom a human couple have passed on their flesh which bears the inheritance of generations, personally bequeathed to them by God, and bearing the potential of future generations.

"Christ Chose to come into the World as a Human Embryo"

Etheredge confronts the problem of the future of frozen embryos with a reminder of the spiritual reality and destiny of each human embryo from the moment of conception, and the need for this tiny human to develop within the warmth of a mother's womb and a father's support. The fact that Christ chose to come into the world as a human embryo conceived in the womb of Mary, in a state that is wholly dependent on the receptivity of the mother, confirms the goodness of this means of development, and God's intention that a woman's womb be the place for the embryo, so that the embryonic child may grow into the love and spiritual destiny in Christ to which the human person is called. To deny this to a child whom God has created with a spiritual soul would be a rejection of God's intention as well as a rejection of the particular child. The fact that the biological parents of a frozen embryo do not make themselves available to be parents to the child does not mean that God does not mean to redeem the child. The adoption of a frozen child is not a perfect situation as it involves a discontinuity for the child from his biological parents and his inheritance, but it appears the better option in an imperfect world that would simply abandon the child to destruction. Some have been concerned that this would be cooperating with the IVF industry, however it is more likely that by shining a light on the humanity of each embryonic child it will give pause to those who are recklessly manipulating the life of embryonic children in a petri dish.

In the artwork that follows, I see a human being beginning life's journey as a single cell enwrapped in the mother's arms and surrounded by the glow of God's creative love.

"Take My Soul" (Blowtorch on steel foil)

by Andrea Colella, Italy[668]

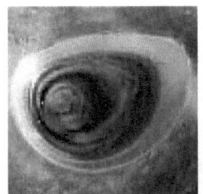

The Artist's Statement

'The cell, the main part of human life, took form due to heat and light. The flame is the same light and flame that shines in our lives by creating a boundary between the physicality of things and the mystery of the universe. The mystery of the universe lies on the edge of a boundary that strikes a balance between science and nature. Steel plates modified for combustion in an informal balance between hot

---

[668] Unesco Chair in Bioethics and Human Rights Art Competition: Reproduced with the Permission of the Director from the 2013 Bioethics in Art Collection (cropped).

and cold in this composition identifies a center from which vital energy is spread over the entire surface of the work.'

CHAPTER FIVE
FINDING A PLACE TO BEGIN: THE "BEING" OF THE BLESSED TRINITY "FOUNDS" HUMAN BEING

Just as the existence of God is "before" the existence of creation, so the truth about God is "prior" to the truth about creation

There are three parts to this chapter, beginning with the mystery of the Blessed Trinity, going on to an examination of the biological reality of human conception and concluding with a dialogue which draws on these preliminary but essential contributions to drawing on faith and reason. Thus, in a certain way, this chapter renews the focus of the whole book and, as it were, exhorts us afresh to the necessity of a new understanding of human conception.

General Introduction to Chapter 5: Part I: The "Being" of the Blessed Trinity "Founds" Human Being. In a certain way, it could be argued, the "help" of the mystery of the Blessed Trinity to the mystery of human being is a dialogue which, once begun, is literally going to go on forever. But, preoccupied as we have been with the difficulty of "understanding" God and distracted by the manifold claims and concerns of life, perhaps we have scarcely begun to appreciate that the mystery of God Himself is a hermeneutical key to human anthropology. In other words, as we begin to recognize that God "contemplated" His own mystery in the creation of man, male and female (cf. *Letter* *to Families*, 6), so this invites us to co-contemplate the Blessed Trinity if we are to understand ourselves (*Gaudium et Spes*, 36). Or, to put it differently, the "question mark" that speaks through the whole search it inspires is "naturally" answered by the mystery of the Blessed Trinity. Thus Revelation is one starting point for the renewed understanding of man, male and female, and the mystery of "our" origin.

Introduction to Chapter 5: Part I: Naming is a Dialogue. While this is not about the beginnings of language, as such, it is nevertheless possible that the naming of the Blessed Trinity[669] is *a beginning: a basic point of departure* as regards the nature and meaning of what exists. In other words, considering my own almost endless questioning of what does and does not exist there is an immense significance in the name of God: God the Father, God the Son and the God the Holy Spirit. It is not for nothing that the reality of God is the *full* meaning of His name. Thus words are fundamentally orientated to the Blessed Trinity as to the inexhaustible fullness of their meaning: the ultimate origin of every expression that reveals the "identity" of "reality"; and, on the basis of the origin of the word in the mystery of the Blessed Trinity, there is the "identifying-word": the word which helps to penetrate the dynamic of created existence and to disclose its reality.

It is almost as if rightly naming what exists is a way of entering into a dialogue with its existence: as if a name is a kind of key *to the interiority* of what it is. Thus, while terms exist in relation to one another with respect to what they mean, and thus one term can be said to be defined by others, there is also the definition that obtains from the existence of the "object" to which the word refers. In other words there

---

[669] Cf. CCC, 234.

exists a similar kind of openness between our understanding of what an "object" is and the object itself *and* the name of an object and the object itself.

God is the "*archetypal form*"[670] *of being*

Now if Scripture expresses the unity in diversity in God, does all that exists as a created good express, on the one hand, *an irreducible diversity,* and on the other hand, *a union in communion?* A theological argument for this could be that the diversity within the created order is irreducible, *because* the *Son* cannot be, as it were, *reduced to the Father,* and the *Holy Spirit* cannot be reduced to the Father or the Son. Therefore, *an irreducibility in the differences between things in the created order could be a trace* of the irreducibility in the difference between the Father, the Son and the Holy Spirit. In other words this could be a *theological reason* for *the sign of irreducible differences in the created order.*

But *the irreducibility* of one thing to another does not exclude communion; indeed, it could be said to be the necessary corollary of it. For if difference was not irreducible then union would not be communion. Secondly, whatever the nature of this irreducibility is, it obviously does not exclude the union necessary to communion. Therefore the origin of this 'sign' in creation is rightly "located" in the definition of the relationship of one Person of the Blessed Trinity to another. In other words, just as the irreducibility of one divine Person to another does not preclude the reality of their communion as "One God", so the presence in

---

[670] I am indebted here to a phrase in an unpublished work by the Rev. Dr. Richard Conrad OP, *Is one human person, or a community such as the family, the better image or model of the*

creation of 'unity-in-diversity' does not preclude an intimately "analogous" relationship within the being of creation and creatures. However, in the case of certain created beings, the human person in particular, the intimate indivisibility of the unity-in-diversity is to the point that the human being is one substance: an indivisible whole[671] – but a substance all the same that exists in relationship to God, others and creation as a whole.

The first principle of being is therefore 'unity-in-diversity'

If the first principle of being is 'unity in diversity', *precisely because* this is itself an irreducible expression of *the* Being which is irreducible, namely God, then being cannot be apprehended more clearly, more simply and more succinctly than this.

Secondly, if this is the first principle of Being, then unity and diversity will be fundamentally evident throughout everything that exists. It does not follow, however, that creation as a whole and each creature will manifest this reality of being identically; for example, creation as a whole is "made up" of beings which are both diverse and yet in relationship to one another. At the same time, the unity-in-diversity of man, male and female, is of another order to that

---

Holy Trinity?, May 1997, p. 3: 'the Holy Trinity ... is the *transcendent* Exemplar of unity-*in*-diversity ...'.

[671] The nature of death is that it is not natural (cf. Wis 2: 24) and that, therefore, it does not contradict the indivisibility of the wholeness of the human being; indeed, as St. Thomas argues, the very nature of human being tends towards the possibility of the resurrection of the body and the restoration of human wholeness (cf. Copleston, *Aquinas,* pp. 161-162). It is not possible to discuss this further at this point, nor to discuss how the resurrection of the body brings with it a new state of human being (resurrection is not resuscitation, a remark often repeated by the Rev. Dr. Ian Ker).

of the whole of creation. Furthermore, the 'unity-in-diversity' within the human person is radically challenging to our understanding; indeed, both because of the individual nature of the human person and because of the social reality of each of us "being-in-relationship".

Thirdly, then, the relation of language to its object is another instance of unity-in-diversity. The connection of a word to a thing is as much an expression of the unity of creation as the difference between a word and a thing is an expression of the diversity within creation.

The relevance of all this to the question of defining the meaning of *integrity* is that the integrity of a thing is *precisely* the being of a thing considered from the point of view of its essential unity; but *because* the being of a thing *is intrinsically a unity-in-diversity, the unity of a thing cannot be understood* except in relation to the diversity which it unifies. In other words, unity and diversity are mutually necessary and equally irreducible terms, *just as reality cannot be reduced to either an undifferentiated single thing or an unrelated diversity of things* precisely because creation manifests the Creator and the Creator is The Unity-in-Diversity.

A definition of an 'integral vision'[672] of man

In *Blackie's Compact Etymological Dictionary*, 'integral' is related to in'teger which comes from the Latin '*integer*, untouched, entire', and thus includes in its sense both whole as related to entire, *but also* 'original perfect state' as related to untouched. Furthermore, there is *integrate: to combine*

---

[672] *Familiaris Consortio*, 32; and cf. *Humanae Vitae*, 7; and cf. The Congregation for the Doctrine of the Faith, *Instruction on Respect for Human Life in its Origin and on the Dignity of*

into a whole and *to complete*; and, finally, an *integer* is a *whole number as distinguished from a fraction*[673]. Thus the many meanings of this word *indicate how well chosen it is to designate a vision of man*. For this word positively includes the union of parts to make a whole; and the fact that the whole is 'greater than the parts'.

Therefore an integral vision of man is one which apprehends him in his *original* entirety, but which implies, nevertheless, the *fall of man*[674], an openness to what can be learnt and expressed in the *present situation*[675], through the progress of time, and is orientated to his *final end*. In other words, this is an "integral vision of man and of his vocation, not only his natural and earthly, but also his supernatural and eternal vocation"[676].

An integral vision, then, is a foundational account of what makes possible the very writing of an investigation of human being. It is what "founds" the breadth and depth of human experience, the natural search for the truth and the encounter with God, the relationships which constitute the dimensions of personal existence, beginning with our parents and siblings and opening, indefinitely, onto a limitless horizon of encountering others and making possible all the daily work, trial and error and everyday activities that are expressed in each human life. In other words, an "integral vision" is in principle non-reductive and open to the amazingly rich reality of the human being-in-relationship; indeed, it is open to the self-evident experience

---

Procreation, (*Donum Vitae*), (London: CTS [S 395], 1987), p. 6. This document uses variations of this expression throughout.

[673] *Blackie's Compact Etymological Dictionary*, p. 173.
[674] Cf. *Humanae Vitae*, articles 20, 25, 29 and 31.
[675] Cf. *Humanae Vitae*.
[676] *Familiaris Consortio*, 32, quoting *Humanae Vitae*, 7.

that each one of us "experiences" ourselves as a living whole in the everyday reality of our lives.

Man is made in the image of God

A first principle of an integral vision of man is that man is made in the image of God, the God who says: 'Let us make man in our image, after our likeness...' (Gn 1: 26; cf. also 5: 2). Thus man is an *image of God*. But this is not because man chose this for himself but because this is the "gift" of God to man: the gift of God *in making the being of man to be in the image of God*. But the 'image of God' has both a singular and a plural meaning, because the God in whose image man is made is both singular and plural.

The singular meaning of *man is made in the image of God* is that man is made in the image of Christ who 'is the image of the invisible God' (Col 1: 15)[677]; and 'only in the mystery of the *Incarnate Word* does the mystery of man take on light'[678]. Therefore man in his singular unity is a person: a manifestation of the mystery of the Person that each member of the Blessed Trinity is and which is expressed in God becoming *a man*. Further, God does not by His own admission exist as an undifferentiated Person. To be God and to be a Person are indissolubly expressed in the mystery of the relationship of Father to Son, of the Spirit to

---

[677] This is not the place to explore the possibility of Christ communicating, in the mystery of His own being, the *"plurality in Being"*, except in passing. For because Christ is the Son of God, *He is necessarily identified by His relationship to the Father and to the Holy Spirit*. However, "plurality" cannot mean a rejection of there being "One God"; and, therefore, the "plurality" of being bears on the mystery of "relationship" in God.

[678] *Gaudium et Spes*, 22, quoted in article 8, on p. 24 of Pope St. John Paul II, *Redemptor Hominis*, translation published by the Vatican Polyglot Press, (London: CTS [Do 506], 1979).

the Father and the Son. *God becoming a man is an articulation, of itself, as it were, of the irreducible particularity of Being-in-relationship*; indeed, in a sense, person "means" to be in relationship. In other words, just as in God, God is the Person of the Father, the Person of the Son and the Person of the Spirit, so when God *became man, God gave concrete expression to His particularity of Being God the Son in becoming a particular man: the one who comes for all*; and, in a certain sense, in God the Son becoming a particular man we can see how manhood is an "enfleshed" expression of personhood as being-in-relationship.

Therefore man is made in the image of a God who is, as it were, a plural being: the one God who is the three persons of the Blessed Trinity. Therefore man in his plurality of being 'male and female', man *in the diversity of being male and female,* is man as a manifestation of the irreducible diversity inherent in God being the Blessed Trinity. Pope St. John Paul II seems to refer to this when he says womanhood and manhood are ontologically complementary, which he further explains to mean: 'It is only through the duality of the "masculine" and the "feminine" that the "human" finds full realization'[679]. Thus, in considering the particularity of Christ expressing the nature of manhood, it is necessary to consider that the Church "expresses" the nature of womanhood. Just as Mary is a visible expression of the mystery of the Church, so the Holy Spirit who animates her would seem to be an "invisible" expression of "woman" as communion. Is it possible, then, to contend that just as the Son is a "sign" of the particularity of personhood, the Spirit is a "sign" of the communion of personhood and, finally, the Father is a "sign" of the origin of personhood?

---

[679] *Letter to Women*, 7.

Conception: An Icon of the Beginning

At the very origin of human personhood what we find is a relationship between three causes: the man, the woman and God. In an irreducible way, therefore, just as man and woman cannot bring a person to exist, so the very act of creation has entailed God giving into the "hands" of human beings the visible expression of divine cooperation at the heart of human procreation. What, however, is both an external manifestation of the mystery of a divine-human cooperation in the act of bringing a human being to exist, is also a wonderful witness to the integrity of human personhood: of a being brought to exist as a creature expressed in the whole language of relationship. In other words, just as God is three persons in One God, so the human person is male and female: each of which is, by definition, a bodily being-in-relationship. It is just as fundamental to being a human person, therefore, as it personal to each one of us to be either male or female. Just as "relationship" is at the root of human personhood in the form of conjugal union, so communion is at the root of the Blessed Trinity; and, just as each human individual is a being-in-relationship so each person of the Blessed Trinity is a Being-in-relationship.

The mystery of human conception, then, is at once a radical expression of the "communion" inseparable to each human person and, at the same time, an amazing expression of this in an indissoluble individuality which is, intrinsically, ordered to communion.

The beginning of an integral vision of man

The 'marriage' of a creation-*event* and a *fact* is at the beginning of each of us; indeed, the creation-event is manifest in the fact and there is a philosophical interface which points to it. This is simultaneously an act of spousal love, bringing about a *manifestly physical occurrence of the activation of an egg by a sperm,* a coming into existence of the relationships of parents to child and, through this of the child's entrance into the human family[680] and, finally, the miracle of the *beginning of being a person, one in body and soul (Gaudium et Spes,* 14), *which mirrors and, in a way, recapitulates the beginning of creation.* For while the "body" of the human being has its antecedent "flesh" in the egg of the mother and the sperm of the father, the soul (cf Gn. 4: 1) *is created by God from nothing: an event which, as it were, re-enacts the event of the absolute beginning of creation*[681] (cf. 2 Mac 7: 22-23).

The term embryo, therefore, like any term which refers to something beyond itself, cannot be separated from the total reality of that to which it refers. For just as God exists and His name is a kind of well down to the ocean of His existence, so did the Creator *intend for us to see* the immense significance between what a thing is and what we call it (cf. Gn 2: 19).

Secondly, and what has become more and more obvious in the course of this study is the following: what is conceived is begun; and what is begun is a process of change; and what governs the process of change is what God has given each created being to be and to become. Therefore the question arises: *what is meant by the beginning of a human life?*

While there are stages to human development, such that it can be asked if this or that stage has been completed, the beginning of human life, as such, is both a fact of the activation of the egg by the sperm and a mysterious moment in which, simultaneously, inseparably and, in a sense, *through* the event of union, God has created an incarnate soul *from nothing.*

---

[680] Cf. Sicari, "Mary, Peter and John", *Communio,* p. 192.
[681] Cf. CCC, articles 296-298.

Conception: An Icon of the Beginning

On the one hand, then, it makes sense to ask at what point the *stage of fertilization is complete* before the *second stage of the first cell division*; but, on the other hand, in that the second stage would not exist but for the first instant of fertilization, then there is no point in seeking a "discontinuity" between one stage and another. In that *what conception is, is that it is a beginning*[682], there is no question of a complete beginning: there is no question of *the duration of the beginning* such that it can be said that the beginning of human life, while begun, has got to extend to some point of completion. In other words, the mystery of the beginning of a human life *recapitulates* the profundity of *the beginning of creation which began with the act of God at the beginning of everything* (Gn 1: 1). This is not to suppose that a soul is created at the beginning of everything and awaits, as it were, its moment of ensoulment; but it is to suggest that the mystery of the beginning of everything is, as it were, recapitulated at the beginning of each and every one of us. In other words, although one part of the process of development can supersede another, the point about the nature of the moment of conception is precisely this: that it is an irrevocable beginning: a beginning that does traverse time: that unfolds through time "without end". Thus the "moment" of that beginning is complete in the very moment it comes to exist. The indivisible reality of that beginning shows itself more and more completely as the whole person, the whole being-in-relationship, unfolds in the son or daughter conceived.

Furthermore, and just by way of emphatic repetition, this is not to say, either, that there is no difference between

---

[682] Cf. *The American Heritage College Dictionary*, senior Lexicographer, David A. Jost (Project Director), (Boston: Houghton Mifflin Company, third edition, 1993), p. 228: con-ception: the archaic sense of which is 'A beginning ... '.

the beginning of everything and the beginning of each one of us. For "before" the very beginning there was no created thing; and in that "before", when there was no created thing, there was the *God Who Is*. Whereas at the beginning of each child of Adam and Eve, there was the life of the sperm and the existence of the egg and the moment of the sperm and the egg's union which, in an expression of the will of the Creator, is when God *repeats a-new His creation from nothing and completes His creation of each one of us*. Thus, while it is possible to say that when the sperm activates the egg[683], I began, because this *involves the inextricable action of God who creates my soul from nothing, and the bodily union to which it is intrinsically ordered, at that same moment,* one has also to say that that *act of God* co-constitutes a moment where time and eternity are, as it were, one. Therefore, if one is truly open to the facts of life and to the data of Revelation one is confronted with *a beginning which is both an act, an event and a moment which is both completely natural and supernatural - both a true act of man and a true act of God: both completely human and at once overshadowed by the intimately active presence of God.*

In conclusion, *because conception is of its nature both an expression of the history of man and the absolute beginning of a new man* - it is not possible to appreciate *the true nature of the beginning that conception is if one does not also apprehend the mystery of the action of God it also and inseparably expresses.* Therefore the marvellous fact of an observable beginning to human life *is the beginning*

---

[683] Cf. *A Child Is Born*, Nilsson and Hamberger, p. 50. Cf. also the extracts from this book published in *The Sunday Times Magazine*, September 16, 1990, *The Winner: The photographs it took Lennart Nilsson five years to get*, particularly p. 45.

which is also and necessarily the data of philosophy and theology - because this is also an act of God as radical as the beginning to which the *Book of Genesis* directs us. The full nature of that moment of beginning is, therefore, as much a question for philosophy as it is an observable fact for embryology, as it is a *fit subject for theological reflection* and a joy, one hopes, to every mother and father to whom this blessing comes as the gift it is.

Finally, while the suffering of infertility is not the subject of this investigation, *true solutions to infertility* will only come through *a method or methods that are ethically acceptable to the natural integrity of the human being and to the Catholic Church.* This is because the 'integral vision of man' that will inform such investigations and methods will be so well informed that they cannot but lead to humane answers to heartbreaking questions. It is because this is also the Church which says that a child is a gift and not a right; and, therefore, it is the voice which preserves the truth concerning everyone and everything that this suffering involves.

CHAPTER FIVE: PART II: GENERAL INTRODUCTION: RELATIONSHIP TO RELATIONSHIP

Francis Etheredge

In general I have written the chapters of this book and others have wonderfully enriched it; however, there is one exception to the structure of this book. Following this *General Introduction* is a paper by Justo Aznar and Julio Tudela; it is a foundational text in its own right. They have written a compelling review of the collective scientific wisdom concerning the beginning of human life.

The "book" position of this paper by Justo Aznar and Julio Tudela

Why, then, does this piece come "between" the Blessed Trinity and the more specific examination of the embryological, philosophical and theological contributions to understanding conception? In brief, this paper establishes more fully the natural foundation to understanding conception; and, indeed, traces the "process" of fertilization to the "first instant" of the changes which come about through the interrelationship between the gift of the father's sperm and the mother's egg or ovum. What is more, this paper "communicates" the equally remarkable interaction between the embryonic child and the mother. In other words, this paper introduces a "concrete" reality to the theme of conception-in-relationship: the real, reciprocal effect of the dynamic between mother and child in the earliest stages of conception and the bearing this has on the development of the child. Thus this paper provides the complementary work of reason and the discerning use of science which both expresses the "traces" of the mystery of the Creator expressed in His work and contributes to the dialogue of reason and Revelation.

Where there is a human being there is a human being-in-relationship

Another way of putting this is that we are each, equally, a gift; indeed, no one gives him or herself being: each one of us has been given existence. On the basis of this reality, each one of us is conceived-in-relationship to others; and, in the unfolding of this reality, lies a profound expression of our identity as human beings: son or daughter; grandson or granddaughter; brother or sister; and the myriad relationships which spread out like light waves in all directions. We can "clothe" this human reality in all kinds of expressions; but, in the end, where there is a human being there is a human being-in-relationship: a child.

Establishing our common humanity establishes the reality of an ethical relationship between us

In the following paper Justo Aznar and Julio Tudela show in majestic detail that our humanity is in the very "grain" of what comes together at conception. In general, then, while there is a basic human genome, or "genomic" human identity, there are also the environmental influences that naturally vary it and constitute a "phenotypic" variety[684]. Between, as it were, the relationship between the "genome", the basic genetic information in the individual embryonic child, and the various influences of the environment, there is what is known as the "epigenetic" interaction between the embryonic child and the mother. The "epigenetic interaction" means that the expression of the basic genome is "through" an interaction with the mother. Thus the basic human genome is expressed "epigenetically", through an interaction with the mother, and "results" in a variety of phenotypic variations of the human genome.

Although, at times, then, this is a very technical paper, yet it is abundantly clear that where a human bodily being exists, there exists a human person; and, therefore, even if the human embryo is made to exist without "obvious"

---

[684] Cf. https://www.biology-online.org/dictionary/Phenotype

parents[685], yet its humanity is expressed in its bodily identity as a human being. Thus even when there is an injustice to the human embryo, in that the child is fertilized or treated as if he or she were a "product", a "biological material" or an expendable research subject, the reality of an embodied humanity manifests itself to the objective observer; and, were he or she to be allowed to thrive, it would be clear that what was begun, in time and innumerable changes, is manifestly a human person present from the beginning.

"Ethics", therefore, is always an expression of a relationship between us; and, in a word, establishing our common humanity establishes the reality of an ethical relationship between us.

---

[685] Parthenogenesis, then, is not just that there is no sexual procreation in the coming-to-be of the child; but, as with a human clone, there is a kind of "virginal" conception. Nevertheless, however, in the reality of bringing about a human clone there is an "insertion" of a whole nucleus into an egg without one and, albeit derivatively, there is the implied human lineage of the person or persons from whom the whole nucleus and egg were taken.

Biographies of Professors Justo Aznar and Julio Tudela:

Biography of Dr. Justo Aznar

Doctor of Medicine, from the University of Navarra. Head of the Department of Clinical Biopathology of the University Hospital La Fe of Valencia, from 1974 until his retirement in July 2006. He is currently Director of the Life Sciences Institute of the Catholic University of Valencia. He has published 508 research papers, has directed 20 doctoral theses and has published 30 book chapters. In Bioethics he has published 58 papers, and has directed 4 doctoral theses. He is a member of the Royal Academy of Medicine of the Valencian Community. He was a member of the Pontifical Academy for Life until March 2018.

Biography of Dr. Julio Tudela Cuenca

Bachelor in Pharmacy, Master in Bioethics and PhD at the Catholic University of Valencia San Vicente Mártir (UCV). He is an Associate Professor at the UCV. He has published more than 20 articles in bioethics, participated in nearly 20 Congresses and directed more than 40 projects at the End of a Degree and the End of Master's Degree. He is currently the Director of the Master in Bioethics at the UCV. Member of the Observatory of Bioethics and the Institute of Life Sciences of the UCV. He is a member of the Scientific Committee of the Tomás Moro Chair and the Ethical Research Comittee of the UCV.

CHAPTER FIVE: PART II: THE BIOLOGICAL STATUS OF THE EARLY HUMAN EMBRYO. WHEN DOES THE HUMAN BEING BEGIN?

Justo Aznar[686] MD PhD and Julio Tudela[687] Pharm PhD

Introduction

In order to determine the nature of the human embryo, we need to know its biological, anthropological, philosophical, and even its legal reality. In our opinion, however, the anthropological, philosophical and legal reality of the embryo — the basis of its human rights — must be built upon its biological reality.

---

[686] Director of the Life Sciences Institute at the Catholic University of Valencia; and, therefore, Justo Aznar has given permission for the use of the four images contained in this paper.

[687] Director of the Master in Bioethics at the Catholic University of Valencia.

Consequently, one of the most widely debated topics in the field of bioethics is to determine when human life begins, and particularly to define the biological status of the human embryo, particularly the early embryo, i.e. from impregnation of the egg by the sperm until its implantation in the maternal endometrium.

Irrespective of this, though, this need to define when human life begins is also due to the fact that during the early stages of human life — approximately during its first 14 days — this young embryo is subject to extensive and diverse threats that, in many cases, lead to its destruction. These threats affect embryos created naturally, mainly through the use of drugs or technical procedures used in the control of human fertility that act via an *anti-implantation mechanism*, especially intrauterine devices (as DIU); this is also the case of drugs used in emergency contraception, such as levonorgestrel or ulipristal-based drugs, because both act via an anti-implantation mechanism most of the time[688]. However, it also affects embryos created by in vitro fertilization – IVF , which are manipulated or even disposed off when techniques such as pre- implantation genetic diagnosis – PGD are used to select healthy embryos and their subsequent gestation, to select children in parents with hereditary or genetic diseases, or to create embryos and later children in order to use their haematopoietic material to treat a sibling with a hereditary or genetic condition. This practice is accompanied by a high loss of human embryos, given the low efficacy of the technique, which is less than 3%, which are manipulated or even disposed off when techniques

---

[688] Aznar J. Mechanism of action of the morning-after pill. Medicina e Morale. 2009; 3: 499-517; Aznar J. Ulipristal acetate. A new emergency contraceptive. Ethical aspects of its use. Medicina e Morale. 2010; 1:15-21.3; and Aznar J, Tudela J. Ulipristal acetate. An emergency contraceptive? Medicina e Morale. 2011; 2:233-45.4.

such as pre-implantation genetic diagnosis (PGD) are used to select healthy embryos and their subsequent gestation, to select children in parents with hereditary or genetic diseases, or to create embryos and later children in order to use their haematopoietic material to treat a sibling with a hereditary or genetic condition[689]. In particular, though, this threat can come from the manipulation of embryos left over from IVF, as a result of the freezing and thawing processes to which they are subjected for possible subsequent use for reproductive or experimental purposes, or even for intended therapeutic ends. There are currently more than 200,000 frozen embryos in Spain and 1.5 million worldwide, not to mention the high loss of embryos entailed in the use of IVF[690].

Finally, this threat also extends to embryos produced by cloning and parthenogenesis, which can then be used for presumably therapeutic and, in particular, experimental ends, mainly to obtain embryonic cell lines that can then be used for biomedical experiments, leading to the inevitable destruction of the embryos created.

A critical point in the current bioethical debate is, therefore, to establish the biological nature of the human embryo, because of the ethical classification that its manipulation merits will depend on the category to which it is attributed

---

[689] Aznar J. Designer babies. A question of ethics. Medicina e Morale. 2009; 59 (6): 1099-119.

[690] Aznar J, Mínguez JA. Loss of human embryos secondary to in vitro fertilisation. Medidina e Morale 4; 613-616, 2012.

Four different positions on the early human embryo's biological nature

There are generally said to be four positions on its biological nature:

1. The first position is that of those who consider that the human embryo, in its first days of life, is a cell cluster with no biological structure, i.e. an unorganized cluster of cells and, accordingly, with no biological or ontological value. While this approach seems anachronistic in the light of current biomedical knowledge, this is not the case, as reflected for example in Spanish Law 14/2006 on Human Assisted Reproduction Techniques (22 May 2006)[691], which in Article 1.2 states that, "a pre-embryo is understood as the embryo constituted in vitro, formed by a group of cells resulting from the progressive division of the oocyte from its fertilization until 14 days thereafter". In other words, this law accepts the obsolete theory that identifies the human embryo as a cluster of cells.

2. The second position is that of those who believe that the human zygote obtained by somatic cell nuclear transfer (SCNT) (cloning) is a different biological entity to the zygote obtained naturally. This has even been given its own unique name, "clonote", with a value less than the zygote obtained by the fusion of human gametes, whether naturally or using human assisted reproduction techniques.

3. The third position is that of those who consider that the single-cell, polarized, asymmetrical human embryo, the zygote, obtained naturally or artificially, is a living being of our species, bearer therefore of the dignity that all human beings intrinsically possess, and consequently worthy of being treated in accordance with that dignity.

---

[691] Ley 14/2006, sobre Técnicas Humanas de Reproducción Asistida. 2006 May 22.

4. There is even a fourth group, which are those researchers or clinicians who circumvent the problem, and who neither affirm nor deny the human identity of the embryo; they simply state that only the scientific aspect concerns them and that discussing the human nature of that biological entity that they use does not affect their job.

But can a scientist set out his experimental objectives without assessing their ethical consequences? Considering scientific research as another human act, it is not illogical to say that, as in any other activity of man, in his research, the scientist cannot fail to take into account the ethical side of his work. For that reason, this aspect should unfailingly be included in the development and assessment of his experimental protocols. A scientist can never stop responding ethically to the acts that he carries out.

As a result of the above, it can generally be said that, from a bioethical point of view, for those who defend the first position, i.e. those who maintain that the early embryo is a cell cluster, there would be no ethical difficulty in using it as a source of stem cells or experimental material, because even though this will entail its destruction, it would be destroying something with no biological or ontological value, never a living human being. However, for those who defend the third position — and I count myself among them — any manipulation of that emerging being would have to be done based on the biological and ontological reality of the human embryo, that is, a living human being.

It is, therefore, essential to establish the biological nature of the early human embryo, in order to be able to delve further into the open bioethical debate on the use of those early embryos for biomedical experiments or intended therapeutic goals.

Is the early embryo a living being of our species?

In this report, our aim is to try to establish that the early human embryo is a living being of our species, a human individual, and thus deserving of the highest respect. If we can do so, the first hypothesis could be ruled out, i.e. the theory that the human embryo is a cell cluster not organized as a living individual. In relation to the second position, that of those who argue that the single-cell embryo obtained by SCNT (clonation) or parthenogenesis is substantially different from the naturally-obtained zygote, which would allow it to be used in some circumstances; we shall return to that later. We shall, therefore, pause to assess whether the human embryo is a living being of our species, an individual human being.

There are numerous biological and genetic arguments to establish that the early human embryo is a living being of our species and not a cell cluster. We shall refer to some of them.

1. The genetic identity of the human embryo

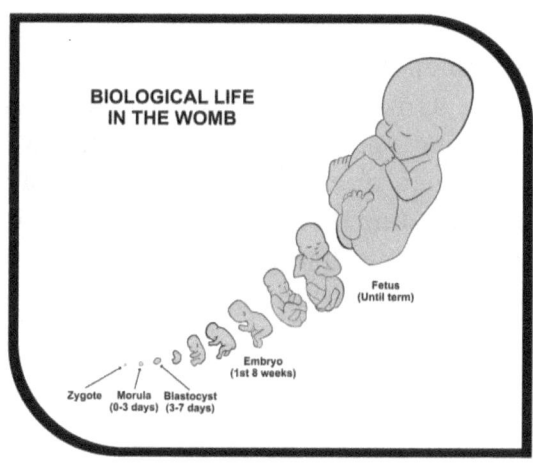

A traditionally used argument in defence of the human nature of the early embryo states that the genome of the zygote already contains all the genetic information necessary for that new being to develop into a state of adulthood. In other words, the genetic identity of the new individual and his membership of a particular species have already been determined in the genome. If nothing organic from outside modifies the genomic content of that emerging biological individual — since it only receives messages that help to regulate its own development from the surrounding world — it is difficult, if not impossible, to establish any leap during the evolution of its life that could mark the start of a genomic reality different from the previous. The evolution of that being is a continuous biological process giving rise to the different phenotypic realities of its development, within the living unit that identifies it as a unique living human being, from the impregnation of the egg by the sperm until its natural death.

However, identifying the individuality of that emerging human being by its genome is a limited and even erroneous concept. Indeed, every day there are more biological arguments to support that a human individual is something more — certainly much more — than its genetic code. In this respect, we have an increasing amount of information on non-genetic mechanisms, the so-called epigenetic mechanisms, that have a major effect on embryo development. These are becoming better understood each day. In fact, biology has reached a clear understanding of the life processes, understanding them as a dynamic collaboration of genes and environment that gives rise to regulated gene expression during the constitution and development of a new being[692]. We thus believe that DNA is necessary, but not sufficient, to identify a human individual. Not everything is in the genome; instead, the genetic information grows with the expression of the genes contained within it, which requires the activation and emission of its specific developmental programme.

This programme is activated as the life cycle of that individual progress, enabling the new being to initiate the complete and orderly emission of the genetic messages necessary for its development to take place in an orderly and complete manner. For this reason, increasing importance is being given to epigenetic factors, which cause minor modifications in the genome but do not affect its nucleotide sequence. These include DNA cytosine methylation, chromatin remodelling through histone acetylation, methylation and phosphorylation, or so called "imprinting", which refers to the ability to impede the expression of some genes in the early stages of embryonic life, especially through selective silencing, depending on whether they come from the male or the female gamete.

That is to say, during the development of the living being, new genetic information not expressed directly in the primitive genome emerges as a result of the interaction of the genome with its environment. This information is what is known as epigenetic information. Therefore, any phenotypic expression of a living being is the result of the gene content of their genome and the epigenetic information that is generated throughout its evolution, as a fundamental consequence of the interaction of the genome with its environment.

---

[692] López Moratalla N, Santiago E, Herranz G. Inicio de la vida de cada ser humano, ¿qué hace humano el cuerpo del hombre? Cuadernos de Bioética. 2011; 22(75):283-308.

2. Is the early embryo an organized and living human being?

In addition, though, there are other reasons that support the position that the early human embryo cannot be considered a simple cell cluster, but an organized and living human being. These most notably include: a better understanding of the mechanisms that regulate the emission of the embryo development programme; everything relative to so-called "position information", i.e. the information necessary for embryo development depends on the interactions between its own cells and the interactions of these cells with the cell niche that they occupy; the role that fusion of the cell membranes of both gametes, male and female, plays in the start-up of the embryo development process and new knowledge on the mechanisms that determine the asymmetry and polarity of the zygote, and how this influences the assignment of functions for each of its cells, as well as the spatial asymmetry of the various organs in the embryo body; various biochemical factors, mainly intra-cellular and extra-cellular calcium levels, which may directly affect embryonic development genetic regulation of cell differentiation mechanisms; control of telomerase function; the biochemical dialogue established between the embryo during its stay the Fallopian tube and its mother, and the related inhibition of the mother's immune response, which allows the embryo to implant in her uterus without being rejected.

A brief review of these biological processes

We will briefly review each of these biological processes, which as a whole and from the harmonious sequence of their actions, seem clearly inconsistent with the hypothesis that

that primordial embryonic being is a cell cluster and not an organized living being.

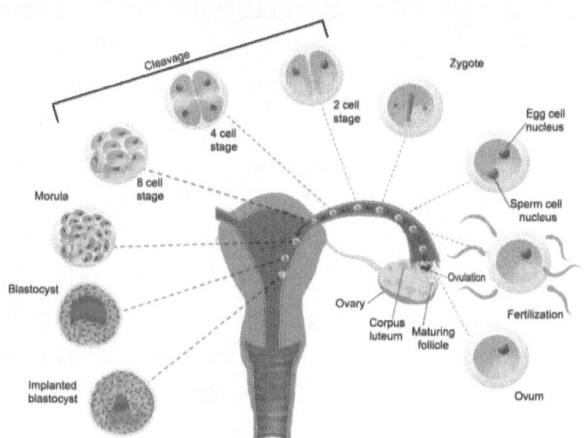

HUMAN DEVELOPMENT FROM OVULATION TO IMPLANTATION

2.1. As already mentioned, in order for human life to begin, it requires not only the existence of a certain human genome, but also activation of a development programme, information contained in the genome itself, which emits the instructions necessary for the life of that embryo to begin[693]. In sexual fertilization, activation of the development programme commences at a very early stage of embryonic life, namely the moment at which fusion of the membranes of the male and female gametes begins. It has even been suggested that it can start with the fusion of their pronuclei, which is already complete at the first cell division. Indeed, during the hours of fertilization, the DNA of both progenitors fuses to achieve the structure and pattern of the new individual.

---

[693] López Moratalla N, Santiago E, Herranz G. Inicio de la vida de cada ser humano, ¿qué hace humano el cuerpo del hombre? Cuadernos de Bioética. 2011; 22(75):283-308.

At the same time, however, there is a "switching on" at fertilization, a start-up, of the expression of the information in the genes. The new fusion of the gametes, insofar as they are carriers of half the genetic inheritance, is not enough but requires that this genome interacts with its environment in order for the so-called epigenetic process to commence. This switches on the motor of embryonic development with which a new human life begins[694].

How, though, is the development programme activated? It is known that immediately after fertilization, a DNA cytosine demethylation process begins, which is the specific trigger for initiating expression of the genome development programme. Indeed, today we know that methylation of the cytosines of certain genes favours their repression, i.e. they cannot express their activity: the coding of a specific protein. Therefore, if these genes are activated as a result of a demethylation process, regulated by certain demethylases, the developmental programme that these genes regulate is activated accordingly. That is, cytosine methylation and histone acetylation and deacetylation, determine epigenetic patterns that differ from one cell type to another and from one moment to another in the life process of the same individual. This delicately regulated mechanism is the first and fundamental step to begin the development of a new human life.

When the zygote is generated by SNCT (cloning), in order for an embryo to be produced, the genetic information contained in the somatic donor cell nucleus must be reprogrammed, i.e. the cell must be dedifferentiated. This action is due to reprogramming factors contained in the cytoplasm of the oocyte receiving the somatic nucleus,

---

[694] López Moratalla N, Santiago E, Herranz G. Inicio de la vida de cada ser humano, ¿qué hace humano el cuerpo del hombre? Cuadernos de Bioética. 2011; 22(75):283-308.

returning its genome to a genomic situation similar to that of the embryonic cells. This is when the nucleus of the transferred cell can express the orders necessary for the life of that new individual to begin.

2.2. Another aspect to consider in the development of the early embryo that, in our view, means that it cannot be considered as a simple cell cluster, are the precise mechanisms that regulate the multiplication and differentiation of its cells; part of these are dependent on the interactions established between the embryonic cells themselves and of these with those of their cell niche.

In fact, as cell development advances — and from the first division of the zygote — an active exchange of information is established between its cells and between these and their environment, especially represented by the cell niche in which each blastomere (cell from an embryo of fewer than 8 to 16 cells) is located. These orders help to activate the differentiation mechanisms of the embryonic cells themselves, mechanisms regulated, among other things, through the expression of new genes, which they only do at certain times in their evolution, as a result of the aforementioned cellular interactions. That is, the behaviour of a cell, as regards principally its biological evolution, does not depend solely on the genetic information contained within its genome, but also on the information exchanged through its own cell surface; this depends first of all on the blastomeres to which it relates, and later the place that that cell occupies in the biological unit that contains it. This is what is called "position information". That is, the development of a living being does not depend only on its genome, but also on other mechanisms that regulate the functional expression of its genes. This is conditioned, among other things, by the interactions between its own cells and the spatial situation of those cells, and by the site in which each of these is located. This regulation determines where, when and for what purpose a cell has to divide in accordance with a unitary and harmonious development. This cell differentiation towards a specific cell phenotype also occurs in adulthood and becomes particularly obvious when an undifferentiated adult stem cell, for example, a bone marrow mesenchymal cell, reaches a certain tissue. There, it is incorporated in a specific cell niche that determines that that undifferentiated cell differentiates towards the specific cells of that particular tissue. This differentiation mechanism is especially dependent on the instructions that the cells in the cellular environment send to the undifferentiated cell incorporated in that cell niche, a clear example of the role played by the "position information".

2.3 Another important aspect to consider in this single-cell human embryo and the embryonic phenotypes subsequently generated, as an organized living unit, is everything related to the role that the cell membranes of the gametes play, and the asymmetric structuring of that first two-cell embryo. This is fundamentally determined by the dividing line (polarization plane) that is established between the point at which the sperm penetrates the zona pellucida of the egg to fertilize it and the polar nucleus of the egg itself. This cellular asymmetry, determined by the polarization plane of the zygote, is an important factor for organization of the embryo into cellular structures with different, precise, well-determined functions, giving rise to two unequal blastomeres with different destinies in the embryo.

Conception: An Icon of the Beginning

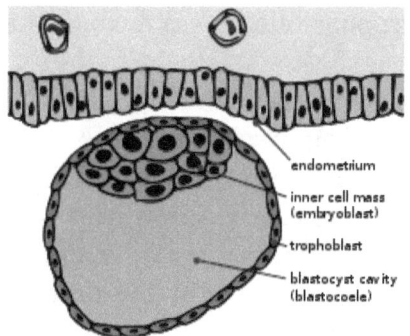

The blastomere with the cellular material that includes the sperm entry point is divided equatorially and asymmetrically, before the other blastomere. These two initial asymmetric cells of the embryo are those that will give rise first to the inner cell mass (ICM), and then to the body of the embryo. The other blastomere then divides, in this case symmetrically, thus giving rise to the 4-cell embryo. The trophoblast and the placenta are generated from the latter two cells. As well as the cellular asymmetry of the first blastomeres, these also possess different cellular biochemical components with particular and different functions, especially related to the specific development and biological function of each of the cells. In fact, the two cells resulting from this first cell division have a different calcium concentration, which helps to regulate the genetic expression of their genome and the kinetics of their cell division. The cell with the highest calcium ion concentration divides earliest, thereby generating the 3-cell embryo. This division takes place on an equatorial plane, then the other is divided along a meridional plane. At around 24 hours of life, the embryo already has four cells. As already mentioned, the first two calcium-rich cells will give rise to the ICM and, subsequently, the body of the embryo, while the two cells with the lowest calcium ion concentration will give rise to the extraembryonic trophectoderm, from which the placenta will be formed.

All of the above, aimed at demonstrating the organization of the human embryo in its early stages of life, and that each of the cells has a specific defined function, has been corroborated by simple, demonstrative experiments by Zernicka-Goetz's group[695], in which the authors labelled the first two cells of a rat embryo with different colours (one red and the other blue). From the red-stained cell arose the ICM of the blastocyst, which, as mentioned, will give rise to the body of the embryo; the extraembryonic trophectoderm was derived from the other, the blue-stained cell, which in turn will give rise to the placenta and the tissues that sustain it. That is, the functional identity of the first two cells of the embryo is determined by the first cell division, with each cell already having a specific role in embryo development. This led Helen Pearson to comment, in an article published in Nature[696], that the biological identity of the human being is established from day one of the embryo's life.

The early embryo has its own cell lineage, timing, and architecture from the beginning.

A new research from scientists at The Rockefeller University shows, for the first time, molecular and cellular processes in human development that occur up to day 14 after fertilization. "We had seen self-organization using this

---

[695] Gardner R. Specification of embryonic axes begins before cleavage in normal mouse development. Development. 2001; 128(6):839-47 and

Piotrowska K, Wianny F, Pedersen R, Zernicka-Goetz M. Blastomeres arising from the first cleavage division have distinguishable fates in normal mouse development. Development. 2001; 128(19):3739-48.

system in the mouse embryo, and also in human embryonic stem cells, but we did not anticipate we'd see self-organization in the context of a whole human embryo," says Brivanlou, one of the authors of the research, together with Zernicka-Goetz. "Amazingly, at least up to the first 12 days, development occurred normally in our system in the complete absence of maternal input... We unveil the self-organizing abilities and autonomy of in vitro attached human embryos. We find human-specific molecular signatures of early cell lineage, timing, and architecture. Embryos display key landmarks of normal development, including epiblast expansion, lineage segregation, bilaminar discformation, amniotic and yolk sac cavitation, and trophoblast diversification"[697].

Some years before, new mechanisms had been described that regulate embryonic cell differentiation towards different lineages. Thus, Plachta et al.[698] found that the capacity of the cells of the 4-8 blastomere embryo to differentiate depends not only on the concentration of Oct 4, as we will discuss later but also on the kinetics of this factor between the embryonic cells. This supports the idea that the embryonic cells, in their initial stages of development, present molecular differences that directly affect their biological destiny.

2.4 Another aspect of interest, which also supports the organization of the human embryo in the early stages of its

---

[696] Pearson H. Developmental biology: Your destiny, from day one. Nature. 2002; 418(6893):14-16.

[697] Deglincerti A, Croft G, Pietila L, Zernicka-Goetz M, Siggia E, Brivanlou A. Self-organization of the in vitro attached human embryo. Nature. 2016; 533(7602):251-4.

[698] Plachta N, Bollenbach T, Pease S, Fraser S, Pantazis E. Oct4 kinetics predict cell lineage patterning in the early mammalian embryo. Nature Cell Biology. 2011; 13(2):117-23.

life, is that small variations in the concentration and diffusion of calcium ions in the zona pellucida of the egg where the sperm penetrates seems to play an active role in the processes of division and organization of its first cell.

Indeed, in order for the sperm to penetrate the egg, two things are basically required: first that it is activated by a glycoprotein from the zona pellucida of the egg, fertilizing, and second, the existence of signals that determine the site where the sperm must penetrate the egg, which appears to be conditioned by the increase in calcium ion levels in that zone.

A recent study provides new findings on the mechanism by which the sperm and egg can recognize each other in the fertilization process, permitting the adhesion and penetration of the sperm through the membrane of the egg, as a previous step for the chromosomal crossover of both gametes and the generation of a new human being. In it, the authors described the three-dimensional chemical structure of an egg membrane receptor called Juno[699], which advances our understanding of how this receptor interacts with the corresponding membrane protein of the sperm, called Izumo1, in the manner of a lock and key.

Furthermore, it seems that the increase in calcium ions at the sperm entry point also helps to regulate the mechanisms responsible for the first cell division of the zygote, while the calcium ion concentration may affect the spatial distribution of the embryo cells. In fact, from the point at which the sperm reaches the egg, there is a release of calcium ions, which diffuse like a wave towards the opposite zone; at this point the dorso-ventral axis of the embryonic body is fixed. Perpendicular to it, the head-tail

---

[699] 13. Han L, Nishimura K, Al Hosseini H, Bianchi E, Wright G, Jovine L. Divergent evolution of vitamin B9 binding underlies

axis is established, in the absence of determining which pole will be the cephalic and which the caudal; this will happen in the second week of embryonic development, with which the right-left axis of the embryo body will be fixed[700]. It is also known that the extracellular calcium concentration also affects the spatial distribution of the embryonic cells, so that whether a cell is located to the left or right of the embryonic body depends on whether a gene, called the nodal gene, is expressed (left) or not (right), which depends on the calcium levels in each of these parts.

More is now known about the asymmetric division of the zygote, since according to a report in Investigación y Ciencia[701], "an essential aspect of the development of multicellular organisms is the generation of multiple and very varied types of cells from a single cell. In certain cases, this is achieved by asymmetric cell divisions, so called because the two resulting daughter cells receive different combinations of factors that determine their cellular destiny, i.e. the molecules that determine the type of cell that each of them will become". In this study, the author makes reference to another study, by Derivery et al[702], who studied the division of cells that organize the sensory organs of the fruit fly, Drosophila melanogaster, demonstrating a complex and well-programmed system of divisions that essentially consists of two phases. In the first, it was found that, towards

---

Juno-mediated adhesion of mammalian gametes. Current Biology. 2016; 26(3):R100-1.

[700] López Moratalla N, Santiago E, Herranz G. Inicio de la vida de cada ser humano, ¿qué hace humano el cuerpo del hombre? Cuadernos de Bioética. 2011; 22(75):283-308.

[701] González C. División celular asimétrica en el desarrollo animal. Investigación y Ciencia. 2016; 478:14- 5.

[702] Derivery E, Seum C, Daeden A, Loubéry S, Holtzer L, Jülicher F, et al. Polarized endosome dynamics by spindle

the end of cell division, a structure composed of microtubules is assembled in the centre of the cell and moves equally towards both sides of the plane that will cleave the cell in two. After this, the endosomes (molecular vesicles) are distributed homogeneously on this structure, moving in both directions along the microtubules forming it. In the second phase, just before the cell divides, the microtubules are destabilized to one side, with the result that the endosomes will spend more time on that side and will end up accumulating in it. As González, the author of the study says, "Taking into account the ubiquitous nature and high degree of evolutionary conservation of the components involved, the mechanism described herein could be operational in other species and cell types in which [there is an] asymmetric distribution of a load — vesicular or another type — transported by proteins that move along an asymmetric bundle of microtubules". This could provide important clues to understand the functioning of fundamental biological processes in higher organisms and among them, why not in the asymmetric division of the zygote?

Some researchers are finding alternative approaches, using human stem-cell technology to construct synthetic embryo-like structures. Recently, in a preprint posted to the BioRxiv server in 2017, Warmflash's group at Rice University in Houston, Texas, demonstrated that the dynamics of growth factors have a role, too; the researchers saw that a surge in signalling by a particular set of proteins — collectively called the Nodal pathway — spreads from the colony perimeter inwards like a wave, leaving different cell types in its wake[703].

---

asymmetry during asymmetric cell division. Nature. 2015; 528(7581):280-5.

[703] Heemskerk I, Burt K, Miller M, Chabra S, Guerra MC. Morphogen dynamics control patterning in a stem cell model of

This would undoubtedly confirm that the human embryo from the zygote phase is a living being that controls its development with very specific biological mechanisms, which could in no way occur in random cell clusters.

2.5 Another aspect to consider, which decidedly goes against considering the early embryo as a simple cell cluster, is the genetic regulation of the mechanisms of cell differentiation, which points towards specifically determined epigenetic control. Indeed, it is known that, as cell division progresses, the cells of the embryo lose plasticity, i.e. they gradually lose the potential to give rise to different cell types. This mechanism arises and is partly regulated by the expression of different genes, especially Oct-4, which already exists in the first embryonic blastomeres, and even in the egg. It functions as a code for a transcription factor, which is necessary in order for each blastomere to maintain its totipotency, by slowing down the differentiation impulses from the cells in its environment. In fact, each of the cells of a 3-5 day embryo maintains its ability to differentiate into cells of all types of tissues through the action of Oct-4. However, as embryo development continues, its cells lose Oct-4 activity and consequently the mechanism they have to remain undifferentiated. When they become differentiated adult cells, the Oct-4 activity has almost disappeared; in contrast, when these differentiated cells are dedifferentiated to return to their embryonic state, in cell reprogramming processes, the Oct-4 levels are recovered. There are other genes that also help these cells to remain undifferentiated, the most significant among them being Nanog.

---

the human embryo. BioRxiv. 2017. (Preprint) doi: https://doi.org/10.1101/202366.

2.6 The enzyme telomerase is also a fundamental factor in the regulation of the life cycle of embryonic cells. Telomerase determines that the telomeres (terminal part of the DNA chains that protects the chromosomes from degradation) do not become smaller with each cell division, which prolongs their life cycle. The size of the telomeres decreases with each cell division, causing the cell to age. Embryonic stem cells and tumour cells therefore contain high levels of telomerase that prevent the telomeres from shortening, favouring the indefinite proliferation of these cells. That is, it seems that the aging mechanisms of the first embryonic cells are finely regulated, which we believe can only occur in well-structured biological entities and never in a cell cluster.

Another biological fact that objectively suggests that the human embryo is an organized living being is the peculiar biochemical dialogue established between the embryo and its mother, which starts from the embryo, and which, in some way, helps to regulate its evolutionary dynamics through the Fallopian tube. In effect, during its journey through the tubes, the early embryo sends specific molecular messages to both the tube and its mother, to which both mother and tube respond. As mentioned, this biochemical dialogue between mother, tube and child allows the embryo to move forward at the right speed to be able to access the uterus at the precise time for its proper implantation[704].

Recently, a further step has been taken in the dialogue between the mother and the embryo, her child, during its passage through the Fallopian tube and implantation in the maternal endometrium. The maternal endometrium produces and secretes other compounds in the endometrial

---

[704] Tudela J, Estellés R, Aznar J. Maternal-foetal immunity: an admirable design in favour of life. Medicina e Morale. 2014; 5:833-45.

fluid in which the embryo is enclosed, which are fundamental for its implantation; these include several integrins (β3, α4 and α1) and interleukins (such as interleukin-1), as well as chemokines (IL8, MCP-1), leptin and human chorionic gonadotrophin.

Now, however, with the publication of an article in Development[705], which we will discuss here, that biochemical and immunological dialogue has been extended to the genetic field, after investigators found that elements in the fluid secreted by the endometrium, and which the child absorbs during the implantation process, may modify the gene expression of the child.

This has major biomedical and bioethical consequences. From a biomedical point of view, this genetic interaction could predispose the embryo to both metabolic and genetic disorders, i.e. it could increase the child's risk of some diseases, such as type 2 diabetes.

This interrelationship between mother and child could also occur in "in vitro" fertilization when donor eggs (i.e. not from the mother) or surrogate mothers are used. In the first case, in the implanted embryos from fertilization of donor eggs, the genetic expression of its genome could be modified by the influence of the maternal messages. In other words, information would be incorporated into the child's genome from the maternal endometrium, so that somehow (and very partially), it would come to constitute an embryo genetically modified by the influence of the biological mother.

Moreover, in the case of surrogacy, the surrogate mother could also influence the child's genome, i.e. biological links

---

[705] Vilella F, Moreno-Moya J, Balaguer N, Grasso A, Herrero M, Martínez S, et al. Hsa-miR-30d, secreted by the human endometrium, is taken up by the pre-implantation embryo and might modify its transcription. Development. 2015; 142(18):3210-21.

could be established with the child carried, beyond those created by the pregnancy.

In both circumstances, by modifying the expression of the child's genome, the relationship between the egg donor or surrogate mother and the child born would be substantially implemented, which could undoubtedly create more biological and social problems than these practices currently entail.

This is, therefore, a very interesting paper that, in our view, supports the human nature of that biological entity that is the early human embryo, and which adds fresh insights, especially in the field of IVF and surrogate motherhood.

Related to the biochemical dialogue discussed above, the phenomenon of "maternal-fetal immuno-tolerance" is particularly significant.

All biological systems have a particular function, aimed at fulfilling a specific purpose in order to facilitate the development and maintenance of the living being that incorporates them. In relation to this, the immune system has the critical purpose of fighting the entry of foreign elements into a living body, so they fulfil a fundamental physiological function, which is to prevent infections; on the other hand, however, they can also give rise to autoimmune processes through which the body attacks itself, causing various major diseases.

However, there is one circumstance — in our opinion unique in the immune system of mammals — which is that the immune system can be inhibited in the mother to allow a foreign body, namely her child, to be implanted in her body without being rejected (it must be remembered that 50% of the child's genetic endowment comes from the father and consequently is foreign to the mother). This is what happens with a so-called immune tolerance between mother and embryo.

As a result of the above, we believe that the complex organization of that living being, the pre-implantation human embryo, responsible for the aforementioned biological processes, is inconsistent with being an unorganized cluster of cells. In other words, that the human embryo is a living being of our species appears to be beyond any reasonable biological doubt.

3. The nature of the human embryo obtained by somatic cell nuclear transfer (cloning) or parthenogenesis

As mentioned previously, among the different positions on the biological nature of the human embryo is that of those who consider that the human embryo obtained by SCNT (cloning) or parthenogenesis has a different biological nature to that of the zygote naturally obtained by fusion of the egg and sperm. In fact, it even has a different name: clonote or parthenote. This biological difference is based fundamentally on the fact that the clonote and parthenote lack the genetic information contributed by the fusion of the egg and sperm, as well as the male genome, information that they consider necessary for that clonote and parthenote to develop into a healthy adult human being. This theory is supported by the biological fact that, until now, it has not been possible to generate human individuals by these techniques[706], although other types of mammals have been cloned, the first being Dolly the sheep.

If this hypothesis were true — given that a living adult human being cannot be generated from a clonote and par-

---

[706] Aznar J. www.observatoriobioetica.org. [Online].; 2010 [cited 2017. Available from: http://www.observatoriobioetica.org/wp-content/uploads/2013/12/clonaci%C3%B3n-c%C3%A9lulas-madre-y-reprogramaci%C3%B3n-celular.pdf.

thenote — that could be used as a source of biological material, especially stem cells, for biomedical experiments. This could be done with no additional ethical difficulties because although it would have to be destroyed to obtain the aforementioned biological material, a biological entity that could never develop into an adult individual would be destroyed. That is, we would not be talking about a human embryo, but rather an embryoid body. However, if the blastocysts produced by cloning or parthenogenesis could continue developing into an adult being, something hitherto unknown, it would be risky to say that the clonotes and parthenotes could be used for biomedical experiments with no ethical difficulties, since the dignity of human nature is not determined by the mechanism used to generate the embryo, but by the nature of the adult individual produced, a nature that, in our opinion, is difficult to argue is not that of a being of our species.

4. Arguments against the position that the zygote is a human individual

For some, however, there are arguments against the classification of the zygote as a biologically defined human individual. Among these, it is the problem of the uniqueness and indivisibility of the zygote, essentially derived from the fact of its possible twinning until 14 days of development, that which arouses most controversy. Those who defend this position argue that if the embryo can divide, it would not be an individual. Against this argument, it could be said that the embryo, in its early stage of life, is unique but divisible; later, as its life cycle advances, it will become a being, equally unique, but indivisible. It should be clarified that individuality and indivisibility are different concepts. The fact that a biological individual can be divided is not contrary to its individuality, just as the fact that they can divide is not contrary to the uniqueness of simpler animals, especially single-celled organisms. This is especially true for those animals that reproduce parthenogenetically. I do not believe that any biomedical expert would dare to say that these animals are not individuals of their species, before dividing, and that those that emerge from that division are not different individuals of the same species. In summary, the biological concept of the individual does not mean that it cannot be divided, but that there is an organized living structure within it with the characteristics typical of individuals of its species. The concept of individual in biology does not refer so much to the inability to divide, as to the fact that there is a real organization that endows that particular individual with the biological category of living.

Others maintain that human life begins with the pregnancy, i.e. that it begins with the implantation of the embryo in the mother's uterus, and that therefore any manipulation of that biological being before the pregnancy begins (in other words, before implantation) is ethically acceptable, because they would not be acting on a developing human being, but on what they call a "pre-embryo".

In our opinion, it is an elementary mistake to confuse viability with living being. Viability requires the previous existence of a living being that can later be eradicated. Furthermore, some of the supporters of this theory contend that, in order to guarantee its viability, it is essential that the embryo can feed itself, something that would not be accomplished, according to them, until it consolidates its implantation in the maternal endometrium. However, these people should be reminded that the embryo already feeds itself with material provided by its mother before implantation, since from the impregnation of the egg by the sperm until its implantation, i.e. during the passage of the zygote/embryo through the Fallopian tube (approximately 5 days) until its definitive accommodation in the mother's womb, the new being feeds itself with the material contained in the cytoplasm of the egg itself, which, of course, has been provided by its mother.

The idea that embryonic life begins with implantation, that is, from day 14 post-fertilization, was proposed in 1979 by the United States Ethics Advisory Board. This notion was later endorsed by the Australian Waller commission and especially the Warnock Commission, which also in 1984 started to use the term "pre- embryo" to describe the pre-implantation embryo.

In relation to the position that human life begins with the consolidation of implantation, a recent article[707] is very illustrative. The article reports that 57% of American gynaecologists believe that gestation, and therefore human life (because if there is no living being, it can hardly be gestated) begins at fertilization, and that only 28% believe that it begins with implantation of the embryo in its mother. This decidedly supports the position that human life does not begin with the pregnancy, but at fertilization.

5. Final considerations

In the light of the above, we believe that we can safely say that the life of a human being clearly begins with the initial penetration of the spermatozoid of the 'zona pellucida', starting the progressive development which leads to the first stage of the 'fusion of the pronuclei', male and female. From the first moment of fertilization, therefore, the primitive embryo is deserving of the respect owed to all adult humans, which will consequently condition that any manipulation of the early human embryo, not intended for its own good, and especially its destruction, is ethically unacceptable.

---

[707] Herranz. Entrevista realizada por Antonio García Prieto. 2001 Febrero 2016.

Conception: An Icon of the Beginning

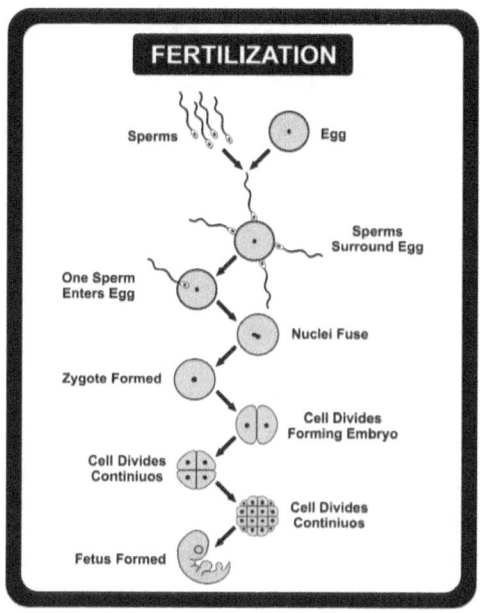

In our opinion, however, there is another, possibly more definitive, argument for defending the inviolability of the early human embryo, which is that human life possesses such dignity, a direct consequence of its own nature that doubts that the newly generated biological entity, the embryo, might be a human being should be sufficient for it to be respected unconditionally. In other words, it would not even be necessary for those of us who say that human life begins at fertilization to prove it — something I believe we have done — but those who argue that that embryo can be destroyed with impunity will have to prove that this newly created life is not human. And no-one, to the best of our knowledge, has yet been able to do so.

Francis Etheredge

CHAPTER FIVE: PART III: THE GIFT AND RIGHTS OF BEING CONCEIVED-IN-RELATIONSHIP: WE ARE AN ICON OF THE BEGINNING

The Help of Faith and Reason: Christian Dogmas, Conception and the Gift of Completing a Homeless Child's Embryological Development

General Introduction to Chapter 5: Part III: The Gift and Rights of Being Conceived-in-Relationship: We are an Icon of the Beginning. We live between where we were and where we are going to be; and, in a sense, that defines our whole reality: a person is what I was at conception, who I am and what I am becoming. In the biblical sense, I am an unfinished work between being conceived and being resurrected from the dead; and, therefore, the whole nature of being a person encompasses both everything to do with beginning and everything expressed in the mystery of rising, God willing, with Christ. A biblical conception of person, therefore, takes account of a trans-temporal understanding of the human person and, in a word, takes us into the realm of the spiritual transformation of all that I am and all that we are: a radical transfiguration of human being.

At the same time, however, we live and work out our salvation in the present; and, in that respect, the being we are to become is also expressed in all its on-going transtemporality. There are many ways of perceiving the human person and it is possible to view ourselves "fractionally", according to the lens of one discipline or another; however, it is necessary to strive for an adequate account of the whole human being, even amidst the kaleidoscoping fragmentation which is so often what becomes of our self-perception. This fragmentation shows itself most tragically in the reductionism which renders one person the "object" of another person's intrusive investigation, manipulation or destruction; and, therefore, there is an urgency in seeking to recover an account of the "whole" that we are which includes our relationship to God, to others and to each other.

Thus it is time to seek and to advance an integral account of the beginning of our whole human nature. At the same time this offers reasons, both religious and realistic, to recover the perception of the humanity of the frozen human embryo and to advance the possibility of housing the "homeless child" in the hospitality of a mother's nurturing womb and the relationships which stem from that beautiful fact. As a whole, while it is both urgent and timely to act for the good of another, it also necessary to widen the debate and to call for a new global ethic which defines the integral individual and social requirements of human development from the first instant of conception onwards. Thus, in this final part of Chapter Five, the resources of both reason and Revelation are brought to bear on the exciting, challenging and ever urgent question of the beginning of the human person and the way forward for the most neglected of our brothers and sisters.

Introduction to Chapter 5: Part III: Beginning an Unfolding of Human Personhood. The complementarity of faith and reason derives, ultimately, from their origin in the being of the Blessed Trinity and the "act of gift" which brought the universe and, in particular, the human race into existence. This is not a discussion, however, of the vast subject of our original beginning and development; rather, it is a specific exploration of the "moment" of human conception (cf. Gn 4: 1) and, in the light of more recent challenges, of the help a "homeless" human embryo needs.

As we shall see, natural and divine truths are both complementary and ordered to one another. While, however, there remains a certain difficulty in proving that conception is the first intimately instant moment that a human being begins to exist there is, nevertheless, the brilliantly illuminating embryological evidence between mother and child collected by Professors Justo Aznar and Julio Tudela and, as we have also seen, the assistance of Scripture, Tradition and the Magisterium of the Catholic Church. On the one hand there are those who hold the view of delayed ensoulment: that God gives the gift of a human soul at a point subsequent to the first instant of fertilisation. On the other hand there are those who see that the evidence "itself" is advocating an increasingly convincing position of a first instant of human conception: a "moment" in which God gives the integral gift of human personhood; indeed, the moment in which the divine-human giving of life is expressed in the whole gift of human personhood: of a being-in-relation – a child. In other words, although there is, as it were, body and soul and the possibility of a "two-fold" giving of human life, it is argued here that the very nature of human wholeness entails an inseparable act of human existence in which God gives there to be "one" being in the first instant of coming to exist as a bodily-expressed-soul. Thus there is the first task of establishing a coherent account of the beginning of each one of us. This author will then advance the position of an "immediately" enfleshed and animating human ensoulment of the human being; and, in addition, that this originating beginning of a particular human person is simultaneously the commencement of all social and spiritual relationships.

On the basis of this brief exposition, it will then be considered what light it is possible that the divine mysteries of the *Immaculate Conception, Incarnation and Eucharist*, can contribute to understanding how to help the "homeless" human embryo. This is not primarily, then, a discussion of the immorality of *in vitro* fertilization or any other procedure which brings about the conception of a human being outside of the marital embrace; rather, the focus of this part of the discussion is on the very existence of a "homeless" human embryo requiring the completing nurture of mothering and the dynamic of human parenting. Thus this author will advance the position that the very deficit of a mothering embrace, which ordinarily begins when a man's wife becomes pregnant, already implies a "need" to rectify the injustice to the child of being "homelessly" conceived. In other words, it is not that this child does not have the parents who contributed to the existence of the child; but, in the very nature of being "instrumentally" conceived, the child is "relationally impoverished" in terms of the very dynamic characteristic of human development: the participation of the "whole" of human parenthood. The utterly poignant situation of the completely incomplete reality of being conceived without the ensuing completion of natural human development is epitomized in the triple tragedy of the freezing of an embryonic human child: of being conceived outside the natural complementarity of the womb; of being conceived in a way that obscures the reality of the "person-as-gift"; of "freezing", as it were, the inherently progressive developmental goal of manifesting the whole humanity of the child. On what basis do those who enjoy the full benefit of human development deprive others of it?

There are a number of parts, then, to this article; however, there are the following five main divisions: What is Conception? (I); Conception in the Teaching of the Church (II); Conception in the Mysteries of Mary, Jesus and Each of Us (III); the Morality of Embryonic Transfer and Adoption

(IV); and the Adoption of the Embryonic Human Child (V)[708].

What is Conception? (I)

Conception, ordinarily, is a beginning. The beginning of a beginning is, as it were, the first instant of that beginning. Therefore the conception of a human being is from the first instant of fertilization. In view, however, of the natural "uncertainty" that "surrounds" the possibility of human conception, it is clear that there is a complementary psychological disposition to the act of being open to the gift of human life: of an integrally grateful giving which both belongs to the marital embrace and "opens" upon the possibility of a child. In other words, even in an account of the "moment" of conception it is necessary to recognize that this belongs to the intimacy of marriage and the language of love's giving; indeed, it is possible that a reason for the very "objectification" of the conception of the human person is the tendency to separate what belongs together: to divorce human conception from the marital act. The popular expression, "making love", bears the intuitive insight that belongs to a wealth of human experience: that love entails the good of the lover and the loved. The integral fruit of the reciprocal good of the love that becomes husband and wife is the good, nascent but begotten in the love of each other, that unfolds and develops in the "passing" from the possibility to the actuality of conceiving a child.

Furthermore, almost as a kind of natural theological outcome of philosophical speculation on the beginning of

---

[708] I acknowledge a particular debt to Dr. Elizabeth Rex for her encouraging and stimulating feedback in response to a prior draft of this part of the work; and, therefore, I am grateful to what

human personhood, there is a threefold argument for the action of God at the first instant of conception. What is beyond the nature of the contributing factors must come from an agent more capable that they are: therefore a soul is created and ensouled by God. Secondly, the very nature of an instant beginning of an everlasting human person implies a uniquely inner determination of what constitutes the ripe moment of the whole beginning of personhood. Thus an ensouling instant that begets a beginning is expressive of the power of God. Thirdly, God so perfects human cooperation in that inward moment of ensoulment being manifest in an outward beginning of embryonic human life that it evidences His completely intimate "involvement" in the mystery of human conception: a truly human-divine act of begetting a child of man, male and female, and a child of God.

The objection that the human embryo is not ready to be "ensouled" at the first instant of fertilization presupposes an ancient account of the human soul as actually bringing about changes in the "matter": as if the changes in the matter were "dependent" on a threefold process of ensoulment. Thus the plant-like level of life required a vegetative soul. Vegetative development matured and was then followed by the requirement of an animal-like soul stimulating sensitive development. Following the maturing of an animal-like development the process culminated in a readiness for the reception of a rational soul and the wholeness of human being[709]. In other words, implicit in this understanding is the view that rational ensoulment requires a specific developmental stage of "bodily" being. However, the human

---

has led to the re-crafting or further development of a number of earlier points.

[709] Cf. Chapter Twelve: Life "from" Life: A Reflection on the Moment a Person Comes to Exist, pp. 289-336, particularly page 304 of Scripture: A Unique Word, Newcastle upon Tyne: Cambridge Scholars Publishing, 2014).

body is not defined by the absence of the human soul but by its presence, except at death; and, therefore, delayed ensoulment points to the need for a more integral understanding of the "whole" of human being.

The reality of the first instant of the sperm's animation of the ovum is expressed by the enclosure of the sperm head "in" the embryonic wall. In other words, up until the penetration of the ovum by the sperm, there are two entities that are nevertheless ordered to each other in the transmission of human life; but, on contact, the inert ovum is animated by the active sperm and becomes, in that instant, a human embryo. The inertia of the ovum is evidenced in the inactivity of the mitochondria: the energy centres of the ovum-as-cell. The formation of the embryonic wall, then, constitutes an outward sign of the new reality of the child conceived[710].

In answer to the main objection to delayed animation, modern embryology makes it very clear that the whole embryo is marvellously coordinated from the beginning, developmentally independent of both parents, while naturally dependent on the mother for psychologically embracing embryonic nurture and, thirdly, the child is an integrated whole whose goal is the progressive manifestation of being the person he or she is. Thus there is no obstacle to ensoulment from conception, by God, which is also a kind of "incarnation" in that the soul constitutes the person, one in body and soul (cf. *Familiaris Consortio*, 11); indeed, if the soul is understood as the "life" of the person, not only does the soul constitute the integrating principle of personhood

---

[710] This summary statement is based on prior research, which can be found in Chapter Twelve: Life "from" Life: A Reflection on the Moment a Person Comes to Exist, pp. 289-336, particularly pages 317-322 of *Scripture: A Unique Word*). But see, too, the middle part of Chapter 5 of this book, by Professors Justo Aznar and Julio Tudela.

but it is, too, the new "life" of the person who comes to exist through the union of the gift of parenthood. Not only is the soul the integrating principle of human life, evidenced by the disintegration which follows death - the human soul is also inseparably one with the matter which constitutes the human being: man is one in soul and body (*Gaudium et Spes*, 14). In other words there is an indescribable intimacy to the union of soul and matter which brings the human person to exist just as surely as the musician's breath brings forth a note from a musical instrument. Just as the saxophone is "dormant" without the breath of a musician, so the first instant of fertilization needs the personalizing presence of the human soul. In other words, it is abundantly clear that the "matter" involved in the transmission of human life is uniquely derived from the man and the woman and is, therefore, intrinsically adapted to the reception and expression of the animating human soul. The human inheritance is, therefore, a deeply rooted reality which is totally taken up in the transmission of human life and the procreation of a child. There is not, then, the "imposition" of a "form" on matter; rather, there is an inward change which manifests the personally humanized inheritability of the human race. On the one hand, then, there is an act of ensouling animation in the moment that the bodily expression of the person comes to exist; and, on the other hand, there is an ensouling animation of what constitutes the bodily expression of the human soul. The "matter" of the body is not, therefore, some kind of "indifferent" substance; rather, in the words of St. John Paul II, the matter of the body is 'the genealogy of the person ... inscribed in the very biology of generation' (*Letter to Families*, 9).

Conception in the Teaching of the Church (II)

We need to begin by recognizing that although the Church has not committed herself to an affirmation of a philosophical nature concerning the moment of ensoulment there is, nevertheless, a tendency in her documents to refer to conception as the beginning of the presence of the human person. A careful consideration, however, of the wording of these documents, particularly *Donum vitae, The Gift of Life,* raises a twofold possibility.

The first possibility is that conception is assimilated to the unification of what were the separate nuclei of sperm and ovum. In the English translation of *Donum vitae* there are two points to note: the first is a reference to a beginning and the second defines that beginning to be when *the nuclei* of sperm and egg have fused. Thus we read in the main text of *Donum vitae*: 'the fruit of human generation, from the first moment of its existence, that is to say from the moment the zygote has formed, demands the unconditional respect that is morally due to the human being in his [or her] bodily and spiritual totality' (*Donum Vitae,* I, 1). In the English text, then, there is the following defining note which goes on to say: 'The zygote is the cell produced when the nuclei of the two gametes have fused'[711]. Thus *Donum vitae* could mean that the first instant of personal individuality is the first instant of the unification of the nuclei of the sperm and the egg[712].

---

[711] *Donum vitae,*
http://www.vatican.va/roman_curia/congregations/cfaith/documents/rc_con_cfaith_doc_19870222_respect-for-human-life_en.html.

[712] This whole discussion of the different translations of *Donum vitae* is more extensively carried out in Francis Etheredge, *The Human Person: A Bioethical Word*, St. Louis, MO 63109: En Route Books and Media, 2017, pp. 361-389: Chapter Five: On the

The Latin text, however, does not include the defining note which says, 'The zygote is the cell produced when the nuclei of the two gametes have fused'; rather, the Latin text of *Donum vitae* simply says that the zygote comes to exist "*orta a fusione*' (arising from a fusion)'[713]. Thus the Latin text could mean that the zygote comes into existence from the first instant of the fusion of the sperm and the egg which, as we know, developmentally unfolds uninterruptedly from then on; but, taking the sense of 'arising from a fusion', it could be argued that the English was simply making more explicit what was in fact the sense of the Latin, namely, that 'fusion' is more of a "step" in the process rather than just a first instant. Therefore, it could be taken that the English note explicates the Latin phrase, "*orta a fusione*' (arising from a fusion)'. In other words, in the English translation of *Donum vitae* conception of the person is assimilated to the first instant of the fusion of the nuclei; but, in the case of the Latin, which is the traditionally more authoritative text, the meaning is more open and could include the very first instant of fertilization.

Thus the second possible meaning of conception is the prior, first instant of fertilization referred to earlier, namely, the sperm's animating penetration of the ovum and the formation of the embryonic wall. In other words, the "delayed animation" type of understanding of conception is that of a "moment" subsequent to the embryo's animation by the sperm's penetration of the ovum; and, while possibly coherent with Church teaching, has the obvious drawback of presupposing an almost dualistic "combination" of "soul" and "body". The original meaning of conception, however, is

---

Development of the Church's Prudential Judgements on Human Conception and the Plight of the Frozen Embryo", particularly page 369.

[713] Etheredge, *The Human Person: A Bioethical Word*, p. 369.

that of referring to a real beginning of an actual entity; and, therefore, there is the possibility that the second meaning of conception, more coherent with its actual meaning, is where the truth is leading us. Thus the integrity of a being formed, whole and entire from the first instant of conception, is both more coherent, consonant with the facts and, it is argued, "falls" within the range of meaning expressed in the Latin text of *Donum vitae*. In other words conception 'arising from a fusion' can denote, specifically, the ovum's reception of the sperm or the sperm's penetration of the ovum which, together and in the "one" moment, "effect" the formation of the embryonic wall.

Conception in the Mysteries of Mary and Jesus and Each one of us (III)

In the following two sections it is necessary to establish what can be known, both naturally and supernaturally, concerning the beginning of each one of us.

The fact of human conception (IIIi)

What can be reasonably established about human conception is that there is an obvious start to the new entity of the human embryo: the formation of the embryonic wall on the penetration of the ovum by the sperm. Delayed animation of the embryo is more "interpretative" of the facts than the more self-evident reality of there being a radically new beginning for a new human being; indeed, it could almost be argued, for relationships to be real there has to be a point at which a child radically exists as "present" to the parents. What better moment, then, than the first instant of "love's" manifestation of the coming together of husband and wife!?

Conception: An Icon of the Beginning

The reciprocal relationship between natural and revealed truth (IIIii)

On the basis of a real, outward sign of the origin of human personhood in the "sperm-inclusive-enclosing" of the embryonic wall, there is a natural "sign" capable of expressing an "inner mystery": the natural outward sign of the enclosing embryonic wall expressing the inner moment in which God determines there to be an animating human soul. Thus we can argue that God acts in a way which gives witness to His action, not because He needs it but because it is a part of the Creator's communication to us of the nature of human being and the mystery of God. Thus creation is a witness to the act of the Creator who brought it about; and, similarly, pouring water over the head of an infant, together with the Trinitarian words of the minister, is an outward sign of the gift of baptism. Just, then, as a sacrament is an "outward sign" of an inward action of God, so the formation of the "embryonic wall" is an outward sign of the inward action of God that brings a person to exist[714]. In other words, God reveals Himself through 'deeds and words' (*Dei Verbum*, 2[715]) which, taken together, are like a hermeneutical principle: a principle through which to understand God as Creator, Redeemer and Sanctifier. Therefore, even in the instance of a natural sacrament, like the first instant of fertilization, God acts in a visible way to communicate the invisible reality of bringing the person to exist – the whole person, one in body and soul (*Gaudium et spes*, 14).

---

[714] Cf. Etheredge, *Scripture: A Unique Word*, Chapter 12.

[715] I am aware that the text of *Dei Verbum* does not apply, specifically, to the beginning of human life; however, in so far as it applies to the action of God generally, it applies specifically to the action of God at conception.

Secondly, there is a kind of "Patristic Principle" based on a number of texts of the Fathers of the Church which, in effect, lead to the conclusion that whatever is true of human conception is redeemed by the coming of Christ; and, therefore, as the nature of human conception becomes better understood, so it is clearer that redemption begins with the beginning of the Conception of Mary and the *Incarnation* of Christ[716]. While, then, God generally acts in a way that communicates His mystery to the creatures He has created, this particularly applies in the conception of Mary. God's conception of Mary is an ensouling action of God which takes up the wholly natural contribution of her parents into the history of salvation. Thus the conception of Mary was, in effect, an act of God as Creator, Redeemer and Sanctifier; and, therefore, it could be said that although human conception is a "deed and word" which would not normally be directly implicated as an act of saving love, on reflection we see that in fact as human conception entails an act of God it is almost intrinsically ordered to salvation history.

There are acts of God in the Old and New Testaments which express, more directly, conception as ordered to salvation history, particularly the conceptions of Isaac, Samuel and John the Baptist. More widely, then, expressing the truth that each person comes to exist in relationship to Christ is indeed to realize that the action of God at conception is in the heart of salvation history; as it says in *Gaudium et spes*: 'For, by his incarnation, he, the son of God, has in a certain way united himself with each man' (22). If, then, it is true of human conception in general that this is an integral expression of how we are "begotten" in salvation history, then how much "more" true is this of the mystery of the *Incarnation* in which, uniquely, the Son of God is expressed in the flesh of human being. Just as the

---

[716] Cf. Etheredge, *Scripture: A Unique Word*, Chapter 12.

Conception: An Icon of the Beginning

'Son of man' (Mt 20: 28) is hypostatically united to God in Jesus Christ, and each one of us is 'in a certain way united' with Christ, so each one of us is, as it were, "in potentia" to the possibility of participating in that hypostatic union. Perhaps, in one sense, baptism and the other sacraments more generally, are an "actuation" of this mystery of our participation in the hypostatic union between God and man in Jesus Christ.

Thirdly, what can be recognized as true of human conception will apply to Mary's *Immaculate Conception*, which was to be humanly conceived in a state of original grace; and, moreover, what follows from her graced conception assists us to understand the first instant of her conception and, therefore, the first instant of our conception. In the mystery of Mary's *Immaculate Conception*, the radical gift of God's grace brings forth the integrity of the woman who is to bear the Christ-child: the mystery of Mary's graced-nature informs our understanding of the conception of each of us. In other words, if Mary is to be free of the "taint" of original sin, the original deprivation of graced-nature which Adam and Eve both lost themselves and passed that "loss" on to us, then it follows that from the first instant that her flesh existed she was conceived without original sin.

Moreover, as it was put by Blessed John Henry Newman, grace is 'a real inward condition or superadded quality of the soul'[717]. Given, then, that a personal grace requires a personal subject[718], it would follow that Mary was "present"

---

[717] The quotation is cited from *Difficulties Felt by Anglicans*, Vol. II, p. 46, published on pp. 22-23 of *Mary: The Virgin Mary in the Life and Writings of John Henry Newman*, edited with an Introduction and Notes by Philip Boyce, Leominster, Herefordshire: Gracewing Publishing, 2001.

[718] References to the following work were suggested by the Rev. Dr. Richard Conrad, OP, (email, 10/3/2019): Cf. St. Thomas Aquinas, *Summa Theologiae*, Methuen, 1992: I-II, Qu 113, Art 10:

from the first instant of her conception; and, in view of what we know of human conception, the first instant of human conception is the formation of the embryonic wall following the sperm's penetration of the ovum. The dogma of the *Immaculate Conception*, it could be argued, while advancing an extraordinary grace for Mary in terms of being conceived without original sin builds on nature to do so[719]; and, in building on nature to do so, the dogma of the *Immaculate Conception* is an implicit confirmation of there being a first instant of human conception from which her redemption follows[720]. While Mary's redemption is different from ours in that it is from the first instant of human conception, Mary's human nature is common to ours in that it is from the first

---

'the soul has a *natural capacity for grace being made in the God's image*' (p. 321); I-II, Qu 63, Art 2: If the standard of virtue 'is God's law then ... [it] can only be caused by an activity of God within us' .... [furthermore, taking account of the possibility of the presence of original sin, it is possible to say with St. Thomas that 'Such divinely instilled virtue cannot co-exist with mortal or fatal sin' (p. 241); I-II, Qu 5, Art 5: 'a nature that can thus achieve utmost perfection, even though needing external help to do it, is of a nobler constitution than a nature that can only achieve some lesser good, even though without external help' (p. 181); I-II, Qu 1, Art 8: 'Men attain their goal by coming to know God and love him' (p. 174); I, Qu 93, Art 4: 'grace adds to some men an actual if imperfect understanding and love of God' (p. 144) which, in the case of the Blessed Virgin Mary, goes to the limit of human perfection and excludes even the possibility of original and personal sin; I, Qu 8, p. Art 3: 'God exists in those actually knowing and loving him, or disposed to do so; and since this is God's gracious gift to reasoning creatures we call it existing by *grace* in his chosen friends' (p. 22).

[719] "Grace builds on nature" (St. Thomas Aquinas).

[720] There is a more complete account of the argument summarized here in Francis Etheredge, *A Little Book on Mary and Bioethics*, a work in progress (forthcoming from enroutebooksandmedia).

Conception: An Icon of the Beginning

instant of human conception[721]. Mary, then, after Adam and Eve, is the pre-eminent case of the human person united to the Son of God; and, in so being, it makes radical sense that she is wholly without sin and completely human, one in soul and body, from the first instant of her conception. In other words, the redemptive mystery that the Son of God, 'has in a certain way united himself with each man', takes on a particularly transparent "completeness" in view of Mary being sinless from conception; and, on that basis, radically unites her to the salvific work of her Son, Jesus Christ, the Son of God made man. Just, however, as the Blessed Trinity is at work in the creation of man, male and female, so the Blessed Trinity is present in the re-creation of the human race through the *Incarnation* of Christ: 'The angel announced to her not just the incarnation but fundamentally the entire mystery of the Blessed Trinity ...'[722].

Fourthly, in the case of the *Incarnation* of the Son of God there is the "originality" of the gift of the second Person of the Blessed Trinity being enfleshed in the womb of Mary. While the eternal Son of God becoming man is a truly extraordinary event, the very "conception" of Christ entails a first moment of the fertilization of the human ovum as it is animated by Christ's human soul and, therefore, begins an unfolding development which expresses the personhood of the Christ-child. In other words, just as the conception of the Virgin Mary entailed a first instant from which "she" was conceived, one in body and soul, so there is a first instant from which Christ was miraculously conceived, one in body and soul; and, if a first instant, then the very first instant of human conception if Christ's soul was not to be united to

---

[721] Cf. Etheredge, *Scripture: A Unique Word*, Chapter 12.

[722] Cf. Hans Urs von Balthasar, Mary for Today, Middlegreen: St. Paul Publications, 1987, translated from the original German, p. 35.

flesh "tainted" with the "loss" of original sin. On the one hand, then, the Son of God is God from God and eternally "of" the Father; but, on the other hand, being "of" Mary in the very nature of human temporality, it follows that He was conceived in a way which united Him to the very depths of human conception: depths from which our redemption proceeded as from the deepest origin of each one of us. If then Christ is God from God uninterruptedly, then it follows that Christ is man from Mary in the first instant of "becoming flesh" (Jn 1: 14).

Fifthly, our understanding of the Eucharistic "presence" of Christ is of an instantaneous change of bread and wine into the *Body and Blood of Jesus Christ*; and, therefore, there is the principle of an "instantaneous" change existing, manifesting itself and being an expression of the action of God. An action of God at conception, then, is no less complete and instantaneous than in the "moment" of changing the bread and wine into the *Body and Blood of Jesus Christ*. In other words, just as the universe did not always exist but was given existence, so a human person did not exist and is given existence. Thus the gift of each human person is in the context of God giving, from all eternity, the gift of creation existing from the moment of His action; and, therefore, there is a kind of "echoing" between " the beginning" (Gn 1: 1) and the "conception" of each one of us: an "Iconic" reverberation between the one and the other: an act of God at conception that "makes present" the beginning of everything in the new beginning of each person – all of which speaks of the "immanent presence of God". Just as having spoken is an irrevocable act, so is the beginning of existence an irrevocable change which conditions the development of what unfolds from it: A human being constitutes a relational whole which is both immersed in the whole history of the human race and, at the same time, is a new beginning of the matrix of relationships in which each one of us is both immersed and expressed.

It is clear, then, from the aforementioned natural and supernatural arguments that there is a "congruence" between natural and supernatural truth in determining the first instant of human conception. The implication of this conclusion is that there is a vital necessity, then, to an action which seeks to save a child conceived – if conception is from the first instant of fertilization. Is there, then, a similar congruence between faith and reason in determining the help necessary to the "homeless" human embryo? "Homeless", not because of being "un-housed", but "homeless" because of being conceived without the nurturing home of the mother's womb.

The Morality of Embryonic Transfer (IV)

There are two sections to this part of the article: the first section concerns a brief exposition of the natural arguments for Embryonic Transfer and Adoption (IVi) and the second section concerns the supernatural arguments for Embryonic Adoption (IVii).

Natural Arguments for Embryonic Transfer and Adoption (IVi)

At its simplest, a child conceived outside of the womb is without the immediate possibility of benefitting from the mother's nurturing contribution to the completion of embryological development; and, therefore, there is a natural injustice to the child who, in "his" own way, cries out for redress: a voiceless cry which appeals to us the more it is almost inaudible in being submerged in freezing temperatures. This is the unnatural drama of the ordinarily "invisible" reality that has been brought into existence by others and is an on-going "rupture" in the universality of the human right to the completing nurture necessary to human beings at the beginning of life; indeed, this human right belongs, inexorably, to the human right to the gift of life once given: the gift of life is an irrevocable gift and entails the whole manifestation of the person conceived. In other words, the child is first and foremost a gift: a gift each one of us is given to be; and, in the case of a frozen human embryo or other abuse of the recipient of this gift, there is an injustice done to the very being of the child. At the same time, there is obviously a problem in perceiving the humanity of the child in storage; and, indeed, perhaps the sophistication of the methods of preserving the child in storage is an indication of the lengths to which "we" will go to "hide" the humanity of the frozen child.

Secondly, then, having been conceived in a way contrary to the very humanity of natural relationships, this child is dependent on being given hospitality in the womb of a woman; and, in order to make this possible, the child must be transferred to her womb from a glass dish or a place of storage. The transference of the frozen child to the womb of the mother confronts the reality of the event of freezing a child: that this is another human being, equally gifted with the gift of existence as you and I.

This procedure of transferring the embryo is radically different from the artificial methods of conception and transportation used up to this point. The reason that the transfer of a child to the womb of a woman is not to be confused or assimilated to *in vitro* fertilization and its methods is that this child now exists; and, intrinsic to his or her existence, is the natural right to completing human development which, in the case of the embryonic stage of a child's development, requires the nurturing presence of a woman willing to be an adopting mother. The natural object of the act of embryonic transfer, then, is that of taking the embryonic child and placing "her" in the womb of a woman; and, as an integral part of this process, following through on the adoption procedure which would help the maturing identity of the child. Embryonic transfer is therefore helping to rectify the relational deficit that was incurred in the very nature of the mechanical method that was employed to conceive the child.

The adopting woman and, by implication, her husband and their family are giving the humanitarian aid that this child needs to live; and, in this essential respect, they are fulfilling the natural gift of womanhood, parental care and family experience that is indispensible to this child's growth and maturation[723].

The Supernatural Arguments for Embryonic Adoption (IVii)

Just as in the case of understanding human conception, the question arises as to the help we may derive from considering the nature of the Christian mysteries particularly, in this case, the mystery of the *Incarnation* of the Son of God; clearly, however, there is an important and irrevocable distinction: the Christian mysteries are acts of God for our salvation, whereas conceiving a child outside the spousal embrace is already abandoning the implicit requirements of relational conception and development. The possible help to us of the mystery of the *Incarnation* of the Son of God is recognizing that a humanitarian act that is different to the natural order is not necessarily contrary to it. The Church has already indicated that embryo transfer is acceptable when it is for the good of the embryo and,

---

[723] Cf. Etheredge, various parts in *The Human Person: A Bioethical Word*, particularly Chapter 7, Parts IV-V.

therefore, the possibility that embryo adoption is also acceptable for the same reason: it is necessary for the good of the homeless embryonic child[724].

It has already been stated that there is an injustice to the child conceived without the natural possibility of completing his or her course of mothering nurture. God, however, even in view of this injustice, has given the gift of personal life; and, therefore, it could be argued, God is not responsible for the injustice to the child conceived but is, as it were, responsible for the life He has given. God, in His salvific acts, is constantly communicating salvation to the human race; and, in one respect, God's saving acts are always in the context of man's prior sin. Thus man's prior sin is not an obstacle to God's saving acts but, rather, the "occasion" of God showing a love greater than the death of sin. God acts for the life and salvation of each one of us, even amidst the tragedies of sin and disorder which arise out of immoral and unnatural human action. In the particular case, then, of the frozen embryonic child, a child whom God 'has in a certain way united [to] himself'[725], it is argued that the very adopting love of the rescuing husband and wife are a concrete expression of redeeming human love: a redeeming human love that is what it is because of the action of God within it that reaches to the needs of the child that was frozen.

God commands us to love the least of our brethren; and, in this situation of an orphaned embryonic child, the requirement of love is expressed in meeting the needs of a radically homeless child: a child conceived with a "deficit" to the right to the completing natural development of the

---

[724] Cf. Dr. Elizabeth Rex, "IVF, Embryo Transfer and Embryo Adoption", NCBQ, Summer 2014; and cf. Etheredge, *The Human Person: A Bioethical Word*, Chapter 7: Parts IV-V.

[725] Slightly adapting *Gaudium et Spes*, 22.

manifestation of his or her personhood. The focus of God's salvific act, then, as always, is not the evil or injustice committed by human beings but what is necessary to remedy the harm that they entail. Thus, in this instance, it could be argued that the natural law expresses the will of God in that we do what we are able to help the orphaned child. At the same time, however, the adopting husband and wife express the gratuitous nature of redeeming love: that just as there is a gratuitous act of giving life – so there is a gratuitous act of saving life. Steering free of all commercial and quality control entanglements, therefore, is essential to the adopting husband and wife's involvement in the rescue of this child; indeed, doing so, purifies the relationship between adopting parents and child and "returns" the child to the gratuitous love from which being conceived "artificially" artificially removed him or her.

The *Incarnation* of the Son of God is an act according to the nature of God the Father's eternal generation of the Son and, through the action of the Holy Spirit, is also according to the relational nature of human conception; it is certainly an extraordinary act in terms of it occurring within the marriage of Mary and Joseph without entailing their marital embrace and indeed implying the preservation of their virginal love of God and each other. In the case, then, of the adoption of the embryonic homeless child, aided as it is by transferring the child to the woman's womb, it is an act of life-giving charity which delivers an innocent child from the possibility of the indeterminate frustration of normal human development, disablement or death by deterioration; and, while this act of adoption occurs, of its nature, outside the context of an original act of spousal love, in providing for a homeless embryonic orphan this adoption begins to communicate the very nature of "redeeming" love as the gift to the child of the good necessary to his or her life.

In a word, just as God's gift of life is completely gratuitous, so an act of redemptive love is completely gratuitous; and, just as God gives human life according to the covenant of the flesh He founded, so His saving acts are according to the needs of the human life conceived. Nevertheless, even the gratuitous nature of redeeming love acts in accordance with the natural law that expresses our human participation in the divine law; and, therefore, what is done to rescue an illicitly conceived child is completely different to the action which caused the child's embryological, developmental and relational "homelessness": the injustice expressed in the conception of a "maternally homeless" child is addressed by the justice of an indispensably generously gratuitous adopting love. In a word, just as redemption goes beyond original sin without endorsing it, so an adopting love goes beyond the injustice of a child conceived "maternally homeless" without endorsing the method through which the injustice was perpetrated.

The Adoption of the Embryonic Human Child (V)

Conception, then, begins a biologically inscribed psychological development that unfolds inseparably socially and spiritually. Just as God acts at the beginning of each one of us, so His action begets the beginning of the spiritual relationship which unfolds in terms of the whole of life and is lived, intensely, in prayer and communion with others. From the beginning, the whole "bio-physiological psychological dialogue" between mother and child is, as it were, in the lived context of spousal love and human fatherhood. The "presence" of the personal communication between mother and child[726] is, then, in the presence of the husband and

---

[726] Cf. Foreword and Biography to Chapter Five by Kathleen Sweeney, *The Human Person: A Bioethical Word*, pp. 226-233.

Conception: An Icon of the Beginning

father – even if this is at times not as possible as it is for the mother. The very personal nature of "mothering" starts to "make visible" that there are personal relationships at the root of human being: the personal relationships which express an interpenetrating parental and divine love which seeks the flourishing of "who" has begun to exist as the fruit of love.

In a sense, then, one of the most challenging tasks of our time is to recover the reality of human conception as an expression of love; and, at the same time, to recover the reality of the person conceived as gift from gift: the gift of the child from the reciprocal gift of human love: the reciprocal gift of human-divine love. It seems all too possible to traverse the myriad paths to an ancient truth and yet never to arrive at it so vividly as Eve did: "I have gotten a man with the help of the Lord" (Gn 4: 1). It is true that there are many wonderful developments in the world around us and in the culture that permeates our everyday world. In one sense, however, there is a failure of reason and imagination - an inability to recognize that each one of us is a living witness to an astounding fact: that the frail temporality of our beginning belies an immutability of "who" comes into existence. God, in His unbounded generosity, "recognizes" a person in and through an "ensouling" act whatever constitutes the real beginning of a human life: that whatever the imperfection of the circumstances of human conception, if it is the conception of a human being, then he or she is a person begotten and beloved by God unto the possibility of eternal life.

Perhaps what we need is the contemplative complement[727] to the analytical approach: to pause in front of our

---

[727] On the back cover of *The Human Person: A Bioethical Word,* Rev. Dr. Nicanor Austriaco says that Etheredge's set of

own identity, the wonder of our children and indeed the mystery of the Christ-child; indeed, in terms of the modern roots of our thinking it may be necessary to revisit the question of the *whole* of human being[728]: an understanding of the mystery of human being as proceeding, as it were, as a whole from the contemplative gaze of God from all eternity. It may even be that we are facing a failure of faith, too, in grasping that if God gazed from all eternity on man, 'male and female' (Gn 1: 27) contemplating, as it were, the creation of human being in the light of His own mystery, that He saw a perfectly whole human personhood: completely integrated from the first instant of fertilization, relational and wondrously manifesting the nature of personal being! Just as we need to enliven our perception of each existing person and the first "moment" of his or her existence so we need to fall again in prayer in front of the mystery of our Creator, Redeemer and Sanctifier.

In conclusion, there is a congruence of reason and faith in both understanding the original moment of human conception and what, therefore, constitutes the good action which expresses the "redeeming" love of an orphaned embryonic child. In a word, the adoption of a radically "homeless" embryonic child, conceived from the first instant of fertilization, is an act of redeeming love: an act that

---

essays 'emerge from a contemplative reflection upon what it means to say that the person is a 'created word'".

[728] This emphasis on the "whole" of human being arose, in a way, from considering various insights in the work of Edith Stein, "A Gift from Edith Stein (1891-1942): http://www.hprweb.com/2017/09/a-gift-from-edith-stein-1891-1942/; but now a part of the published book, *The Family on Pilgrimage: God Leads Through Dead Ends*:
http://enroutebooksandmedia.com/familyonpilgrimage/.

participates in the mystery of God's adopting love of the human race (cf. Eph 1: 5).

Progress in the Church's teaching, then, not only proceeds in terms of the relatively recent discoveries concerning the nature of human conception; but, in addition, can be further enabled by the "organic" dialogue between the dogmas of the Christian Faith and their "implied" foundation in the mysterious fact of human existence. Thus it is necessary to argue for a more coherent exposition of the dogma of Mary's *Immaculate Conception* and the nature of every human conception: the action of God from the first instant of fertilization.

Just as creation and redemption require a radically original moment of human conception, so do human and divinely redeeming adoption reciprocally illuminate each other as gratuitous gifts of love; and, if adoption is the work of the redeemer, and grace builds on nature, then the radical adoption of a "homeless" embryonic person is yet a further expression of the lengths to which love goes in the "homing" of the homeless. Thus this essay argues for the clarification of the teaching of the Church on the right to embryo adoption: the reciprocal right of offering and being offered the possibility of embryo adoption[729].

---

[729] Cf. Conclusions: 'Regardless of the above comments, we [are] of the opinion that the statements in Dignitas Personae offer no settled moral assessment of embryo adoption. Thus, we certainly believe that there is no impediment to continue investigating the moral foundations of this practice, until such times as the Catholic Church issues a definitive moral judgement on it' (Acta Bioethica 2017; 23 (1): 137-149, p. 147 of "Moral Assessment of Frozen Human Embryo Adoption in the Light of the Magisterium of the Catholic Church", Justo Aznar, Miriam Martinez-Peris and Pedro Navarro Illana: http://www.bioethicsobservatory.org/wp-content/uploads/2018/07/Moral-assessment-of-frozen-human-embryo-adoption.pdf.

In a word, then, if there is progress in understanding the irrevocable moment of human conception then it beholds the human community to articulate this truth in a newly formulated charter of human rights; indeed, from what begins as a whole comes the unfolding of what began from the first instant of that beginning. As truth and goodness are inherently ordered to one another, then the whole gift of human personhood entails the immutable right of the full unfolding of what has begun. 'If we are all equal in the receipt of the gift of human life'[730] then the unfolding of that gift is a common good. Thus the human person, the human being-in-relation, the child, has the right to an integrally human conception, development and manifestation of the human person. Thus this book argues for a new instrument of human rights to be debated and clarified for the benefit of the whole human race.

---

[730] Etheredge, *The Human Person: A Bioethical Word*, p. 347.

Conception: An Icon of the Beginning

The Reality of two Children: Spencer and Caroline

"Spencer and Caroline were conceived during *in vitro* fertilization (IVF) and were cryopreserved for some years before being lovingly placed for adoption through the Nightlight Christian Adoption Agency and its Snowflakes Embryo Adoption Program. Over 650 "Snowflake Babies" have been adopted as frozen human embryos since 1998. For more information please visit: www.snowflakes.org. (Permission was granted to use this photograph.)"

Francis Etheredge

FIVE CONCLUSIONS

The conclusion of this book is in five parts: The virtue of simplicity (I); A summary of the arguments as to why the soul is ensouled in the body from its beginning (II); A summary of the contra-indications of a theory of evolution which would suppose an actual development of one kind of being into another kind of being (III); A universal call to witness to the truth of the beginning of human being (IV); The Gift of Faith: Convergence from different philosophical and religious traditions (V: I) and A warning from St. Mother Teresa (V:II) and A blessing.

Contrary, however, to the usual custom of not introducing new material in the conclusion, there were some marvellous references to a variety of points from different legislative and bioethical statements which were too helpful to be omitted, and were therefore included in these conclusions. This additional material was added, however, in support of an existing conclusion rather than in terms of generating a new point of departure.

First Conclusion (I): *The virtue of simplicity*

In the opening chapters of the book a variety of analogies were employed in order to imagine the instant of an irrevocable beginning. Indeed, even if we reverse the decision, the act of beginning to write is irreversible. In other words, even if the initial piece of writing was scrapped or rewritten, the beginning it expressed remains an indelible act. Thus a book, however long, would not exist but for the beginning; and, in that sense, a beginning is a decisive change from desire and idea to bringing paper and pen together. From the first contact, as it were, there is the

Conception: An Icon of the Beginning

formation of a letter, then a word and a sentence. Given the intentionality of the writer in the act of writing, the first instant of the pen coming into contact with the paper begins the writing. Thus a beginning is not a matter of completing a word or a sentence, although this follows; rather, a beginning is a beginning of the relationship between author, pen, paper and possible publisher and readers. The beginning, then, is expressing an intentionality that unfolds and develops; and, in view of the book to be written, the beginning is literally a necessary point of departure. At the same time, then, without the very instant of beginning, before anything is clear to anyone else, nothing can follow, unfold and be made fully manifest.

What is the human embryo if not the absolutely "first jot" of a person's life story (cf. Ps. 139: 16)? What makes this evident is that sperm and egg are two independent entities, one small and active and one large and inactive; however, on contact, they are one: the sperm head embeds in "the outer opening in the wall of the ovum" and is immediately enclosed in a "locked down" embryonic wall. The "outward activity" expresses "inward activity". The inward activity "translates" into "outward" development and, just as the book follows the first jot of the writer, so the manifestation of the person follows the ensouling moment of conception; and, just as a word expresses a thought, so the outward sign of the "embryonic wall" signifies an inward action of God bringing the ensouled human being to exist.

But just as a mark begins a word which begins a book, so we need to remember that the person is a whole: a whole as embedded in relationships as our participation is enabled by our being differentiated from each other. Thus, whether at the beginning of life or at the end, or at any point in between, we cannot understand ourselves without reference to the other, whether the other is God or each other. The primordial origin of each and every human person, then, is

God as "Author"; and, therefore, the ultimate origin of each and everyone of us is in the "imagination" of God: an "imagination" of each one and everyone of us that must be as holistic as it detailed. Even if, then, there tends to be an expression of the soul as distinct in its existence from the body, as when it is said that 'The immortal soul is a spiritual substance (or a subsistent form) with its own act of existence'[731], it is possible that just as "form" determines "matter" to be what it is, so the moment that God brings the soul to exist is the moment that God determines, as it were, the existence of the body's expression of the soul[732]. In other words, although we tend to think "after the fact" about how to understand the unity of the person, one in body and soul, God acts *from the single point of view of bringing each and all of us into existence – both as completely individual beings and as a community of "beings-in-relation"*. Thus there is a single act of God which conceives the whole of each human being and makes it possible that 'it is because of its spiritual soul that the body made of matter becomes a living, human body; spirit and matter, in man, are not two natures united, but rather their union forms a single nature' (CCC, 365). In a word, if each human being has a 'single nature'

---

[731] "Bioethics and the Human Soul: Pope St. John Paul II's Reflections on Ensoulment", Richard A. Spinello, *National Catholic Bioethics Quarterly,* 18.2 (Summer 2018), pp. 291-316, p. 308. Notwithstanding my use of this expression, this article has many excellent insights, notably its insistence on the interiority of human being as a convincing argument for the existence of the soul. It is possible, moreover, that the author would actually share the conclusion of the unitary nature of the existence of the human person from conception. At the same time, however, this article prompted me to "recover" the origin of our unity in the "Authorship" of God.

[732] Cf. St. Thomas Aquinas, *Summa Theologiae,* Methuen, I, 76, 1: 'The existence the soul itself has it shares with the physical

then there is a single act of existence at the root of each one of us.

Second Conclusion (II): *A summary of the arguments for the existence of the soul from conception*

In the first place, the activity and reactivity of the sperm and the ovum are analogous to sensations. Thus the formatively "embedding" contact between sperm and ovum elicit the formation of the embryonic wall - bringing to exist the embryonic being. The manifestation of the psychological relationship of parent and child, the unfolding of human identity and the expression of intelligent imagination all exceed the "sensory" level of existence and express the presence of what is called the human soul. Just as the effects of the human soul exceed the "sensory" nature of sperm and ovum, so the creation and ensoulment of a human soul brings to exist what did not exist; and, therefore, the creative act integrates, seamlessly, the human soul and body, expressing an intimately powerful creativity that "echoes" the beginning of creation (cf. Gn 1: 1).

Thus God is a cause of the soul's existence-as-ensouled. The human soul is by definition the life and 'form' of the body-as-ensouled; and, therefore, the human soul is not created and then ensouled: the human soul is "created-as-ensouled". The creation of the human soul's existence-as-ensouled is the constitutive moment of the body's beginning and, therefore, expresses the truth that *each one of us is an icon of the beginning*: each one of us is a manifestation of the creative power of God expressed in the very act of creation itself. It could be argued, then, that the very existence of the ensouled human body goes beyond animal

---

matter it forms, so that the existence of the composite whole is the existence of the soul itself.'

reproduction and, therefore, of itself implies the existence and creative action of God.

Secondly, the Church teaches that there is a 'personal presence' from conception. There is an "outward" and human sign of the "inward" and divine act of our creation. Thus the conception of a human being is "analogous" to our understanding of a sacrament: an outward sign of an inward grace. An act of God, namely the creation and infusion of the human soul "in" the first instant of fertilization is a sacramental act: the external act of fertilization is an outward sign of the inward act of God which brings a whole person to exist.

The evidence of an outward act of a moment of conception is the moment of fertilization: the contact between sperm and egg resulting in the formation of the embryonic wall. In terms, then, of the formation of the embryonic wall being an ensouling moment of beginning - to begin is to beget the whole.

Thirdly, a metaphysical account of the existence of the body-soul unity from conception is an account which follows on the nature of a "moment" in which body and soul are constituted one. In St. Thomas Aquinas' discussion on the origin of Adam and Eve there is a wonderful grasp of the value of the argument for the creation of the whole person, one in body and soul, from the very beginning; St. Thomas says: 'Adam's body was formed by God immediately, there being no preceding human body that could generate a body of like species to itself'[733]. Echoing then, the idea of it being

---

[733] St. Thomas Aquinas, *Summa Theologiae*, I, 91, 2; indeed, St. Thomas saw a 'perfection of the production of things' in the creation of Adam (I, 91, 4, Reply Obj. 3, http://www.newadvent.org/summa/1091.htm).

Conception: An Icon of the Beginning

more perfect to create man as a whole from the beginning[734], it is now clearer that it is possible for the first instant of ensoulment to be the first instant of fertilization; because, in the end, the sophistication of the human embryo is adequate to receiving the animatingly personalized principle of the human soul. Therefore the first moment in which the reciprocal relationship of body and soul can be established, irrevocably determining the inward nature of what exists to be the unfolding of a personal nature, is the first possible act of existence of the whole being: the first instant of fertilization.

In the philosophical language of 'form' and 'matter', the human soul is the 'form' and the transmitted flesh of sperm and ovum is, on being ensouled, the 'matter' of the body. At conception, the human body does not exist unless ensouled; and, therefore, there is not a "body" and a "soul": there is an ensouled body. The human soul co-constitutes the "matter" a human body; and, at the same time, there is no human soul if there is no human body. In other words, a "blob of cells" is not a human body: a human body is the personally transmitted "flesh" of human sperm and ovum which, on being ensouled, is the "outward" expression of an "inwardly" personalized matter; and, even if the human gametes of egg and sperm are treated as "commodities", in view of their nature, they retain their potential to express the human person.

'Matter' entails both inheritance and the personal expression of the universal identity of being a member of the human race. 'Matter' and 'form' are a philosophical expression of what enables there to be both change and continuity in the identity of the human person; and, therefore, 'form' entails determining the 'matter' to be

---

[734] Indeed, St. Thomas saw a 'perfection of the production of things' in the creation of Adam (I, 91, 4, Reply Obj. 3).

personalized and 'matter' transmits our inheritable humanity and manifests the personalizing human soul. Thus the act of existence which expresses the inextricable interrelationship of soul and body is the same act of existence which, simultaneously, expresses the beginning of all relationships: to God, to the parents and to the whole human family.

Fourthly, a metaphysical expression of the biblical *unity-in-diversity* is that each created personal being "imitates" *Uncreated Being*; and, therefore, the unity-in-diversity of three Persons in One God is, as it were, "replicated" in the body-soul unity-in-diversity of human being. In the social terms of relationships, men and women constitute a created expression of the "unity-in-diversity" of the "personal being-in-relationship" of the Blessed Trinity. In other words the principle of human being *immediately* imitating its origin is a personal expression of the following general principle: that created being "imitates" the *being of the Creator*.

In the original *Biblical Hebrew* Psalm 139, verse 16, uses a unique word for the beginning of the person; this word *golmi,* has an etymological meaning of 'unfinished vessel'. This phrase is not only an imaginative, analogous expression of the beginning of what it is to be a person, but in some way expresses the essential nature of what it is to be a human creature. Thus to be an 'unfinished vessel' is to be constituted as orientated "to receiving"; and, therefore, to be both a living "symbol" of a "received being" and, at the same time, to be open to the reception of the graced indwelling of God. In other words a biblical understanding of the conception of the human being is, in one sense, an understanding of the "whole human being"; and, unlike the philosophical possibility of a 'form' informing a pre-existing 'matter', is that of a "whole" human being coming to exist as a "whole human being" from conception[735].

We are all creatures who will remain incomplete in this life, and indeed even in purgatory if, that is, we are fortunate enough to make it even to there; moreover, it could be said that the unfortunate creature which is damned is a creature which will be *eternally unfinished*. This is because what is begun in our beginning is an end which is only and ever accomplished in the mystery of communion with God and our neighbour. The psalmist, therefore, could be said to have so well defined our essential nature that it applies, *by definition*, to both the first moment of his life and to his entire life until, that is, the definitive 'end' of it in heaven or hell. If on the level of human nature we are "beings-for-relationship" – how much more expressive and explanatory is it that we are "beings for an eternal relationship with God" and each other!

One image which "makes sense" of the reality of the inseparability of body and soul is the biblical image of a rock in the light intimated, as it were, in the language of Mary being "overshadowed" by the Holy Spirit (cf. Lk 1: 35). When a rock is placed in a light, the rock casts a shadow; and, therefore, just as a rock casts a shadow in the light, so a human body cannot be what it is without a human soul. Another aid to our understanding is the biblical image of the 'burning coal' in the vision of Isaiah (cf. Is 6: 6). On the one hand, the difference between ontological life and ontological death is well expressed in the image of a "dead" coal infused by fire from the presence of God. In other words, a soul "dead" in sin can nevertheless be infused with the grace of eternal life: an image which expresses a relationship to fire as being as necessary to the coal burning as a living relationship to God is necessary to the life of the person. On

---

[735] Cf. Etheredge, *Scripture: A Unique Word*, p. 305.

the other hand, the image of a burning coal, however, could equally well express the relationship of 'soul' to 'body'. For, just as coal needs to be heated to be a burning coal, so 'matter' needs to be ensouled to be a living human being.

The scriptural witness is also, typically, an account of how God is the true author of human life; nevertheless, the biblical authors demonstrate a growing, imaginative and realistic grasp of the mystery of human conception (cf. Job 10: 8-12[736]). This perception of the male and female contribution to human fertility both brings to light when God acts to heal infertility; and, at the same time, is a remote preparation for understanding the extraordinary nature of the conception of Christ.

Fifthly, the *Incarnation* of the Son of God redounds, in a certain way, throughout the whole of Scripture and inspires an incarnational vision of the nature of creation: of the "incarnation" of divine ideas expressed in each act of creation (cf. Gn 1); and, therefore, both "introduces" the embodiment of the soul (cf. Gn 2: 7) and the groundwork of the unthinkable: the *Incarnation* of the Son of God (cf. Jn 1: 14). If the soul is *incarnately* expressed in the body, then the whole human person is inextricably one. This mystery of *being* one person, one in body and soul, is a mystery which

---

[736] Job is a very rich example of a specific writer who almost sums up the whole development of a biblical understanding of conception. He begins with 'thou hast made me of clay' (Job 10: 9) then he draws on an image which implies an understanding conception as being poured 'out like milk and curdle[d] like cheese' (10: 10) and goes on to express the "hidden" nature of the soul in the anatomical language which communicates bodily realism, when he says, 'Thou didst clothe me with skin and flesh' (10: 11 etc.).

nevertheless has to be understood in the light of human conception, death[737] and man's eternal destiny.

Christ recapitulates the history of the whole human race. Therefore, just as Christ's conception is from the first instant of His incarnation, *or an animal would be united to God*, so is our conception "modelled" on His and, in its own way, reflects the dignity of being made in the image of God. At the same time, just as Christ is Himself a "Being-in-relationship" to the Father and the human race, it is clearer, too, that the nature of human personhood is to be a "being-in-relationship". Thus personhood, whether divine or human, is inherently relational. If, then, the Son of God is God from God, 'becoming flesh' imitates this from the first instant of fertilization in which Christ as the son of man is, by the power of the Holy Spirit, an ensouled man from the flesh of Mary.

The dogma of the *Immaculate Conception* and the doctrine of original sin together constitute the following argument for ensoulment from the first instant of conception. The dogma of the *Immaculate Conception* is that Mary is conceived free from original sin and full of grace. The doctrine of original sin is that the deficit of original grace is communicated to all the descendants of Adam and Eve except Mary and her son Jesus Christ. If Mary is the perfect creature then at conception, while full of grace, she is conceived according to nature. Therefore whatever can be said according to nature of the moment of her conception, can be said of our conception. Mary was conceived without original sin. Original sin is transmitted

---

[737] The question of whether or not there is a "virtual" corporeality which manifests itself on the departure of the soul is a question which remains outstanding; cf. Kenny, *Aquinas*, p. 41 and cf. also E. McMullin, "Matter", p. 477 of Vol IX, NCE. What is clear, however, is that there cannot co-exist two "substantial forms" in the same being, at the same time, in the same way.

through generation and is, therefore, a "privation" in which body and soul share. For Mary to be conceived with a graced body and soul would be for Mary to be conceived and sanctified, body and soul, from the first instant of her ensouling conception.

Furthermore for Mary to be conceived full of grace is to be conceived "in-relationship" to God. Therefore, for Mary to be conceived "full of grace" and in-relationship to God, she has to be conceived from the first instant of fertilization. Otherwise, if there is no soul at conception then there is no grace, as the soul is the recipient of grace, and if there is no grace then there is an effect of original sin. If there is an effect of original sin then there is an impediment in the relationship to God. If Mary, then, is conceived as one, at one and the same moment of the conception of body and the creation and infusion of the soul, her conception defines *this* moment of our creatureliness for us. Therefore we are all conceived as one, body and soul, from the first instant of our conception.

In conclusion, *"Where the body lives, there the soul is, and where both are is the human person"* is a principle which developed out of the "riddle" of how to express the fact that human life comes from human life and yet is "created" by a uniquely personal act of God bringing to exist a uniquely personal *identity of the human being-in-relationship*. The physical, philosophical and theological reasons advanced in this book, God willing properly understood and properly expressed, *taken together*, are a proof of the following proposition: the person is one in body and soul; and, *from conception, wholly individual and wholly "embedded" in relationship to God and the human family*. This can be expressed more succinctly by saying *conception is the "outward" sign of the inward mystery of each one of us coming to exist through a divine-human personal act.*

Third Conclusion (III): *A summary of the arguments against the theory of an evolutionary development from one kind of being to and from another*

If creation imitates the being of the Creator[738], *at the instant of its creation*, then the being which is a *unity-in-diversity* from that first instant of its beginning is a being which is necessarily a unity of what is in reality as diverse as heaven and earth (cf. Gn 1: 1). In other words it is the fact of an immediate *unity-in-diversity* which is what excludes the possibility of a true development of one kind of being into another. This is because such a compositional being reflects a decision of "design" which is different from, but complementary to, the developmental design of an object through time. Thus a washing machine, while conceived as a whole and modified by feedback, is a developmental design through time; and, as such, it depends on a process to bring about what is envisaged, as it were, from the beginning. By contrast creation in general and the creation of the human person in particular are, as it were, conceived as a whole from the beginning; and, in their very nature, they express what they are from the first instant of their beginning. At the same time, however, being conceived as a "whole" from the beginning does not preclude the development that makes manifest what and who began to exist at conception. There

---

[738] The "distance" and the *intimacy of communion* between one person of the Blessed Trinity and another could be said to be a parallel way of approaching the "problem" of God as the absolute origin of all unity-in-diversity. Cf. Hans Urs von Balthasar, *Glory of the Lord, A Theological Aesthetics*, I: Seeing the Form, translated by E. Leiva-Merikakis, (Edinburgh: T & T Clark, reprinted 1989), p. 328.

exists, then, a necessary presumption of an entity as a whole and the processes which are an integral part of it. Therefore, the processes which are a part of the whole cannot come before the whole of which they are a part, nor can the whole exist without the processes which unfold its existence[739].

There exists, then, a hierarchical order of created being beginning with physical matter and ascending to plant, animal, human and angelic life[740]. Each and every created being "expresses" a variety of created existence which does not imply a chronological development of one being to another. These "differences in being" could be called "discontinuities"; however, they are "discontinuities" in the context of a real "continuity": that each variety of created being exists "in-relationship" to the Creator and to each

---

[739] Cf. Frederik Andersen, Rani Lill Anjum and Elena Rocca, "Philosophy of Biology: Philosophical bias is the one bias that science cannot avoid", on p. 2 of 5, they say: 'Biology, for example, is concerned with both entities and processes (Nicholson and Dupre, 2018). The standard ontological assumption is that entities (such as proteins) are more fundamental than processes, and that processes are produced by interacting entities. Molecular biologists have traditionally taken this as the default position. The ability of entities, such proteins, to interact with each other is determined by their chemical structure, so to understand processes (such as interactions between proteins), we need to understand the entities themselves in detail.

However, some scientists take the view that processes are more fundamental than entities (Guttinger, 2018). In this view, entities are understood as being the result of processes that are stable over some length of time, and the best way to understand the behaviour of an entity is to study the relations it has with other entities, rather than its internal structure. Ecologists tend to take this view, thinking in terms of systems in which the properties of individuals and species are determined by their relationship with each other and their environment': https://www.academia.edu/38645400/Philosophy_of_Biology_Philosophical_bias_is_the_one_bias_that_science_cannot_avoid.

[740] Copleston, *Aquinas*, p. 156.

other. At the same time, as this variety of created being exists as a kind of "complementary composition" in its own right, it exists as a kind of created image of the unity-in-diversity of the mystery of the *Uncreated Being* of God. These "discontinuities" take a variety of forms, somewhat characteristic, as it happens, of the aforementioned hierarchy of created being. The first "discontinuity" is, therefore, between creation and Creator. The contrast is between the Creator and the created; and, therefore, there is a profound difference between a Being who brings to exist and the "being" of creation which has been brought to exist. The difference between the power to create and the nature of being created constitutes the gratuity of creation: that to be created is to be a "gift".

A second discontinuity would be between the nature of an angel and the nature of a human being; however, this would be in the context of the continuity of the variety of intellectual forms which the Creator chose to manifest in this hierarchy of being. On the one hand an angel is like the top rung on a "ladder of bridging being": bridging the nature of "incarnate" creatures and God. On the other hand the angel is a "stepping stone" between the mystery of visibly created human being and the mystery of invisibly existing Uncreated Being. At the same time, however, the variety of created being opens up a vast canvass "echoing" the mystery of God and envisaging an unimaginably wide communion between intelligent beings.

A third example of this discontinuity is the whole human person: the human being-in-relationship. The bodily integrity of the human being manifests a unique individuality and, at the same time, each person is an expression of the human race. What distinguishes us in our humanity, however, is not only the characteristic of a personalized bio-physical being but, in the very detail of our being, the way that dexterity expresses intelligence, sensitivity and skill. Our bodily expressibility is indeed an expressibility of the "face" of the person; and, therefore, our whole being is intelligently ordered to the sensitive expression of meaningful emotion. Whether as artists, craftsmen, writers, musicians or parents and children, our communication is a profoundly personal exteriorization of our interior life. In other words, in the very integral nature of the hand being an expression of the heart and the mind that, in and of itself, there is the objection to the possibility of a pre-human body becoming human: the bodily expression of our humanity is so profoundly integral to the expression of human meaning that the body cannot be understood to be a kind of "artificial addition" to the expressibility of the person. Just as a human being does not become human gradually but is so from the beginning, so there cannot be a bio-physical process of an animal kind of being gradually becoming a human kind of being.

Even if, then, there are many ways in which coexisting on planet earth entails that animals and human beings have overlapping dietary, muscle, nerve, digestive and motor characteristics, the personalization of a bio-physical being that is constitutionally receptive to human ensoulment constitutes a radical "discontinuity" between human and animal being.

The question of human death raises a particularly relevant point precisely because the act of existence through which the person begins is an act of existence which brings to *one-being* the diverse "parts" of 'form' and 'corporeal matter'. For whether one explains the division of body and soul in relation to the one act of existence of the human being or in terms of a *form of corporeality which exists as virtual*[741] and which, on death, manifests itself, it is nevertheless the case that the body is no longer "simply" matter. The physico-biological matter, which either became the body of the human being at conception or subsequently through digestion[742], is physical matter which has entered into the "identity", in a way appropriate to it, of the person whose body it now is.

A fourth example of a "discontinuity" is that a virus cannot be an intermediary form to that of physical matter and biological life if it requires a biological cell in which to reproduce itself. The natural habitat of the virus is the cell. In other words, the virus cannot be an "intermediary" between an inorganic and an organic type of life, if the cell needs to exist for the virus to exist. For the virus needs the cell to exist if it is to exist itself; and, therefore, the virus cannot be an intermediary, evolutionary "step", between organic and inorganic life.

Similarly, if the sperm and the ova are present from the earliest stages of the development of the sexual organs of the male and the female human being respectively, then how can they transmit a "useful" modification of human being to their descendants? For a modification that occurred in the life of the growing or mature human being would not be encoded in the genetic inheritance of the child of that adult. If the genetic inheritance of the next generation is already "in place" in the infant, awaiting the developmental characteristics of adolescence and, in due course, the fruition of the conjugal act, then it is clear that the only kind of change that can be transmitted from one generation to

---

[741] E. McMullin, "Matter", p. 477 of Vol IX, NCE; cf. also Kenny, *Aquinas*, p. 41.

[742] Kenny, *Aquinas*, p. 40.

another is that of a non-characteristic or idiosyncratic mutation or type of change.

Furthermore, if the nucleus is what particularly governs cell division, then the nucleus itself cannot develop in isolation from the whole human body of which it is itself a part. Indeed, to imagine that a nucleus could develop from a part of what comes to be the "whole" is itself somewhat like imagining that a particle of dust could evolve into a seed. In other words there is in fact a considerable difference between physical matter and organic life.

The fifth discontinuity, therefore, is between inorganic and organic plant life. On the one hand there are innumerable material components which "pass" from the inorganic to the organic realm; and, in that sense, there is a continuity between the existence of the plant and the capacity of the plant "to take up" inorganic matter and "to incorporate" it in the growth of the plant. On the other hand, then, the whole principle of organic growth is very different from, for example, the combining of oxygen and hydrogen to form water[743]; and, while water is a liquid at the temperatures at which hydrogen and oxygen are gases, it is nevertheless a molecular change in accord with the "pattern" of possibilities inherent in the oxygen and hydrogen atoms. In other words, the difference between the molecular building blocks and the growth of a plant is not with respect to each doing what it is natural for it to do; rather, there is a difference of "capability": each is doing what it is capable of doing. The capability of molecular building is a very specific change in accordance with the atomic properties of both oxygen and hydrogen, temperature and proximity to each

---

[743] The example is used in "The Dumb Ox on Evolution" by Rob Agnelli, http://www.hprweb.com/2013/11/the-dumb-ox-on-evolution/.

other. The capability of a plant is as different from the formation of water as making bricks is from the Architect's house plan which makes use of them.

The 'discontinuities'[744] to which one has referred, whether that between physical matter and viruses, the kind of being an animal is and a person is or that between man and the angels are all discontinuities which are sufficiently different to require a different determination by which they are what they are. To use the philosophical terminology, each type of being, whether it be physical, plant, animal, human or angelic, each requires that which brings it to exist as it is: each requires a different 'form' to determine what it will be. These differences between what is created, however, exist in the context of the continuity of creation and of the common fact that all created being is a "work" of the Creator. It is these "discontinuities" which are the contra-indications to the theory of one kind of being developing into another.

The theory of 'form' and 'signet first matter' is an argument in its own right for the need to understand the cause of what comes to exist. Just as we cannot account for the change of the wood of a tree into a table without an account of the activities of the carpenter, so we cannot account for the existence of a "ladder of being", each rung of which exceeds the capability of the previous rung, just as anything coming to exist at all "exceeds" non-existence. In

---

[744] In an article entitled, "The Dumb Ox on Evolution", by Agnelli, there is the same term, 'discontinuities'. There is a similarly in our understanding of the reason for this term in that there exists changes which cannot be explained without recourse to a cause that is capable of bringing them about. In a word, the expression is: 'no effect can be greater than its cause' (Agnelli's footnote 17 cites Clarke, W. Norris. *One and the Many: A Contemporary Thomistic Metaphysics*. Notre Dame: University of Notre Dame Press, 2001, p.247).

other words it is a radically insufficient account of creation to suppose it can simply consist, *as a kind of viable minimum*, of one act at the absolute beginning of created existence; for, just as the act of creation at the beginning of each one of us is an ensouling act that brings the human person to exist, one in body and soul, so it is possible that there be "several" acts of creation which were, as it were, a discreet part of the whole act of creation[745].

One of the earlier Church Fathers, St. Augustine, says: 'There are those who consider that only the world itself was made by God, and that other things come into being through the world itself, just as He ordained and commanded, but without God's doing the work Himself. The statement of the Lord, however, is proposed against them: "My Father is working even until now"'[746]. St. Augustine clearly admits the possibility of a kind of "multiple-unitary" act of creation; and, at the same time, rejects the "apparent" simplicity of a uniquely singular act of creation. At the same time, however, there was obviously a point at which creation "stood out" from nothingness or non-existence. In one sense, then, there was an absolute beginning[747]: a beginning from which all development began; however, what also began was a relationship: a relationship in which the act of creation was both a point of departure and an expression of an "on-goingness" of the active presence of God in His work. In

---

[745] This is not to take Genesis literally except, in a sense, to see the possibility that the author or editor of the early chapters was sufficiently astute to see that "discontinuities" in the very nature of creation could imply an "unfolding" but "singular" act of creation.

[746] *The Literal Interpretation of Genesis*, p. 84, excerpt 1694 (5, 20, 40), of Vol III, *The Faith of the Early Fathers*.

[747] According to St. Thomas Aquinas, this is one of the truths of Revelation which is a particular aid to human reason (cf. Chris John-Terry, *For the Love of Wisdom*, pp. 10-11, 31, 57-59.

Conception: An Icon of the Beginning

biblical terms, the "on-goingness" of the creative presence of God is expressed in terms of the history of salvation which unfolds from "covenant" to "covenant": from the Old Testament's universal "outwardness" of the rainbow to the New Testament's inwardness of the universal vocation to communion with Christ[748]. Equally personalistic is the coming into existence of each one of us through relationships and the saving of each one of us through our relationship to Christ.

Finally, the *First Book of Moses* gives two accounts of our creation: the first one in the context of the mystery of God's creation of all that exists; and the second one in the context of the fact that God made us in a way which as personal as the style of literature which conveyed it could communicate it to be. Therefore a question for a *Christian evolutionary theory* would be how well does it address, if at all, the fact that God made man male and female in such a way as to express a particularly personal love of what and whom He had made? God's Love is 'immanent'[749] in such a way as the creation of each and every one of us proceeds, as it were, through the 'sign of conjugal love' which manifests an inwardness turning outwards[750]: a Love insolubly expressed in love. At the same time, however, a rational account of human existence has to account, too, for the personal nature of human existence; and, therefore, it is

---

[748] Cf. Francis Etheredge, Chapter Thirteen: The Covenant is 'The Interior Thread of Scripture Itself' (Cardinal Ratzinger) in *Scripture: A Unique Word,* Newcastle upon Tyne: Cambridge Scholars Publishing, 2014; and cf. also, *Volume III-Faith is Married Reason* (of the trilogy *From Truth and truth*), Newcastle upon Tyne: Cambridge Scholars Publishing, 2016, pp. 258-263.

[749] Cf. Balthasar, *Glory of the Lord*, Vol. I: Seeing the Form, p. 22.

[750] Balthasar, *Glory of the Lord*, Vol. I: Seeing the Form, p. 112.

necessary to philosophize from the depths of human experience and not just from particular aspects of it[751].

More widely, then, one can say that the author of Genesis, when describing the 'breath of life' as that which gives life (Gn 2: 7), is not just giving us an imaginative account that "envisions" an act of creation - but is giving us a deeply rational account of both the personal nature of bringing a person to exist and that the spiritual nature of human life requires a transcendent cause.

Fourth Conclusion (IV): A Universal Call to Witness to the general advance of Truth Concerning Conception

As we have seen throughout this book's dialogue with people from the past and the present, there is a growing universality to the witness to the truth that each of us is begotten from the first instant of fertilization. There is a convergence from a variety of directions; and, while convergence is not of itself completely compelling it is yet pointing in that direction. In the first place, there is a convergence from the compelling evidence of those both capable of communicating the findings of embryology and recognizing the conclusion to which this material leads: that each of us is conceived-in-relationship to others. On the basis of the philosophy that regards reality as a source of its speculations there is a process of thinking through the philosophical arguments raised by evidence, their limitations, contextual qualifications and their need for further elaboration and refinement, all of which is gathering momentum in the articulation of the view that what actually takes place exceeds the "ingredients" of what is "there" and points to a divine action which makes a coherent whole of human conception.

---

[751] Cf. Chris John-Terry, *For the Love of Wisdom*, pp. 5, 9 etc.

Conception: An Icon of the Beginning

Finally, following a variety of examples of how this growing consensus is being expressed in a variety of legislative documents: Kenya' Constitution; US Department of Health and Social Services; and Germany's Embryo Protection Act of 1991, there is the European initiative: One of Us.

In Kenya, 'the Constitution advances that "life begins at conception"'[752] – but it is beginning to be recognized that conception needs to be further clarified by stating that life begins from the first instant of fertilization. Thus a new book by Supreme Court Judge Isaac Lenaola and Bioethical Researcher Prof. Marion Mutugi[753] says that "It follows that if life begins at fertilisation, stopping the embryo from growing ... [by injecting unwanted embryos with a chemical that stops them from growing] like in the case of test tube babies is equivalent to murder"[754]. Although, then, it is probably received wisdom that conception, which means a beginning, is equivalent to understanding that beginning to be the first instant of fertilization, there is now a need for this to be clarified in legal definitions.

---

[752] "New book stirs debate on 'life starts at conception' stand", article by Michael Chepkwony:
https://www.standardmedia.co.ke/health/article/2001302994/new-book-stirs-debate-on-life-starts-at-conception-stand.

[753] 'The book, titled *Bioethics of Medical Advances and Genetic Manipulation*, [published by Longhorn] interrogates the grey area in the legal system in Kenya and challenges scholars in medicine and law to offer clear explanations [of fertilization and conception]' (from the above article by Michael Chepkwony.

[754] "Does Life Begin at Conception or Fertilization? The Answer Could Make a Huge Difference", Micaiah Bilger, November 16, 2018: https://www.lifenews.com/2018/11/16/does-life-begin-at-conception-or-fertilization-the-answer-could-make-a-huge-difference/

Even if it is not obvious what has brought about the following change in America[755], another concrete expression of this convergence of the truth concerning the origin of each human being at conception is the recognition, for the benefit of all, of the change in the wording of the U.S. Department of Health and Human Services (HHS) strategic plan for 2018-2022. 'Formerly, the document stated: 'HHS accomplishes its mission through programs and initiatives that cover a wide spectrum of activities, serving Americans at every stage of life.' Now the new edition of this document states: 'HHS accomplishes its mission through programs and initiatives that cover a wide spectrum of activities, serving and protecting Americans at every stage of life, beginning at conception'[756]. Not only, then, does this document now communicate the truth concerning the origin of each one of us, but it does so comprehensively, as it says: 'serving and protecting Americans at every stage of life, beginning at conception'. In other words, this document could become a "blueprint" for a renewed international order "protecting human beings at every stage of life, beginning at conception".

---

[755] Nevertheless, well before this current change back to a more pro-life policy, there is an interesting account of the conversion of the late and great President, George Bush ("The Amazing Story of How President George H.W. Bush Became Pro-Life", Brad Mattes:

https://www.lifenews.com/2018/12/05/the-amazing-story-of-how-president-george-h-w-bush-became-pro-life/).

[756] "HHS to define human life as 'beginning at conception'", by Nancy Flanders, October 12th, 2017, https://www.liveaction.org/news/new-hhs-strategic-plan-protects-american-lives-beginning-conception/?fbclid=IwAR3yAIfAPcrOdm5luJoEcdGQ46UGsoYpJill-DrWmAPwvQ59eNB2G59-rEk.

Germany, however, has gone before the world and enacted the following, 1991 legislation: "Act for the Protection of Embryos" (The Embryo Protection Act)[757]. This "word" of law, as it were, has become a world-wide teacher and a noted Muslim bioethicist commented, approvingly, on the German law: Hassan Hathut (1924-2009) 'referred to Germany, which banned all use of human embryos in biomedical research. As for the surplus of fertilized ova in the IVF processes, the law even banned initiating such a surplus .... Hathut concluded that this law goes in line with Islamic ethics (Hathut 1994, 175)'[758].

On the 23rd February, 2019, a European initiative, "[T]he Cultural Platform One of Us", was launched in Paris at the *Palais du Luxembourg*; the 'One of Us Federation and its forty member organizations of 19 European Union countries gathered' to recognize the value of life from conception until natural death. In the words of 'Professor Rémi Brague (from the *Institut de France)*', the 'French philosopher who is the face of the European Cultural Platform and author of the "Manifesto For a Europe Faithful to Human Dignity"': "Today, what we are committed to, is the life, the reason, the freedom, the equal dignity of every human from his conception to his or her natural death. We live in a time we

---

[757] German "Act for Protection of Embryos", in force from 1991, https://www.rki.de/SharedDocs/Gesetzestexte/Embryonenschutz gesetz_englisch.pdf?__blob=publicationFile.

[758] "Islam, Paternity, and the Beginning of Life": "The Beginning of Human Life: Islamic Bioethical Perspectives" with Mohammed Ghaly, (*Zygon: Journal of Religion and Science*, vol. 47, No. 1, (March 2012), pp. 175-213: https://core.ac.uk/download/pdf/43497555.pdf, p. 207.

must reaffirm these values"759. 'Herman Van Rompuy, Former Prime Minister of Belgium and first President of the European Council' said at the meeting: 'The debate on identity must not make us forget that what our society needs is respect, dignity and to show love. Our society needs a soul outside money and hate, something that gives meaning. The sense of life only comes to its sense when it focuses on the other". Finally, 'Mrs. Obianuju Ekeocha, the Nigerian founder of "Culture of Life Africa"' gave a speech in which she 'talked about the Primacy of Reproductive Rights and Ideological Colonialism in Africa. She explained that in her native language – the Igbo language – abortion always has a negative connotation no matter how it is said. "At the core of my people's value system is the profound recognition that human life is precious, paramount, and supreme. For us, abortion, which is the deliberate killing of little ones in the womb, is a direct attack on innocent human life. It is a serious injustice, which no one should have the right to commit"'.

If it is almost impossible to express the seriousness of the threat to human life and integrity; but, in a way, the words of Martin Heidegger (1889-1976) come as close as any to expressing the mentality in which we live: 'In 1951, Heidegger wrote, "Since man is the most important raw material, one must reckon with the fact that some day factories will be built for the artificial breeding of human material"'760. If, by 'man', then, Heidegger means the whole

---

759 Slight typological alterations to quoted text, eg. italics etc.: https://oneofus.eu/2019/03/final-press-release-3rd-one-of-us-forum/.

760 Quoted at footnote 9, "Dépassement de la métaphysique", in *Essais et Conférences* (1954), trad. André Préau, Paris, Gallimard, col. "Tel", 1980, pg. 110, in the article, "The deconstruction of nature: an anthropological crisis" by

human being, one in body and soul from conception, this is almost the "new hell" from which only God can rescue us: the harvesting hell of the unborn. Is it any wonder, then, "One of Us" has 'worked to officially collect 1,721,626 signatures across Europe, from its registration to its closure, on 1 November 2013. This initiative called for a ban of European funding of programs involving the destruction of human embryos and foetuses'[761].

> Fifth Conclusion in two parts, Part One (V: I): *Faith in God:* Convergence from Different Philosophical and Religious Traditions

Even amidst the difficulties of our time the *providence of God*[762], however, is more and more clearly seen in the history of the world. Not only is there the actual evil of elective abortion and the impending evil of a nuclear war but also, as St. John Paul II says in *Evangelium Vitae*, there is the culture of life. We live, too, in a time when the widespread existence of the *Christian Faith* is both itself a providential fact and is, in the context of the ecumenical movement[763] and inter-faith dialogue, what makes possible an almost universal call to repentance. Thus it is clear that there is a common witness for the Russian Orthodox and the Catholic Church to give as regards the most fundamental of

---

Olivier Rey https://oneofus.eu/2019/03/the-deconstruction-of-nature-an-anthropological-crisis/.
[761] "On of Us at the Court of Justice": https://mailchi.mp/eclj/one-of-us-at-the-court-of-justice?e=42a982a712.
[762] Cf. *Tertio Millennio Adveniente*, 17.
[763] *Tertio Millennio Adveniente*, 16.

human rights[764]. On the one hand 'The protection of life is an issue on which the two Churches [Orthodox and Catholic] completely agree, also in terms of theology'[765]. On the other hand 'The Orthodox Church has always spoken out against abortion, of course, as did its Catholic sister Church. But now there is a growing awareness that concrete deeds and initiatives need to be developed to help the women. On the whole, the Russian people are beginning to become aware of this problem—if for no other reason than the low birth rate in Russia, as well as across the Western world'[766].

At the same time, in a Jewish-Christian dialogue we almost see a contemporary expression of the very roots of the research which has contributed to this book. On the one hand there was a common recognition of the ethical roots of the 'inviolability of human life' in 'our shared biblical patrimony that declares that the human being is created in the Divine Image (cf. Gen 1:26-27; 5:1-2)': 'We are ... children of One God'[767]; and, on the other hand, 'All of this

---

[764] "Pope's Appeal: Human Rights Must Be at Center, Do Not Fear Going Against the Grain", Deborah Lubov, December 10th, 2018:

https://zenit.org/articles/popes-appeal-human-rights-must-be-at-center-do-not-fear-going-against-the-grain/: 'I think, among other things, of the unborn who are denied the right to come to the world'.

[765] "In Russia, Orthodox and Catholics Are 'Saving Unborn Children Together'", Eva-Maria Kolmann, February 23rd, 2017: https://zenit.org/articles/in-russia-orthodox-and-catholics-are-saving-unborn-children-together/.

[766] Kolmann, "In Russia, Orthodox and Catholics Are 'Saving Unborn Children Together'".

[767] "Joint Declaration released after 16th Meeting of Jewish-Vatican Commission", November 22nd, 2018: https://zenit.org/articles/joint-declaration-released-after-16th-meeting-of-jewish-vatican-commission/.

Conception: An Icon of the Beginning

demands that we refrain from any instrumentalization of another person, whose dignity should always be seen as a goal in and of itself'[768].

Furthermore, 'In January 1985, about 80 Muslim religious scholars and biomedical scientists gathered in a symposium held in Kuwait to discuss the broad question "When does human life begin?"'[769]. In a wonderfully thorough account of the different views prevalent in Islamic bioethics, which echoes the discussion throughout this present book[770], there emerged a voice which really encapsulates at least one major line of agreement between us: Hassan 'Hathut, ... opined that human life starts at the very moment of conception'[771]. But then, more comprehensively, 'Hathut added, the beginning of this life should be counted from the earliest stage in which the following five conditions are all applicable to a being: (1) the being has a clear and well-known start; (2) he has the potential to grow as long as he has not been deprived of the causes of growth; (3) his growth would result in a human being as fetus, neonate, child, boy, young man, adult, old

---

[768] "Joint Declaration released after 16th Meeting of Jewish-Vatican Commission".

[769] "Islam, Paternity, and the Beginning of Life": "The Beginning of Human Life: Islamic Bioethical Perspectives" with Mohammed Ghaly, (*Zygon*, p. 175).

[770] I note that at two points in the Islamic text explicit reference was made to the resemblance, as it were, of certain Muslim positions and that of the Catholic (on p. 200) and Christian Church (on p. 203) of "Islam, Paternity, and the Beginning of Life": "The Beginning of Human Life: Islamic Bioethical Perspectives" with Mohammed Ghaly, (*Zygon*).

[771] "Islam, Paternity, and the Beginning of Life": "The Beginning of Human Life: Islamic Bioethical Perspectives" with Mohammed Ghaly, p. 180.

man, and so forth; (4) this being in an earlier stage cannot grow to become a human being; and (5) the being carries the full genetic code of the human race in general and of this being in specific that distinguishes him from all others throughout the ages. To Hathut, all these conditions are only applicable to the fertilized ovum and thus not to any of the stages before or after conception (Hathut 1985, 58-59)'[772]. Furthermore, lest it be unclear that there is common ethical ground, as noted earlier, Hathut agreed with Germany's banning of all human embryos in biomedical research and 'As for the surplus of fertilized ova in the IVF processes, the law even banned initiating such a surplus .... Hathut concluded that this law goes in line with Islamic ethics (Hathut 1994, 175)'[773].

More generally providence has put before us, through the ministry of His priest, Pope St. John Paul II, in *Tertio Millennio Adveniente*, a program for our conversion: a recognition of human sin, both personally and socially, and the need to beg God to help us. We are called to work for the evangelization of the world concretely, now, in order to save the world from the probably unforseen consequences of our personal and cumulatively social sins. For the possibility of a nuclear war arises out of, but is not identical with, the multitude of our individual sins[774]. The providence of God is, therefore, nowhere more clearly evident than in granting

---

[772] "Islam, Paternity, and the Beginning of Life": "The Beginning of Human Life: Islamic Bioethical Perspectives" with Mohammed Ghaly, p. 182.

[773] "Islam, Paternity, and the Beginning of Life": "The Beginning of Human Life: Islamic Bioethical Perspectives" with Mohammed Ghaly, p. 207.

[774] Cf. Pope St. John Paul II, *On Reconciliation and Penance in the Mission of the Church Today*, otherwise known as *Reconciliatio et Paenitentia*, articles 16-18.

us, *even at this late hour*, the celebration of the third millennium as the occasion for our gift of thanksgiving to God our Creator and Redeemer, for delivering us from the possibility of a nuclear war if, that is, we repent of our rejection of His law. There exists, then, the two social factors that make the possibility of a universal call to repentance both a practical proposition and one that can be expressed in effective, international social action. On the one hand there is the gift of the means of social communication[775]. And, on the other hand, there is the growth, recognized as legitimate and therefore of God, by Pope St. Paul VI and Pope St. John XXIII, of the timeliness of the following: 'Who but must see the necessity of arriving by degrees at the establishment of a world-wide authority capable of acting effectively on the juridical and political plane?'[776]

In conclusion, then, let us praise the providence of God and repent (cf Lk 3: 4-6). For now is the favourable time (cf Ps 85: 1-2): the time for a "jubilee"; the time for the Church to prepare to *rejoice in the salvation of the world*. In the sober words of Pope St. John Paul II, we see both the reason to rejoice and the reason to repent: '*the Second Vatican Council was a providential event, whereby the Church began the more immediate preparation* for the Jubilee of the Second Millennium. It was a Council similar to earlier ones, yet very different; it was a Council *focused on the mystery of Christ and his Church and at the same time open to the world*. This openness was an evangelical response to recent changes in the world, including the profoundly disturbing experiences of the Twentieth Century, a century scarred by the First and Second World Wars, by the

---

[775] Cf. *Inter Mirifica*, 1.
[776] Pope St. Paul VI, *Populorum Progressio*, 78.

experience of concentration camps and by horrendous massacres. All these events demonstrate most vividly that the world needs purification; it needs to be converted'777.

Fifth Conclusion in two parts, Part Two (V: II): A warning from Mother Teresa: Abortion leads to nuclear war

Ethical decisions proceed from a rational recognition of the truth; and, therefore, what assists us to recognize the truth assists us to recognize the ethical imperative which follows from it. If we are a person from conception, a human being-in-relationship to the family of man, then our human rights are inherent in the relationships which we both express and are immersed in.

On the one hand, if there is no clear recognition of the benefit of the truth, even the truth of how a person came to be conceived as a part of a programme of reproduction, stripping "procreation" of its explicit, spousal and parental relationships, then it follows that the disorientation of an individual will increasingly be reflected in society as a whole: "How could the government, charged with protecting the most vulnerable members of the community, its children, legislate to make it illegal for me to know the identity of my biological father? How can its institutions subject me to the psychological torture of knowing that records exist, but I am forbidden to know the contents?"[778] On the other hand, if

---

[777] *Tertio Millennio Adventiente*, 18.

[778] Anonymousus.org, "Jaws of Life," http://anonymousus.org/stories/story.php?sid=1413 (accessed June 1, 2011) – cited as footnote 13 in the following article: Paige Comstock Cunningham, "Baby-Making: The Fractured Fulfillment of Huxley's Brave New World, Part I,"

there is no truth about the moment of conception, the nature of the benefits to the child conceived in the spousal embrace or the real depths to human identity, the more it is possible for a whole variety of factors to influence the direction we go in, as individuals and as a society, including the possibility that the more anonymous we become the more the indiscriminately destructive tendencies emerge and predominate in a "relation-less" world.

Thus we live in a society in which there is an almost deliberate mix of issues and concerns so as to indiscriminately heap upon the consciences of men and women the impossibility of thinking through the differences, the interrelationships and the hierarchy, as it were, of global concerns and, therefore, to both paralyze thinking through what is happening and to press for a kind of panic assent to anything. Thus Marguerite Peeters summarises the situation by saying that those who will advance, indiscrimately, the control of populations: 'Having indoctrinated the masses about the alleged threat of "overpopulation" of the planet, they strove to "prove" its link with risks of famine, the rise of poverty, the general deterioration of "quality of life", the extinction of species and the "depletion" of natural resources – all to the end of gaining acceptance for the *absolute priority* which they wanted to give to population control objectives in international development programs'[779]. There is, in addition, the vast industry of contraceptives[780] and

---

Dignitas 18, no. 1 (2011): 1, 5–9: https://cbhd.org/content/baby-making-pt-1the-fractured-fulfillment-huxleys-brave-new-world.

[779] *The Globalization of the Western Cultural Revolution: Key Concepts, Operational Mechanisms*, translated from the French by Benedict Kobus, published by the Institute for Intercultural Dialogue Dynamics, asbl, 2012, p. 113.

[780] In an article by Dr. Thomas Ward, "The War on Parents and Humanae Vitae", Professor Winter is quoted as saying 'after

their human and environmental pollutants, quite apart from their occasional constructively medicinal use of regulating excessive menstrual periods, not to mention that they can often result in the loss of a child's life and the inhuman means of their chemical development[781]. Then there is growing number of companies that exploit the suffering of infertility[782], having done so from the beginning[783], with its whole mentality of freezing, discarding and experimenting on human embryos. In other words, whatever the subjective good of the intention to help the infertile, there is an objective harm being done to individuals in all kinds of ways. In the words of one writer: 'I wonder whether ART [Assisted

---

the armaments industry the contraceptive and abortion industry was the second largest multi-national industry in the world' (http://voiceofthefamily.com/dr-thomas-ward-the-war-on-parents-and-humanae-vitae/).

[781] 'Dr. Philippe Schepens says: 'Going back to the evening I spent with the Puertorican doctor, in addition to explaining all kinds of technical details of the experiments conducted by Pincus, he gave me a staggering account of the suffering of thousands of young women subjected to scandalous experiments, comparable to those conducted by Dr Mengele in Auschwitz. Because Pincus required an accurate assessment of the risks, he therefore administered hormonal doses more than a thousand times greater than the present dosage. The results were more than "convincing", because hundreds of women suffered the complications indicated in the leaflets in the "pill" boxes' ("*Humanae Vitae*: My testimony as a doctor" by Philippe Schepens, General Secretary of the World Federation of Doctors who Respect Human Life, delivered at "*Humanae Vitae* at 50: Setting the Context", Pontifical University of St Thomas Aquinas, Rome, 28 Oct 2017', http://voiceofthefamily.com/dr-phillippe-schepens-humanae-vitae-a-medical-doctors-testimony/).

[782] Cf. "Global In Vitro Fertilization Market Forecasts upto 2024", https://www.infoholicresearch.com/report/global-in-vitro-fertilization-market/.

[783] Cf. Francis Etheredge, "On Regulating IVF": https://www.ncbcenter.org/files/5714/6601/7762/NCBC_Ethics Medics_July2016.pdf.

Reproductive Technology] has not derailed an important aspect of medical research, specifically in the area of resolving male and female infertility. With most resources devoted to the highly lucrative, and virtually unregulated $3 billion fertility practices, have we diverted financial and intellectual capital that could have addressed this deeper medical research need? Not only could this help couples who long to have "a child of their own," it also might remove the temptation to commission, produce, select, or modify future children through ART"[784].

St. Teresa of Calcutta, otherwise known as Mother Teresa, saw clearly that the deliberate, systematic and prevalent destruction of innocent human life, a manifestation of what Pope St. John Paul II called the 'culture of death', is what makes a third world war an unimaginably horrific possibility. As a modern "Mother"[785] of all Mother Teresa said, quite simply: "The fruit of abortion is nuclear war"[786]. This is because deliberate abortion and nuclear war have in common the following two things: the widespread and indiscriminate killing of the innocent; and,

---

[784] Paige Comstock Cunningham, "Baby-Making: The Fractured Fulfillment of Huxley's Brave New World, Part II," *Dignitas* 18, no. 2 (2011): 1, 6–9: https://cbhd.org/content/baby-making-pt-2the-fractured-fulfillment-huxleys-brave-new-world.

[785] Although she is not cited in the following article, Mother Teresa certainly qualifies to be called a modern Mother of the Church: Francis Etheredge: "A Gift from Edith Stein (1891-1942): A Modern Mother of the Church", http://www.hprweb.com/2017/09/a-gift-from-edith-stein-1891-1942/.

[786] "A Tale Of Two Questions", an article on p. 5 of *Human Concern*, No 32, (London: The Society for the Protection of Unborn Children, Autumn 1991).

secondly, the widespread rejection of the law of God written on our hearts: "to do good and to reject evil".

Whether, therefore, from the ancient expression of the *Hippocratic Oath* which required a doctor not to take the life of a child or from deep within the conscience of each one of us, reason urges us to recognize that each one of us has a beginning which, if rejected, rejects the whole life of the person. This law of life and of God is expressed, classically, in three ways: the law of civilized society and that of medicine[787] particularly, which considered it a rational development to protect the life of the unborn child. Secondly, there is the first principle of natural law which commands us to do good and to avoid harm and the first practical act of which is to preserve innocent human life[788]. Finally, the law of God, as expressed particularly in the Scripture, is that you shall not kill the innocent (Ex 23: 7)[789].

St. John Paul II has rightly expressed, sympathically, the plight of the mother, while recognizing that these reasons 'can never justify the deliberate killing of an innocent human being'; and, indeed, the same can be said of governments, institutions and private individuals who dedicate themselves to the destruction of human life: that being sympathic to the fears and anxieties that the people of the earth face does not justify any kind of abortion, either coercive or otherwise. Sympathy, then, is intended to be directed at helping people

---

[787] Cf. "Hippocratic Oath", on p. 210, and cf. also the "Hippocratic Tradition", by V. Nutton, pp. 210-212 of the *Dictionary of Medical Ethics*, ed. by A. S. Duncan et al, (London: Darton, Longman & Todd, revised and enlarged edition, 1981).

[788] J. C. H. Wu, "Thomistic Analysis", p. 257 of Vol X, NCE.

[789] Cf. *Humanae Vitae*, 4, pp. 7-8; and cf. also *Gaudium et Spes*, articles 25-26, 39, and 79-93.

not at suffocating the sufferer. Thus what St. John Paul II says could equally well apply to all who recognize the difficulties of life to remember the objective nature that *all who live* need help: 'It is true that the decision to have an abortion is often tragic and painful for the mother, insofar as the decision to rid herself of the fruit of conception is not made for purely selfish reasons or out of convenience, but out of a desire to protect certain important values such as her own health or a decent standard of living for the other members of the family. Sometimes it is feared that the child to be born would live in such conditions that it would be better if the birth did not take place. Nevertheless, these reasons and others like them, however serious and tragic, can never justify the deliberate killing of an innocent human being' (*Evangelium Vitae*, 58).

Pope Francis, however, putting the matter from the point of view of the innocent human life who bears the brunt of the act of abortion, says in his own inimitable way: 'Abortion, Pope Francis said today, is a way of "eliminating someone" that is similar to the services of a "hired assassin"'[790]. In a word, if it is permissible to take the life of one innocent human being, what makes it impermissible to take the life of many innocent human beings?

Human rights are relational: establish the relationship establish the rights. If we are human, then we have rights. Being human is a gift that each one of us receives. Human rights, therefore, are not obtained, lost or acquired. If we are not all equally a gift, then we are not equal. If we are not equal, then the inequality implies that we are not realists: no

---

[790] Deborah Castellano Lubov, October 10th, 2018: https://zenit.org/articles/pope-decries-abortion-one-can-not-do-away-with-human-being-even-if-small-to-resolve-a-problem/.

one gives themselves life and therefore everyone is equally a gift. Human rights are an expression of a realistic recognition of our relationship to one another; and, therefore, everyone has a right to the integrity of being human. The right of a child to parents is inseparable from conception; however, while that right requires that it is possible for the child to know who the parents are, so the child can refuse to foster that relationship if it is contrary to the good of the child's human development.

In conclusion, we need a new and simple definition of the rights of the human being from the first instant of fertilization and the completing good of human development. Thus there needs to be a world-wide collaboration in the search for human rights: 'This is why global bioethics is an important front on which to engage'; and indeed, 'This also means engaging in dialogue regarding human rights, clearly highlighting their corresponding duties. Indeed these constitute the ground for the common search for universal ethics, on which we find many questions that tradition has dealt with by drawing on the patrimony of natural law'[791]. The ultimate motive in seeking the truth-in-love is the Love by which we are loved: 'Our commitment to valuing, supporting and defending the life of every human being is ultimately motivated by God's unconditional love [of each one of us]'[792].

---

[791] Pope Francis' Address to Pontifical Academy for Life's Plenary Assembly for 25th Anniversary (Full Text), February 25, 2019: https://zenit.org/articles/pope-francis-address-to-pontifical-academy-for-lifes-plenary-assembly-for-25th-anniversary-full-text/.

[792] Pope Francis also sent a letter to the Pontifical Academy for Life to mark its 25th Anniversary, as it was founded 11 February 1994. Here is the Vatican-provided text of Pope Francis' letter, which was signed, Jan. 6, 2019, and published a couple days

Conception: An Icon of the Beginning

"Death of Birthright"

by

Natacha Horn[793]

---

afterward: *Humana Communitas,* https://zenit.org/articles/pope-francis-address-to-pontifical-academy-for-lifes-plenary-assembly-for-25th-anniversary-full-text/.

[793] Unesco Chair in Bioethics and Human Rights Art Competition: Reproduced with the Permission of the Director from the Finalists of the 1st Global Art Competition: Bioethics in Art Collection. The appeal of this picture is simply in the help that a young man gives a child; and, indeed, therein is its encouragement to us all! At the same time this picture, and the one that follows prayer-poem, the "Afar women of Ethiopia", bring to life the reality of many peoples lives and that, therefore, the context of the blessings of God is an almost heroic living of everyday life.

Francis Etheredge

Artist's Statement

'The one characteristic all humans have in common, regardless of color or creed, is that they began their life by being born. It is our common inheritance. This boy carrying a younger child to safety incarnates the hope that persisted all through the cruel wars of the 20th century. It does not matter if it was taken during WW2 or in Kosovo or in Chechnia or in any of the many places where each individual birthright was forgotten.

What matters is that innate knowledge of the right to live born out of our birth survived. Out of the flames of hell blossomed love and a profound sense of responsibility. The defiance in the posture and expression of the toddler carried by the child personifies the indomitable will to claim their birthright: the right to live free and to care for each other, even if they have to shoulder on the task to defend that right from early in life.'

BLESSINGS

Blessed be God
in my beginning.

Blessed be God
in my wife and children.

Blessed be God
in my husband and children.

Blessed be God
in our mothers and fathers.

Blessed be God
in our brothers and sisters.
Blessed be God
in our relatives and friends.

Blessed be God
in our enemies and in our end.

Holy Mary Mother of God, pray for us.
St. Joseph, pray for us.
Jesus Christ, Son of God and son of man, save us.
Amen.

Conception: An Icon of the Beginning

"Afar Women of Ethiopia" (photograph)

by

Jerry Galea (Australia)[794]

Artist's Statement

'Lakqo is forty four and has nine children, six sheep, ten cows and fifteen goats. Lakqo is a strong, able and confident woman. Her understanding of life is day to day, caring for her cattle and feeding her family. All she wants is her children to have a better life then hers.'

---

[794] Unesco Chair in Bioethics and Human Rights Art Competition: Reproduced with the Permission of the Director from the Winners of the 2nd Global Bieothics in Art Competition. It was

Conception: An Icon of the Beginning

EPILOGUE

If authors can imagine cosmeres and the peoples in them, if manufacturing companies can design their vehicles and products to draw on what is available throughout the world, if companies can encompass the earth in marketing strategies, if cultures expand and contract globally, if political cooperation is spanning vastly different centres of civilization, then what obstructs us having a global vision of the human person: a transnational, enduring and open ended vision of the reality that each of us witnesses day by day: that each of us is a witness to day by day: that each of us is an unrepeatably equal gift of a being-in-relationship? Even if we live in uniquely modern times in rapidly changing and unpredictable cultures, nevertheless we exist in continuity with the past: we inherit the heritage of the human race and the experience of living on this planet. The history of thought is our history and the history of that thought-in-action is our history, just as the history of salvation is our history.

While, therefore, we must begin to understand who we are as if it is a new point of departure, we must remember that we are receiving from those who have gone before as well as we will leave a trace of our passing and the possibility of a contribution to the future self-understanding of humanity. In other words, while there are many changes, fashions and influences of all kinds, there is a "presence of the present" which is always with us and with which we dialogue, day in day out; and, therefore, our investigation is, in a sense, always in the present tense: we are always turning

---

the woman's smile which attracted me to this picture: a simply profound expression to her life and hope.

to what exists and to the possibility of explaining, exploring and enriching our perception of it further[795].

A book about ourselves, then, is a renewable work; but, at the same time, it takes up those who passed, too, to the present task of understanding ourselves. There is no possibility, however, of addressing all those who have visited the reality of human identity; and so, in the end, this book is like a word in a conversation: a perennially urgent conversation in that it always involves recognizing, afresh, our forgotten brothers and sisters, whether frozen, aborted or otherwise tragically neglected. There is indeed the need for constant vigilance so that scientists and their sponsors actually contribute to the good of human life and are not architects of new and complex problems which, deriving from a fundamental disrespect for the integrity of human beings, open up problems which beset real human beings owing to their unwarranted interventions, manipulations and experiments[796].

Even, then, amidst all the limitations of time and ingenuity, there can emerge what endures. Just as music, fashion and reading changes with the times in which we live and so there is a growing treasure of old and new works, so our relationships to each other enduringly exist and encountering the challenge of understanding ourselves entails constantly turning to the reality of human being.

---

[795] Cf. Francis Etheredge, "Chapter Two: A History of Being in the "Present": A Dialogue with the Past in the Present", from *Volume I-Faithful Reason* (of the trilogy *From Truth and truth*), Newcastle upon Tyne: Cambridge Scholars Publishing, 2016, pp. 103-152.

[796] Cf. Kathy Schiffer, "Science Without God: Researchers' Bold Usurpation of Divine Authority: The scientific and therapeutic use of human embryonic stem cells is always wrong": http://www.ncregister.com/blog/kschiffer/science-without-god.

Conception: An Icon of the Beginning

Thus the principle espoused in this book, "where the body lives, there is the soul, and where both are is the human person" however useful is also an inadequate account of our profoundly enfleshed relational nature. In other words, in constantly turning to the human reality expressed in our daily lives, the gift of personhood is concrete and complex; and, at the same time, radically simple: each one of us is a relational being: a human person. Thus the language of 'form' and 'matter' expresses, at its most abstract, the mystery of the human soul determining the body to be the outward expression of itself. However, the human person is not only an individual and relational but is also a graced reality.

On the one hand there needs to be a renewed appreciation of the reality of "matter": that the human being is integrally bodily and in every respect human. There needs to be a new realism about the bodily expression of human personhood. In other words, the language of 'form' and 'matter' may express how intimately 'form' determines 'matter' to be what it is; however, the whole transmission of human life "demands" a realistic reappraisal of the "matter" that "receives" the 'form'. It therefore has to be a task of our times to communicate the whole of human personhood: the whole integrity of each man and each woman: the whole unity-in-diversity of being a male and being a female person: the whole mystery of being totally embedded in the relationships in which each one of us is both source and recipient of the gravitational grace of the heart of God.

On the other hand, then, just as the human embryo's development shows the personalistic nature of "who" is begun and is literally an expression of the inner reality shaping the outward expression of human personhood, so the "grace of our relationship to God" completes and perfects our relationship to to each other. Beginning with being conceived "in relationship" to Christ, the grace of God in the sacrament of Baptism comes to us like a warmth to thaw the development of love that sin obstructs; and, like warmth, it is God's relationship to us "in action": travelling through the being of man, male and female, to the ends of all our relationships. At the same time as we stand out of nothingness to exist in the myriad relationships of everyday life, so we dialogue "out of our relationship" with God our Creator, Redeemer and Sanctifier; and, conversely, we take all our relationships and their multidimensional aspects into our daily prayer, begging God to act throughout human life and culture to the good of all. What is more, the mystery of the resurrection of the body communicates the goal of the "complete" spiritualization of the whole person: one in body and soul – one being-in-relationship among all; and, therefore, it is not so much that there is a limited personalization of matter as that there is a blessing, like the beauty of light in Autumn leaves, that awakens the good in everything and everyone.

The suffering we encounter, then, needs an anthropological answer[797]: an answer that speaks to the heart of human personhood. Just as the heart of a person circulates the blood to bring about the health of the body, so each person needs the flow of relationships to bring about the health of the community. Just as a plant cannot exist without the moist soil in which it grows, neither can a human being flourish without the "ground" of graced relationships. The frost bitten sinner needs the warmth of Love to unfold fully. In a word, planet home is the beginning of an encounter: the beginning of encountering our need to be in communion with God and each other. Each one of us is an *icon of the beginning*, then, because our conception expresses an act of

---

[797] Cf. also Francis Etheredge, *The Human Person: A Bioethical Word*, 5705 Rhodes Avenue, St. Louis, MO, 63109: En Route Books and Media, 2017.

Conception: An Icon of the Beginning

creation as communal and individual as the mystery of the Blessed Trinity: the beginning and the end of every relationship in between.

In view of the times in which we live and the nature of our subject, we need more than ever a collaborative response to understanding our own nature and providing for it; in the words of Pope Francis: 'I am certain that there is no shortage of men and women of good will, scholars included, with differing approaches to religion and with a variety of anthropological and ethical visions, who are agreed on the need to propose a more authentic wisdom about life in view of the common good. Open and fruitful dialogue can and must be pursued between all those committed to seeking meaningful foundations for human existence'[798]. At the same time, just as a healthy realism recognizes that there are many points of departure in the pursuit of wisdom and, ultimately, holiness[799], so there are many insights that may begin our search for understanding the wholeness of human being; and, therefore, it is hoped that this book will encourage that pursuit among us all and, in time, contribute to the groundswell collaboration which helps us to provide for the needs of all, beginning with the least among us.

If it is true, then, that we are "conceived-in-relationship" then it is also true that there are many who are suffering the withering rupture of those relationships; and, therefore, we live in a time when there needs to be a "resurrection" of the

---

[798] Address of His Holiness Pope Francis to Participants in the General Assembly of the Pontifical Academy for Life, 5th October, 2017, https://w2.vatican.va/content/francesco/en/speeches/2017/october/documents/papa-francesco_20171005_assemblea-pav.html.

[799] Cf. Pope Francis, *Gaudete et Exsultate*, http://w2.vatican.va/content/francesco/en/apost_exhortations/documents/papa-francesco_esortazione-ap_20180319_gaudete-et-exsultate.html.

recognition, renewal and revitalization of the truth of the goodness and beauty of the human being-in-relationship. Thus, to draw on St. Paul, we are not only God's 'workmanship' (RSV, Eph 2: 10) – but we are His workmanship from the beginning. Thus, just as the conception of each one of us is an "living" icon of the beginning, so "we" are a living icon of the Blessed Trinity. Therefore let us work together to express the reality that there is "one gift of life, one right to life to govern one and all".

"An End Word: A New Beginning" and Biography

Elizabeth Bothamley Rex, PhD

Biography

Dr. Elizabeth Bothamley Rex is an adjunct professor of Catholic Bioethics at Holy Apostles College & Seminary and the President and Co-Founder of the *Donum Vitae* Institute, an international bioethics institute dedicated to the defense of human life in its origin. Dr. Rex received a BA from Barnard College at Columbia University, an MA and Ph.D. in Thomistic Ethics at the University of Navarra, an MBA from Baruch College (CUNY), and is currently pursuing a Th.D. in Theology at Pontifex University. Dr. Rex has been a frequent contributor to the National Catholic Bioethics Quarterly where she has repeatedly defended the licitness of therapeutic embryo transfer[800] and of the morality of embryo adoption as the only moral option to resolve the plight of millions of endangered "spare" frozen human embryos around the world. Her NCBQ submissions include: Embryo Adoption and Conscience (Winter 2011); IVF, Embryo Transfer and Embryo Adoption (Summer 2014); Embryo Adoption and the Bodily Relationship of Biological Mother and Child (Summer 2015); The Magisterial Liceity of Embryo Transfer (Winter 2015); and Impregnation versus Implantation in the Embryo Adoption Debate (Autumn 2017).

In the year 2000, Dr. Rex co-founded The Children First Foundation to promote and support adoption as the only moral choice for all unplanned or unwanted children, including children who are currently frozen human embryos.

Dr. Rex lives in Cromwell, Connecticut with her husband and three children, two of whom were adopted as newborns. The Children First Foundation was named in honor of birthparents and genetic parents who lovingly put the lives of their "Children First" by choosing life and adoption.

---

[800] Cf. *Catechism of the Catholic Church* n. 2275 and *Donum vitae*, I,3.

Conception: An Icon of the Beginning

AN END WORD: A NEW BEGINNING

"The human being must be respected as a person – from the very first instant of his conception."~ Donum vitae

Introduction

I have chosen this beloved portrait of Saint John Paul II to introduce this End Word because it is only fitting that this magnificent work should also *end* as it *begins* on its first page:

"This book is a thanksgiving to God for the spiritual fatherhood of the late Pope St. John Paul II; and more generally, for the ways that papal writing and the ministry, the work, and the presence of many others have enriched my life."

Conception: An Icon of the Beginning by Francis Etheredge is a profound, scholarly, and masterful presentation of the most important scientific, philosophical, theological, scriptural, and magisterial evidence that explores, defines, and answers the single most important question facing the entire human race today: When does human life begin?

It was a great – but very humbling – honor to be asked by Francis Etheredge to provide an End Word. When I pleaded with him for some guidance, his advice made perfect sense:

> "*Do not worry about an extensive review of the book. The point is to look ahead and around, not back;*
>
> *although historically, in terms of the **reality of human life**, we do need to **look back in order to look ahead.***
>
> *But as regards the book, **only refer to what is in the book so that you can go forward.***"
>
> *Go, therefore, for what is manageable and, as you say, **indicate new developments, whether in the law or elsewhere**. A bit like the end of a PhD thesis, it is important to **acknowledge where work needs to be done** and, if you see clearly, **to end with some bold points about these possibilities**"*[801].

Therefore, inspired by Francis Etheredge's comments, this End Word will first *"look back in order to look ahead"* by providing an important historical timeline that begins with the relatively simple and fairly unnoticed developments that led from the scientific discovery of fertilization to the current myriad of highly significant scientific, ethical, legal, and magisterial events *"in terms of the reality of human life."*

---

[801] Email on 7/18/2018, with emphasis added.

For many of us who are not professional research scientists, it may come as a surprise to learn that the scientific discovery of fertilization did not occur until 1843. Regardless, however, of our field of scholarly expertise, we must learn from history and take seriously the prohibition to experiment on any human being, regardless of his or her age or stage of biological development. Medical and technological advances must be therapeutic and ethical at all times. Why? Because, as it is so carefully and thoroughly discussed in this outstanding book, every human conception is an icon of the beginning; every human being is a child of God whose spiritual soul is directly and immediately created in the image and likeness of God at the transformative first moment of human conception.

Finally, in order to *"acknowledge where work needs to be done,"* I will briefly refer to just five of the many significant contributions made by Francis Etheredge in order to "end with some bold points about these possibilities."

A LOOK "BACK"

A History of Human Fertilization & Conception From 1818 to the Present

We must "look back in order to look ahead...
in terms of the reality of human life."
~ Francis Etheredge

Louise Joy Brown is the world's first test-tube baby, and her birth in 1978 was considered to be a major milestone in the history of what is now called ARTs, the acronym that is used for Assisted Reproductive Techniques. Her birth was heralded as the beginning of a new era that would be filled with promising new technological advances in the service of human life.

But as history has so often demonstrated, technology itself, if not restrained by ethical regulations and by the law, can also be used as a powerful weapon to dehumanize, manipulate, and destroy human life. Sadly, Aldous Huxley's warnings, in his 1932 futuristic novel Brave New World, have already become a global reality that is in desperate need of ethical boundaries and strict international regulations before it is too late.

Louise Joy Brown was born in England on July 25, 1978, after being conceived in a Petri dish on November 10, 1977, during a procedure which is now known as *in vitro* fertilization or IVF. Today, Louise lives in the UK with her husband and their two sons who were born in 2006 and 2013.

By 1990, just twelve years after her birth, roughly 90,000 IVF babies had been born. In 2008, a worldwide study prepared by the International Committee for Monitoring Assisted Reproductive Technologies (ICMART) estimated that over 5 million babies had been born using IVF; and by 2018, just 40 years after the birth of Louise Brown, ICMART estimated that 8 million babies had been born using IVF. What is rarely reported, however, is that tens of millions of other human embryos perish during IVF because they were often discarded, donated to destructive embryonic research, or remain frozen in cryostorage tanks filled with liquid nitrogen.

Who, when, where, why and how did all this happen? While it would be impossible to list every relevant event and development, the following historical timeline nevertheless presents a history of some of the major developments in every discipline regarding human conception and fertilization. I am very grateful to the following web site and its timeline for documenting many, but not all, of these important events:

Conception: An Icon of the Beginning

http://www.pbs.org/wgbh/americanexperience/babies/timeline/index.html/

1818 - 1978: From *Frankenstein*, to the Scientific Discovery of Fertilization, to the First Test-Tube Baby

1818 – On January 1, the first edition of the novel Frankenstein; or, The Modern Prometheus was published anonymously. It was written by 18-year old Mary Shelley and tells the story of a young scientist, Victor Frankenstein, who creates a monster as a scientific experiment in his laboratory.

1827 – Karl Ernst von Baer discovers that the female body contains egg cells called ova (plural) or ovum (a single egg).

1833 – On July 26, the Abolition of Slavery Bill passed in the House of Commons in England, 3 days before the death of William Wilberforce, who had led the long parliamentary campaign to end slavery throughout the British Empire.

1843 – Martin Berry, a physician, discovers that fertilization occurs when a single sperm penetrates the ovum.

1854 – On December 8, the Apostolic Constitution *Ineffabilis Deus* is promulgated *ex cathedra* by Pope Blessed Pius IX. The Dogma of the Immaculate Conception of Mary settles a 600-year debate regarding the first and second instance of Mary's Conception. "[Our Predecessors, the Roman Pontiffs] never thought that greater leniency should be extended toward *those who, attempting to* **disprove** *the doctrine of the Immaculate Conception of the Virgin,* **devised a distinction between the first and second**

instance of conception and inferred that the Conception which the Church celebrates was not that of the *first* instance of conception but the *second. In fact, they held it was their duty* not only to uphold and defend with all their power the Feast of the Conception of the Blessed Virgin but also *to assert that* **the true object of this veneration was her conception considered in its first instant (in primo instanti)"**[802].

1855 – Woman's Hospital opens in New York City. Over the next two years, its chief doctor, Dr. J. Marion Sims performs artificial insemination 55 times during which he injected sperm from the husband into the uterus of the wife. Only one pregnancy was ever achieved, and it ended in a miscarriage.

1856 – On March 6, the U.S. Supreme Court infamously ruled (7-2) in Dred Scott (slave) v. Sanford (owner) that Scott was not a citizen based upon racial arguments that were enforced by those "who held the power." Regrettably, it was Chief Justice Roger B. Taney, a devout Roman Catholic, who delivered the majority opinion: "The question before us is whether the class of persons described in the plea in abatement compose a portion of this people, and are constituent members of this sovereignty? We think they are not, and that they are not included, and were not intended to be included, under the word "citizens" in the Constitution, and can therefore claim none of the rights and privileges which that instrument provides for and secures to citizens of the United States. *On the contrary, they were at that time considered as a subordinate and inferior class of beings who had been subjugated by the dominant race, and,*

---

[802] Emphasis and italics added. Cf. http://www.newadvent.org/library/docs_pi09id.htm.

whether emancipated or not, yet remained subject to their authority, and had no rights or privileges but such as those who held the power and the Government might choose to grant them...."[803].

1863 – On November 19, President Abraham Lincoln delivers his famous Gettysburg Address, in the midst of the Civil War that ultimately ends slavery. Lincoln reaffirms the Nation's dedication *"to the proposition that all men are created equal."*

1865 – On January 31, the 13th Amendment to the United States Constitution abolishes slavery in the United States.

1868 – On July 9, the 14th Amendment to the United States Constitution is ratified. It legally establishes that "States may not deprive any person of life, liberty, or property, without due process of law; nor deny to any person within its jurisdiction the equal protection of the laws."

1876 – Oskar Hertwig observes the fusion of spermatozoa with ova (of a starfish) for the first time.

1884 – A doctor in Philadelphia, Dr. William Pancoast, performs the first known case of artificial insemination by donor (not by husband), by injecting sperm from a medical student while the woman was under anaesthesia. Nine months later a baby boy was born, but Dr. Pancoast never told either the husband or the wife what he had done.

---

[803] Emphasis added to the citation from: https://billofrightsinstitute.org/dred-scottv-sanford-1857-excerpts-majority-dissenting-opinions.

1909 – 25 years later, an article about artificial insemination by donor appeared in the *Medical World Journal*, and Dr. Pancoast was severely criticized.

1926 – On January 30, the American Eugenics Society (AES) was formally incorporated to promote eugenics education in the United States with the goal of improving the genetic composition of humans through controlled reproduction. Irving Fisher from Yale was its first president. In 1972, AES was renamed the Society for the Study of Social Biology.

1926 – Funded primarily by the Rockefeller Foundation, the Committee for Research on Problems of Sex is founded. For the next 20 years, this well-funded Committee does research on reproductive endocrinology, i.e. reproductive hormones.

1928 – The ovarian hormone *progesterone* is discovered by scientists. The role of progesterone is to thicken and enrich the lining of the uterus each month in order to receive and nourish the embryo. Following the embryo's implantation in the womb, progesterone continues to be produced in the placenta during the pregnancy.

1929 – The ovarian hormone *estrogen* is also discovered. Estrogen affects the development of the female body and prepares her genital tract for fertilization, implantation, and the nutrition of the human embryo. Too much or too little estrogen can adversely affect the female body. Birth control pills contain estrogen and affect ovulation and implantation.

1932 – Novelist Aldous Huxley publishes the futuristic novel *Brave New World* that portrays a society that is primarily comprised of test-tube babies. This shocking novel continues to affect the ongoing debate regarding assisted reproduction.

1944 – Dr. John Rock at Harvard and his lab assistant Miriam Menken conduct successful human *in vitro* fertilization experiments but they do not implant any of the embryos. Their IVF research generates public interest and concern.

1947 – On August 20, the International Medical Tribunal in Nuremberg, Germany, convicted 23 Nazi doctors for crimes against humanity. The tribunal issued a set of 10 international rules for all future human experimentation. The first rule of the Nuremberg Code states: **"The voluntary consent of the human subject is absolutely essential"**[804].

1948 – On December 10, the Universal Declaration of Human Rights (UDHR) was proclaimed by the United Nations General Assembly in Paris as a common standard of achievements for all peoples and all nations. It sets out, for the first time, fundamental human rights to be universally protected and is considered a milestone in human history. Article 3 states, "Everyone has the right to life, liberty and security of person"[805].

1949 – Pope Pius XII publicly condemned the fertilization of any human ova outside the body of a woman.

---

[804] Emphasis added to the citation from: https://history.nih.gov/research/downloads/nuremberg.pdf.
[805] https://www.un.org/en/universal-declaration-human-rights/.

Those who do so, he said, are taking "the Lord's work into their own hands."

1961 – An Italian scientist, Daniele Petrucci, fertilized 40 human ova. He allowed one embryo to develop for 29 days and even attain a heartbeat before destroying it. The Vatican publicly denounced his experiment as "sacrilegious."

1968 – An American doctor, Robert Edwards, and an English gynaecologist, Patrick Steptoe, agree to work together using a new abdominal surgery technique, called laparoscopy, to retrieve a mature human egg for *in vitro* fertilization.

1968 – Pope St. Paul VI issues a papal encyclical called *Humanae vitae* that forbids the use of artificial contraception because it immorally violates the "inseparability principle" between intercourse and procreation. While IVF is not mentioned, the "inseparability principle" equally applies to IVF because it also separates intercourse and procreation.

1969 – A Harris poll claims that a majority of Americans believe that IVF is "against God's will."

1970 – New York State legalized abortion and stunned the Nation[806].

1971 – At a Washington, DC conference on medical ethics, the Noble laureate James Watson, who collaborated in the discovery of the double helix structure of DNA, warns the conferees that IVF research necessarily involves

---

[806] https://www.nytimes.com/2000/04/09/nyregion/70-abortion-law-new-york-said-yes-stunning-the-nation.html.

infanticide. Dr. Edwards (mentioned above in 1968) stood up, publicly defended his IVF research, and was given a standing ovation.

1972 – The American Medical Association (AMA) urged a *moratorium* on all IVF research involving humans; but the American Fertility Society urged further work.

1972 – On April 16, ten thousand New Yorkers gathered in Central Park to protest New York's 1970 abortion law. After the protest, the NYS legislature votes to repeal the law; but one man, Gov. Rockefeller (R), vetoes the will of the people.

1973 – On January 22, the U.S. Supreme Court legalizes abortion in Roe v. Wade. The majority decision uses 13th century theology and science to support their erroneous decision about when human life begins, stating: *"Christian theology and canon law came to fix the point of animation at 40 days for a male and 80 days for a female,* a view that persisted until the 19th century.... *Due to continued uncertainty about the precise time when animation occurred, to the lack of any empirical basis for the 40-80 day view, and perhaps to* **Aquinas'** *definition of movement"*[807]. Anti-abortion advocates also opposed IVF research and experimentation that involved the deliberate destruction of human embryos.

1974 – A couple in New York City sues Columbia-Presbyterian Hospital for $1.5 million dollars when the hospital deliberately destroyed the couple's IVF embryos. The hospital feared it would lose its government grants.

---

[807] Roe v. Wade, 410 U.S. 113 (1973) IV.3, with emphasis and italics added.

1976 English gynaecologist, Dr. Patrick Steptoe, meets with Lesley and John Brown. Lesley has blocked fallopian tubes. The doctor recommends *in vitro* fertilization to them.

1977 – On November 10, Dr. Steptoe surgically removes one egg from Lesley's ovary and fertilizes it in a petri dish. After two days, the eight-cell IVF embryo is transferred into Lesley's uterus. In December, her pregnancy is confirmed.

1978 – Anticipating a media frenzy, the Browns sell the rights to their story to a British tabloid for half a million dollars.

1978 – On July 25, the birth of Louise Brown makes headline news around the world and raises legal and ethical questions.

1978 – On October 16, Cardinal Karol Josef Woytyla is elected as Pope John Paul II. He is inaugurated on October 22.

1978 – 1998: 20 Years After the Birth of the First IVF Embryo, the First "Adopted" Frozen Embryo is Born

1979 – Following discussions by bioethicists and theologians regarding the ethics of IVF and the moral status of human embryos, the Ethics Advisory Board of the then-Department of Health, Education and Welfare of the United States published a document recommending a 14-day limit to the growth of a human embryo *in vitro*. It became known as the "14-Day Rule" and several countries pledged to prohibit *in vitro* experimentation on human embryos beyond 14 days, i.e., the 14-day old embryos involved would all be destroyed.

1986 – On August 29, Lewis E. Lehrman, a distinguished businessman, philanthropist, writer, historian, and Lincoln scholar publishes, *The Right to Life and the Restoration of the American Republic.* His compelling article explains that America "was founded 'under God,' begotten as Thomas Jefferson wrote, according to the 'Laws of Nature and of Nature's God, a nation dedicated, in fact, to a religious proposition, a principle of natural theology." As such, the "unalienable right to life is not, for America, a single issue, but a first principle, a self-evident truth established at its Founding.... The truth is that life, liberty, and the pursuit of happiness are a logically ordered sequence. The rights to liberty and to the pursuit of happiness derive from every man's right to his own life and are meaningless without it"[808].

1987 – On February 22, *Donum vitae* is promulgated during the pontificate of Pope St. John Paul II. It forbids IVF and all other Assisted Reproductive Techniques. But it also declares as *"licit"* and *"desirable"* therapeutic procedures that are carried out on the human embryo that "are directed toward its healing, the improvement of its condition of health *or its individual survival"*[809].

1990 – Germany, in compliance with the Nuremberg Code, passes the world's first "Embryo Protection Act." Under penalty of fines and/or imprisonment, human

---

[808] https://www.crisismagazine.com/1986/the-right-to-life-and-the-restoration-of-the-american-republic.

[809] *Donum vitae* I, 3. Emphasis added.

embryos may not be used for scientific experimentation, harmed, or killed[810].

1990 – The Human Genome Project (HGP) begins to research is the DNA sequence of the entire human genome.

1993 – On August 6, as a response to pervasive and global moral relativism, Pope John Paul II promulgates *Veritatis Splendor*, a profound encyclical that reflects upon the solid moral foundations of the teachings of the Catholic Church.

1995 – On March 25, Pope John Paul II promulgates the encyclical *Evangelium vitae: on the Value and Inviolability of Human Life*. It defends the sanctity of life and prohibits abortion at any stage of human development *from the first moment of conception*. It prohibits contraception, *in vitro* fertilization, and all destructive research on human embryos.

1996 – A female sheep called "Dolly is the first mammal to be cloned but the controversial news is not revealed until 1997.

1996 – The U.S. Congress bans federal funding for research on embryos through "the Dickey-Wicker Amendment that prohibits the use of federal funds for the creation of human embryos for research purposes or for research in which human embryos are destroyed, discarded or know-

---

[810] https://www.rki.de/SharedDocs/Gesetzestexte/Embryonenschutz gesetz_englisch.pdf?__blob=publicationFile.

ingly subjected to risk of injury or death greater than that allowed for research on fetuses in utero"[811].

1997 – On August 15, the *Catechism of the Catholic Church* is approved and promulgated during the pontificate of Pope St. John Paul II. It states, "Since it must be treated from conception as a person, the embryo must be defended in its integrity, cared for, and healed, as far as possible, *like any other human being*"[812].

1998 – Hannah Strege, the world's first adopted frozen embryo is born in San Diego, California on December 31, 1998. Nightlight Christian Adoptions, a fully licensed adoption agency located in Santa Ana, California, assisted Hannah's adoptive parents, Marlene and John Strege, with the adoption of several frozen embryos who were relinquished for adoption by a loving placing family.

1998 - Present: Scientific Evidence Reveals the Beginning of Human Life at the First Instant of Fertilization

1998 – On November 1, the Human Fertilisation and Embryology Act 1990 is approved by the Parliament of the United Kingdom. Its official title states that it is "An Act to make provision in connection with human embryos and any subsequent development of such embryos; to prohibit certain practices in connection with embryos and gametes; to establish a Human Fertilisation and Embryology

---

[811] https://www.researchamerica.org/advocacy-action/issuesresearchamerica-advocates/stem-cell-research/timeline-majorevents-stem-cell.

[812] CCC, n. 2274, with emphasis added. CCC, n. 2275, also cites *Donum vitae* I, 3 (Cfr. 1987 above).

Authority; to make provision about the persons who in certain circumstances are to be treated in law as the parents of a child; and to amend the Surrogacy Arrangements Act 1985." Among its many policies, it limits the storage of human embryos to a maximum of five years.

1998 – On November 9, the UK passes the Human Rights Act. It compels all public organizations, including the Government, police and local councils, to treat everyone equally, with fairness, dignity, and respect. Article 1 defends the Right to Equality, and Article 2 defends the Right to Life.

2003 – In January "Dolly," the cloned sheep is euthanized due to premature arthritis, lung disease and premature aging.

2003 – In April, the Human Genome Project is completed.

2003 – A Harris poll finds that a majority of American believe that infertility treatments should be covered by insurance.

2004 – Italy passes a Medically Assisted Reproduction Law, also known as Legge 40, that strictly regulates the fertility industry. A maximum of three IVF embryos may be created and every embryo must be transferred. Pregnancy reduction is prohibited. The cryopreservation of human embryos and destructive embryonic experimentation are both prohibited. Frozen embryo adoption is legally permitted and encouraged[813].

---

[813] https://www.ieb-eib.org/nl/pdf/loi-pma-italie-english.pdf.

Conception: An Icon of the Beginning

2005 – On April 2, Pope St. John Paul II dies in Rome.

2005 – With the Vatican's support, Italy's Medically Assisted Reproduction Law survives a public referendum to repeal it[814].

2006 – The National Catholic Bioethics Center and the Westchester Institute for Ethics and the Human Person jointly publish *"Human Embryo Adoption: Biotechnology, Marriage and the Right to Life."* Edited by Rev. Thomas V. Berg, L.C. and Dr. Edward J. Furton; and Foreword by Robert P. George.

2006 – On July 19, President George W. Bush vetoes the Stem Cell Research Enhancement Act. Many *"Snowflake"* children, i.e., children who were adopted as frozen embryos, and their adoptive parents attend the White House ceremony.

2007 – On January 16, a previously frozen embryo named Noah is born in New Orleans. Following Hurricane Katrina, a cryostorage tank containing 1,400 frozen embryos was rescued from a flooded hospital on September 11, 2005. Noah's rescue and birth 16 months later make national news.

2007 – Dr. Maureen Condic, a researcher and professor of Neurobiology and Anatomy, publishes the article, *Life: Defining the Beginning by the End* in the scholarly journal, *First Things*. Dr. Condic scientifically argues that "Embryos are not merely collections of human cells.... Embryos are genetically unique human organisms, fully possessing the integrated biologic function that defines life at all stages of

---

[814] https://www.nytimes.com/2005/05/31/world/europe/in-political-step-pope-confronts-law-on-fertility.

development, continuing throughout adulthood until death"[815].

2007 – Editors Sarah-Vaughan Brakman and Darlene Fozard Weaver publish, *The Ethics of Embryo Adoption and the Catholic Tradition: Moral Arguments, Economic Reality, and Social Analysis*. The publisher is Springer.

2008 – Authors Robert P. George and Christopher Tollefsen publish, "*Embryo: A Defense of Human Life.*" They argue that no one should be excluded from moral and legal protections on the basis of age, size, or stage of biological development.

2008 – During the pontificate of Pope Benedict XVI, the "Instruction *Dignitas personae* on Certain Bioethical Questions" is officially dated September 8, 2008, the Feast of the Nativity of the Blessed Virgin Mary, but it is not publicly released by the Congregation of the Doctrine of the Faith until December 12th at a Vatican press conference. *DP* begins by teaching that "[t]he dignity of a person must be recognized in every human being from conception until natural death" and that the "teaching of Donum vitae remains completely valid, both with regard to the principles on which it is based and the moral evaluations which it expresses"[816].

2008 - At the Vatican press conference, the President of the Pontifical Academy for Life tells the *Catholic News*

---

[815] http://www.firstthings.com/article/2007/01/life-defining-thebeginning-by-the-end.

[816] http://www.vatican.va/roman_curia/congregations/cfaith/documents/rc_con_cfaith_doc_20081212_sintesi-dignitas-personae_en.html.

Conception: An Icon of the Beginning

Service that "the discussion is still open" on the matter of embryo adoption and specifically *states that "the Vatican did not rule out the practice"*[817].

2008 – On December 9, the United States Conference of Catholic Bishops releases a summary that states that while *Dignitas personae* "raises cautions and problems" about proposals for the adoption of abandoned frozen embryos, it "*does not formally make a judgment against them*"[818].

2012 - On December 31, The Telegraph reports that more than 3.5 million human embryos have been created between 1991 and 2012: approximately **1.4 million embryos** were transferred to the womb, with only about one in six resulting in a pregnancy (16%); about **1.7 million** embryos were discarded; about 270,000 embryos remain in cryostorage; 23,480 were discarded after being taken out of cryostorage; and about 5,900 were set aside for scientific research[819].

2015 - On February 24, the United Kingdom becomes the first country in the world to allow creating "3-parent" IVF babies. The IVF technique involves creating a genetically modified human embryo by combining: 1) the nuclear DNA (nDNA) from the mother; 2) the mitochondrial DNA (mDNA) from a female donor's egg; and 3) fusing the genetically modified ovum with a sperm from the father

---

[817] Emphasis added. Cindy Wooden, "Adopting Embryos Raises Moral Questions, Vatican Officials Say," *Catholic News Service*, 12/12/2008.

[818] http://www.usccb.org/issues-and-action/marriage-and-family/natural-family-planning/resources/upload/Winter-spring2009.pdf.

[819] https://www.telegraph.co.uk/news/healthnews/9772233/1.7-million-human-embryos-created-for-ivf-thrown-away.

using *in vitro* fertilization. Critics fear it will lead to creating "designer babies." "Where will it lead?" said Conservative lawmaker Fiona Bruce during the debate, "The answer has to be that we stop here. The answer has to be that we say this is a red line in our country, as in every other country in the world, that we will not cross"[820].

2015 – On June 17, the U.S. Congress introduces a bill to prevent the FDA [U.S. Food and Drug Administration] from using federal funds for research that involves creating viable embryos with heritable genetic modifications, or genetically modifying human sperm or eggs to create such an embryo[821].

2015 – On September 15, the European Court of Human Rights, in a surprise ruling, upholds Italy's 2004 ban on destructive embryonic research and "affirmed Italy's right to protect human embryos as it sees fit"[822].

2015 – On December 22, the Thomas More Society files an amicus brief in two court cases, i.e., *McQueen v. Gadberry* (in Missouri) and *Loeb v. Vergara* (in California), that cites the irrefutable scientific proof that human life begins at fertilization. The amicus brief states that the "current, not antiquated, scientific understanding regarding human embryonic development should drive the Court's ruling. As a matter of scientific fact, the frozen embryos are not potential human life, but actual living human beings.

---

[820] https://www.scientificamerican.com/article/britain-votes-toallow-world-s-first-3-parent-ivf-babies/?print=true.
[821] https://nature.com/news/us-congress-moves-to-block-human-embryo-editing.
[822] https://www.lifesitenews.com/news/in-surprise-ruling-european-court-of-human-rights-allows-italys-ban-on-embryo-research.

Conception: An Icon of the Beginning

Their 'potential' is for further development consistent with the embryo's body plan that came into existence at the time of the binding of sperm and egg membrane.... Human embryos may not be treated as property and are not merely 'entities deserving of special respect.' They are human beings and should enjoy equal protection of the laws as persons"[823].

2016 – On February 5, James Clapper, the U.S. Director of National Intelligence, added "gene editing" to the official list of threats that are considered "weapons of mass destruction."

2016 – On April 26, research scientists at Northwestern University in Chicago observe for the first time in human history the "transformative" moment of human conception. The paper is titled, "The Zinc Spark is an Inorganic Signature of Human Egg Activation." Sperm enzyme was used to activate human eggs and their "activation" was made visible using a fluorescent dye to view the release of billions of zinc ions that are expelled from the human ovum at the instant of egg activation, i.e., human conception.

2016 – On September 27, *New Scientist* publishes an article, "Exclusive: World's first baby born with new '3-parent' technique." The method used was approved in the UK. It is called pronuclear transfer and "involves fertilising both the mother's egg and a donor egg with the father's sperm. Before the fertilised eggs start dividing into early-stage embryos, each nucleus is removed. The nucleus from

---

[823] https://www.thomasmoresociety.org/thomas-more-society-asserts-scientific-fact-embryos-are-human-not-property.

the donor's fertilised egg is discarded and replaced by that from the mother's fertilised egg"[824].

2016 – On November 7, a conference at the Center for Bioethics at Harvard Medical School on the "Ethics of Early Embryo Research" proposes to *extend* the "14-Day Rule."

2016 – On November 23, the Human Fertilisation and Embryology Authority (HFEA) reports to Parliament that since 1990, a total of 1,687,260 human embryos were transferred to uteri and a total of "2,315,262 human embryos were deliberately discarded during IVF treatment" in the United Kingdom[825].

2017 – On January 7, research scientists publish an article titled, "Zinc sparks induce physiochemical changes in the egg zona pellucida that prevent polyspermy" in *Integrative Biology*. (N.B. The experiment observed fertilization in mice.)

2017 – "Embryo Adoption Before and After *Dignitas personae*: Defending an Argument of Limited Permissibility" by Sarah-Vaughan Brakman and Darlene Fozard Weaver is published by Springer International Publishing in *Contemporary Controversies in Catholic Bioethics*. They argue that Embryo Adoption (EA) "is not excluded in *DP* and that it is grounded in the moral and social teaching of the

---

[824] https://www.newscientist.com/article/2107219-exclusive-worlds-first-baby-born-with-new-3-parent-technique/.
[825] https://catholicherald.co.uk/2016/11/23/almost-2-5-million-human-embryos-destroyed-ivf-in-britain-since-1990/.

Church." It is the only moral option for spare frozen embryos[826].

2017 – On November 24, a baby girl was born who had been frozen for 24 years. Her adoptive parents were 26 years old. Emma Wren Gibson was frozen as an IVF embryo in 1992.

2018 – On March 3, a cryostorage tank containing 4,000 frozen human embryos and ova malfunctioned causing the death of all of the embryos in Cleveland, Ohio. On the same day, a second cryostorage tank failed in San Francisco, destroying at least another 2,000 frozen embryos. Class-action lawsuits are being filed by hundreds of affected patients. Many are suing for the "wrongful death" of their "children."

2018 – On November 26, a Chinese scientist announced that he had defied international norms and genetically edited the human genome of two baby girls using CRISPR-Cas 9 to disable a gene that would make the babies resistant to infection with H.I.V. Scientists, ethicists, and policymakers around the world have reacted with alarm. The long-feared genetic engineering of human embryos had become a reality.

2019 – On January 16, U.S. Senator Rand Paul introduces the Life at Conception Act "to implement equal protection under the 14th Amendment to the Constitution of the United States for the right to life of each born and

---

[826] https://link.springer.com/chapter/10.1007/978-3-319-55766-3_12.

preborn human person"⁸²⁷. This Act "declares that the right to life guaranteed by the Constitution is vested in each human being" and that the "terms 'human person' and 'human being' include each member of the species homo sapiens at all stages of life, including the moment of fertilization or cloning, or other moment at which an individual member of the human species comes into being." In the words of Senator Rand Paul, "it is time for Congress to recognize the right to life is guaranteed to all Americans in the Declaration of Independence, and it is the constitutional [duty] of Congress to ensure this belief is upheld. (...) The Life at Conception Act legislatively declares what most Americans believe and what science has long known – that human life begins at conception, and therefore is entitled to legal protection from that point forward"⁸²⁸.

2019 - On March 13, the world's leading CRISPR scientists, including its two discoverers, published an article in Nature, a British journal considered by many to be the world's leading multidisciplinary science journal, calling "for a global moratorium on all clinical uses of human germline editing — that is, changing heritable DNA (in sperm, eggs or embryos) to make genetically modified children." The scientists also recommend that "there should be a fixed period during which no clinical uses of germline editing whatsoever are allowed. As well as allowing for discussions about the technical, scientific, medical, societal, ethical and moral issues that must be considered before germline editing is permitted, this period would provide time to

---

⁸²⁷ Senator Rand Paul's quote was taken from his press release: https://www.paul.senate.gov/news/sen-rand-paul-introduces-life-conception-act.

⁸²⁸ https://www.congress.gov/bill/116th-congress/senate-bill/159/text.

establish an international framework." Finally, they recommend that while many nations "might choose to continue the moratorium indefinitely or implement a permanent ban" other nations "might well choose different paths, but they would agree to proceed openly and with due respect to the opinions of humankind on an issue that will ultimately affect the entire species"[829].

2019 – On May 2, the 8th District Ohio Court of Appeals rules that frozen embryos are not persons. The 2-1 decision states that "the pre-implanted embryos being stored at University Health System facilities were not capable of independent survival." Bruce Taubman, the attorney for the families who lost their frozen embryos, says he will appeal the appellate court's decision to the Ohio Supreme Court because it is a scientific fact that "embryos are human beings"[830].

2019 - On May 15, Alabama becomes the first U.S. state to pass a bill that bans abortion even in cases of rape and incest. The bill was signed into law by Governor Kay Ellen Ivey, Alabama's first female Republican governor, who said, "this legislation stands as a powerful testament to Alabamian's deeply held belief that every life is precious and that every life is a sacred gift from God." The new law could set up "a court fight that Republicans hope will end with the Supreme Court overturning *Roe v. Wade*"[831].

---

[829] Emphasis added to the citation from: https://www.nature.com/articles/d41586-019-00726-5.

[830] https://www.cleveland.com/news/2019/05/universityhospitals-fetility-case-appellate-court-rules-lost-embryoswere-not-living-person.html.

[831] https://politico.com/story/2019/05/15/alabama-governor-abortion-1327389.

Francis Etheredge

2019 – By Divine Providence, it is at this critical moment in human history that *Conception: An Icon of the Beginning* by Francis Etheredge is published as an invaluable resource for every concerned citizen, scientist, bioethicist, philosopher, theologian, priest, religious, doctor, lawyer, statesman, and politician. It uniquely brings together, into a single volume, the collective wisdom found in philosophy, theology, science, and the law that defines and defends the beginning of human life at the first instant of conception.

The purpose of looking back at the past 200 years – since the scientific discovery of human fertilization – is to help explain the major historical importance of *Conception: An Icon of the Beginning* written and compiled by Francis Etheredge. The human race is at an existential crossroads and a fierce battle is being waged worldwide between a Culture of Life built upon the "laws of nature and of Nature's God" versus a culture of death that is attempting to defy these God-given laws. Human conception is the very heart of this battle.

Conception: An Icon of the Beginning should be read cover to cover in order to fully understand the urgency for coming together as the children of God that we truly are, made in the very image and likeness of God who so loved us that He became one of us at the first instant of His own conception, in order to reveal to us the great mystery of man.

Conception: An Icon of the Beginning

A LOOK "*IN THE BOOK*":
Five Points from Chapter Five

"But as regards the book, only refer to what is in the book so that you can go forward."
~ Francis Etheredge

It would be impossible to list all of the significant and truly visionary contributions that are contained within this interdisciplinary masterpiece by Francis Etheredge that is dedicated to exploring and revealing in greater depth the profound natural and supernatural truths that are have been hidden for so many centuries deep within the first instant of human conception. But five contributions that Etheredge examines in his Fifth Chapter are of such great importance for all humanity that they deserve to be *referred to* – and briefly quoted – in order to *go forward* and conclude this End Word. These five exceptionally significant contributions are best presented using direct quotes from Francis Etheredge himself.

Conception – like Creation – is an Irrevocable Beginning

"In other words, the mystery of the beginning of a human life *recapitulates* the profundity of the beginning of creation which began with the act of God at the beginning of everything."

"[T]he moment of conception is precisely this: that it is an irrevocable beginning: a beginning that does traverse time: that unfolds through time 'without end". Thus the 'moment' of that beginning is complete in the very moment it comes to exist."

"[T]he moment of the sperm and the egg's union which, in an expression of the will of the Creator, is when God *repeats anew His creation from nothing, and completes His creation of each one of us."*

"Therefore the marvellous fact of an observable beginning to human life *is the beginning which is also and necessarily the data of philosophy and theology* – because this also an act of God as radical as the beginning to which the Book of Genesis directs us."

The Conception of Mary and the Incarnation of Christ

"[T]here is a kind of "Patristic Principle' based upon a number of texts of the Fathers of the Church which, in effect, lead to the conclusion that whatever is true of human conception is redeemed by the coming of Christ; and, therefore, as the nature of human conception becomes better understood, so it is clearer that redemption begins with the beginning of the Conception of Mary and the Incarnation of Christ."

"God's conception of Mary is an ensouling action of God which takes up the wholly natural contribution of her parents into the history of salvation."

"[W]hat can be recognized as true of human conception will apply to Mary's *Immaculate Conception*"... and "what follows from her graced conception assists us to understand the first instant of her conception and, therefore, the first instant of our conception."

"Moreover, given that a personal grace required a personal subject, it would follow that Mary was 'present' from the first instant of her conception; and in view of what we know of human conception, the first instant of human conception is the formation of the embryonic wall following the sperm's penetration of the ovum."

"Mary, then, after Adam and Eve, is the pre-eminent case of the human person united to the Son of God; and, in so being, it makes radical sense that she is wholly without sin and completely human, one in soul and body, from the first instant of her conception."

"In the case of the Incarnation of the Son of God (...) the very conception of Christ entails a first moment of the fertilization of the human ovum as it is animated by Christ's human soul and, therefore, begins an unfolding development which expresses the personhood of the Christ-child."

"In other words, just as the conception of the Virgin Mary entailed a first instant from which 'she' was conceived, one in body and soul, so there is a first instant from which Christ was miraculously conceived, one in body and soul."

"If then Christ is God from God uninterruptedly, then it follows that Christ is man from Mary in the first instant of 'becoming flesh' (Jn 1:14)."

The Sperm-Inclusive-Enclosing of the Embryonic Wall

"What can be reasonably established about human conception is that there is an obvious start to the new entity of the human embryo: the formation of the embryonic wall on the penetration of the ovum by the sperm."

"[I]n the 'sperm-inclusive-enclosing' of the embryonic wall, there is a natural 'sign' capable of expressing an 'inner mystery': the natural outward sign of the enclosing embryonic wall expressing the inner moment in which God determines there to be an animating human soul."

"Thus we can argue that God acts in a way which gives witness to His action, not because He needs it but because it is part of the Creator's communication to us of the nature of human being and the mystery of God."

"Orta a fusione" in the Latin Text of Donum Vitae

"[T]he Latin text of *Donum vitae* simply says that the zygote comes to exist "orta a fusione" (arising from a fusion).

"The Latin text (...) does not include the defining note which says, 'The zygote is the cell produced when the nuclei of the two gametes have fused.'"

"Thus the Latin text could mean that the zygote comes into existence from the first instant of the fusion of the sperm and the egg which, as we know, developmentally unfolds uninterruptedly from then on."

The Morality of Embryo Transfer and Adoption

"At its simplest, a child conceived outside the womb is without the immediate possibility of benefitting from the mother's nurturing contribution to the completion of embryological development; and, therefore, there is a natural injustice to the child, who in 'his' own way, cries out for redress: a voiceless cry which appeals to us the more it is almost inaudible in being submerged in freezing temperatures."

"[T]he sophistication of the methods of preserving the child in storage is an indication of the lengths to which 'we' will go to 'hide' the humanity of the frozen child."

"[The] procedure of transferring the embryo is radically different from the artificial methods of conception" ... "The reason that the transfer of a child to the womb of a woman is not to be confused or assimilated to *in vitro* fertilization and its methods is that this child now exists; and, intrinsic to his or her existence, is the natural right to completing human development which, in the case of the embryonic stage of a child's development, requires the nurturing presence of a woman willing to be an adopting mother."

"The Church has already indicated that embryo transfer is acceptable when it is for the good of the embryo and, therefore, the possibility of embryo adoption is also acceptable for the same reason: it is necessary for the good of the homeless embryonic child."

A LOOK "FORWARD": Starting from the 'awe-inspiring and "transformative" first moment of human conception'

In order to *look forward* to a new beginning I can think of no better starting point than by studying the aweinspiring and "transformative" first moment of human conception – which is the primary subject of this entire book – which became visible for the world to see, for the first time in history, on August 27, 2016.

Francis Etheredge

"Seeing Life in a New Light: Scientists Capture 'Transformative' Moment of Human Conception"

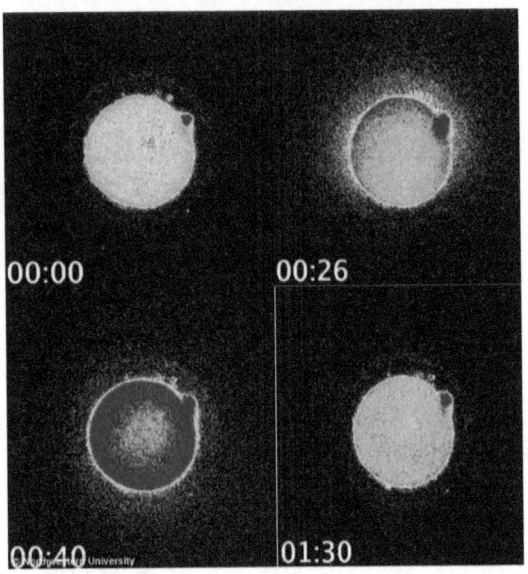

(Photo and Article Published in Northwestern University News on 4/27/2016: https://on.rt.com/7b5z)

On April 26, 2016, *Scientific Reports* published, "The Zinc Spark is an Inorganic Signature of Human Egg Activation" that documents the transformative moment of human conception and also explains the scientific significance of egg activation which is caused when the sperm and egg first fuse.

"Egg activation refers to events required for transition of a gamete into an embryo, including establishment of the polyspermy block, completion of meiosis, entry into mitosis, selective recruitment and degradation of maternal mRNA, and pronuclear development. [...]

Conception: An Icon of the Beginning

zinc dynamics and establish the zinc spark as an extracellular marker of early human development"[832].

Teresa Woodward, one of the study's two senior authors at Northwestern, commented, "All biology starts at the time of fertilization, yet we know next to nothing about the events that occur in the human [...] to see zinc radiate out in a burst from each human egg was breathtaking"[833].

Let us now carefully observe each of the four photographs above which capture the image of the *human egg* moments before human conception occurs, and the two photographs that capture the image of what would be the *human embryo* immediately *after* the 'transformative' moment of human conception when the sperm-activated human egg has become a living human embryo, a living human being; i.e., a person.

In the first photograph, taken at 00.00 seconds, a sperm's enzyme has entered the human ovum, but fertilization has not yet occurred. The next photograph, however, which is taken at 26 seconds, reveals the "transformative" moment of human conception as billions of zinc ions, referred to as "zinc sparks," suddenly burst through the cellular wall of the newly fertilized human egg that has become a human embryo.

This powerful expulsion of billions of excess zinc ions triggers the "polyspermy block" constituting an independent act in which the newly conceived human being protects itself within a hardened and impenetrable membrane.

The two gametes, one egg and one sperm, have fused with each other and have been transformed into a single

---

[832] https://www.nature.com/scientificreports/articles/srep24737.

[833] https://www.rt.com/usa/341063.

living *organism*, a living *one*-cell human embryo, who is now a unique human being, completely distinct from its parents, with its own pronuclei, and who is already a male or a female.

This earliest stage of the human embryo is scientifically known as an "ootid" and the new human being has already begun its own self-directed process of fusing together its own two *pronuclei* into a single nucleus. When the single-cell human *ootid* completes the fusion of its two pronuclei, approximately 24 hours later, the *ootid* will then be known as a single-celled human *zygote* with a completely fused nucleus.

In the next two photographs, taken respectively at 40 seconds and at 01:30 minutes, the "zinc sparks" are clearly diminishing because *fertilization* has taken place and the outer membrane of the new human embryo has immediately hardened to protect itself and its integrity from polyspermy.

The following diagram shows the moment before and the moment after the transformative instant of fertilization:

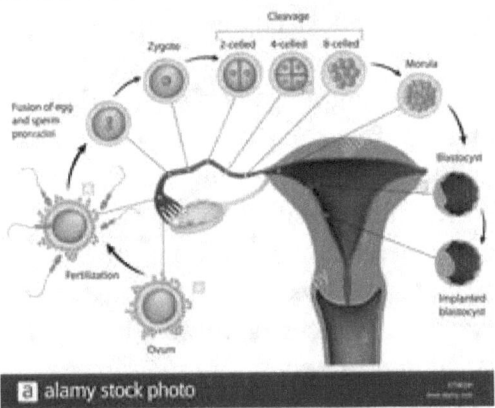

In particular, the third and fourth photographs taken immediately after fertilization capture the amazing first images of what each one of us looks like immediately after conception. As the diagram above also clearly shows, as

Conception: An Icon of the Beginning

newly conceived human embryos, we were already progressing toward our *second observable act*, namely, the *self-directed* fusion of our two haploid pronuclei into a single nucleus with the unique set of 46 chromosomes that each one of us possesses, as *ootids*, from the very first instant of fertilization. From that first instant onward, each one of us will continue to possess those very same 46 chromosomes during our entire earthly lives and, after our death and resurrection from the dead, for all eternity.

How do we know this? Because faith and reason, along with science and theology, must necessarily lead to the same ultimate truths regarding the mystery of God and the mystery of mankind. These new, breathtaking and irrefutable scientific facts can and should help every one of us to better understand what God has so magnificently revealed to all humanity through the magisterially defined dogmas of the Immaculate Conception of Mary and the Incarnation of the Second Person of the Blessed Trinity, Our Lord and Savior, Jesus Christ.

What can these absolutely stunning photographs reveal to us about Mary's Conception and Jesus' Incarnation, and about every human being who has ever been conceived?

How wonderful it is that, once again, faith and reason so perfectly support each other. In 1854, in *Ineffabilis Deus*, the Magisterium teaches as divinely revealed that Mary's "soul, in the first instant of its creation and in the first instant of the soul's infusion into the body, was, by a special grace and privilege of God, in view of the merits of Jesus Christ, her Son and the Redeemer of the human race, preserved free from all stain of Original Sin." Today, science has made it easier for humanity to understand and accept the truth of this dogma which must have occurred at the transformative moment of Mary's conception when her father's sperm first activated her mother's egg. As loving spouses, Mary's parents were predestined from all eternity to co-create their daughter, Mary, together with the Blessed Trinity: God the Father who created and infused her spiritual soul; God the Son who redeemed her; and God the Holy Spirit who sanctified her at the first instant of her Conception.

To Mary "did the Father will to give His only-begotten Son – the Son, Whom, equal to the Father and begotten by Him, the Father loves from His Heart – and to give this Son in such a way that he would be the one and same common Son of God the Father and of the Blessed Virgin Mary. It was she whom the Son Himself chose to make His Mother and it was from her that the Holy Spirit willed and brought it about that He should be conceived and born from whom He Himself proceeds"[834].

Beautifully implicit, therefore, in the Dogma of the Immaculate Conception of the Blessed Virgin Mary, is the necessary truth that God must also immediately create and directly infuse our spiritual and rational souls into our one-cell human bodies at the very first instant of human conception. To deny that this is true for each human being would be tantamount to denying that it is true for Mary who is as fully human as we are, except for sin.

When these beautiful pictures that capture the transformative moment of human conception were first made public, it was not surprising that many commentators hailed them as a tiny glimpse, as a miniature "icon," of the very beginning of Creation itself, when God the Creator summoned the entire universe into existence from nothing, *ex nihilo*, with His almighty command, "Let there be light!"

In Mary, we clearly can see that her human conception was truly an "icon" of the beginning because from "the very beginning, and before time began, the eternal Father chose and prepared for His only-begotten Son a Mother in whom the Son of God would become incarnate and from whom, in

---

[834] http://www.papalencyclicals.net/pius09/p9ineff.htm.

the blessed fullness of time, He would be born into this world."

Likewise each of us has been known and loved by God from all eternity, since before the beginning of the world. We, too, like Mary and Jesus, have divinely created spiritual souls made in the image and likeness of God that are immediately created and directly infused in our wondrous, one-cell human bodies at the first moment of our human conception. "In our bodies," Saint John Paul II once said, "we are mere specks in the vast created universe, but by virtue of our souls we transcend the whole material world"[835].

Conclusion: A Bold New Beginning

It is my sincere hope that this End Word has served to highlight the historical importance of this great work as we continue together to forge a bold new beginning for humanity.

May "A Look *Back*" provide helpful information to better understand and confront our present day challenges and inspire us to research, write, and actively pursue important legislative efforts such as Germany's Embryo Protection Act, Italy's Medically Assisted Reproduction Law, and America's ongoing effort to pass a Life at Conception Act.

May "A Look *in the Book*" inspire us to ponder and further investigate so many of the profoundly significant and visionary contributions that Francis Etheredge has proposed.

May "A Look *Forward*" encourage us to work diligently in every professional field and academic discipline. There is

---

[835] The quotation from St. John Paul II was found in the following book: *Lessons for Living*, edited by Joseph Durepos, Loyola Press, Chicago, Illinois, 2004, p. 47.

an urgent need to promote a greater international clarity and consensus that defends human life at conception. Science must be required to ethically regulate itself, and strict laws must be enacted to protect vulnerable human life from the first moment of conception until natural death. Within the Church, given the global assault and destruction of human lives before birth, and given the now irrefutable scientific evidence that human life begins at conception, there is a great need for a definitive formulation regarding God's immediate creation and infusion of the spiritual soul at conception. Following the example of Francis Etheredge himself, let us invite people of goodwill from every religious tradition to collaborate in a vigorous defense of human life at conception.

Finally, on behalf of all of his contributors, I want to thank Francis Etheredge for inviting us to join him in this exceptional work and serving as a great inspiration to us all.

May these final words which were spoken on the Feast of the Presentation of the Lord by our beloved Holy Father, Saint John Paul II, to whom Francis Etheredge has dedicated this entire book, express in some small way our gratitude.

The Light of Life

"Today the Church blesses the candles which give light. These candles are, at the same time, a symbol of the other light, the light of Christ. He began to be light from the moment of his birth. He was revealed as light to the eyes of Simeon on the fortieth day after his birth. Then he remained as light for thirty years in the hidden life of Nazareth. Subsequently, he began to teach.... He said: *I am the light of the world: he who follows me will not walk in darkness, but will have the light of life* (Jn 8:12). When he was *crucified there was darkness over all the land* (Mt 27:45) but on the third day this darkness made way for the light of the Resurrection.

"The light is with us! What does it illumine? It illumines the darkness of human souls. The darkness of existence. *Man makes a perennial and immense effort to open up a way and arrive at light; the light of knowledge and existence. How many years does not man at times dedicate to clarifying some fact for himself, to finding the answer to a given question!* And how much personal toil it costs each one of us in order that – through everything in us that is "dark," shadowy through our "worse self," through the man subjugated by the lust of the flesh, the lust of the eyes, and the pride of life (cf. 1 Jn 2:16) – we can reveal what is luminous: *the man of simplicity, of humility, of love, of disinterested sacrifice; the new horizons of thought, of the heart, of will, of character. The darkness is passing away and the true light is already shining* (1 Jn 2:8).

"If we ask what is illumined by this light, recognized by Simeon in the Child forty days old, the answer is as follows... It is the answer to your life"[836].

---

[836] Emphasis added. The quotation comes from the Magnificat, Vol. 20, No. 12, February 2nd, 2019, "Feast of the Presentation of the Lord, Meditation of the Day, St. John Paul II, pp. 45-46.

www.ingramcontent.com/pod-product-compliance
Lightning Source LLC
Chambersburg PA
CBHW030512230426
43665CB00010B/597